American Wine Economics

American Wine Economics

An Exploration of the U.S. Wine Industry

James Thornton

UNIVERSITY OF CALIFORNIA PRESS

Berkeley • Los Angeles • London

University of California Press, one of the most
distinguished university presses in the United States,
enriches lives around the world by advancing
scholarship in the humanities, social sciences, and
natural sciences. Its activities are supported by the UC
Press Foundation and by philanthropic contributions
from individuals and institutions. For more information,
visit www.ucpress.edu.

University of California Press
Berkeley and Los Angeles, California

University of California Press, Ltd.
London, England

Library of Congress Cataloging-in-Publication Data

Thornton, James, 1955–.
 American wine economics : an exploration of the U.S.
wine industry / James Thornton.
   p. cm.
 Includes bibliographical references and index.
 ISBN 978-0-520-27649-9 (cloth : alk. paper)
 1. Wine industry—United States.   I. Title.
 HD9370.5.T546   2013
 338.4′7663200973—dc23   2013013423

Manufactured in the United States of America

22 21 20 19 18 17 16 15 14 13
10 9 8 7 6 5 4 3 2 1

In keeping with a commitment to support environmen-
tally responsible and sustainable printing practices, UC
Press has printed this book on Rolland Enviro100, a
100% post-consumer fiber paper that is FSC certified,
deinked, processed chlorine-free, and manufactured with
renewable biogas energy. It is acid-free and EcoLogo
certified.

To Julie, Robert, Sarah, and the memory
of my parents

Contents

Illustrations

Tables

Preface

The wine industry in the United States is growing rapidly, and wine consumption is becoming an increasingly important part of American culture. The United States now consumes more wine than any other nation in the world. The wine market has recently received increased attention within the discipline of economics. The American Association of Wine Economists, an educational organization started in 2006, is dedicated to promoting economic research on topics related to the wine industry and publishes *The Journal of Wine Economics*. Colleges are beginning to offer courses in wine economics. As wine consumption increases, so does the demand for wine knowledge. Today, wine is a popular topic that interests and mystifies many people. Numerous books have been written about wine appreciation, wine tasting, wine history and culture, and different facets of wine business. While many of these describe various economic aspects of wine, they fail to provide a unified and systematic treatment of the wine industry from an economic perspective. The purpose of my book is to fill this void. This book has three specific objectives. First, it gives a detailed description of the economic organization of the U.S. wine industry. Information is provided about wine's unique attributes; grape growing, wine production, and wine distribution; wine firms and consumers; and grape and wine markets. Second, the book uses economic principles to shed light on the behavior of wine producers and consumers in a manner that is accessible to noneconomists as well as students of economics. Lastly, it summarizes findings and presents insights from the growing body of studies related to the economics of the wine industry.

This book is intended not only for students of economics but for anyone interested in learning more about the U.S. wine industry from an economic perspective. No formal background in economics is assumed. Analytical material emphasizes the application of economic concepts and principles, which are clearly explained before they are used, supplemented by numerous anecdotes and examples. As a result, this book can be read on its own by wine enthusiasts or used as a supplement to a source that contains more formal and rigorous methods of economic analysis by advanced students of economics. Instructors may find it useful as an organizing text for courses in wine economics or as a supplemental text for courses in the economics of industrial organization or applied economics. It might be read with some benefit by professors of economics interested in the emerging field of wine economics. It could also serve as a primer for wine professionals who have a limited background in economics.

Acknowledgments

I would like to thank all the economists who have contributed to the development of the emerging field of wine economics. Articles in *The Journal of Wine Economics* and working papers published by the American Association of Wine Economists were particularly valuable sources for this book, and their authors were a source of inspiration.

I also owe a debt of gratitude to my teachers who inculcated the economic way of thinking. Special thanks to my mentor, Kelly Eakin, who taught me never to lose sight of basic economic principles and their many applications.

I am especially grateful to Blake Edgar of the University of California Press. His vision of a book on wine economics and the guidance he provided made this book possible. Copyeditor Peter Dreyer and several anonymous reviewers also made suggestions that significantly improved the organization, presentation, and content of this book.

Thanks to Rod Johnson and the other wine professionals who have taken the time to talk with me about the wine industry.

Last, I thank family members for their contribution and support. Sarah McIntire urged me to write a book and enthusiastically followed my progress. Robert McIntire and Janet Daly provided much appreciated moral support. Charlie Thornton read an early draft and shared his knowledge of viticulture. Mary Thornton stoked my interest in wine. Paul and Valerie Thornton endured a week-long vacation of wine "lectures" by me and asked many thought-provoking questions about wine-related issues. My parents, Arthur and Paula Thornton, always encouraged me to make the most of my abilities, and for that I am very grateful. Most of all, I thank my wife, Julie. Her enthusiastic encouragement and support motivated me to devote the long hours necessary to write this book.

Introduction

This book focuses on the organization, structure, and institutional features of the wine industry in the United States, and on how U.S. grape growers, wine producers, distributors, retailers, and consumers interact and behave in the market for wine. Wine production and consumption are becoming an increasingly important part of American culture. The U.S. wine industry is growing rapidly and now embraces thousands of firms, ranging in size from small family-run businesses to large modern corporations, including multinational conglomerates. Many of these firms have nonprofit as well as profit objectives. The wine market includes not only buyers who are brand-loyal but also wine snobs and consumers who engage in conspicuous consumption and often equate price with quality, sometimes therefore exhibiting seemingly uneconomic or irrational behavior.

Wine is a complex and intriguing product with unique qualities that make it significantly different from a typical manufactured good. It arouses the intellect, pleases the senses, enhances food, promotes good health when consumed in moderation, and has a long and interesting economic history. Because of these attributes, the wine industry lends itself to an interesting and entertaining application of economic concepts and microeconomic analysis. Finally, wine economics is emerging as a new specialized field of study within the discipline of economics. A new breed of economist, the wine economist, is starting to populate economics departments, and students are beginning to enroll in wine economics classes. Practitioners of the dismal science have caught the wine bug.

THE ECONOMIC IMPORTANCE OF THE WINE INDUSTRY

There are more than 7,000 domestic wine firms in the United States.[1] In the decade prior to 2012, their number increased by about 7 percent annually, and this trend is predicted to continue unabated. There is at least one wine producer in each of the fifty states, including five in Alaska, and twelve states have more than 100 wineries. Wine tourism has paralleled the growth of wine firms. Estimates suggest that each year, close to 30 million people now visit wineries. In addition, there are more than 23,000 grape growers in the United States, and about half of these produce wine grapes. The dollar value of grape production is higher than that of any other type of fruit grown in the country. Hundreds of distributors are involved in delivering wine to consumers through thousands of retailers. Wine-related activities create in excess of a million jobs and contribute more than $160 billion to the U.S. economy each year. One hundred million Americans drink wine. About eleven million of these do so daily, and another forty-five million imbibe at least once a week. Per capita wine consumption has increased each year since 1994, even during the severe recession of 2007–9. Total wine consumption in the United States is now higher than in any other country in the world, but per capita consumption still lags behind thirty-two other wine-consuming nations, which suggests that there is plenty of room for the industry to grow in the future.

THE STRUCTURE OF THE WINE INDUSTRY

From an economic standpoint, the most important characteristics of the structure of a market are the number and size distribution of sellers and buyers, the degree of product differentiation, and the ease with which new firms can enter the industry. These attributes significantly influence the behavior of firms in an industry.

As in most competitive markets, there are a large number of sellers and buyers of wine: thousands of domestic wine firms and millions of wine consumers. However, a handful of large firms dominate sales of wine by the case. The three largest, E. & J. Gallo, The Wine Group, and Constellation Brands, account for 50 percent of domestic case sales; Gallo alone sells 75 million cases of wine per year in the United States, and another 5 million in eighty foreign countries. The twenty largest firms have a combined market share of roughly 90 percent. This means that the remaining 7,000+ wine firms account for only 10 percent of the U.S. wine market. However, the degree of market power that large wine firms possess is mitigated by significant competition from foreign wine producers, whose exports to the United States account for roughly one-third of sales. What is more, the wine industry can be separated into several submarkets based on the perceived quality and price of wine products. The lower-priced segment of the market is dominated by big firms that strategically consider the reactions of their rivals when making pricing and product decisions, while the higher-priced luxury submarket is occupied by a relatively large number of small boutique firms who act independently. The mid-price premium segment is a hybrid of the low- and high-quality submarkets and includes a substantial number of small proprietors, many medium-sized firms, and relatively few large producers.[2]

From an individual wine firm's perspective, the large number of wine consumers does not necessarily translate into an equally large number of wine buyers. Ninety percent of wine produced in the United States is sold to retailers and consumers through distributors, as to a large degree required by state laws. The distributor segment of the wine market is highly concentrated. The five largest distributors purchase 50 percent of the wine produced by domestic wine firms. The largest twenty distributors have a market share of about 75 percent. The remaining 25 percent of purchases are accounted for by a few hundred smaller distributors. This means that thousands of wine firms must compete to sell their products through a relatively small number of highly concentrated distributors. The alternative is for wine firms to sell their products directly to consumers, which given the restrictions imposed by current state laws governing wine distribution and sales can be very difficult.

The extremely large number of highly differentiated products offered for sale by firms, and the large range of prices that consumers are willing to pay for these products, are typical of the wine industry. Wine firms in the United States produce and sell more than 15,000 wine products. No other industry offers consumers so many product choices. Consumers believe that these products have significantly different characteristics. Because of product differentiation, all wine firms, both big and small, have a degree of market or monopoly power. Consumers make buying decisions by comparing wine characteristics as well as price. The greater the degree of differentiation of a wine firm's product, the less sensitive consumers will be to a price change, which gives the seller more discretion in setting its price. Differences in wine products can be real or imagined. Wines may differ in terms of their appearance, smell, taste, grape variety, location where the grapes are grown, viticultural practices, vinification methods, vintage, label, brand image, prestige, and wine critics' scores, as well as other ways. These perceived differences result in enormous differences in prices among wine products. Consumers can purchase a bottle of Charles Shaw wine for as little as $2 in California. On the other hand, a bottle of Screaming Eagle wine sold at auction in 2007 for $3,117.

Unlike in most industries, the ease with which firms can enter the wine industry depends in large part on the segment of the market in which they want to compete. New firms face few barriers in entering the premium and luxury submarkets, as evidenced by the hundreds of new wine firms launched each year. By contracting with an independent vineyard to buy grapes and a custom-crush winery to produce and bottle the wine, one can start a small virtual winery that sells a premium or luxury wine with an investment of less than $25,000. A fulfillment agent can handle the logistics of processing orders and shipping the wine to consumers who submit orders on the proprietor's website. Most of these activities can be organized and coordinated by telephone or Internet thousands of miles from the location where the grapes are grown and the wine is produced, if the proprietor so chooses. On the other hand, new firms face substantial barriers in entering the commodity segment of the wine market, which is characterized by economies of large-scale production. To achieve the low unit costs necessary to compete with large firms like Gallo and The Wine Group would require a multimillion dollar investment in plant and equipment, as well as millions more for the advertising necessary to persuade brand-loyal consumers to purchase the new wine product.

GOVERNMENT REGULATION OF THE WINE INDUSTRY

The wine industry is characterized by a complex maze of government regulations. Wine, beer, and spirits have the dubious distinction of being the only product class in the U.S. economy to have merited a constitutional amendment. The Twenty-First Amendment to the Constitution gives each state the right to regulate the production, distribution, and sale of alcoholic beverages within its borders. States have responded by enacting about 4,000 different laws to regulate suppliers of wine, beer, and spirits. While each state promulgates its own laws, most states require wine to be delivered to consumers through a regulated three-tier distribution channel. Wine firms are required to sell their products to licensed distributors, who sell them to licensed retailers, who sell them to consumers. In some states the distributor or retailer is the government itself. Moreover, wine firms are prohibited from vertically integrating forward; that is, they cannot own a distributor or retailer. Virtually all states impose additional regulations on the behavior of the producers, distributors, and retailers that operate within the three-tier channel. These may include franchise and territory laws; quantity discount, minimum markup, "post and hold," and uniform pricing regulations; prohibitions on credit transactions; and warehousing restrictions; as well as various other regulations. Most states have exceptions to the three-tier distribution requirement that allow wine firms a limited opportunity to sell their products directly to consumers, and a few permit direct sales to retailers. However, the direct-to-consumer and direct-to retailer channels in most states are subject to burdensome rules and regulations that make using these channels either challenging or unfeasible.

Why do states regulate the distribution and sale of wine? Why do wine regulations differ across states? What are the economic effects of these regulations on consumers, producers, distributors, and retailers? Do these regulations serve the public interest or special interest? Economic analysis can be used to address these questions.

WINE FIRMS

A wine firm is an entity that produces and sells wine. However, to qualify as such, must this entity grow its own grapes or can it purchase grapes from independent vineyards? Must it own a winery, or can it contract with another firm to produce its wine products? Must it be involved in selling wine to consumers, or can it contract with other firms to do so? What if wine is sold under the brand name of an entity that performs none of these activities itself? Should this entity be considered a wine firm? Everyone would agree that E. & J. Gallo is a wine firm. It grows grapes on thousands of acres of company-owned vineyard, produces a variety of wine products in seven Gallo wineries, and is directly involved in distributing and selling millions of cases of wine to consumers. But what about the legal entity named Castle Rock Winery? In 2011, consumers purchased 600,000 cases of wine sold under the Castle Rock label, but the Castle Rock Winery does not own a single vineyard or wine-production facility. It contracts with a variety of independent vineyards, wineries, and distributors to produce and sell Castle Rock products. Can Castle Rock Winery really be considered a wine firm? If so, then what about Whole Foods Market? Whole Foods contracts with a number of independent wineries to produce more than 100 private-label wine products that it sells directly to consumers in its retail stores across the United States. Surely, if Castle Rock is a wine firm, then Whole Foods qualifies as a wine firm also, does it not?

To produce and sell wine, a wine firm must make a number of choices. How should it organize and coordinate grape growing, wine production, and wine distribution? What tasks should be performed within the firm and which should be contracted out to other firms? What particular technology and method of production should be used for tasks done by the wine firm itself? How many and what types of wine products should be offered for sale to consumers? What qualities should these products have, and what prices should be charged? How much effort should be devoted to marketing and promoting these wines? The choices a wine firm makes determines how it will behave. Some firms choose to specialize in producing high-quality premium or luxury products, and others focus on lower-quality commodity wine. Some choose to convey information about wine quality to consumers by building a reputation based on past performance, while others spend a large amount of money to establish a brand name. Some grow their own grapes and make wine in their own production facilities; others contract with independent vineyards and custom-crush producers. Among those who grow their own grapes, some harvest them by hand and others use mechanical harvesters. Why do wine firms make such different choices and display such different behavior?

To explain and predict wine firms' behavior, it is necessary to make an assumption about what motivates a wine firm to make the choices that it does. Economists typically assume that the objective of a firm is to maximize profit. This implies that it will choose a course of action only if the amount it will add to total revenue is expected to exceed the increment in total cost. The major advantage of making this assumption is that it yields specific explanations and predictions. For instance, a firm will always choose the technology and method of production that minimizes cost. It will contract with an independent grape grower or winery to produce grapes or wine only if doing so is cheaper than performing these tasks itself. It will choose the profit-maximizing quantities and prices of wine products it sells. It will strive to increase the quality of the wine products it sells if this is expected to result in increased profit.

The assumption of profit-maximization would seem to be reasonable for large wine firms that are legally organized as corporations. However, it may not be a valid assumption for the vast majority of smaller wine firms, many of which are sole proprietorships. Anecdotal evidence and surveys of the attitudes of proprietors suggest that owners of these wine firms often have nonprofit objectives. Many seem willing to trade off profit for the prestige or aesthetic value of making a high-quality wine product that gets accolades from wine aficionados and high scores from wine critics. Others appear to willingly trade off profit for the enjoyment they experience from the lifestyle of a wine proprietor who owns a picturesque vineyard and winery, tends the land, and employs family members.

This raises several interesting economic questions. Can wine firms with nonprofit objectives survive over time in an industry that includes profit-maximizing wine firms? A standard economic argument is that firms that fail to minimize cost and maximize profit in a competitive environment are not viable in the long run. Does this argument apply to the wine industry? If not, how will these non-profit-maximizing wine firms behave? How does this behavior differ from that of profit-maximizing wine firms?

WINE CONSUMERS

A fundamental assumption in economics is that consumers behave as if they are rational when making buying decisions in the marketplace. When considering a wine purchase, a rational consumer evaluates the benefit and cost of a wine product and buys it only if the benefit outweighs the cost. The benefit of purchasing additional units of a product declines as more is consumed, because each additional unit has a lower value to the consumer than the previous one. This implies that a rational individual will buy more of a wine product over the course of say a month if the price falls and less if the price rises, assuming that income or other factors that may affect wine consumption do not change. This relationship, called the law of demand, is used by economists to explain and predict consumer behavior and has been validated by numerous empirical studies for a wide range of goods and services.

Many observers of the wine market maintain that wine consumers often display irrational behavior, however, and that the law of demand may therefore be violated for individual wine products, or even for wine purchases in the aggregate. Stories of seemingly irrational wine consumers abound. Here are a few. Price has little if any influence on the wine-buying decisions of many people who are in the habit of drinking wine with meals. Not only are some people unresponsive to price changes because of brand loyalty, but wine snobs and conspicuous consumers abound in the luxury segment of the wine market, and those who buy wine to be exclusive or advertise their wealth tend to buy less of a luxury wine when price falls and availability increases. A typical wine buyer uses price to assess quality: a higher price is always equated with higher quality. Lower the price of a wine, and these consumers will buy less, because they now see it as a lower-quality product, even if the smell and taste have not changed. Wine consumers typically cannot taste a wine before purchasing it, so how can they rationally evaluate its sensory qualities? And many who buy wine are unduly influenced by wine critics, whose quality scores affect and shape their preferences. How can this be rational?

Do most wine consumers behave as if they are rational? Do wine products, like other goods and services, obey the law of demand? How do income, tastes and preferences, the prices of beverages related to wine, like beer and spirits, and wine quality affect wine consumption? How do consumers assess wine quality, and what characteristics of wine do they value most highly?

THE WINE PRODUCT

Wine looks nice. It can be clear, brilliant, and sparkling, with a range of intense, distinctive, and stunning colors. Wine smells and tastes good. It can have a variety of interesting aromas and flavors, including fruit, flowers, spice, earth, vanilla, chocolate, smoke, and meat, as well as a mouthfeel that is firm, crisp, or silky. Wine enhances food. Wine and food are natural complementary goods because the acidity, alcohol, tannin, and residual sugar in wine make most types of food taste better. In moderation, wine promotes good health. Hundreds of studies find evidence that a glass or two of wine each day reduces the risk of heart disease, stroke, diabetes, and possibly certain types of cancers.

The complexity of wine arouses the intellect and makes it interesting to study, contemplate, describe, and discuss. It is a complex agricultural good, deriving from grapes of a particular vine variety, climate, soil, landscape, farming practices, production technology, and maturation and storage conditions. Its more than 300 natural compounds produce a seemingly infinite number of possible aromas and flavors. These compounds can give different wines a distinctive character and personality, which varies depending on where the grapes are grown, the viticultural techniques used, and the vinification methods employed.

Winemaking began more than 5,000 years ago and was regarded in antiquity as a gift from the gods. Throughout the history of civilization, wine has played an important role in commerce, social interaction, religion, and even public health, since historically it was safer to drink than water, and it was often used for medicinal purposes. Today it is an integral part of European culture and is fast becoming an inextricable component of American lifestyles.

THE ORGANIZATION OF THIS BOOK

The remainder of this book is organized into six parts. Chapter 1 discusses important concepts and principles that underlie the economic approach to the study of wine and illustrates how they can be applied to wine-related phenomena.

Chapters 2 and 3 discuss the complex nature of wine, viewed as a class of differentiated goods composed of a common bundle of sensory and nonsensory characteristics. These characteristics and the important notion of wine quality are examined.

Chapters 4 through 8 focus on the three important activities required to produce and sell wine: grape growing, wine production, and wine distribution. Chapter 4 discusses wine-grape planting, growing, and harvesting decisions and the potential trade-off between grape yield, cost, and quality. Chapter 5 describes the spot and long-term contract markets for wine grapes and provides an economic explanation of regularly recurring wine-grape supply-and-demand imbalances that culminate in periods of financial boom and bust for grape growers. Chapter 6 covers the economic activity of wine production and emphasizes the pivotal role of the winemaker in the determination of the style, quality, and cost of wine products. Chapter 7 focuses on three important topics related to wine production: bulk wine, private-label wine, and wine alcohol. The pivotal role of the bulk-wine market is explained, and a supply-and-demand framework is used to analyze factors that affect the price and quantity of this intermediate good. Next, the forces underlying the trend toward private-label wine and its implications for wine firms are discussed. Finally, the controversial issue of the high and rising alcohol content of wine is examined. Chapter 8 delineates wine distribution and focuses on the three principal channels available to wine firms to deliver their products to consumers. The complex maze of government regulation of the distribution system is described, and the economic effects of these regulations and the behavior of regulators are examined.

Chapters 9 and 10 are devoted to the wine firm. Chapter 9 develops the notion of a wine firm as a legal entity that organizes and coordinates grape growing, winemaking, and wine distribution. The different ways in which a wine firm can be legally organized, the types of contracts it can enter into, and the economic implications of different organizational forms and contractual arrangements are discussed. The objectives of wine-firm owners and the structural characteristics of the wine market that impose constraints on their choices are discussed. Chapter 10 analyzes wine firms' behavior. It provides an explanation of how they determine the quality of their products, price them, and communicate information about their quality to consumers.

Chapters 11 and 12 concentrate on the wine consumer. Chapter 11 begins by describing the demographic characteristics of wine consumers, and trends and patterns in wine consumption in the United States. It then analyzes the effect on wine consumption of price, income, prices of related goods, and consumer tastes and preferences. The results and implications of empirical studies of wine consumption are summarized and discussed. Chapter 12 explains how economists measure the value consumers place on the sensory and nonsensory characteristics of wine and analyze the effect of these attributes on prices. The findings of empirical studies of wine quality and price are presented and used to address a number of issues related to consumer behavior, the influence of wine critics, and the informational efficiency of the wine market.

Chapter 13 discusses the trend toward wine globalization, the structure of the global wine industry, and the degree to which the United States participates in the global wine market. Lastly, the conclusion highlights and summarizes insights about wine in America obtained from the economic principles and empirical studies presented in this book.

1

The Economic Approach to the Study of Wine

To explain the economic organization of wine production and consumption and the behavior of American wine firms and consumers, it is necessary to apply a set of basic economic concepts and principles. This chapter begins by explaining the important ideas of scarcity, choice, opportunity cost, rational self-interest, and economic incentives. These concepts are then used to develop the logic of choices by wine consumers and wine firms and the principles of individual demand and supply. Lastly, supply-and-demand analysis is presented as an analytical tool that can be used to organize our thinking about how buyers and sellers interact in the wine market, and how the quantities of wine grapes and wine traded and their prices emerge from these interactions.

SCARCITY AND CHOICE

The fundamental economic problem that confronts all of humanity is scarcity, which arises from two incontrovertible facts of life: human wants and desires are unlimited, but the resources available to satisfy those wants and desires are limited. As a nation, the United States does not have enough labor, capital, and natural resources to produce all of the wine, food, automobiles, cell phones, computers, education, healthcare, and countless other goods and services that Americans want.

Because resources are scarce in relation to wants and desires, individuals, business firms, and entire nations must continuously choose among alternative uses for their scarce resources. Choosing is a direct consequence of scarcity. Someone with limited money and time must decide whether to spend $50 on a bottle of luxury wine, or two bottles of premium wine, or a new sweater, or a new garden tool; sleep an extra hour or read the morning paper; work an extra hour or take an additional hour of leisure. A farmer must decide whether to use his own time, land, and capital equipment to grow grapes, apples, peaches, nuts, or some other crop. A wine firm must choose the type of varietal or blended wine to employ its winemaker, cellar workers, fermentation tanks, maturation vessels, and bottling line to produce. The nation as a whole must determine the amount of wine and other goods and services to produce with its scarce labor, capital, and natural resources.

OPPORTUNITY COST

Whenever a choice is made, a cost is incurred. Economists call this *opportunity cost*. The opportunity cost of a choice is the benefit forgone from not using the resources engaged for their next best alternative. This forgone benefit is the value the decision maker places on the alternative. For example, if one chooses to use $100 to purchase a bottle of Silver Oak Cabernet Sauvignon, the opportunity cost is the benefit forgone from not using this $100 to buy something else, such as a new shirt and pair of pants. If one chooses to use two hours to attend a "free" wine-tasting event sponsored by a local wine shop, the opportunity cost is the benefit forgone from not using this time for another activity, such as watching a football game. If one owns five acres of land and chooses to grow grapes on it, the opportunity cost is the benefit forgone from the most highly valued alternative use of the land. Suppose the land has two alternative uses. One can also use it to build a house or sell it for, say, $25,000. If the perceived next best use of the land is for a house, the opportunity cost of using it as a vineyard is the satisfaction of living in a home on the land. On the other hand, if the perceived next best use of the land is to sell it for $25,000, the opportunity cost is the benefit of the other goods and services the money could have purchased or the return on investing the money. The concept of opportunity cost tells us that in a world of scarcity, there is no such thing as a free lunch: you can't get something for nothing.

The above examples illustrate that opportunity cost may or may not involve money, and if it does involve money, the real cost is the resources, goods, or services those dollars could have purchased. It is useful to make a distinction between two types of opportunity costs. An *explicit cost* is a money payment that an individual or business firm makes to another party; an *implicit cost* does not entail a money outlay. Because explicit costs arise from expenditures that are actually made, such as paying $25 for a bottle of wine or $1,000 for an acre of land, they are relatively easy to observe and measure. However, implicit costs are typically not obvious and are revealed by careful consideration of a choice situation. Economists often impute a monetary value to these costs so that they can be compared to explicit costs. In fact, whenever possible, economists measure opportunity cost in dollars, facilitating comparison of different types of costs.

Implicit costs associated with wine firms' choices often involve money payments forgone. Consider the following applications of the concept of implicit cost. The most important input used to produce wine is grapes. Many wine firms own vineyard land and grow some or all of the grapes used to produce their wine. While these firms incur no explicit cost in the form of rent, the implicit cost is the money payment forgone from not renting the land to someone else. Conceptually, there is no difference between making a money payment of, say, $1,000 to rent vineyard land from someone else or forgoing a money payment of $1,000 by not renting vineyard land you own to someone else: both of these alternatives involve giving up $1,000. The implicit cost these firms incur from choosing to use the grapes they grow to produce their own wine is the money forgone from not selling them at the going price. To increase grape quality, some of these firms choose to reduce the number of grape clusters per vine several months before harvest by sending workers into the vineyard to cut off grape bunches, allowing them to fall to the ground and rot. The explicit cost of this choice is any money outlay required for the services of the workers who perform the cluster pruning. However, there is also an implicit cost, which is the money payment forgone from not harvesting and selling these grapes or the wine they could have produced. A choice that wine producers must make is whether to mature wine in a stainless-steel tank or an oak barrel. Unlike in a stainless-steel tank, wine evaporates in an oak barrel at a rate of as much as 10 to 12 percent per year. The opportunity cost of choosing an oak barrel is the sum of the money outlay for the barrel and the revenue lost to this evaporation. Many wine firms are owned and operated by self-employed proprietors who perform many of the winemaking tasks. The implicit cost of the time provided by the proprietor to his firm is the money forgone from not providing winemaking services to other firms who hire winemakers as employees or consultants.

Implicit costs associated with wine consumers' choices typically do not entail a money payment forgone, and usually involve the value of an individual's time in its next best use. When a consumer purchases wine, she or he typically incurs both an explicit cost and an implicit cost. Making a wine purchase usually involves gathering information about the prices and qualities of available wines, traveling to a store where wine is sold, and paying for it. The explicit cost is the price of the wine, transportation, and any out-of-pocket payments for sources of information on available wines and their prices, such as wine guides. The implicit cost is the opportunity cost of the time devoted to gathering information and purchasing the wine. This may include time spent visiting different stores to obtain information on prices and wines recommended by salespeople, reading wine labels, magazines, studying wine-related websites, and talking with friends. The implicit cost of purchasing wine is the value of this time in its next best alternative use. It is sometimes estimated by a person's wage rate: a higher wage is associated with a higher implicit cost for any given amount of time devoted to a wine purchase.[1]

The same wine often sells at different prices in different stores in the same market area. However, the opportunity cost of purchasing the higher-priced bottle may actually be less than that of the lower-priced bottle, taking into account the implicit cost of the time required to search for the cheaper wine. For example, suppose that a computer programmer who makes $30 per hour desires to purchase a bottle of Caymus Cabernet Sauvignon. He knows this wine is selling for $70 at a wine shop close to his house, so that it would require only ten minutes to make the purchase. Suppose that by spending an hour searching other stores in his town, he could find one that charges the lower price of $60 for the same wine. If we use his wage rate as an approximation of the value he places on his time, the actual cost of purchasing the cheaper wine is $90 and that of the high-priced wine is only $75.

RATIONAL SELF-INTEREST

Scarcity requires individuals to make choices, and the choices people make determine how they behave. But exactly how are these choices made? Economists assume that people make rational choices that are in their own self-interest.

People act in their own self-interest when they attempt to go as far as possible to satisfy their own wants and desires. Self-interest does not necessarily imply that people are greedy or selfish; it allows them to have a variety of wants and desires. One person's wants may be limited to material goods, while another may have wants that are aesthetic or include the welfare of others. For example, some people may want to donate time or money to charitable organizations to benefit the less fortunate. A wine proprietor may want to produce wine as an artistic expression or grow organic grapes to benefit the environment. Anything a person wants is considered a good. The more a person values a good, the more satisfaction he or she gets from the good. Economists call this satisfaction *utility*.[2] Therefore, an individual acts in his own self-interest when he attempts to maximize his utility.

To maximize utility, individuals make rational choices. When making a rational choice, people behave as if they consider the benefit and cost of an alternative and choose the alternative only if the benefit exceeds the cost. Cost is always opportunity cost, which is the benefit forgone from not choosing the next best alternative. In the nomenclature of economics, *benefit* is another word for the value a person places on a good or the utility he or she derives from a good. To say that people maximize utility is another way of saying they maximize net benefits. Rational behavior can be thought of as subjective cost-benefit analysis.[3]

Rational decision-making also considers *marginal benefit* and *marginal cost*. These are the additional benefit and the additional cost of choosing an alternative. For example, when deciding how many bottles of wine to buy, a rational consumer considers the marginal benefit and marginal cost of each additional bottle and buys more if marginal benefit exceeds marginal cost. When deciding how many cases of wine to make, a proprietor considers the benefit and cost of each additional case produced, and expands production as long as marginal benefit exceeds marginal cost. Marginal cost does not include any cost not affected by choosing an alternative. These unaffected costs are called *sunk costs*. For example, when a proprietor is deciding whether to produce an additional case of wine, overhead costs such as rent on the winemaking facility and property taxes are sunk costs. A rational proprietor will ignore these costs, because they do not vary with the number of cases of wine produced.

Finally, rational decision making does not require that people have complete information about the set of alternatives from which they are able to choose. Information itself is scarce and expensive. When making a choice, a rational individual will continue to gather additional information as long as the marginal benefit exceeds the marginal cost. Rational behavior can result in mistakes. A rational consumer may regret purchasing a bottle of wine despite having expected the benefit to exceed the cost based on the available information when making the choice.

The assumption of rational self-interest implies that wine consumers choose the combination of wine products and other goods and services that maximize their utility, given their money and time resources, which limit their available alternatives. They do this by purchasing additional units of a wine, other good, or service only if the marginal benefit exceeds the marginal cost. But what does it mean for wine firms to make rational self-interested choices? Wine firms do not make choices; individuals make choices. The individuals who typically make choices in firms are the owners or managers. Like consumers, the owners of wine firms attempt to maximize their utility. To maximize utility, economists typically assume that the owners of a firm, or managers who act on their behalf, attempt to maximize the firm's profit. Profit is the difference between total revenue and total cost. By maximizing the firm's profit, the owners maximize their personal income or money resources. And by maximizing their money resources, they maximize the amount of goods and services they are able to purchase and consume, and therefore the level of utility they can attain.

This argument suggests that profit maximization is a logical consequence of utility maximization. However, there are certain conditions under which utility maximization does not necessarily imply profit maximization, and profit maximization may not therefore be a reasonable approximation of what motivates wine firms to make the choices they do. Consider a large wine firm that is a publicly traded corporation with thousands of owners who are stockholders, such as Constellation Brands or Treasury Wine Estates. The managers who make business decisions in these big firms are not necessarily the owners. In seeking to maximize their utility, these managers may choose to trade firm profit for sources of personal satisfaction such as posh offices, private planes, country club memberships, and the prestige of managing a large and growing firm, albeit one that exceeds the most efficient size. Alternatively, consider a relatively small wine firm whose owner does make the decisions for the firm. Suppose that the owner derives utility from a good that cannot be purchased in the marketplace, but can only be obtained through ownership of a wine firm. These types of nonmarket goods may include nepotism, living the wine proprietor's lifestyle, and the aesthetic value of making a high-quality wine. To maximize personal utility, the owner may choose to trade off a certain amount of profit for these sources of satisfaction. For example, recall that some wine firms choose to use cluster pruning to decrease the number of grape bunches per vine to increase wine quality. A rational proprietor will choose to undertake cluster pruning only if the expected benefit exceeds the opportunity cost. The opportunity cost of cluster pruning is the money payment made to workers who perform this activity plus the revenue forgone from the lower grape yield and wine output. If the objective of the proprietor is to maximize profit, the benefit of cluster pruning is the increase in revenue the proprietor expects to receive from selling a wine of higher quality. Suppose that the opportunity cost of cluster pruning of $20,000 exceeds the expected revenue gain of $15,000. A profit-maximizing proprietor would choose not to cluster-prune; doing so would decrease firm profit and his personal income by $5,000. However, suppose the proprietor derives aesthetic utility from the improvement in wine quality and would be willing to pay $10,000 for this nonmarket good if it could be purchased in the marketplace. The benefit of cluster pruning for this utility-maximizing proprietor is $25,000, and he would therefore rationally choose to trade $5,000 of profit for the utility he gets from the improvement in wine quality.

The assumption of rational profit maximization may still be reasonable for large corporate wine firms and wine firms whose owners derive utility from nonmarket goods. A standard economic argument is that these types of wine firms must make profit-maximizing choices to survive in the industry. The applicability of this survival-of-the-fittest argument to the wine industry is discussed in detail in chapter 9. Moreover, through the board of directors, the owners of large wine firms can provide economic incentives to managers to induce them to make profit-maximizing decisions.

ECONOMIC INCENTIVES

Rational individuals respond to anything that affects the benefit or cost of choosing an alternative. Anything that increases benefit or decreases opportunity cost gives a rational individual an economic incentive to choose the alternative. Anything that decreases benefit or increases opportunity cost gives a rational individual an economic incentive not to choose the alternative. Economic incentives may or may not involve money. Those that involve money are called *financial incentives*.

For example, an increase in the price of a wine gives wine consumers an economic incentive to choose to buy less of it, because the higher price increases the opportunity cost. A decrease in the amount of time required to search for a wine product lowers the opportunity cost of choosing to purchase it, and therefore gives wine consumers an economic incentive to buy more of it. When the board of directors of a large wine firm link the compensation of managers to profits through stock ownership, this provides an economic incentive for these managers to make profit-maximizing decisions. When a wine firm contracts with an independent vineyard to buy grapes at a fixed price per ton, this gives the wine firm an economic incentive to request riper fruit with a lower water content, which weighs less, because this decreases the opportunity cost of purchasing grapes. On the other hand, the grape grower has an economic incentive to harvest the grapes when they are less ripe and weigh more, since this increases the benefit received from grapes sold.

Economists believe that economic incentives have an important influence on the behavior of individuals and firms. To understand how wine consumers and wine firms behave, it is necessary to understand the economic incentives they face.

WINE CONSUMERS' CHOICES AND DEMAND

Economists have developed a simplified theory of choice to explain how consumers make decisions about what goods and services to purchase and how much of each of these to consume.

The objective of a rational wine consumer is to maximize the utility of wine products and other goods and services, given the amount of money available, determined by income. The utility derived from a good is measured in dollars by the maximum amount of money the consumer is willing to pay for it. To decide how to spend in a manner that yields the greatest amount of utility, the consumer compares the benefit of a feasible consumption alternative to the cost, and chooses the alternative only if the benefit is greater than or equal to the cost. A rational consumer makes decisions by considering marginal benefit and marginal opportunity cost, where opportunity cost is the benefit forgone as a result of not spending money on the next best consumption alternative.

To better understand the logic of rational consumer decision-making, consider the following example. Suppose that at the beginning of each week, Jill Oenophile shops for the wine she will drink during the subsequent seven-day period. Jill must decide whether to purchase a particular wine, such as Kendall-Jackson (KJ) Chardonnay, and, if so, how many bottles of it to buy. Assume that she is willing to pay $16 at most for one bottle of KJ, $12 for a second bottle, $8 for a third, and $4 for a fourth, but nothing at all for a fifth. This tells us that the marginal benefit of the first bottle is $16. This is a dollar measure of the utility she would derive from consuming one bottle of KJ during the week. It is the maximum amount of money she is willing to spend to purchase this first bottle. The marginal benefit of a second bottle of KJ is only $12. Her willingness to pay less for a second bottle indicates that while consuming this bottle would be enjoyable, it would yield less utility than the first. The marginal utility, and therefore the marginal benefit, of each additional bottle diminishes as evidenced by the successively smaller amount she is willing to pay for extra bottles. Consuming a fifth bottle of KJ during the week would provide Jill with no additional utility. This example reflects what economists call "the law of diminishing marginal utility." This law asserts that a typical individual eventually experiences less utility from each additional unit of a good consumed during a given period of time, and is therefore willing to pay less and less for these extra units.[4]

Suppose that the retail store where Jill does her shopping is selling KJ at a price of $12 per bottle. This price is a dollar measure of opportunity cost. She must forgo the benefit of $12 of other goods she could have consumed for each bottle of KJ purchased. If she is rational, how many bottles will Jill buy for the week? All those for which the marginal benefit, measured by the maximum amount of money she is willing to pay, is greater than or equal to the marginal cost as measured by price. Jill will buy a first bottle since she is willing to pay $16, but has to pay only $12, so she gets a net benefit of $4. She will purchase a second bottle because the amount she is willing to pay is equal to what she must pay. She will not buy a third bottle since the $8 she is willing to pay is less than the $12 price. For this bottle, the marginal cost exceeds the marginal benefit. To maximize her utility, or net benefits, Jill will purchase two bottles of KJ for consumption that week.

Now, consider five alternative prices at which KJ might be sold: $20, $16, $12, $8, and $4. How many bottles will Jill purchase at each of these prices? Applying the above logic, to maximize utility, she would buy none at $20, one at $16, two at $12, three at $8, and four at $4. The inclination of a consumer to demand a larger quantity of a good when price falls and a smaller quantity when price rises, all else being equal, is called "the law of demand." It is a logical consequence of rational

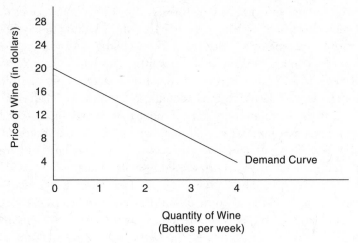

FIGURE 1. Demand curve for wine.

decision-making and the law of diminishing marginal utility. Because a typical individual is willing to pay less for each additional bottle of KJ, to induce her to buy more, the price would have to be lower and lower. If the five price-quantity possibilities are plotted on a two-dimensional graph with price on the vertical axis and quantity on the horizontal axis, a demand curve is obtained (see figure 1). This demand curve has two useful interpretations. It tells us the quantity of wine demanded at each possible price. Alternatively, it tells us the maximum price an individual is willing to pay for each additional bottle of wine.

The amount of money a consumer like Jill is willing to pay for a wine such as KJ, and therefore the quantity she demands, depends upon several factors in addition to her tastes and preferences. An increase in Jill's income increases her ability to buy KJ, but may either increase or decrease her willingness to do so. If Jill is drinking KJ because she can't afford a more expensive Chardonnay, an increase in income may decrease the desirability of KJ, and she would then be willing to pay less for any given amount and want to buy less at any given price. Economists call a product an *inferior good* when demand decreases after a rise in income and increases after income falls. However, it is typically the case that at a higher income, an individual is both able and willing to pay more for a wine product, and will therefore want to buy more at the prevailing price. The opposite occurs at a lower level of income. Economists call this a *normal good*. The desirability of a particular good also depends upon the prices and quantities of related goods consumed.

Suppose Jill enjoys drinking KJ with salmon and also finds Beringer Founders Estate to be a desirable substitute for KJ. The amount she is willing to pay for KJ is influenced by the prices she has to pay for salmon and the Beringer Chardonnay. At higher salmon prices, Jill eats less of it. This makes KJ less enjoyable, since these two complementary goods are consumed together. Alternatively, at lower prices of Beringer, it is a relatively better buy, and Jill may therefore find KJ to be less desirable. This is because she views these two brands of Chardonnay as goods that can be substituted for each other. The amount Jill is willing to pay for KJ, therefore, is less at higher fish and lower Beringer Chardonnay prices. Alternatively, she is willing to pay more at a lower price of fish and higher price of Beringer. Lastly, the higher the quality of a good, the more an individual is willing to pay for any given quantity. Jill would be willing to pay a higher price for KJ if she perceived an improvement in appearance, smell, and taste.

WINE FIRMS' CHOICES AND SUPPLY

Like wine consumers, the owners of a wine firm want to maximize their utility. As stated previously, if the owners control the firm and do not derive utility from firm-specific nonmarket goods, then to maximize utility, they will maximize profit. A rational profit-maximizing wine firm will choose to increase wine production, improve wine quality, invest in a new fermentation tank, devote more effort to marketing, or any other course of action only if the marginal benefit, measured by the additional revenue the firm expects to receive, is greater than or equal to the marginal opportunity cost.

Two important choices a wine firm makes are the interdependent decisions of how much wine to produce and what price to charge. To better understand the logic of profit-maximizing decision making, consider a wine firm that must choose whether to increase wine output. It is currently producing 3,000 cases of a wine per year and receives a price of $11 per bottle, or $132 per twelve-bottle case. The wine is made in a leased winery from grapes grown in a vineyard that it owns. Surplus grapes not used to make this wine are sold on the wine-grape market. To grow the grapes and produce the wine, it purchases the services of hired labor, fuel, electricity, and other inputs that vary with the amount of grapes grown and wine produced. These inputs are called variable inputs, and the outlays made for them are called a variable cost. The winery and vineyard land are called fixed inputs and the cost associated with them fixed cost, because they do not vary with the amount of wine produced. The firm must decide whether to produce and sell an additional 1,000 cases of this wine next year. It faces a downward-sloping demand curve, and to induce consumers to purchase an additional 1,000 cases, it would therefore be required to reduce the price to $10 per bottle, or $120 per case. The marginal benefit of increasing production by 1,000 cases in the coming year is the additional revenue the firm would receive. Total revenue of 3,000 cases at $132 per case is $396,000. Total revenue of 4,000 cases at $120 per case is $480,000. The marginal benefit, therefore, is $84,000. The wine firm has a five-year winery lease and is contractually obligated to make an annual rental payment of $25,000. The cost of the variable inputs required to increase production is $49,500. The wine firm uses fifteen tons of its own surplus grapes, which it could have sold on the wine-grape market at $300 per ton. The marginal cost of producing the additional 1,000 cases of wine is $54,000. This measure of opportunity cost includes both the money payment made for variable inputs of $49,500 and the $4,500 money payment forgone because the extra fifteen tons of grapes used in the production of wine can no longer be sold on the wine-grape market. Both of these costs measure the dollar value of benefits forgone. The rental payment for the winery of $25,000 is a sunk cost, and therefore not included in the measure of marginal cost. The wine firm is obligated to make this payment regardless of whether it produces 3,000 or 4,000 cases per year. The cost of leasing the winery is unaffected by the decision to produce an extra 1,000 cases of wine. Because the marginal benefit of increasing production by 1,000 cases ($84,000) exceeds the marginal cost ($54,000), the wine firm will choose this alternative. By doing so, it increases annual profit by $30,000.[5]

Since the objective of the wine firm is to maximize profit, it will continue to increase production as long as the marginal benefit measured by the additional sales revenue generated exceeds the marginal cost measured by the money outlays for required variable inputs and money payments forgone from not using self-owned variable inputs in their next best area of employment.[6] As the firm expands output, the marginal revenue of additional cases produced will fall: given consumer demand, more of this wine can be sold only by lowering price. Also, the marginal cost of production will typically rise as a consequence of the law of diminishing returns. This results from the constraint imposed by the size of the winery and the rate of production it can efficiently handle. As larger amounts of labor services and other variable inputs are used in the fixed wine production facility, the combination of inputs becomes less efficient and the cost of producing additional cases rises. As production approaches the capacity of the winery, marginal cost will rise sharply. The profit-maximizing level of output occurs where marginal revenue is equal to marginal cost. By behaving in this manner, the firm maximizes the difference between its total revenue and total cost and makes as much money as possible for the owners, given the constraints it faces.

How will a profit-maximizing wine firm respond to a change in the demand for its product resulting from a change in consumer tastes, income, or prices of related goods? For example, suppose the marginal revenue of the last case of wine produced equals the marginal cost at an annual rate of production of 5,000 cases and a price of $9 per bottle. Now, consumers experience an increase in income, and therefore want to buy more of the wine at the current price. The increased demand allows the firm to charge a higher price, which increases marginal revenue. Because marginal revenue exceeds marginal cost at the current output level of 5,000 cases, the firm has an economic incentive to expand production. As it produces more wine the marginal cost of additional cases increases. Eventually, marginal revenue equals marginal cost at both a higher level of output and a higher price; for example, 6,000 cases at a price of $11 per bottle. Alternatively, if demand decreases, the profit-maximizing output and price would both decrease.

How will a profit-maximizing wine firm respond to a change in cost arising from a change in the price of a variable input or the excise tax on wine? Extending the above example, suppose that the government increases the excise tax on wine. Because the firm must now pay a higher tax on each bottle of wine produced, this increases the marginal cost of producing the current output of 6,000 cases, and marginal cost therefore now exceeds marginal revenue. To maximize profit, the firm will respond by reducing the number of cases it produces, and marginal cost therefore falls. At the lower output level, the firm is able to charge a higher price, which results in an increase in marginal revenue. Eventually, marginal revenue once again equals marginal cost, but at a lower rate of production and higher price, say 5,000 cases at a price of $12 per bottle. By a similar line of reasoning, a profit-maximizing wine firm would respond to a lower excise tax by expanding production and reducing price. The same logic applies to changes in variable input prices.

It is important to understand that a wine firm's fixed cost is a sunk cost, and therefore a change in fixed cost does not affect the profit-maximizing level of output. This is because the firm's profit-maximizing output choice involves marginal cost, which only includes those costs that vary with the level of output produced. For example, suppose that the government increases the property tax on the firm's vineyard land. This would have no effect on output and price, since property taxes are a fixed cost that do not change when the rate of production increases or decreases. However, the increase in fixed cost resulting from higher property taxes does decrease the firm's profit. In the long run, lower profits or losses may induce the firm to the leave the industry, which would reduce its level of output to zero.

The logic of wine firm's choice presented above applies to profit-maximizing wine firms. However, suppose the owner of a wine firm derives utility from a nonmarket good that can only be obtained from the ownership of a wine firm, and he is therefore willing to trade off profit for this firm-specific source of utility. A non-profit-maximizing wine firm, like a profit-maximizing wine firm, will choose an alternative only if the marginal benefit exceeds the marginal cost, but now marginal benefit is not necessarily captured by revenue alone. To better understand the logic of non-profit-maximizing decision making, consider the example of an owner who gets satisfaction from profit and the prestige of producing a high-quality wine; given his preferences, he is willing to trade off profit for wine quality. Assume that quality and prestige are measured by wine critic scores. A higher score is associated with a higher-quality wine and more prestige for the owner. The firm must decide whether to improve the quality of a wine it currently sells and raise critic scores from say 85 to 90 points on a 100-point scale. To do this, it would need to hire an expensive winemaking consultant and purchase better-quality, higher-priced grapes, and the marginal cost of this quality improvement is therefore $100,000 per year. The higher quality of the wine would enable the firm to charge a higher price and earn an additional $75,000 in revenue. If the objective of the firm was to maximize profit, then it would choose not to undertake the quality improvement. This is because the marginal benefit, measured by the additional revenue of $75,000, is less than the marginal cost of $100,000, and the firm would consequently reduce its profit by $25,000 per year. However, because the owner derives satisfaction from wine quality as well as profit, the marginal benefit of quality improvement is not accurately measured by the dollar value of additional sales revenue alone; it must also include the benefit the owner gets from the prestige of quality enhancement. Suppose the owner is "willing to pay" a maximum of $40,000 in the form of reduced profit for the satisfaction of making a higher-quality wine. In this case, the marginal benefit of $115,000 exceeds the marginal cost of $100,000 and the firm will choose to trade off $25,000 in profit for the five-point improvement in quality. To maximize owner utility, the firm will continue to enhance the quality of the wine product as long as marginal benefit exceeds marginal cost.

It is much easier to explain the behavior of profit-maximizing than non-profit-maximizing wine firms, since the choices of the former are more predictable than those of the latter. Because a non-profit-maximizing wine firm is willing to trade off profit for other sources of utility, it is necessary to know what those sources of utility are and the benefit the owner experiences from them. For example, if the objective of a wine firm is to maximize profit, then it follows logically that it will always choose the method of production that minimizes the cost of producing any given quantity and quality of wine output. A non-profit-maximizing wine firm, on the other hand, may not necessarily behave this way. If the owner derives utility from owning vineyard land and employing family members, he may choose a method of production that has more than the cost-minimizing amount of vineyard land and labor. To predict these non-cost-minimizing choices, it is necessary to know that the owner derives utility from vineyard land and nepotism, as well as the value the owner places on these nonmarket sources of utility.

DEMAND, SUPPLY, AND THE WINE MARKET

A market is any set of arrangements by which buyers and sellers make an exchange. Most market transactions involve the exchange a good or service for money. For our purposes, the wine market refers to the markets on which wine grapes and wine are bought and sold. The type of wine traded in this market can be either wine that a firm packages in a bottle or box and sells to consumers or bulk wine that one wine firm sells to another. The market for newly released wine is called the primary market; the market for previously released wine is called the secondary market.

A market can be organized as a direct-search market, brokered market, dealer market, or auction market. The wine market incorporates all four of these organizational mechanisms.

In a direct-search market, buyers and sellers seek out and find one another directly without the assistance of a third-party intermediary. About 95 percent of wine-grape and bulk wine sales are direct-search transactions. On the other hand, less than 10 percent of packaged wine sales involve wine firms selling their products directly to consumers at a tasting room or shipping wine to consumers by package carrier to fulfill wine club or Internet orders.

A brokered market is organized by third-party intermediaries called brokers. Brokers specialize in collecting information about opportunities for exchange and matching potential buyers and sellers of a good. They never take ownership of a good, and they are paid a commission for the services they provide. Brokers exist in the market for wine grapes and bulk wine. Although it is still relatively small, a growing proportion of transactions are taking place through brokers who have specialized knowledge of wine-market conditions, and these often assist buyers and sellers in negotiating contract terms and mediating disputes. Many wine firms also use brokers to arrange transactions with wine distributors and retailers. The major advantage of trading through a broker is that it reduces the cost of searching for another party with whom to make a satisfactory exchange. Of course, a rational wine firm will only choose to use a broker if the expected reduction in search cost exceeds the broker's commission.

A dealer market is organized by third-party intermediaries called dealers. Dealers purchase goods for their own inventory and attempt to resell them at a higher price than the purchase price. The difference between the buy price and the sell price is the dealer's markup, which is compensation for services provided. These services include reducing the search cost of exchanges to parties who buy from and sell to the dealer, and assuming the risk of reselling the goods held in inventory should market conditions change. The primary market for packaged wine products is largely organized by wine distributors and retailers who function as dealers. Wine firms sell more than 90 percent of their newly released wine to consumers through distributors and retailers. On the other hand, dealers do not exist and therefore play no role in organizing wine-grape and bulk wine transactions.

In an auction market, buyers and sellers submit bid and asked prices for a good either at a physical location, such as an auction house, or on a website. Transactions are carried out through a human or electronic auctioneer at prices that are mutually agreeable for the participating parties. The secondary market for wine products is largely organized as an auction market. Previously released, age-worthy, luxury wine products, such as first-growth red Bordeaux and Napa Valley "cult" wines, are typically traded on the secondary auction market at large auction houses like Christie's and Sotheby's, a number of smaller auction houses, some retail wine stores, and several websites.

SUPPLY-AND-DEMAND ANALYSIS

Supply-and-demand analysis is the cornerstone of economics. It is a theoretical construct used by economists to organize their thinking about how buyers and sellers interact in a market setting, and how the price and quantity bought and sold of a product emerge from these interactions. It was conceived to explain price and output determination in a competitive market with a large number of buyers and sellers of an identical product who individually have no power to influence price, but it is also useful in analyzing markets that deviate somewhat from this perfectly competitive structure, such as the wine market.

Figure 2 illustrates market demand and supply curves for wine. The average price of a 750 ml bottle of wine is measured on the vertical axis and the quantity of wine in billions of bottles per year is measured on the horizontal axis. The demand curve is downward-sloping, reflecting the law of demand: at higher prices, consumers desire to buy less wine, and at lower prices more, all else being equal. The supply curve is upward-sloping, reflecting what economists call the law of supply. All else being equal, at higher prices, producers are willing to increase the quantity of wine they supply on the market. When wine firms receive a higher price for their product, they are able to cover the higher marginal cost of production that results from the law of diminishing returns and earn greater profits by expanding output. The opportunity to make greater profits provides a strong economic incentive for a typical wine firm to offer more of its product for sale to consumers. Given these supply-and-demand conditions, the market clears at an average price of $7.50 per bottle and 4 billion bottles of wine bought and sold per year where the demand curve intersects the supply curve. This intersection point is called market equilibrium, and the price and quantity are called the equilibrium price and quantity. A price of $7.50 is the only price at which the number of bottles of wine consumers are willing to buy equals the quantity firms are willing to sell. Since the rational decisions of buyers and sellers are consistent, there is no economic incentive for either party to change its behavior, and the wine market is in a state of balance.

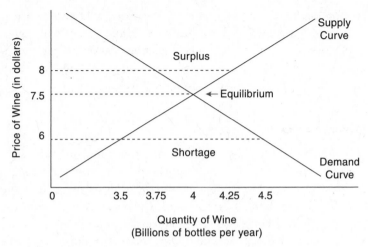

FIGURE 2. Supply and demand curves for wine.

In a competitive market, any price higher or lower than $7.50 is not sustainable, since the decisions of buyers and sellers are inconsistent. For example, at an average price of $8 per bottle, wine firms produce and are willing to sell 4.25 billion bottles per year. However, wine consumers desire to purchase only 3.75 billion. As a result, there is a surplus of 500 million bottles on the market, and wine firms therefore experience an unwanted increase in inventories. To reduce excess inventory, a typical wine firm cuts its price to entice consumers to purchase more, while at the same time lowering its rate of production. The lower price provides consumers with an economic incentive to buy more wine, and the quantity of wine demanded therefore increases. The market will continue to adjust until the price of wine falls to $7.50 and quantity demanded equals quantity supplied at 4 billion bottles per year. What happens if price is below $7.50, say, $6.00 per bottle? At this price, consumers desire to purchase 4.5 billion bottles of wine, but wine firms produce and are willing to sell only 3.5 billion, so the market is characterized by a shortage of 1 billion bottles of wine per year. Consumers find that a number of wines they want to buy at the current price quickly sell out and are difficult to find. The excess demand for wine puts upward pressure on price. As price rises above $6.00, this gives wine firms an economic incentive to ramp up production, and the quantity of wine supplied increases. At the higher price, some consumers are willing to buy less, and the quantity demanded falls. This adjustment process will continue until equilibrium prevails in the market.

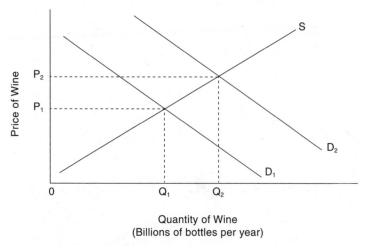

FIGURE 3. Change in wine demand.

A change in any factor, other than price, that affects the amount of wine consumers desire to purchase and the quantity producers are willing to sell will shift the demand or supply curve, temporarily disrupt market equilibrium, and result in a change in the equilibrium price and quantity of wine bought and sold. Anything that increases (decreases) the amount of wine consumers desire to buy at any possible price will increase (decrease) demand, shift the demand curve to the right (left), and increase (decrease) the equilibrium price and quantity. This is illustrated in figure 3. An increase in demand moves the demand curve to the right from D_1 to D_2, increases equilibrium price from P_1 to P_2, and increases equilibrium quantity from Q_1 to Q_2; a decrease in demand moves the demand curve to the left from D_2 to D_1, resulting in a lower price and quantity. Any factor that increases (decreases) the amount of wine that firms are willing to produce and sell at any possible price of wine will increase (decrease) supply, shift the supply curve to the right (left), decrease (increase) equilibrium price, and increase (decrease) equilibrium quantity. This is illustrated in figure 4. An increase in supply moves the supply curve to the right from S_1 to S_2, resulting in an decrease in price from P_1 to P_2 and an increase in quantity from Q_1 to Q_2; a decrease in supply moves the supply curve to the left from S_2 to S_1, increasing price and decreasing quantity.

Economists maintain that the most important factors that affect market demand and shift the demand curve are income, prices of substitute and complementary goods, tastes and preferences, and population.

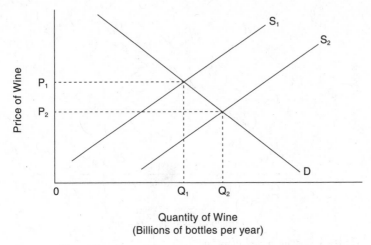

FIGURE 4. Change in wine supply.

If wine is a normal good, then an increase in income increases demand, and a decrease in income decreases demand. For example, supply-and-demand analysis predicts that wine demand will increase during periods of economic expansion, when aggregate output and income are rising, and decrease in periods of economic recession, when aggregate output and income are falling. Ignoring other possible factors that might change over the business cycle, the rise in wine demand during an economic expansion shifts the demand curve to the right, resulting in higher wine prices and a larger volume bought and sold. Conversely, during a recession, the wine demand curve shifts to the left, and price and quantity fall.[7]

An increase in the price of a substitute good increases demand, while an increase in the price of a complementary good decreases demand. Conversely, demand decreases when the price of a substitute falls and increases when the price of a complement falls. For example, many people consider wine to be a substitute for other alcoholic beverages such as beer and spirits. Between 2006 and 2010, the average price of wine decreased by about 12 percent relative to the average price of beer and spirits. All else being equal, this would have resulted in increased wine demand, higher wine prices, and greater wine consumption as some consumers substituted wine for the relatively higher-priced beer and spirits. On the other hand, during the same period of time, beef prices increased by about 11 percent. If consumers view wine and beef as complementary goods, then the increase in beef prices would have had the effect of reducing wine demand, wine prices, and wine consumption as consumers chose to have fewer meals with beef and its complement, wine. Many consumers view imported wine as a substitute for domestic wine. As a result, supply-and-demand analysis predicts that an increase in the value of the dollar relative to the currencies of foreign wine-producing countries such as France and Australia will decrease the demand for domestic wine as consumers substitute relatively lower-priced imported wine.

Tastes and preferences for wine may be influenced and shaped by a wide range of factors. These include advertising, wine critic scores, health considerations, cultural influences, and demographic characteristics. Anything that results in a favorable change in consumer taste for wine will increase demand. A shift in preferences away from wine will decrease demand. Some wine-market analysts argue the most important factor affecting wine consumption is consumer perception of the health effects of wine. They contend that the demand for wine has increased dramatically because of the large and growing number of medical studies that find evidence that moderate wine consumption promotes good health. Supply-and-demand analysis predicts that, all else being equal, this shift in preferences toward wine resulting from the perception of wine as a healthy beverage will increase wine prices and the quantity produced and consumed.

The last important factor influencing market demand is the size and age distribution of the population. A rising population increases the number of potential consumers in a market, which translates into a bigger demand for most products. For example, total wine consumption in the United States is higher than in any other country in the world, including France and Italy, where wine is an integral part of culture and lifestyle. However, this can be largely explained by the fact that the population of the United States is more than five times bigger than the populations of France and Italy. A major reason the United States consumes more wine than these countries is that we have a larger demand for wine, because we have substantially more potential wine consumers. On a per capita basis, France and Italy each consume more than five times as much wine as the United States. The proportion of the population falling into different age groups can also have a significant effect on demand. Studies of the U.S. wine market find that individuals thirty-five years of age and older consume substantially more wine per capita than those under the age of thirty-five. All else being equal, supply-and-demand analysis therefore predicts that the aging of the population will increase wine demand, price, and quantity.

Economists argue that the most important factors that affect market supply and shift the supply curve are input prices, excise taxes and subsidies, technology, prices of substitute goods in production, and the number of firms in the industry.

Anything that increases (decreases) cost will decrease (increase) supply. The most important factors that affect the cost of producing a given quantity of wine are the prices a wine firm pays for its inputs, the excise tax on alcoholic beverages, government subsidies, and advances in grape and wine technology. The most important input used to produce wine is grapes. Lower grape prices reduce the cost of producing any given output of wine, increase profit, and give wine firms a strong incentive to raise production. All else being equal, the increase in market supply leads to a lower price and greater wine consumption. The opposite occurs when grape prices rise. Grape prices, in turn, are significantly influenced by year-to-year variations in weather and other growing conditions. In years with favorable growing seasons, grape and wine supply tends to be higher and prices lower than in years with poor growing seasons. Federal and state governments impose excise taxes on wines that are collected directly from producers. Wine firms view these as another variable cost of production. Higher excise taxes raise costs and reduce profits and wine supply. Lower excise taxes lead to greater production and consumption of wine and lower prices. When government provides a subsidy to a producer, this typically reduces the firm's cost of production and increases supply. Some states give subsidies to growers to provide an economic incentive to grow more grapes. One midwestern state gives growers a money payment of up to $1,000 per acre to develop new vineyard land. Another provides a tax credit to growers to reduce the cost of expanding grape production. Supply-and-demand analysis predicts that these types of subsidies will lead to increased grape and wine production and consumption, and lower prices, all else being equal. Advances in grape and wine production technology increase productivity, reduce cost, and increase supply. During the past fifty years, the wine industry has witnessed dramatic advances in grape-growing and wine-production knowledge. Much of this knowledge is embodied in capital equipment such as mechanical harvesters, pruners, and sprayers; computerized, temperature-controlled fermentation tanks; and pneumatic presses. Supply-and-demand analysis predicts that these sorts of technological advancements contribute to lower grape and wine production costs, increased wine supply, and lower prices for consumers.

Two important non-cost factors that affect supply are the prices of substitute goods in production and the number of producers in the industry. Two goods are substitutes in production if they can be produced by a firm with similar resources and production processes. For example, Merlot grapes and wine are a substitute in production for other types of grapes and wine such as Zinfandel. In the early 1990s, the TV news show *60 Minutes* aired an episode summarizing medical evidence suggesting that drinking red wine resulted in a longer life span for the French, even though they smoked more, consumed more red meat, and exercised less than Americans. In response to this "French paradox," the demand for red wine increased dramatically, particularly soft, fruity, sweet tasting Merlot, which many Americans started to consume in place of the popular sweet White Zinfandel. As a result, the price of Merlot increased and that of White Zinfandel fell. This gave grape and wine producers an economic incentive to produce more of the relatively higher-priced Merlot and less of the relatively lower-priced White Zinfandel. In response, the supply of Merlot increased and the supply of White Zinfandel decreased. Supply-and-demand analysis predicts that the increase in the supply of Merlot, considered by itself, would lead to an increase in equilibrium quantity and put downward pressure on price. Lastly, an increase (decrease) in the number of grape growers and wine firms in the industry will increase (decrease) supply. All else being equal, the entry of new grape growers and wine firms into the industry shifts the supply curve to the right, increases equilibrium quantity, and decreases equilibrium price.

2

The Wine Product

An important characteristic of the structure of a market is the nature of the product bought and sold. Wine is a complex and intriguing product with unique qualities that make it significantly different from a typical manufactured good. To understand the wine market and how consumers and producers behave, it is necessary to have sufficient knowledge of the characteristics of the wine product. This chapter views wine as both an agricultural and economic good, and relates it to the economic activities required for its production and sale to consumers.

WINE AS AN AGRICULTURAL GOOD

Wine is an agricultural good made from grapes by the natural process of fermentation.[1] Unlike a typical manufactured good, the production of wine requires minimal human intervention in the form of the services of labor, capital, and entrepreneurship. The most important input used to produce wine is grapes. Wild grape vines grow naturally in forested areas using trees and other plants as a supporting trellis to seek out sunlight and bear ripe fruit that contains sugar, acid, and a variety of aroma and flavor compounds. To make wine all that is necessary is to pick ripe grapes and place them in a container; nature will do the rest of the work. The weight of the grapes that occupy the top of the container will eventually break the skins of the grapes on bottom releasing juice. Single cell microorganisms, called yeast, that exist naturally in the atmosphere and on the skins of the grapes spontaneously initiate a process of fermentation that transforms the sugar in the grape juice into alcohol. Once the fermented grape juice is separated from the solids, the resulting liquid is an agricultural good, called wine, that can be consumed.

FERMENTATION

The most important stage in the natural process of wine production is fermentation. Fermentation transforms the grape input into wine output. Sugar exists naturally in the juice of ripe grapes. Wild yeasts circulate in abundance in the environment. When grapes are crushed, juice comes into contact with yeast. The yeast secrete an enzyme that initiates a chain of chemical reactions that convert sugar in the juice to alcohol and carbon dioxide in roughly equal proportions. The carbon dioxide dissipates into the air. In addition, small amounts of a large number of by-products are produced. Many of these are aroma and flavor compounds that contribute to wine complexity. Fermentation ends when all of the sugar is converted to alcohol or the alcohol reaches a level high enough to kill the yeast, typically around 15 percent. The fermented grape juice that emerges from this process is wine.[2]

MODERN WINE PRODUCTION

If wine is a natural agricultural product that almost produces itself, then why does modern wine production involve a significant amount of human intervention? Grapes are grown in vineyards and wine is produced in production facilities called wineries. Grape growers make decisions about vineyard location, grape variety, vine trellising and pruning, fungicide and pesticide use, irrigation, and timing and method of harvest. Winemakers make choices about grape crushing and pressing, yeast strain, fermentation vessel and temperature, maturation container, clarification and stabilization, blending, aging, storage, and much else.

The reason for substantial human intervention in grape growing and winemaking is inherently economic. Wine is an economic good governed by the market forces of demand and supply. Grape growing and winemaking choices are heavily influenced by consumer tastes and preferences and production costs. Decisions to intervene in the natural wine production process invariably involve quality and cost considerations related to the satisfaction of consumer wants and desires.

WINE AS AN ECONOMIC GOOD

Wine is an economic good because people value it and derive utility from its consumption.

Wine as a Bundle of Characteristics

A useful way to think about certain types of economic goods is in terms of their qualities or characteristics.[3] For example, an automobile can be viewed as a bundle of characteristics that includes engine size, interior space, fuel economy, and style. A house is a bundle of characteristics of which a few are square footage, number of bedrooms, and location. Consumers derive utility not from a good such as an automobile itself, but rather from the types and amounts of characteristics it possesses. While different types of automobiles are similar products with common characteristics, they differ in terms of the amounts of utility-bearing attributes they offer consumers. One automobile type may have a larger engine size; another offers more miles per gallon of gasoline. The utility a consumer derives from an automobile depends upon its engine size, fuel economy, and other characteristics.

Like automobiles it is useful to view wine as a bundle of characteristics. Wine is a complex good with a variety of qualities. It is convenient to distinguish between sensory and nonsensory characteristics. Sensory characteristics are utility-bearing attributes perceived by the senses. The three important sensory characteristics of wine are appearance, smell, and taste. Appearance is the look of the wine. Smell is the wine's aroma as perceived by the olfactory system. Taste is the impression the wine gives when placed in the mouth; it includes both flavor and feel. These attributes, in turn, are related to more basic sensory qualities such as color, clearness, alcohol, acidity, tannin, residual sugar, and fruit, oak, and yeast aroma and flavor compounds. According to this view, wine is a liquid beverage with specific appearance, smell, and taste attributes that a consumer finds satisfying or pleasing. The utility derived from a particular wine depends upon these sensory characteristics.

Nonsensory characteristics are factors related to sensory characteristics. In general, they do not yield utility to wine consumers directly, but rather indirectly by their effect on sensory characteristics. Five important categories of nonsensory characteristics are grape variety, grape location, viticulture, vinification, and transportation and storage. Grape variety is the type of grape produced by a particular grapevine, such as Cabernet Sauvignon, Chardonnay, and Pinot noir. Grape location refers to the specific geographic location where the grapes are grown, for instance, the Napa Valley, California, and the Willamette Valley, Oregon. Viticulture is the planting, growing, and harvesting of grapes. Vinification refers to the techniques of winemaking, or winegrowing (many wine producers believe that wine is made in the vineyard and therefore prefer the latter term). Lastly, transportation and storage is the manner in which wine is moved from winery to consumer, and the conditions under which it is kept until final consumption.

Nonsensory characteristics are associated with the three major economic activities required to produce and sell wine: grape growing, winemaking, and wine distribution. These activities, which entail hundreds of choices that affect the sensory characteristics of wine, are organized and coordinated by a legal entity called a wine firm and can be performed either within the firm or outsourced to other firms. For instance, a wine firm can grow its own grapes or contract with independent vineyards to buy grapes. It can produce wine in its own winemaking facility or outsource this to a custom-crush winery. Most wine firms rely on contracts and relationships with other firms to transport, store, and distribute wine to consumers. When making the multitude of choices that affect wine attributes, the wine firm may be motivated by the desire to maximize profits, or it may have nonprofit goals.

Wine as a Class of Differentiated Goods

From an economic standpoint, it is useful to view wines as a class of goods that have a common set of sensory and nonsensory characteristics; that is, each good in the class is a liquid beverage that has a particular appearance, smell, and taste resulting from grape variety and vineyard location, viticultural and vinification practices, and transportation and storage conditions. Different wines in the class possess different bundles of these common characteristics and are identified by a unique label that is attached to a bottle or alternative package, such as a box. By this definition, more than 15,000 different wine products are available to consumers in the U.S. wine market.[4] Wine is a differentiated good, as opposed to a homogeneous good, because the bundles of characteristics offered by different wines are imperfect substitutes for each other.[5]

Wine as an Experience Good

When a good is viewed as a bundle of characteristics, a distinction can be made between a search good and an experience good depending upon whether the consumer learns about the utility-bearing attributes of the good before or after it is purchased. For example, an automobile is a search good, because information about fuel economy, engine size, and other features can be gathered prior to purchase. However, it is useful to think of wine as an experience good, since the appearance, smell, and taste of a particular wine can rarely be evaluated before it is purchased.[6]

When making decisions about the first-time purchase of a wine, consumers often lack subjective information about its sensory characteristics, and therefore may use a variety of nonexperiential sources of information. This may include the wine firm's reputation, brand name, wine critic quality ratings, wine guides and magazines, wine bottle labels, and recommendations from friends and salespeople at retail establishments. Consumption decisions about repeat purchases of the same wine are obviously better informed, but even these may have an experience good aspect as a result of bottle variation and aging. The appearance, smell, and taste of a typical wine tend to change over time as the wine chemically transforms in the bottle. Sensory characteristics may also be affected by the manner in which wine is transported and stored, as well as the condition of the cork closure, which can vary across bottles of the same wine.

Wine Quality

An important dimension of wine as an economic good is quality. The term quality is regularly used by grape growers, winemakers, wine distributors and retailers, wine writers, wine critics, and other wine professionals. However, the concept of wine quality is often left undefined and used in a nebulous manner. While there appears to be a general consensus that the notion of quality in wine is important, differing opinions exist about its precise nature.[7]

From an economic perspective, it is useful to think of quality in terms of the amounts of characteristics contained in a particular wine. Wines vary in quality because of differences in the bundles of characteristics they possess. For example, a bottle of vintage 2007 Caymus Cabernet Sauvignon differs in quality from a bottle of 2005 Duckhorn Merlot because of differences in appearance, smell, and taste. Differences in these sensory characteristics reflect differences in color, alcohol, acidity, tannin, and fruit, oak, and yeast flavor compounds that result from differences in grape variety, geographic location where the grapes were grown, viticultural and vinification practices, and vintage-related age and weather conditions.

Assessment of differences in wine quality requires valuation of the bundle of sensory characteristics embodied in a particular wine. A distinction can be made between subjective and objective (or absolute) quality based on how wine characteristics are valued. Subjective quality involves consumer evaluation of wine attributes based on personal tastes and preferences. Consumers may differ in terms of the value they place on the bundle of wine characteristics. The more a consumer values a bundle of characteristics, the more she or he is willing to pay for the wine product. Subjective wine quality, therefore, is defined in terms of the degree to which a wine satisfies consumer wants and desires, and is revealed by consumer willingness to pay in the marketplace.

Objective quality involves the identification or discovery of a set of absolute standards related to sensory characteristics and independent of personal preferences that define wine quality. The more closely a particular wine conforms to these ideal standards, the higher its quality. Different sets of standards have been proposed by wine professionals. For instance wine tasting, as opposed to wine drinking, is typically defined as the sensory evaluation of wine to determine quality. Professional wine tasters usually suggest a set of standards by which they attempt to objectively value wine sensory characteristics and assess quality, which may include such criteria as balance, complexity, finish, concentration, flavor intensity, and varietal and geographic typicity. Judged by these standards, the taster may well conclude that a particular wine is of high quality on grounds that it has balanced taste components, a variety of interesting aromas and flavors, a long aftertaste, and expresses the location where the grapes were grown, even though the taster personally dislikes it.

The most visible application of the notion of objective quality is professional wine criticism. Wine critics attempt to provide an objective assessment of wine quality. To do this, they typically give a description of the appearance, smell, and taste of a wine, along with a rating or score as a measure of quality. The most prominent and influential wine critic of the past three decades is Robert Parker.[8] Parker's quality rating system employs a 100-point scale similar to an educational grade system. Each wine begins with a base score of 50 points. Additional points are then assigned for appearance (5 points), smell (15 points), taste and finish (20 points), and overall quality and aging potential (10 points). Higher point scores indicate higher-quality wine.[9] While Parker does not claim that his scores measure a set of absolute quality standards, the cover of his bimonthly newsletter *The Wine Advocate* states: "There are specific standards of quality that full-time wine professionals recognize." However, the precise standards that wine critics use is not always clear.

The concept of subjective quality is more relevant to the economic decisions of wine consumers and producers than the notion of objective quality. Ultimately, consumers who seek to satisfy subjective wants and desires determine wine quality by the maximum amount of money they are willing to pay for wine characteristics in the marketplace. A typical producer who makes decisions based solely on objective quality and ignores consumer preferences will likely not be in business very long. From an economic standpoint, the notion of objective quality is relevant only insofar as it affects consumer tastes and preferences or producers' perceptions of those preferences.

3

Wine Sensory Characteristics

Wine is a complex good. To provide a better understanding of its nature, this chapter discusses its sensory characteristics in some detail, drawing from the literature on wine appreciation and wine science.[1] Knowledge of how wine professionals think about and describe the appearance, smell, and taste of wine is germane to wine economics. These professionals are either direct participants in the wine industry or may influence others who make economic decisions in this market. Moreover, information on factors that influence the sensory characteristics of wine is necessary for an understanding of grape growing and wine production, and the economic choices and trade-offs that confront producers in the wine industry. Finally, sensory characteristics play an important role in the hedonic theory of wine consumers' behavior. Knowledge of the nature of these characteristics and how they may be measured is useful for interpreting economic studies of wine quality and price.

APPEARANCE

Clarity and Color

Appearance refers to how a wine looks. The most important qualities of wine appearance are clarity and color. Wine can be clear and bright, or dull and cloudy with noticeable sediment. The range of possible colors includes different shades of purple, red, garnet, pink, gold, yellow, and green. Wine critics generally believe appearance is the least important sensory characteristic of wine. For instance, Robert Parker's quality wine rating system assigns a 10 percent weight to appearance, while smell and taste are given weights of 30 and 40 percent. However, it is common knowledge in the wine industry that consumers often refuse to accept or return cloudy wines with noticeable but harmless sediment. This suggests that the appearance of wine, like the appearance of fruits and vegetables, is a characteristic highly valued by many. Moreover, experimental studies find evidence that a consumer's perception of the smell and taste of a wine depends on its appearance. For example, subjects give the same description of the smell and taste of red wine and of white wine with flavor-neutral artificial red coloring.[2]

Nonsensory Characteristics Affecting Appearance

The major source of wine color is chemical pigment found in grape skins. Juice obtained from grape pulp is essentially clear. Color is added to wine when grape juice absorbs pigment from the skins. Grape variety determines whether a wine is red or white, as well as influencing shades of difference. For instance, wine made from the Chardonnay grape typically has a yellow or golden color, while wine from the Cabernet Sauvignon grape has a bluish purple color. The location where grapes are grown can affect color. Grapes grown in cool climates tend to be lighter in color than those from warmer locations. Wine color is also influenced by vinification techniques. Color intensity can be augmented by increasing the amount of time the juice is in contact with grape skins, thereby extracting more pigment into the wine, or blending in a small amount of wine made from a deeply colored, flavor-neutral grape. Adding grape concentrate, like Mega Purple, is an easy way to deepen and enrich the color of red wine.[3] All of these methods have been used by winemakers to improve the appearance of wine. Maturing a white wine such as chardonnay in oak barrels can result in a deeper yellow or golden color preferred by many consumers, but is usually not the primary motivation by winemakers for oak aging. Lastly, the length of time a wine is stored and storage conditions can affect wine color. White wine gets darker and red wine lighter with exposure to oxygen, and both eventually turn brown. This typically happens to a wine as it ages because of inevitable oxidation.

The most important determinant of wine clarity is vinification. After grapes are crushed and the juice is fermented, the resulting wine is invariably hazy with pieces of skin, pulp, yeast, and other suspended particles. To produce a clear wine, one or more winemaking techniques must be used. Most winemakers have responded to consumer preference for clarity by racking, fining, and filtering wine to remove innocuous foreign objects and sediment that consumers may find undesirable. Some producers refuse to use filtration because they believe it militates against the flavor, character, and overall quality of the wine.

SMELL

Smell refers to wine aroma. Wine is a naturally volatile liquid that readily emits an invisible gas in the form of a vapor. This vapor contains molecules, called aroma compounds, that can exist in a gaseous state and be detected by the sense of smell via the olfactory system. A single wine may contain hundreds of different aroma compounds, which are largely responsible for its complexity. When wine vapor is inhaled, the aroma compounds travel up the front nasal passage and attach to receptor cells in the olfactory system. The receptor cells transform the chemical input provided by these compounds into electric impulses, which are then transmitted to the brain and interpreted as smell.[4]

Important qualities of smell are pleasantness, complexity, and intensity. Many critics maintain that aroma is the most important sensory characteristic of wine; however, Robert Parker's rating system gives a somewhat smaller weight to smell than taste.

Describing Smell

Wine professionals typically attempt to describe wine aroma by making comparisons with other familiar smells or using metaphorical expressions that recall smells. A wide variety of words and expressions are used to describe the complex aroma of wine. In the 1980s, the enologist Ann Noble developed the wine aroma wheel in an attempt to provide a standardized language to describe the smell of wine.[5] As a result, many wine professionals describe wine aroma using terms related to her framework, such as *fruity, floral, vegetative, herbaceous, spicy, earthy, oaky, animal, nutty,* and *chemical.* Within these broad categories more precise aroma descriptors are also frequently used, such as *green apple, pineapple, black currant, raspberry, rose pedal, green pepper, cinnamon, wet stones, fresh dirt, vanilla, leather, almond,* and *tar.* In spite of Noble's work, a lack of consensus exists among wine professionals on the best way to describe wine aroma.

Sources of Aroma Compounds

The aroma compounds in wine that give it a distinctive smell come from three main sources: grapes, wood, and yeast. Grape aroma compounds emanate from the grape itself and can produce smells reminiscent of a variety of fresh fruits, flowers, and vegetables. The amounts and types of grape compounds vary across grape varieties. Most grape compounds come from the skins, but some are also found in the pulp. A distinction is typically made between free aroma compounds and aroma precursors.[6] The scent of free aroma compounds can be detected in the grape juice prior to fermentation; the more plentiful aroma precursors are inactive compounds, which need to be unlocked during fermentation, maturation, or bottle aging to contribute to wine smell.

Many wines are fermented or matured in wood barrels. The most common type of wood used is oak. Wood contains aroma compounds that are absorbed into wine and are capable of producing smells suggestive of vanilla, caramel, toast, smoke, meat, and other non-fruit scents.

Moreover, during the process of fermentation, yeasts produce their own aroma compounds as a by-product of transforming sugar into alcohol. Different strains of yeast are capable of contributing different smells to wine. When fermentation ends, the yeast die and fall to the bottom of the fermentation vessel, contributing to a sediment called lees. The spent yeast cells are capable of creating additional aroma compounds reminiscent of toast, fresh bread, biscuit, or roasted grain.

Some wine professionals distinguish between primary, secondary, and tertiary aromas, depending upon the stage in the wine production and aging process when various types of aroma compounds are created or released.[7] Primary aromas come from compounds found in grapes before fermentation and are sometimes referred to as a wine's fruit. Wine with a large amount of primary aroma compounds, rich in fruit aromatics, is often said to have "lots of fruit," "high-quality fruit," or "oodles of fruit" (Robert Parker's phrase). Secondary aromas arise from compounds created during fermentation. In the process of alcoholic fermentation, scents locked in aroma precursors are released, primary aroma compounds are modified, and new aroma compounds are created by yeast. Some white wines and most red wines also go through a secondary nonalcoholic fermentation performed by lactic bacteria. During this malolactic fermentation, which transforms malic acid into lactic acid, new compounds are produced that may be suggestive of butter, milk, yogurt, or butterscotch. If wine is allowed to remain in contact with spent yeast cells in lees, it may develop additional yeast-related aromas.

Tertiary aromas, also called a wine's bouquet, result from compounds produced during wine maturation and bottle aging. After fermentation is completed, wine is typically matured for a certain period of time in either a stainless steel tank or an oak barrel. Maturation in an oak barrel can result in the creation of additional non-fruit aromas in two ways. Oak is porous and may expose the wine to a small amount of air, which can foster the creation of new aroma compounds. More important, the oak itself contains aroma compounds that can be absorbed into the wine as it matures. The smells created by these oak compounds, as well as their intensity, depend upon the type of oak (American or French), the newness of the oak (new or used), and how it was toasted (light, medium, or dark). Maturation in a stainless steel tank does not promote the creation of tertiary aromas, because it consists of an inert material with no aroma compounds and prevents oxidation. Once wine is placed in an airtight bottle, it enters a stage called reduction, which may affect its smell. Most wines do not develop new aroma compounds in the bottle and may lose their attractive primary and secondary aromas, or possibly develop unpleasant odors, if not consumed within a couple of years. However, a select group of wines with certain characteristics, such as substantial amounts of rich fruit, tannin, and acidity, may develop new smells as a result of complex chemical changes that occur as these wines age in the bottle. Additional smells may be unlocked and released from aroma precursors, and fruity primary and secondary aromas may be transformed into more complex non-fruit scents reminiscent of truffles, mushrooms, oregano, game, leather, honey, or even kerosene.

The notion of primary, secondary, and tertiary aromas indicates that the smell of a typical wine will change over time. Primary fruit and secondary fermentation aromas are characteristic of a young wine. If the fruit aromas dominate those resulting from non-grape winemaking treatments, such as malolactic fermentation, lees contact, and barrel maturation, the wine is often called "fruit forward" or "fruit driven."[8] Most wines tend to lose their fruit- and vinification-derived aromas over time; a relatively small subset possess the ability to gain more complex and interesting smells with age.

TASTE

Taste is the impression wine gives when placed in the mouth. When wine is taken into the mouth, it is felt by the sense of touch. This is referred to as "wine mouthfeel" and relates to the perceived weight, resistance, texture, and warmness of the wine. In addition, nonvolatile chemicals in the liquid are sensed by the taste buds (groups of receptor cells on the tongue) and interpreted by the brain as any of four major tastes: sweet, sour, bitter, or salt. Finally, the liquid wine releases aromatic vapor that travels up the retro-nasal passage, located in the back of the mouth, to the olfactory system and is interpreted by the brain as smell. What is usually referred to as flavor is the combined sensation of sweet, sour, bitter, and salt detected by the taste buds and aroma compounds detected by the olfactory system. As anyone who has ever tasted wine with a head cold knows, the most important element of its flavor is smell; we largely smell flavor. For this reason, aroma compounds are also called flavor compounds; the two expressions are interchangeable.

Describing Taste

To describe wine flavor, professionals use language similar to that used to describe wine smell. In addition, a variety of words and expressions are used to describe wine mouthfeel. For example, the word *body* is used to convey the impression of weight or fullness that a wine leaves in the mouth. Wines are often classified as light, medium, or full-bodied and compared to skim milk, whole milk, and cream. Viscosity describes the degree of resistance of wine as it moves over the tongue. Words used to describe wine texture include *hard, firm, crisp, soft, silky, velvety,* and *flabby*. Metaphors such as *opulent, voluptuous, hollow, well-knit,* and *linear* are also frequently used to create an image of mouthfeel.

Taste Components of Wine

It is useful to think about the taste of wine as consisting of seven major components: alcohol, acidity, tannin, residual sugar, fruit, oak, and yeast. These components are largely responsible for the flavor and mouthfeel of wine.[9]

Alcohol is the most important taste component by volume, accounting for about 8 to 16 percent of a bottle of wine. It is largely responsible for wine body and viscosity. Wine with relatively high alcohol tends to feel heavy, full, viscous, and powerful. Alcohol can also make wine feel soft and warm, and leave the impression of sweetness in the absence of sugar.

Wine contains six major types of acids. Tartaric, malic, and citric acids come from grapes; acetic, lactic, and succinic acids are produced during the process of fermentation. Acidity accounts for only about 0.5 to 1 percent of the volume of wine; nevertheless, it has an important effect on the way wine feels in the mouth, particularly white wine. Adequate acidity results in a crisp, clean, refreshing taste. Too much acidity leaves a tart or sour taste; too little makes wine feel flabby and flat. Different types of acid can leave the impression of different tastes. For instance, malic acid is often compared to the harsh taste of a green apple, lactic acid to sour cream or yogurt, and acetic acid to vinegar.

Tannin is a group of compounds found in grape skins, seeds, and stems, and the wood of oak barrels. Red wine typically has more tannin than white wine, because red wine is fermented with grape skins, seeds, and occasionally stems. Tannin gives wine structure and a firm mouthfeel, but too much can leave the impression of bitterness and dryness.

Residual sugar is the amount of sugar that remains in wine after fermentation is completed. It can range from about 0.1 percent to more than 10 percent of the volume of wine depending on whether the style is dry or sweet. Residual sugar creates the impression of sweetness and can make wine feel soft and viscous, but too much can have a cloying effect.

Fruit, oak, and yeast, refer to the aroma and flavor compounds deriving from grapes, oak barrels and treatments, and the variety of yeast strains used to ferment wine. These three components are the major source of wine flavor.

The Taste Qualities of Wine

Wine professionals have defined a number of qualities of taste of possible importance to consumers. The most common of these include faultlessness, balance, complexity, finish, concentration, flavor intensity, and varietal and regional typicity. These taste attributes are sometimes used by professionals as criteria by which to evaluate wine quality and objective standards of quality.[10]

Faultlessness is the absence of wine defects, such as cork taint, brett-anomyces, oxidation, and acetification, which give wine an obvious off-taste to most consumers. Cork taint occurs when the cork closure becomes contaminated with a chemical called TCA, resulting in a musty or wet cardboard taste. Brettanomyces is an unwelcome strain of yeast that produces wine flavors many consumers describe as reminiscent of a barnyard. Oxidation is excessive exposure to oxygen resulting in a dull, flat, tasteless wine. Acetification occurs when bacteria in wine called acetobactor transform alcohol into a distinct taste of vinegar.

Balance refers to the relationship among the major taste components of wine. A wine is balanced when the alcohol, acidity, tannin, residual sugar, fruit, oak, and yeast complement one another and no single component stands out. An unbalanced wine is often described as being too hot, or astringent, or sweet, or tart, or fruity, or oaky, or yeasty. A complex wine is typically described as one that is interesting to drink because it has a variety of attractive aromas and flavors that tend to change during the period it is being consumed. Finish refers to how long the taste of wine remains in the mouth after it is swallowed; a pleasant, lasting taste is called a long finish. Concentration is the richness and distinctiveness of grape flavor compounds, while flavor intensity is the degree to which these compounds are sensed. Typicity refers to how well a wine expresses its grape variety or the location where the grapes were grown. Different grape varieties have different characteristic flavors, but may vary in taste depending upon the geographic location where the grapes are grown and the wine is produced.

Nonsensory Characteristics Affecting Smell and Taste

Grape variety is largely responsible for the smell and taste of wine and predisposes it to various aromas, flavors, and mouthfeels. Most of the world's wine is produced from about twenty to thirty varieties that belong to the grapevine species *Vitis vinifera*. These varieties have the most appealing taste profiles for a majority of consumers. Each grape variety has its own signature smell and taste. For example, Cabernet Sauvignon is naturally predisposed to an intense aroma reminiscent of black currant, high tannin, and medium acidity. Pinot noir has comparatively little tannin, higher acidity, and characteristic flavors of cherry, strawberry, and other red fruits. Riesling is known for its crisp acidity and intense fruit and floral aromas. Chardonnay is predisposed to relatively high sugar and alcohol levels, and lower acidity, particularly when grown in warmer climates. It is often described as having little natural flavor of its own; rather, its smell and taste are highly dependent on the specific location where it is grown and the winemaking techniques used to produce it.

The inherent smell and taste of a grape variety are significantly influenced by the geographic location where it is grown, vineyard practices, and vintage-related weather conditions. Geographic locations differ in terms of climate, soil, and landscape; all of these can have a substantial effect on the natural characteristics of grapes. Some grapes better express their natural smell and taste in warmer climates, while others prefer cooler climates. Cool locations tend to produce grapes with higher levels of acidity, and therefore wine with a lighter mouthfeel and a fresh, crisp, refreshing taste. Grapes grown in warm locations tend to yield wines with more alcohol, body, richness, and flavor intensity. Too much rain can result in dilute grapes and wine with little flavor and a thin mouthfeel. Too little rain can preclude grapes from achieving their full potential. Vintages with a sunny, warm, and dry summer and fall growing season permit grapes to fully ripen and mature, allowing for balanced sugar and acid levels and rich flavor compounds. For instance, when grown in a cool climate or a vintage with too much rain and too little sunshine, Cabernet Sauvignon can have a sour taste, harsh mouthfeel, and aromas reminiscent of green peppers and weeds. Grapes can have a noticeably different taste profile depending upon the physical and chemical properties of the soil, and the elevation, slope, and nearness to water of the vineyard where the grapes are grown. For example, when the Riesling grape is grown in infertile soil containing a large amount of slate stone in close proximity to a river on steeply sloped hillside vineyards in Germany, it is often said to have a mineral or wetstone aroma in addition to its characteristic fruity and floral flavor. Chardonnay grown in soil rich in limestone and fossilized seashells in the Chablis region of Burgundy, France, often is said to have a chalky, flinty taste. Many professionals believe that this flavor characteristic of Chablis comes from aroma compounds in the soil itself, although this assertion has yet to be scientifically verified.[11]

Viticultural choices of grape growers regarding planting, tending, and harvesting vines can dramatically alter varietal grape characteristics These choices include selection of vines, vineyard layout, trellis and irrigation systems, herbicide, pesticide, and fungicide use, pruning, and harvesting methods. Many believe the viticultural decisions that have the biggest effect on grape quality are yield and timing of harvest.

Grapes from high-yield vineyards often lack concentrated and distinctive flavors, and grape growers who desire to produce high quality grapes may therefore use cluster pruning to reduce the number of grape bunches per vine. The assumption is that a trade-off exists between quantity and quality of grapes. The date when grapes are harvested affects the amount of sugar, acid, and flavor compounds they contain. If harvested too soon, they can have too much tart acidity and lack varietal flavor characteristics. If harvested too late, they can be overripe and full of sugar resulting in hot, flabby wine with a high alcohol content and jammy fruit flavors.

The smell and taste of wine produced from specific grape varieties are also heavily influenced by winemaking techniques. The production of wine involves crushing, pressing, and fermenting grapes, and clarifying, stabilizing, maturing, and bottling the resulting wine. Decisions are made regarding yeast type, addition of sulfur dioxide, adjustments to acid, sugar, and tannin levels, stainless steel or wood fermentation vessel, skin maceration, malolactic fermentation, lees contact, racking, fining, filtration, and many more. Each step and decision in the winemaking process can potentially affect the smell and taste of wine by preserving, enhancing, detracting, or in general altering the natural aroma, flavor, and mouthfeel characteristics of the grape input. Wine made from the Chardonnay grape provides a good example of the influence of winemaking techniques. Chardonnay fermented and aged in stainless steel tanks with minimal winemaking manipulation tends to have a crisp, clean mouthfeel with flavors that range from citrus to tropical fruit, depending on whether it is grown in a cool or warm climate. However, winemakers often use techniques involving oak treatment, malolactic fermentation, or lees contact to modify the natural flavor and mouthfeel of Chardonnay. Winemakers view oak as a spice that can enhance the taste of wine. When Chardonnay is fermented or matured in oak barrels, this adds a sweet vanilla, butterscotch, or toasty flavor to the wine. Inducing malolactic fermentation to transform malic to lactic acid contributes a buttery taste and soft, creamy mouthfeel. Allowing the fermented wine to soak on spent yeast cells in lees imparts richness, and often aromas of fresh-baked bread or roasted grain. Excessive oak, malolactic, and lees treatment can produce a wine with a dominant vanilla and butter taste, with little or no natural fruit flavor, that bears little resemblance to the Chardonnay grape from which it is made.

The final nonsensory characteristic that can affect the smell and taste of wine is transportation and storage. After a wine is produced, it is transported by truck, rail, ship, or air to distributors, retailers, and consumers. It is stored in warehouses and retail stores until resold. It is then placed in wine cellars, closets, cupboards, and almost any other place in a home or restaurant until consumed. During this period between production and consumption a number of factors may affect the flavor of wine, such as movement, vibration, humidity, and light, but a consensus exists among wine professionals that the most important influence comes from temperature. Wine exposed to temperatures above 75 to 80 degrees for an extended period of time can develop a smell and taste of cooked fruit or lose its fruit flavor altogether. Unfortunately, transportation and storage conditions are not always ideal. Often wine is not transported and stored in temperature-controlled containers and warehouses, and it may be exposed to high heat, particularly in the summer months. Retail stores may also be warmer than optimal, and a wine may therefore lose some of its fresh fruit flavor before it is purchased and consumed.

THE USEFULNESS OF EXPERT WINE SENSORY DESCRIPTIONS TO CONSUMERS

As stated previously, wine is an experience good; its utility-bearing sensory characteristics can be known with certainty only after it is consumed. As a result, when making wine buying decisions, consumers often lack information about how a wine will smell and taste until after it is purchased and the bottle is uncorked. One possible source of information a consumer can use to guide buying decisions are the descriptions of the aroma and flavor of wines provided by wine critics in wine guides, magazines, and on websites. A question of interest to wine economists is: how useful is this type of information for a typical wine consumer?

The economist Richard Quandt argues that critics' tasting notes that profess to offer a description of the sensory characteristics of a wine are nonsensical and vacuous and provide no useful information to consumers.[12] For example, it is not uncommon for wine descriptions to include terms like "scorched earth," "raspberry ganache," "sweaty fruit," and "chewy tannins," which have little or no meaning to a typical consumer. Many tasting notes describe five or more aromas, but studies suggest that individuals do not have the capacity to detect more than four different smells in a beverage.[13] Roman Weil provides empirical evidence in support of this view. In a blind experiment, nonprofessional wine drinkers are able to perform no better than chance in matching a wine to the description provided by critics.[14] This suggests that a given wine product may smell and taste significantly different to a consumer and a critic, or that the description provided by the critic is contrived. Research on professional wine tasting by cognitive psychologists indicates that expert wine descriptions tend to be subjective and depend on the personal preferences of the taster.[15] As a result, a wine description may provide more information on the types of wine products critics prefer than on the aroma and flavor of the wine itself based on its chemical attributes. A study by Carlos Ramirez finds evidence that wines with longer metaphorical descriptions—as opposed to technical words used by wine critics such as *balanced, complex, tannic,* and *dry*—have higher prices, after controlling for other factors that may affect price.[16] One interpretation is that the information content in tasting notes is more persuasive than descriptive. That is, wines preferred by the critics induce them to write longer, more enthusiastic tasting notes, using nontechnical, metaphorical language, which affects consumers' preferences and the amount they are willing to pay for the wine.

4

Grape Growing

The most important input used to produce wine is grapes. This chapter focuses on the economic activity of grape growing, which encompasses three important nonsensory aspects of wine production: grape variety, grape location, and viticulture. Basic knowledge of grapes and viticulture is necessary for a fuller appreciation of the nature of the complex wine product, as well as an understanding of wine-firm behavior and the wine market. As this chapter will highlight, numerous options are available to commercial vineyards and wine firms in growing wine grapes, and the specific decisions that are made affect both the quality of the wine and the cost of producing it. In general, a trade-off exists between the goals of improving grape and wine quality and lowering production costs. To provide consumers a higher-quality product, wine firms must typically incur higher costs. There is no such thing as a free lunch.[1]

GRAPE VARIETY

Producing wine begins with the grape input choice. This involves selecting a vine species, variety, clone, and rootstock.

Vine Species

Vitis, the genus of all grape-bearing vines, includes roughly sixty different species. Most of the world's wine is produced from a single species,

Vitis vinifera, which is native to the Middle East and Europe, but today is grown in wine-producing countries throughout the world. *Vinifera* vines bear grapes that have the aroma and taste characteristics preferred by most wine drinkers. The rest of the world's wine is produced from a small number of species native to North America. Most wine consumers find wine made from these less appealing, and they are often grown to produce table grapes or grape juice. However, as discussed below North American grapevine species play an important role in wine-grape production by providing pest-resistant rootstock for *vinifera* vines, without which they would not survive in most wine-producing countries, including the United States.

Vine Variety

The species *Vitis vinifera* has as many as 10,000 different vine varieties, each of which produces a distinct grape. Hundreds of these varieties are used to make wine; however, most wine is produced from a relatively small subset of about twenty to thirty grapes with the greatest appeal to consumers. Popular varieties include Cabernet Sauvignon, Merlot, Pinot noir, Syrah, Cabernet Franc, Zinfandel, Grenache, Sangiovese, Tempranillo, Chardonnay, Sauvignon blanc, Riesling, Pinot gris, Chenin blanc, Gewürztraminer, Semillon, and Viognier.

All grape varieties have four common characteristics: stems, seeds, pulp, and skin. Stems and seeds contain tannin. Pulp yields juice with acid and sugar. Color pigment, tannin, and flavor compounds reside in the skin. Varieties differ in terms of berry size, skin color, skin thickness, acid and sugar levels, vine vigor, grape yield, ripening time, maturation time, and other characteristics. These attributes give each vine and grape its own unique varietal character. As a grape ripens, the amount of sugar increases and acid decreases, but some varieties naturally have more acid and others more sugar at any given stage in the ripening process. Varieties with smaller grapes and thicker skins have a higher concentration of color pigment, tannin, and flavor compounds. The amount of time required during a growing season to achieve ripeness and physiological maturity varies among varieties. A grape is typically considered to be ripe when sugar accounts for about 21 to 25 percent of the volume of juice in the grape. Maturity occurs when color pigment, tannin, and flavor compounds are fully developed. Some varieties ripen or mature early, while others take much longer. Varieties also differ in terms of the amount of shoots, leaves, and grapes they produce, with some naturally producing more foliage or fruit than others.

Wine can be made from a single grape variety, in which case it is called a varietal wine; if made from two or more varieties in combination, it is called a blended wine. Wines made from different grape varieties are often combined either to increase quality by producing a blended wine with a more appealing flavor than a single grape would yield, or to lower cost by combining a cheaper variety with one that commands a higher price.[2]

Vine Clones

In addition to selection of grape variety, the grape choice may also involve selection of a clone within a given variety. New grapevines have not been produced from seed for centuries; instead, they have been obtained through a process called cloning. To generate a new grapevine by cloning, a cutting is taken from an existing vine, called the mother vine, and nurtured until it roots and develops into an autonomous plant. The population of all vines reproduced from the same mother vine, or offspring of this parent vine, is called a clone. Vines that belong to a given clone have the same characteristics. However, because grapevines are genetically unstable and can mutate into different strains of potential mother vines, this historically gave rise to different clones with somewhat different attributes within a given vine variety. It has been estimated that a typical grape variety has ten to twenty clones, but some, like Pinot noir and Sangiovese, may have several hundred.[3]

Clones within a given vine variety can have noticeably different characteristics, which may affect wine taste, quality, and cost. Possible differences include vine vigor and grape yield, virus and disease resistance, time required to ripen, cluster density, berry size and color, and aroma compounds. Over the past fifty years, viticultural researchers have identified and experimented with a wide range of varietal clones in an attempt to determine which have the most favorable quality and cost characteristics. Today, vine nurseries provide a relatively large selection of clones for many vine varieties.

Clonal selection is becoming an increasingly important part of the grape input choice process. To minimize cost, some producers choose a single clone for its disease-resistant and high-yield qualities. Others attempt to improve wine quality by planting different clones in different blocks of the same vineyard and produce a varietal wine, like Pinot noir, by blending wines made from these different clones. This may increase the complexity of the wine by giving it a wider variety of interesting flavors.[4]

Clonal selection can influence the economic viability of a grape variety grown in a particular geographic location. When grape growers in Oregon's Willamette Valley initially planted Chardonnay vines, they selected a clone popular in California that is well suited for a warm climate. A characteristic of this clone is that it requires a relatively long time to ripen, which is not appropriate for Oregon's cooler climate and shorter growing season. The result was low-quality, high-cost Chardonnay grapes and wine for which there was little consumer demand. Once Oregon growers started planting a clone prevalent in Burgundy, France, that is better suited to cool climates, demand for Oregon Chardonnay increased as quality improved and cost declined.[5]

Vine Rootstock

Input choice does not end with the selection of a vine variety and clone. Wine producers must also choose a particular rootstock for their chosen grapevine. Rootstock is the root system at the base of the vine plant embedded in the soil. Most *Vitis vinifera* vines are not allowed to grow on their own root system; rather, the fruiting part of the *vinifera* vine is grafted onto a non-*vinifera* rootstock almost always taken from one of three North American species: *Vitis berlandieri, Vitis riparia,* and *Vitis rupestris,* or a hybrid of these.[6]

The original reason for this practice involves a microscopic insect called phylloxera. Phylloxera can kill grapevines by feeding on sap and depositing waste into a vine's root system. Its original home is the East Coast of the United States, where native American vine species developed a resistance to this lethal pest. However, phylloxera readily destroys the root system of vulnerable, non-native *vinifera* vines, resulting in their demise. In the mid-nineteenth century, American grapevines, and unknowingly phylloxera, were exported to Europe. Eventually, phylloxera spread to other regions of the world, including the West Coast of the United States, destroying much of the world's *vinifera* grapevines. By the late nineteenth century, it was discovered that cuttings from the fruitful part of *vinifera* vines could be attached to the rootstock of phylloxera-resistant North American species to produce healthy *vinifera* vines. After this discovery, vineyards in California and throughout Europe were replanted with *vinifera* vines on American rootstock.[7]

Over the past century a wide variety of phylloxera-immune rootstocks have been developed from which to choose. Like clones, rootstocks have different characteristics that can affect grape and wine quality and cost. Most producers choose rootstock for its soil, climate, and yield qualities. Vineyards primarily concerned with producing high-quality grapes with concentrated flavors may select a rootstock with less vine vigor and a lower grape yield. Those located in cooler climates, such as the Finger Lakes region of New York, will likely opt for a cold hardy rootstock.

GRAPE LOCATION

Grape location refers to the natural environment where grapes are grown. It encompasses the climate, soil, and landscape properties of a viticultural area. Wine professionals call this *terroir,* a French word frequently used in the wine industry, which may describe a geographic region, a particular vineyard within a region, or even a specific block within a vineyard. Variation in climate, soil, or landscape exists at each of these levels.[8] The source is thus a factor that producers must consider in choosing a grape. This choice has important economic implications for wine quality and cost.

A consensus exists among wine professionals that naturally occurring differences among grape-growing locations have an important effect on wine quality and style, independent of factors such as grape variety, viticultural practices, and vinification methods. For example, two wines made from the same grape variety grown, harvested, fermented, and matured in exactly the same way will taste different if the grapes come from different geographic regions and vineyards. These differences in taste are said to reflect differences in quality and style attributed solely to the location where the grapes are grown, or *terroir.* Locations with a more favorable natural environment are more likely to achieve optimal ripeness and physiological maturity, producing grapes with characteristics related to wine quality such as concentrated and complex flavors, supple tannins, and crisp acidity. Not only do wines from superior locations taste better to most consumers, they also tend to have a distinct style that expresses the natural characteristics of the location. That is, these wines taste as though they come from somewhere, which gives them their own unique character and personality, while those made with grapes sourced from less favorable locations taste more generic; they could come from anywhere. Many professionals believe this characteristic of "somewhereness" is what ultimately separates a great wine from one that is merely good or mediocre.[9]

The cost of vineyard land and grapes sourced from specific vineyard sites varies widely across locations. Much of this variation can be explained by differences in the natural environment of a location, which is discounted in market price. In California's Napa Valley vineyard land with a superior natural environment, capable of producing distinctive, high-quality wine costs as much as $300,000 per acre, and grape varieties like Merlot or Cabernet Sauvignon sourced from these vineyards can command prices as high as $25,000 per ton.[10] In contrast, the least favorable vineyard land in the same region can be purchased for as little as $500 per acre, with grape prices as low as $400 per ton for the same two grape varieties. This suggests that the location from which the grapes are sourced is an important determinant of the cost of the wine produced and its potential quality.

The question naturally arises: What type of environment constitutes a favorable grape growing location? The answer is geographic regions and vineyards with particular climate, soil, and landscape characteristics.

Climate

The long-run average behavior of atmospheric variables, such as temperature, sunshine, rainfall, humidity, and wind, characterize the climate of a location. Temperate locations with moderately warm or cool temperatures, gentle rather than strong sunshine, mild humidity and breezes, and adequate but not excessive rainfall, primarily during winter and spring months, tend to be associated with higher-quality grapes. Heat and sunshine affect grape ripeness and physiological maturity. In cold locations with relatively little sunshine, grapes have too much acid and not enough sugar, and they may fail to ripen to a level sufficient for wine production. In hot locations with strong sunshine, grapes ripen too fast and lose too much acidity. They may not achieve physiological maturity, and therefore fail to fully develop their aroma, flavor, tannin, and color. Strong winds can damage vines; high humidity can promote fungal diseases. Too much rain, particularly in the fall, causes grapes to become waterlogged, which dilutes acid, sugar, and aroma compounds, resulting in thin, flavorless wines.

Closely related to climate is weather. Weather is the behavior of atmospheric variables during a short period of time in a specific geographic location. The most relevant weather-related time period for grape production is the year in which the grapes are harvested, or vintage. A number of variables associated with vintage may affect wine quality, but weather conditions that influence grape quality are arguably the most important. Studies by economists find evidence that the quality of a vintage for age-worthy wine depends largely on temperature and rainfall during the growing season. Moreover, these two variables can predict the future quality and price of mature wine sold on the secondary auction market with reasonable accuracy.[11] Vintage-related weather is more important in a geographic location with greater year-to-year variations in temperature and rainfall, such as Oregon, than in a location like California, where weather varies much less from one growing season to the next.

Soil

Many wine professionals, particularly those associated with the Old World wine-producing nations France and Germany, maintain that the most important factor influencing grape and wine quality is the soil in which vines are planted.[12] Grapes used to produce high-quality wines tend to come from geographic regions and individual vineyards characterized by soil with good drainage and heat absorption, and relatively poor fertility. Soil with a high rock and stone content with the ability to drain water and absorb heat promotes the best vine growth and grape ripening. Vines do not like saturated soil and respond by producing low-quality fruit; if too wet, they may even die. Grapes tend to ripen more fully when soil absorbs heat during the day and releases it at night. Unlike many fruits and vegetables, grapevines do not perform well when grown in nutrient-rich soil high in organic matter. In this type of fertile soil, vines devote most of their energy to producing leaves rather than grapes. Not only does excess leaf production decrease grape quality by precluding proper grape ripening and maturity, it also lowers grape yield and consequently increases production cost.

Somewhat more controversial is the role of the mineral content of the soil. A number of professionals argue that soil rich in minerals produces grapes and wine with the most complex and interesting flavors, and is largely responsible for giving wine a unique character and personality; that is, its "somewhereness" characteristic. An extreme view taken primarily by French grape growers is that minerals in the soil contain aroma compounds that are absorbed by the roots of the vine and then transmitted to the grapes and wine. According to this view, consumers can literally taste the soil in the wine. So wines produced from grapes grown in limestone soil smell and taste like limestone, and those made from grapes with a large gravel content have an aroma and flavor reminiscent of wet stones. While it is generally accepted that wine made from identical grape varieties grown in different types of soils can taste noticeably different, there is no scientific evidence to support the argument that aroma compounds exist in the soil and are directly transmitted to the grapes and wine.[13]

Landscape

Landscape refers to the topographical features of a grape-growing location such as mountains, hills, valleys, elevation, and proximity to water. Landscape affects the quality and cost of grape and wine production primarily by modifying the climate and soil of a location. The soil of sloped hillside vineyards is less fertile and drains better than that of vineyards on flat land. Sloped land also promotes grape ripening in cool regions by magnifying the effect of sunshine. In many geographic locations, higher elevations are often preferred for their cooler climates and longer growing season. Vineyards located in close proximity to oceans and lakes tend to have more moderate climates with less temperature variation, and those located next to rivers tend to be warmer due to reflected sunlight.

Although steeply sloped vineyards frequently produce the highest-quality grapes, they are usually difficult and costly to maintain. Cost-reducing capital equipment like tractors and mechanical harvesters often cannot be used on this terrain, and grape growers must therefore adopt relatively high-cost labor-intensive methods of production.

VITICULTURE

Viticulture comprises everything related to the production of grapes. Viticultural activities are performed both by wineries that produce their own grapes and by commercial vineyards that sell their grapes to wineries. The vast majority of wineries contract with independent grape growers to supply some or all of their grape input.

There are more than 23,000 grape growers in the United States, including both independent vineyards and wineries that grow grapes. About half of these are located in California. California vineyards produce 90 percent of the grapes in the United States, and more than half of these are wine grapes. Ninety percent of vineyards are less than 100 acres in size, and about 50 percent are smaller than 5 acres. However, vineyards 100 acres and larger account for about 90 percent of the vineyard land planted in the United States and the majority of grapes produced.[14] Large wine-grape growers tend to specialize in producing lower-quality grapes for bulk commodity wines, while smaller vineyards often concentrate on growing higher-quality grapes for premium and luxury wines. Wine grapes are a differentiated rather than a homogeneous product. Grape heterogeneity results from the diversity of grape varieties produced, as well as differences in grape quality among producers. The cost of entering the wine-grape industry as an independent vineyard can be significant. Startup costs include the cost of vineyard land, trellises, grapevines, irrigation systems, and other types of equipment. Moreover, once vines are planted it usually takes three years or longer before they begin yielding enough grapes for harvest. During this initial period, a vineyard incurs substantial startup costs but generates no revenue.

Yield

Yield is the term generally used for the quantity of grapes produced by a vineyard. In the U.S. wine industry, it is measured as tons of grapes per acre of land, which depends on the number of grapevines planted and the weight of grapes produced by each vine. Vine yield, in turn, depends on the number of grapes per vine, as well as the size and weight of the individual grapes.[15]

The greater the productivity of vineyard land, the lower the cost of producing grapes and wine. This is because a higher grape yield per acre allows vineyards to produce the same amount of grapes with less land, which reduces the cost of producing both grapes and wine. It has been estimated that vineyards located in the Napa Valley, where land is relatively expensive can decrease the average cost of producing a ton of grapes by as much as 40 percent by increasing yield from three to five tons per acre.[16] Given fixed grape and wine prices, the reduction in cost results in increased profit. Vineyards and wineries therefore have a strong economic incentive to maximize yield. However, most professionals maintain that a trade-off exists between the quantity and quality of grapes produced; specifically, a higher yield per acre results in lower-quality grapes and wine. If so, increasing yield to reduce cost also lowers quality. To the extent that grape and wine quality is reflected in price, the lower-quality product will result in a lower price. Consequently, grape producers that maximize yield may find that while they minimize cost, the product they sell commands a relatively low price.

If such a trade-off does exist, vineyards must choose a point on the quantity-quality curve that describes this inverse relationship. The point chosen will have important implications for grape quality, production cost, and vineyard and winery profitability. Given the nature of the relationship between quantity and quality, is it possible for vineyards to take actions that shift the entire curve so that for any given quantity of grapes produced, quality will be higher?

The Quantity-Quality Trade-Off

Throughout the history of winemaking, it has been assumed that a trade-off exists between grape quantity and wine quality. This belief has been codified into the wine laws of European countries such as France and Italy. For their wine to be classified as a quality wine rather than an ordinary table wine, producers in these countries must satisfy strict grape yield limits. French winegrowers generally believe that high-quality red wine requires a grape yield of less than 3.7 tons per acre; the yield for quality white wine is somewhat higher.[17]

Most of the evidence supporting the inverse relationship between quantity and quality is anecdotal and observational, not scientific. It has been observed that the highest-quality wines tend to come from grapes grown in low-yield vineyards. Great wine estates in Burgundy limit yields to as little as two tons per acre. High-quality wines from the coastal regions of California typically have yields of two to five tons per acre, while most bulk commodity wines are made with grapes from vineyards in the San Joaquin valley, with yields that typically exceed ten tons per acre.[18] The often observed negative correlation between quantity and quality has a supporting biological explanation. The more grapes a vine has, the longer it takes for them to ripen. In cool climate locations, they may fail to achieve the degree of ripeness necessary for quality wine. In warm climate locations, the grapes may ripen but fail to achieve physiological maturity, and therefore lack desirable flavor compounds.[19] Also, higher-yielding vines tend to produce larger grapes with less acidity and flavor intensity, which can compromise wine quality.

Winegrowers also recognize that a number of factors are capable of shifting the quantity-quality curve, and by doing so produce a positive relationship between grape yield and quality. Vine viruses, diseases, and extreme drought can greatly reduce yield and result in poor quality grapes. Proper use of fungicides, pesticides, and irrigation can be used to obtain a larger quantity of better grapes. Canopy management is another way winegrowers can potentially increase both quantity and quality. The canopy of a grapevine includes the leaves, shoots, cane, and grape clusters. Canopy management involves techniques that increase leaf and grape exposure to sunlight. These techniques can not only improve grape ripening and maturity but prevent development of fungal diseases, and they therefore result in higher yields of high-quality grapes.[20] Weather is also capable of shifting the relationship. An example often cited is Bordeaux, where the highest-quality vintages have been associated with both the highest grape yields and the most favorable weather conditions.

From an economic standpoint, it is reasonable to assume that growers desire to maximize yields of high-quality grapes at minimum cost. However, the prevailing evidence seems to indicate that many situations require them to sacrifice quantity for quality, or quality for quantity. Unfortunately, given the current state of knowledge, the exact nature of the trade-off is uncertain. A number of vineyard practices are available for those who choose to limit the natural productivity of the vine in the expectation of improving grape and wine quality. These practices involve decisions related to the planting, growing, and harvesting vines.

Planting Decisions

When developing a vineyard, growers must first choose grape variety, clone, and rootstock. Today, wine producers recognize the importance of matching grape variety to location. Some varieties such as Cabernet Sauvignon and Zinfandel grow better in warm locations; others like Pinot noir and Riesling prefer cool climates. Clones and rootstock are selected based on considerations such as taste characteristics, grape yield, climate, soil, pest and disease resistance, and water requirements. New vineyards are often divided into different blocks based on soil and drainage tests, and clones and rootstocks are chosen accordingly. One way for growers to limit yield in an attempt to produce higher-quality grapes is to choose a clone and rootstock that offer relatively low vigor and yield.

After grape variety, the most important vineyard development decision is choice of vine density. This involves choosing the number of vines to plant per acre. Many growers, particularly in Old World countries like France and Italy, believe that less space between and within vineyard rows promotes better-quality grapes. Planting vines in close proximity, it is argued, stresses vines by forcing them to compete for the available water and soil nutrients. As a result, each vine produces fewer and smaller grapes that have more concentrated and intense flavor. The evidence to support this quality effect is largely anecdotal, based on the observation that the highest-quality wines often come from high-density vineyards.

The yield per acre of a high-density vineyard is similar to that of a low-density vineyard. This is because the potential increase in grape output of planting more vines on each acre of land is largely offset by the reduction in yield per vine. As a result, a high-density vineyard has little if any productivity advantage. However, the cost of developing and cultivating a high-density vineyard is significantly higher than a low-density vineyard. A low-density vineyard requires a smaller initial investment in vines, lower planting costs, lower cultivation costs, and can be farmed using capital intensive methods of production that take advantage of tractors, mechanical harvesters, and machine pruners. The narrow rows of a high-density vineyard often preclude the use of machines, and must therefore be cultivated using more expensive, labor-intensive methods. It has been estimated that the development cost alone of a high-density California vineyard with 2,722 vines per acre is as much as 60 percent higher than that of a low-density vineyard with 907 vines per acre.[21]

Virtually all modern vineyards attach vines to a trellis typically made of wood and wires. By doing so, growers can determine the shape and position of the vines in the vineyard. Shaping and training vines reduces cost by facilitating vineyard operations such as spraying, pruning, and harvesting, and allowing grape growers to use capital-intensive methods of production. It can also influence vine yield and other factors that affect grape quality. A large number of trellis and training systems exist. When developing a vineyard, growers must choose one of these systems. Many vineyards in the United States use a vertical trellis system that forces vines to grow upward rather than sideways and allows grapes to get maximum sun exposure. While this trellis system improves grape ripening and quality, shaping vines in this manner requires a large amount of manual labor and therefore tends to be more costly than many alternative trellis systems.[22]

Another decision related to vineyard planting is when to rip out existing vines and plant new ones. The grape yield of a vine is related to its age. Once a vine is planted, it typically takes about three years for it to produce enough grapes for harvest. It achieves maximum grape productivity roughly from six to twenty years of age. After age twenty, grape yield tends to decline, and by age fifty, a typical vine produces relatively little fruit. However, many professionals believe grapes from lower-yielding, older vines make higher-quality wine, so the decision regarding when to replace old vines with new ones is related to the quantity-quality trade-off.

Growing Decisions

Once vines are planted, they have to be cultivated. The most important grape-growing activities are irrigating, pruning, trimming, and spraying vines.

Irrigation occurs when a vineyard supplies water to grapevines from a source other than rainfall. A grower must decide whether to use irrigation, and if so how much water to supply to vines. If vines receive too little water and experience drought conditions, this results in a low yield of poor-quality grapes. Under these conditions irrigation can increase both quantity and quality. Alternatively, when vines receive an overly generous supply of water from either rainfall or irrigation they produce a large amount of big diluted grapes that may not adequately ripen, and therefore make wine of unacceptably low quality. Within these two extremes, there is general agreement, at least in New World countries such as the United States and Australia, that irrigation can be used as a tool to adjust the quantity and quality of grapes. If the goal of a vineyard is to maximize the yield of lower-quality grapes for commodity wine, then generous irrigation is appropriate. On the other hand, if the objective of the grower is to produce higher-quality grapes for premium and luxury wine, then limited irrigation can be chosen to make vines struggle more for water. Most professionals believe the restricted yield that results from a degree of water stress promotes better grape ripening and more concentrated flavors, but the optimal amount of stress is still widely debated. The use of irrigation can be a particularly effective tool in choosing a point on the quantity-quality trade-off curve in drier locations with relatively little rainfall.

Grapevines are naturally productive plants and left to their own devices tend to produce more grapes than they can adequately ripen. To prevent this type of "overcropping," most growers prune vines during the winter months to limit the number of buds capable of producing grape clusters in the subsequent growing season. During spring and summer months, many growers also thin shoots and leaves as part of a canopy-management strategy to increase grape and leaf exposure to sunlight in an attempt to improve quality without sacrificing yield. However, canopy management can be labor-intensive and costly. The most draconian tool vineyards have at their disposal to reduce yield in an attempt to enhance quality is cluster thinning. In midsummer if a grower determines the vines have produced too many grapes to achieve a desired quality level, workers may be sent into the fields to cut off grape bunches allowing them to fall to the ground and rot. This would appear to be uneconomic behavior, since the vineyard chooses to employ more labor services at increased cost to decrease output. But growers that use this technique believe lowering yield by removing grape bunches increases quality by promoting better ripening of the grapes that remain on the vine.[23] However, studies suggest the benefits of cluster thinning may be relatively small, particularly when compared to the cost.[24]

Grapevines are vulnerable to damage by a variety of diseases and insects. The most common infections are from fungal diseases such as powdery mildew, downy mildew, and botrytis. Growers must decide the method of farming they will use to prevent damage from insects, disease, and uncontrolled weeds. Conventional farming uses synthetic sprays as fungicides, pesticides, and herbicides; it is the least costly way to prevent crop destruction. Sustainable farming employs synthetic spray alternatives when possible, and relies on manmade fungicides as a last resort only when fungal disease threatens to destroy the grape crop. Organic farming involves the exclusive use of natural substances and techniques to keep vines disease-free and healthy, such as copper and elemental sulfur sprays, plant oils, cover crops, and canopy management. Many vineyards that practice organic viticulture obtain a government certification that allows wine producers to indicate on the bottle label that the wine was made from organically grown grapes. Organic certification informs consumers that the grapes were grown without synthetic fungicides, pesticides, or herbicides. Biodynamic farming, the most costly method of grape growing, is an extreme form of organic viticulture based on principles propounded by Rudolf Steiner. The vineyard is viewed as a living system and homeopathic preparations such as fermented cow manure, ground quartz, and horsetail-plant tea are sprayed on vines to prevent disease and maintain a healthy vineyard organism.[25]

Many wine producers believe grapes grown organically or biodynamically make the highest-quality wine, and are therefore willing to incur the higher cost necessary to procure these grapes. A recent study provides some support for this belief. Researchers used a sample of 13,426 wines from 1,495 wineries in California to analyze the relationship between method of farming, wine quality measured by critic scores, and wine price. They found that wines made from organic and biodynamic grapes had an average quality score of more than one point higher, on a 100-point scale, than grapes grown using conventional and sustainable methods of farming. Oddly, producers of wines made from organic grapes received a 7 percent higher average price for their products than conventional wine producers provided they did not reveal the method of farming on the bottle label. Those producers who stated on the label that the wine was produced with organic grapes received a 20 percent lower price than those who did not, and a 13 percent lower price than conventional wines.[26] The researchers speculate that people may mistake organic grapes for sulfite-free organic wine, for which they are unwilling to pay a higher price.[27]

Harvesting Decisions

Harvest is the activity of picking grapes at the end of the growing season each year. In the United States, this typically occurs during the months of September and October. The most important decision related to harvest is when to pick the grapes.

Quality is maximized when grapes achieve optimal ripeness and physiological maturity. As grapes ripen during summer and fall, the amount of sugar increases and the amount of acid decreases. Grapes are considered to be ripe when they have the desired balance between sugar and acid as determined by the grape grower or winemaker. The amount of sugar in grapes is related to the alcohol content of wine. It can be measured by grape juice weight in Brix units using a device called a refractometer. This measure of grape sugar is called must weight. If grapes have a must weight of 20 Brix, then approximately 20 percent of the juice is sugar. Because yeast transforms sugar into alcohol at a rate of about 55 percent, the resulting wine would have an alcohol content in the neighborhood of 11 percent. Acidity is related to wine freshness. It is often measured by the percentage of acid in grape juice, called total acidity. Until recently, most growers picked grapes strictly "by the numbers" when they reached a level of about 21 to 25 Brix and total acidity of about 0.60 to 0.85 percent. U.S. viticultural researchers argued that grape quality is maximized when the ratio of Brix to acidity falls within a range of 30 to 35, which is the best time to harvest. However, harvesting grapes scientifically by the numbers ignores physiological maturity. Today, many growers and winemakers recognize that it is possible for grapes to achieve physiological maturity either before or after this quantitative definition of ripeness.

Physiological maturity is determined by grape constituents other than sugar and acid that affect wine quality, primarily tannin and flavor compounds. These taste components are related to skin, pulp, and seed color and texture, and the smell and flavor of the grape. Unlike ripeness, there is no chemical or scientific measure of physiological maturity. To assess it, a grower must touch, examine, and taste the fruit.[28] The rate at which grapes ripen depends on climate; the warmer the location, the faster they accumulate sugar and the earlier they ripen, all else being equal. However, physiological maturity progresses at a similar rate in both warm and cool climates. As a result, in warm or hot locations, it is not uncommon for grapes to achieve traditional levels of ripeness before reaching physiological maturity.[29] If grapes are harvested when ripe, they may result in wine with desirable amounts of alcohol and acidity, but with a bitter, herbaceous taste and lacking expected varietal characteristics. For some growers, the solution is to let grapes hang longer on the vine to ensure physiological maturity. But this type of harvesting strategy can result in an unbalanced wine with excessive alcohol, because overripe grapes picked late in the growing season have a high sugar content. In cool locations, where physiological maturity often occurs before ripeness, picking by the numbers tends to be the preferred harvesting strategy, since the biggest concern is sugar accumulation.

The decision about when to pick grapes is also influenced by factors other than grape quality. A grower takes an economic risk when choosing to wait until grapes achieve optimal ripeness and physiological maturity before harvesting. The longer grapes are allowed to hang on the vine, the greater the risk of inclement weather. Hail, frost, and rot may destroy part or all of a crop, and unexpected rain can result in waterlogged and diluted grapes of low quality. Wine producers who purchase grapes from vineyards under contract at a fixed price per ton have an economic incentive to ask growers to harvest overripe fruit. The reason is that grapes with a sugar content in excess of 25 Brix have a lower water content and weigh less than those with Brix of 25 or less. Lower grape weight reduces winery grape cost. Grape weight and input cost can be cut by as much as 25 percent if grapes are harvested at or above 27 Brix.[30] Water lost from over-ripeness can be easily added back during the winemaking process at negligible cost. Of course, vineyards have a financial incentive to harvest grapes at the traditional ripeness of 21 to 25 Brix to maintain fruit weight and generate higher revenue.

Method of Production Decisions

Vineyards must choose a method of production to implement their planting, growing, and harvesting decisions. This involves either choosing a specific combination of labor and capital given available technology, or deciding whether to adopt a particular technology. As with any business, the specific method of production used by a vineyard is an important determinant of production cost. However, unlike in many businesses, the relative amounts of labor services and capital equipment chosen may well affect the quality of the output produced. An important question related to viticultural decisions is: How and to what extent do methods reducing the cost of grape production affect the quality of fruit and wine output?

Winter pruning of vines can be done with either a labor-intensive method that relies almost exclusively on manual labor or a capital-intensive method that uses a machine pruner and relatively little manual labor. It has been estimated that hand pruning requires worker input of about 45 to 65 hours per acre, accounting for as much as half of the annual operating cost of a typical vineyard. Machine pruning reduces labor usage to less than 5 hours per acre, resulting in a substantial decrease in labor cost. Many vineyards have adopted the capital-intensive method of pruning to lower cost, but some believe it is too imprecise, results in higher yield, and contributes to a decrease in grape quality. While there is little evidence to support this adverse quality effect, these vineyards are willing to trade-off pruning cost for what they believe are higher-quality grapes from labor-intensive manual pruning.[31]

Growers must decide not only when but also how to pick grapes. Vines can be harvested using either a labor- or capital-intensive method of production. The labor-intensive method employs a large number of workers to handpick grapes. A tractor or truck is typically used to transport grapes in bins from the vineyard. Alternatively, the capital-intensive method uses a harvesting machine operated by a single worker. A typical mechanical grape harvester has arms that strike the vines to detach the berries, which then fall onto a conveyor belt, which carries them to a receptacle. It has been estimated that machine-picking can reduce the cost of harvesting grapes by as much as 75 percent.[32] However, the fixed capital cost of a mechanical harvester can exceed $300,000 and represents a substantial investment, particularly for small vineyards and grape-producing wineries. An alternative is for a grower to contract with an entity that provides mechanical harvesting services.

While choosing a capital-intensive method of harvesting has the potential for significant cost savings, its effect on grape quality is widely debated. Many vineyards choose a labor-intensive method of harvesting, because they believe it results in higher-quality grapes and wine. Workers can select ripe and healthy grapes and discard those that are rotten or diseased. Machine harvesters are incapable of selective picking and harvest all types of grapes regardless of their condition, as well as a certain amount of leaves and vine fragments. Harvesting machines also beat grapes off the vine, detaching most individual grapes from the stems and often breaking the skins. Skin breakage can result in oxidation and reduce grape quality. Harvesting individual berries limits winemakers' choices by eliminating whole grape bunch fermentation or use of stems to facilitate drainage when pressing juice from grapes. However, studies suggest that wine quality from grapes harvested by a capital-intensive method is at least as high as a labor-intensive method. There are several possible reasons for this. A capital-intensive method that employs a machine harvester is flexible and reduces the amount of time it takes to harvest grapes. Grapes can be harvested at night when the temperature is lower to reduce deterioration and increase acidity. Harvest can be completed quickly before inclement weather causes crop destruction. Adverse effects of oxidation from skin breakage is also minimized, because grapes are immediately moved from vineyard to winery without delay.

A majority of growers and grape-producing wineries eschew mechanical harvesting and employ largely seasonal workers to handpick grapes. There are several possible reasons for this choice. A large supply of adequately skilled, low-wage immigrant grape pickers exists. This keeps the price of labor relative to the price of capital low enough to justify labor-intensive harvesting. However, this may change if the supply of these workers is limited by future immigration legislation. A number of wineries that produce premium and luxury wine products demand and are willing to pay a higher price for handpicked grapes of higher perceived quality. This may justify the higher cost of manual harvesting. Mechanical grape pickers cannot operate on steeply sloped terrain or in vineyards with narrow rows of vines, so capital-intensive harvesting methods are not feasible for either hillside or high-density vineyards. Finally, most grapes harvested by machines are in the form of individual berries, but some wineries demand whole grape bunches for better juice drainage or partial and whole cluster fermentation.

An increasingly important choice growers must make is whether to use information technology and data-based decision making in vineyard management. A variety of technologies now exist that enable growers to collect substantial amounts of data about vineyard characteristics for purposes of making growing and harvesting decisions. These include remote sensing, yield monitors, global positioning systems, geographical information systems, automated weather monitoring systems, and evapotranspiration measurement to estimate vineyard water consumption.[33] Grape growers have long recognized that significant variation can exist in soil, landscape, and even climate across different blocks within the same vineyard. Until recently, information about this natural variation could only be obtained from decades of careful observation by owners and managers of long-established vineyards. Today, data collection and imaging technologies can be used to construct maps of this variation in a relatively short period of time. Information provided by these maps can be used to decide how to irrigate, prune, thin, spray, and harvest different vineyard blocks to reduce cost and improve grape quality.[34]

5

Grape Markets and Supply Cycles

Growers must choose the quantity of grapes to produce and the manner in which to sell them. Grapes can be sold either on a spot market or a long-term contract market. Many wine-market observers believe the way in which growers make output decisions produces regularly recurring grape supply and price cycles that culminate in repeated periods of boom and bust. This chapter provides a description of the institutional features of the market for wine grapes and an economic analysis of the cyclical nature of wine-grape production and prices.

CHARACTERISTICS OF THE WINE-GRAPE MARKET

Wine grapes are sold on both a long-term contract market and a spot market.[1] The long-term contract market consists of growers and wineries that make contracts to buy and sell grapes with a duration of one year or longer.[2] These contracts are negotiated prior to the year in which the grapes are harvested. The spot market consists of growers and wineries that make agreements to buy and sell grapes in the year when the grapes are harvested. These agreements are typically made between early summer and the time grapes are picked, usually in September or October. Given the difficulty of storing wine grapes and the potential for rapid deterioration in quality, few spot-market transactions are made after harvest time. Estimates suggest that as much as 90 percent of wine grapes in California are bought and sold under long-term contract.[3] It is not unusual for a grower with a single vineyard to have contracts with twenty or more wineries that agree to purchase grapes from different blocks within the vineyard.[4]

The Spot Market for Wine Grapes

The spot market is loosely organized by wine-grape brokers and marketing cooperatives, with the majority of transactions negotiated directly between growers and wineries without the assistance of a third-party intermediary. Grape brokers perform a search function and bring together growers and wineries that desire to buy and sell grapes on the spot market. They also provide services to facilitate these transactions. A broker never takes ownership of the grapes and is paid a commission for the search and other services provided, which is typically around 3 percent of the value of the transaction. Brokers specialize in gathering information on potential wine-grape buyers and sellers, as well as market supply and demand conditions. They use this information to match growers and wineries, and assist them in negotiating prices for grape transactions given prevailing spot-market conditions. The two largest brokers in the California wine-grape market are Joseph Ciatti Company and Turrentine Brokerage. A marketing cooperative is an association of growers that assists its members in selling grapes by providing services similar to those rendered by brokers. An example is Allied Grape Growers, a California wine-grape cooperative with more than 500 growers as members that sells grapes to over 75 wine-related firms. In spite of the valuable economic function performed by brokers and marketing cooperatives, a preponderance of spot-market transactions continue to be made directly between growers and wineries, who search the market for one another by phone, mail, word of mouth, established relationships, and occasionally the use of a website.

Spot-market prices differ by grape variety, quality, vineyard location, and grower reputation, and are determined by the supply and demand for grapes in the year when the fruit is harvested. Spot-market prices can vary widely from year to year and are significantly influenced by the size of the grape harvest in any given year, which is largely determined by unpredictable weather conditions. Years with favorable weather that produce a bumper crop often result in excess grape supply and low prices; excess grape demand and high prices are common in poor weather years with low grape yields. Growers who choose to sell grapes on the spot market face substantial economic risk from this uncertain price variability.

The Long-Term Contract Market for Wine Grapes

Most wine grapes are bought and sold under long-term contract. While brokers also operate in the long-term contract market, a majority of these contracts are arranged and negotiated directly by growers and wineries. A 1999 survey of California grape growers reported that about one-third had one-year contracts, while half had contracts with a duration of three years or longer.[5] New one-year contracts are negotiated at the beginning of the calendar year, after the size and quality of the prior harvest is better known, and wineries have forecast their production, sales, and grape input demand for the coming vintage. Some of these contracts have an evergreen provision that automatically renews the contract each year, provided that neither the grower nor winery chooses to terminate it.

A large proportion of growers and wineries prefer contracts of longer than one year in duration that don't need to be renegotiated or renewed each year. Growers favor these contracts because it enables them to better manage the risk of year-to-year variation in grape supply and prices that result from uncertain weather conditions and abrupt changes in wine demand. It also lowers the annual cost of marketing grapes and makes it easier to get bank loans to finance vineyard operations. Wineries benefit from longer-term contracts because it allows them to lock in a steady supply of grapes with desired quality characteristics for the style of wine they want to produce. A number of long-term contracts are planting contracts that are negotiated before a grower plants a new vineyard. The winery agrees to purchase fruit produced by the new vineyard, often for ten years or longer. Locking in a steady source of future grape demand enables the grower to borrow the money necessary to cover the significant cost of developing a new vineyard until it yields enough grapes for sale, typically in three years after vines are planted.

A typical long-term contract has provisions related to grape quantity, price, and viticultural practices. The quantity provision specifies the amount of grapes a winery agrees to buy each year over the life of the contract. The vast majority of contracts do not specify a specific amount of grapes to be purchased. Instead, they specify a specific number of acres to harvest, and the winery agrees to buy all grapes produced from this acreage in a given year. Contracts that do contain a specific quantity provision typically state the maximum number of tons per acre the winery agrees to purchase, in addition to the number of acres to be harvested.

The price provision establishes the price a winery agrees to pay for grapes. A typical contract specifies the price per ton of grapes. This price can be either fixed over the duration of the contract or vary from year to year. A fixed price contract specifies a price for each year over the life of the agreement that is negotiated prior to the start of the contract. This may be the same price for all years or a schedule of prices that differ by year. A variable price contract does not fix a price in advance, but allows it to vary over the life of the contract according to a predetermined formula usually based on market conditions. Some variable price contracts state that the price per ton of grapes for the current year is equal to the spot-market price for the previous year. In more sophisticated contracts, price is determined by two components: a base price and a price adjustor. The base price is fixed for the duration of the contract and depends upon such factors as grape variety, grape quality, grower reputation, and expected future market conditions at the time the contract is negotiated. The price adjustor is typically the percentage change in the average price of grapes for the prior harvest year in the geographic region where the vineyard is located; however, some contracts use as the adjustor the percentage change in the price of the wine produced from the grapes. An alternative to specifying a price per ton of grapes is to state a price per acre harvested. Under this type of contract, the grower receives a fixed amount of revenue for each acre harvested regardless of the number of tons of grapes that acre yields.

Viticultural provisions specify grape growing and harvesting techniques. This may include guidance on canopy management, irrigation, desired yield per acre, and manual or mechanical method of harvest. Viticultural provisions may also specify measures of grape quality such as sugar and acid levels, and grape defects. Some contracts include bonuses or penalties for achieving or not achieving agreed-upon quality measures.

In the spot market, prices adjust to eliminate excess grape supply and demand. However, in the long-term contract market, price provisions make grape prices sticky and rigid, so in any given year they cannot adequately perform this rationing function. Here, wineries typically play a key role in the mechanism that clears the grape market. As stated above, under a typical contract, the winery agrees to buy all grapes produced from a given tract of vineyard land each year over the life of the contract. This is because wineries are better able to adjust to unanticipated year-to-year changes in the quantity of grapes produced than growers. It is difficult for growers to store grapes, which deteriorate rapidly. In good weather years with an unexpectedly large crop, wineries purchase surplus grapes. They use the superfluous grapes to produce more wine than planned and store the excess for aging or sell it on the bulk wine market. In bad weather years with an unanticipated small crop, wineries buy fewer grapes and produce less wine than planned. To cover the shortfall, they sell more of their inventory of aging wine or buy wine on the bulk market.

Contractual arrangements create economic incentives for growers and wineries to behave in a manner that can significantly influence the quality and cost of grapes. For instance, consider a multiyear contract that specifies a fixed price per ton of grapes and contains a viticultural provision that allows the winery to determine the sugar content at which the grapes will be harvested each year. The grower has an economic incentive to maximize yield per acre by increased irrigation and other farming techniques to generate greater revenue and profit. However, high yield may result in poor-quality grapes. The winery, on the other hand, has an economic incentive to ask for grapes to be harvested at relatively high sugar levels. This requires picking grapes later in the growing season when they have a lower water content and weigh less. Lower grape weight reduces the winery's grape input cost. The economic incentives the grower and winery face are significantly different if the price provision of the contract is renegotiated to specify a fixed price per acre harvested. Under this new price provision, the grower no longer forgoes revenue when yield per acre is limited to enhance grape quality. The winery no longer reduces grape input cost by asking growers to harvest overripe fruit.

Some vineyards offer wineries different contract options that are designed to take economic incentives into account. Bien Nacido, a large independent vineyard located in Santa Barbara County, California, allows wineries to choose one of two alternative contracts. The first specifies a fixed price per ton, with little or no winery involvement in how vineyard blocks are farmed. The second specifies a fixed price per acre regardless of yield, and allows the winery to manage the land in such a way to limit yield to achieve a desired quality level.[6] Other contractual arrangements that explicitly consider economic incentives are also starting to gain popularity. For instance, Beckstoffer Vineyards in Northern California writes contracts that tie grape prices to the price of the wine produced from the grapes, and farms vineyard blocks in a manner that satisfies the specific needs of each winery to which it sells fruit.[7] This type of contract may result in a more optimal risk-sharing arrangement for both the vineyard and winery. Harlan Estates winery has a long-term profit sharing plan with three independent growers to provide grapes for vineyard-specific wines.

SUPPLY CYCLES AND THE WINE-GRAPE MARKET

An economic cycle exists when an economic variable or set of related economic variables display a pattern that repeats itself over a given period of time. Many wine-market observers believe there is an inherent tendency for wine-grape production and prices to behave in a cyclical manner. Over time, the wine-grape market exhibits systematic supply and demand imbalances that culminate in recurring periods of financial boom and bust for grape growers. This cycle continues to persist, although it may be amplified or dampened by growing season weather, economic recessions and expansions, and other unpredictable factors beyond the control of grape growers. Similar cycles have been recognized for other agricultural products, such as potatoes, lemons, onions, cotton, and hogs.

The notion of a wine-grape cycle is illustrated in figure 5. Aggregate grape supply is measured on the vertical axis, and time on the horizontal axis. The straight line represents the long-run upward trend in grape production in the United States. For example, the annual production of California wine grapes, which accounts for more than 90 percent of grape output in the United States, increased from 1.46 million tons in 1977 to 3.59 million tons in 2010.[8] The undulating curve around the trend line describes the inherent tendency for actual wine-grape supply to vary cyclically around its long-run trend. When actual production is above the trend, the market is said to be characterized by grape overproduction and relatively low prices. Because many growers experience financial distress when grape supply is at a peak, this is sometimes referred to as the bust phase of the cycle. When actual production is below the trend, the wine-grape market is said to be characterized by underproduction and relatively high prices. This is sometimes called the boom phase of the cycle, since many growers earn large profits when grape supply is at a trough. Over time, the wine-grape market is said to travel through these repeated cycles of rising production, falling prices, and below-normal profits, and declining production, rising prices, and above-normal profits.

FIGURE 5. Wine-grape supply cycle.

Turrentine Brokerage, a large grape and wine broker located in California, has studied grape and wine supply cycles in the United States and publishes the Wine Business Wheel of Fortune, which attempts to describe the cycle and time-stamp phases of overproduction and under-production. According to this, periods of overproduction leading to relatively low prices have occurred from 1982 to 1985, 1990 to 1993, and 2000 to 2006. Periods of underproduction resulting in relatively high prices have occurred from 1986 to 1989, 1994 to 1999, and 2007 to the present.[9]

When discussing the grape-supply cycle, many wine market observers describe the phase of overproduction and low prices as a period of surplus wine grapes and the phase of underproduction and high prices as a wine-grape shortage. However, this description of the grape-supply cycle is inconsistent with traditional supply and demand analysis. To see why this is, consider figure 6, which illustrates the demand and supply curves for wine grapes. Suppose the price of grapes is currently P_1. At this price, the quantity of grapes that growers harvest and desire to sell is Q_1, but the amount that wineries are willing and able to purchase is only Q_0. As a result, a surplus of grapes exists on the market. This surplus may be the result of a decrease in demand for wine grapes arising from falling consumer income that leads to a reduction in wine demand. However, this state of grape-market disequilibrium is inconsistent with the overproduction phase of the cycle, because prices are unsustainably high, not low, and market forces will cause them to fall toward the equilibrium price P^*, not rise. As prices fall and grapes become less profitable to produce, growers respond by producing fewer grapes as they move down along the supply curve. Eventually, the market achieves equilibrium at the lower price and output level of P^* and Q^*. Alternatively, suppose the price of grapes is currently P_0. At this price, the quantity of grapes wineries desire to purchase of Q_1 exceeds the amount that growers harvest and want to sell of Q_0 and a shortage of grapes exists on the market. This wine-grape shortage may be the result of an increase in the demand for wine, and therefore wine grapes, that results from a shift in consumer preferences in favor of wine. Because price is unsustainably low and will rise to the equilibrium level of P^*, this period of underproduction is characterized by relatively low grape prices followed by rising prices and increased production as grapes become more profitable to produce. To conclude, the concepts of surplus and shortage as used in traditional supply and demand analysis describe periods of overproduction and unsustainably high prices and underproduction and unsustainably low prices. A grape-supply cycle of alternating phases of surplus and shortage would lead to a pattern of declining production and prices followed by rising production and prices, which is inconsistent with the supply cycle that is said to exist in the U.S. wine-grape market. Moreover, alternating periods of grape surplus and shortage would require a repeated pattern of leftward shifts in the grape demand curve (or rightward shifts in supply) followed by rightward shifts in the demand curve (or leftward shifts in supply), which would be very difficult to justify.

A well-known theory in economics, called the cobweb theory, provides an explanation of the phenomenon of agricultural supply cycles in the context of supply and demand analysis.[10] This theory assumes that demanders of wine grapes make their buying decisions based on the supply of grapes available in the current vintage. Given their downward-sloping demand curve, they are willing to pay higher prices when the grape harvest is smaller and lower prices when it is larger. However, the growers who supply grapes make their production decisions based on prices that prevailed in previous vintages. This is because the grape-production process involves a lag between the initial decision about how much to produce and the final output available to be sold on the market. The most important factor determining wine-grape supply is grape-bearing acreage. After a grower plants new acreage, it takes three years for the new vines to produce grapes. In making the acreage decision, the grower does not know what the price will be when the grapes are eventually sold on the market and must form an expectation of the future price. To do this, he uses information both on current

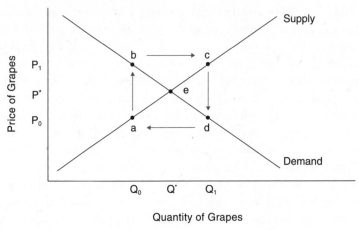

Quantity of Grapes

FIGURE 6. Grape surplus, shortage, and cycles.

grape prices and on those that have prevailed in the recent past. As a result, the size of the current vintage, which determines the current price of grapes, is influenced by prices that prevailed in previous vintages.

To see how these conditions can generate a self-perpetuating cycle of overproduction and low prices, and underproduction and high prices, once again consider the wine-grape demand and supply curves in figure 6. Suppose grape price is currently P_0. Given this price, growers plant acreage that will produce Q_0 grapes in future years (point a on the supply curve). Because Q_0 is relatively small, when this vintage is eventually sold on the market wineries are willing to pay the high price of P_1 (point b on the demand curve). Growers now use this relatively high price to reevaluate their production decisions and respond by increasing acreage, which produces the relatively large vintage Q_1 in future years (point c on the supply curve). Given this large vintage, wineries are only willing to pay the low price of P_0 when it comes to the market (point d on the demand curve). Given this low price, growers once again reevaluate their production decisions and reduce acreage, resulting in a relatively small vintage and high price several years later. This leads to a rectangular-shaped cycling of grape prices and output around the equilibrium price and output of P^* and Q^*. During the phase of underproduction and high price, grape output and price are below and above their respective equilibrium levels (point e). During the phase of overproduction and low price, the opposite is true.

In the above scenario, the grape market never achieves a state of equilibrium; rather, it perpetually swings back and forth between disequilibrium states of underproduction and high price, and overproduction and low price. This occurs because the production decisions of growers and buying decisions of wineries are equally responsive to price changes, and therefore the demand and supply curves have equal slopes. If growers are less responsive than wineries to price changes, the supply curve has a steeper slope than the demand curve. Given these supply and demand conditions, periods of overproduction and underproduction become successively smaller over time, and eventually the grape market reaches a state of equilibrium. In this case, the systematic cycling of output and price around equilibrium looks like a cobweb that converges to the point of intersection of the supply and demand curves.[11] The equilibrium price and output, P^* and Q^*, can persist from vintage to vintage, since the price growers expect to receive when they sell their grapes in future vintages turns out to be the same as the actual price wineries are willing to pay when the vintage is sold on the market, and therefore the lagged production decisions of growers are consistent with the current buying decisions of wineries. A new cycle begins when the grape market experiences a big change in demand or supply that throws it into disequilibrium. This type of supply shock may result from consecutive vintages of abnormally good or bad weather that induce a big shift in the grape-supply curve. Examples of demand shocks that may significantly displace the grape demand curve include the severe economic recession of 2007–9, the red-wine health craze of the early 1990s, and terrorist attacks of 2001.

The cobweb theory provides a simplified explanation of what actually happens in the complex wine-grape market. According to this theory, the length of the wine-grape cycle depends solely on the amount of time that elapses between altering acreage and harvesting grapes from the expanded or contracted acreage. Because it takes three years for new vines to produce grapes, but a minimum of one year to remove acreage from production, the cobweb theory predicts it would take at least four years to complete one cycle from peak to peak or trough to trough. For example, if 2012 is a period of underproduction and high price, growers will increase acreage. When grapes from these new vines are harvested and sold in 2015, this results in overproduction and a low price. Growers now respond to the low price by reducing acreage. If acreage is taken out of production for the next vintage, underproduction and a high price would prevail in 2016, and this would complete a four-year cycle. On the other hand, if contracting acreage in response to a low price takes growers two years or more, then the cycle would be completed in five years or longer.

While this type of supply-cycle mechanism may be inherent in the wine-grape industry, a number of institutional features of the market may alter the amplitude and length of the phases. First, grape production depends on yield per acre as well as grape-bearing acreage. Yield, in turn, is influenced by fertilizer, irrigation, canopy management, and other discretionary actions of growers, as well as unpredictable weather conditions. When prices are high in the underproduction phase, growers can respond in the short term by using vineyard-management practices to increase yield. Output can be cut immediately by abandoning vines and letting grapes go unharvested in the face of overproduction and low prices. Second, while spot-market prices may be set by the amount wineries are willing to pay for the available grape supply in a given year, this is not necessarily the case in the long-term contract market. For grapes produced under contract, the terms of contract may have a bigger influence on price in a given year than the available supply. Moreover, during the underproduction phase, more long-term contracts are typically negotiated as wineries attempt to secure an adequate supply of grapes. In the overproduction phase, wineries negotiate fewer contracts and contracts of shorter duration, and rely more heavily on spot-market purchases. Third, wineries have the option of purchasing wine on the bulk market from foreign producers when grapes are in short supply, or selling wine on this market when grapes are abundant.[12] Finally, different grape varieties grown in different geographic locations can have their own cycles, which may obscure the cycle for aggregate grape supply. Cuellar and Lucey (2005) find evidence that the grape-supply cycle for California North Coast Chardonnay is shorter and more pronounced than that for North Coast Cabernet Sauvignon. Six years elapse from the peak of Chardonnay overproduction to the trough of underproduction; the same phase of the cycle takes thirteen years for Cabernet Sauvignon.

6

Wine Production

This chapter discusses the economic activity of wine production. In economics, production is defined as the transformation of inputs into output. Economists typically use an analytical device called a production function to represent or describe a production process. A production function treats a production process as a "black box." Inputs—such as grapes, the services of cellar workers and a winemaker, and the services of fermentation and maturation tanks—enter the box at one end and maximum wine output emerges at the other end. The activities that take place within the box are ignored. The production function, which is a simplification of a complex real-world production process, is a useful analytical tool for both theoretical and empirical analysis. For example, economists do not necessarily need to know the details of a production process to formulate a valid theory to explain the input and output choices a profit-maximizing firm will make, or to use data to empirically estimate various measures of input and firm productivity.[1] That said, the purpose of this chapter is to open the "wine production function black box" and describe the important activities and choices that take place inside. Wine production involves choosing one or more grape varieties for a particular wine type, crushing and fermenting the grapes, and maturing, blending, clarifying, stabilizing, and packaging the resulting wine. These activities represent some of the most interesting and unique institutional features of the wine market, and reveal the important role the winemaker plays in a wine firm. In each of the stages of the wine production process, a variety of choices must be made. Different choices result in different vinification methods, affecting the quality and cost of the wine produced. As with grape growing, a trade-off generally exists between improving wine quality and lowering cost. Producing a higher-quality wine inevitably entails higher cost. Without adequate knowledge of the details of wine production and the crucial function performed by the winemaker, it would be difficult to gain a good understanding of the economics of the wine industry.

WINE TYPE AND STYLE

A wine firm must first decide what type and style of wine to produce.

Wine-Type Classification

The three main types of wine are fortified, sparkling, and still. A fortified wine is one that includes the addition of a spirit, such as brandy, to increase the alcohol content, usually to a level of 17 to 21 percent. The difference between sparkling and still wine is that the former contains bubbles from carbon dioxide, while the latter does not. Red and white still wine is the most popular type of wine, and the one discussed below.

In the United States, wine falls under two legal classifications for labeling and tax purposes. A table wine has an alcohol content of 14 percent or less. Any wine with alcohol by volume in excess of 14 percent is a desert wine. The federal excise tax on dessert wine not exceeding 21 percent alcohol is 10 cents per 750 ml bottle higher than table wine. Most wines legally classified as dessert wines are neither fortified nor sweet, but rather still wines with an alcohol content typically between 14 and 16 percent. The distinction between a table wine and high-alcohol still wine is becoming increasingly important in the choice of wine type. Over the past decade, the proportion of still wines that are high in alcohol has increased dramatically. Many retailers and consumers are beginning to question the quality of these wines, arguing that they are too alcoholic and not "food friendly."

Choice of Wine Style

Still wine can be produced in a variety of styles. Different wine styles result from different combinations of the seven taste components discussed previously: alcohol, acidity, tannin, residual sugar, fruit, oak, and yeast.[2] A producer's desired wine style has an important influence on winemaking decisions, and therefore on the quality and cost of the wine produced.

The two most important factors affecting wine style are the objectives of the wine firm and the characteristics of the grape input. The objective of a large profit-maximizing wine firm may be to produce a commodity wine of consistent quality made from inexpensive grapes grown in large vineyards in the Central Valley of California, with a flavor profile that appeals to the largest possible number of consumers. The choice of this particular style may be influenced by results from consumer focus groups and test marketing. Alternatively, the objective of a small artisanal producer may be to make a limited quantity of a luxury wine with complex flavors that expresses the climate, soil, and landscape of the vineyard where the grapes are grown, and appeals to a more sophisticated wine consumer. This small winery proprietor may be willing to trade off a certain amount of profit for the utility of producing a "wine work of art."

An argument made with increasing frequency is that many wine firms choose styles that will get the highest scores from influential wine critics, such as Robert Parker and *Wine Spectator,* whose ratings can have a significant effect on wine sales and winery prestige. Consulting firms now exist that use chemical analysis and computer technology to identify wine styles that consistently achieve scores of 90 points or higher.[3] A growing number of wine firms are using this information when making wine-style choices, while others are giving bonuses and other financial incentives to their winemakers to achieve high scores from critics. Winemaking philosophy may also have a significant influence on wine style. Winemakers who subscribe to the "Old World philosophy" argue that wine should have subtle aromas and flavors that reflect the location where the grapes are grown. Fruitiness is less important than non-fruit flavors reminiscent of soil, forest, herbs, leather, game, and roasted meat. They believe that winemaking itself is an art, not a science. Good wine is made in the vineyard from high-quality grapes, and the winemaker should therefore avoid intervening in the winemaking process as much as possible and let nature take its course. Alternatively, those winemakers who adopt the "New World philosophy" believe that because wine is made from grapes, and grapes are a fruit, wine should have fruity aromas and flavors. Intense flavor, rather than subtleness and "somewhereness," is the most important characteristic of a good wine.

Moreover, winemaking is a science that uses modern technology, and it is therefore perfectly acceptable to intervene in the winemaking process and manipulate the wine by making adjustments to alcohol, acidity, tannin, and sugar, as well as using other techniques that alter its natural taste components.

Grape Input

Grape input constrains the potential quality and style of the wine to be produced. There is a general consensus among wine professionals that a high-quality wine cannot be produced from low-quality grapes regardless of the vinification practices used. The grape characteristic of most concern to a wine firm that desires to produce a commodity wine is sugar content. Alternatively, a producer that wants to make a premium or luxury wine typically seeks ripe grapes with additional characteristics such as concentrated flavors. However, for any given set of characteristics of the grape input, vinification decisions will have an important effect on the style, quality, and cost of the wine produced. It is possible to make bad wine from good grapes, and the same grapes can be used to make varying styles of wine.

Crush

Crush includes all those activities performed to prepare grapes for fermentation. This involves making decisions about sorting, destemming, crushing, and pressing grapes; and chilling, sulfiting, clarifying, macerating, chaptalizing, acidifying, and watering back grape must.[4]

Sorting, Destemming, Crushing, and Pressing Grapes

When grapes arrive at the winemaking facility, the first decision a producer must make is whether to sort them to remove those that are rotten, diseased, sunburned, or unripe, along with any leaves and vine fragments that may exist. Damaged and unripe grapes and debris can adversely affect wine quality. Sorting is costly if performed by hand, since it is labor-intensive and requires a degree of skill. Labor-saving sorting tables have been developed recently that employ vibration to separate grapes from debris. A floatation device and optical scanner can then be used to cull unripe and damaged fruit, thereby minimizing labor.[5] However, this type of equipment is expensive. Sorting may not be necessary if grapes are harvested manually, since it can be done in the process of handpicking grapes in the vineyard.

The next decision a producer must make is whether to detach the stems and crush the grapes to release the juice. Most winemakers choose to perform both of these activities, and do so with destemming and crushing machines.[6] Stems contain a significant amount of tannin and allowing them to soak or ferment with juice can make a wine taste harsh and bitter. However, some producers purposely increase the tannin in wine made from red grapes like Pinot noir that have a naturally low amount by using whole grape clusters in fermentation. Crushing grapes results in a mix of juice and solids called must.

To make white wine, the liquid from crushed grapes is almost always separated immediately from the solids, resulting in free-run juice. The juice is then fermented without the skins. To make red wine, the juice and solids are fermented together. Some winemakers allow the juice to soak with the solids at a relatively low temperature for up to ten days before fermentation to maximize the extraction of flavor compounds and color pigment from the skins. This practice, called cold maceration, is typically used for red wine only.

Virtually all grapes are pressed using some type of mechanical device to obtain juice. When making white wine, grapes are pressed after being crushed to extract juice that does not run free when the skins are broken. This is called press juice. Some winemakers choose not to crush white grapes, but rather press whole grapes or clusters. The grapes are pressed several times resulting in separate batches of juice. High-quality white wines are typically made from delicate free-run and first-press juice. This is the most costly juice because of its higher quality and limited quantity. When making red wine, the juice is fermented with the solids, so grapes are pressed after fermentation to maximize the amount of wine produced.[7]

Chilling, Sulfiting, Clarifying, and Adjusting Grape Must

After the grapes are crushed and pressed, a producer must decide whether to chill, sulfite, clarify, and make adjustments to the resulting must. Unfermented must is vulnerable to damage from exposure to oxygen, inimical bacteria, and undesirable yeast that can initiate fermentation prematurely. This is particularly true of white wine must, since the juice has been separated from the protective antioxidants of the skins. Many producers cool the must to protect it, particularly if they plan to use it for fermentation in the future. Almost all wine firms choose to add sulfur dioxide to must to prevent oxidation, kill harmful bacteria, and inhibit undesirable yeast strains.[8] In the United States, wine regulations specify maximum permissible sulfur dioxide levels and require the label to state "contains sulfites" if sulfur dioxide has been added. It is very difficult to produce a wine of acceptable quality without using sulfur dioxide, and if a firm is successful at making such a wine, it must be transported and stored at a cool temperature until it is consumed, which is very unlikely given the current wine distribution system. Because of these difficulties and related cost, relatively few producers attempt to make a sulfite-free wine, even those who use organic grapes. Firms that do produce wine with no added sulfur dioxide usually market it as a highly differentiated product and charge a price accordingly. However, even this wine is not "sulfite-free" because a small amount of sulfur dioxide is created naturally by yeast during the process of fermentation.

Even though the juice from white grapes has been separated from the solids, it contains very small pieces of pulp, skin, and other debris that make it cloudy. A producer must decide the degree to which to clarify white grape must before it is fermented. If none of these particles are removed, this may result in an off-taste in the wine. If all of these particles are removed, the resulting wine may be stripped of its aroma and flavor. The traditional and most natural method of clarification, called settling, involves cooling the must to prevent fermentation from starting and letting it sit for about twenty-four hours to allow the solid particles to sink to the bottom of the container. An alternative is to use a centrifuge machine to spin out the particles. The advantage of this method is that the juice can be clarified in a couple of hours. The disadvantage is that the machine is expensive, and some winemakers believe it has an adverse effect on the must.[9]

The final decision a producer is required to make before fermentation is whether to alter the acid, sugar, or water content of the must. All wine-producing countries, including the United States, have regulations that limit one or more of these adjustments to the must or finished wine. For example, California prohibits sugar but allows acid to be added to must; New York, on the other hand, permits the addition of sugar but not acid. Acidification is common among California wine producers who use grapes with a low level of natural acidity from warm locations, often harvested later in the growing season to achieve optimal physiological maturity. Adding acid to must can prevent the finished wine from being flat and unbalanced. Deacidification techniques can be used to remove excess acid from must or wine that may occur when grapes are sourced from a cool location, and this is a regular practice in some parts of New York State. Adding sugar to must to increase the amount of alcohol in wine is a common winemaking technique, called chaptalization. It is used by most producers in cool locations and growing seasons when grapes fail to achieve a level of ripeness necessary to produce the desired level of alcohol in a wine. Too little alcohol can make a wine feel thin and unbalanced. Chaptalization is typically prohibited only in warm locations such as California, where it is never needed, but allowed in places like New York and Oregon, where it is viewed as occasionally necessary to produce wine of acceptable quality. Some winemakers, particularly those in California, add water to must from overripe grapes high in sugar to prevent the wine from being too high in alcohol, a controversial practice called "watering back." Watering back is prohibited in most European countries. Others use techniques to remove excess water from diluted grapes by either freezing the must and removing ice crystals (cryo-extraction) or filtering it out through a semiporous membrane (reverse osmosis). This serves to concentrate the sugar and flavor compounds in the must, and if done judiciously, it can result in dense, concentrated wines of sufficient alcoholic strength, even in rainy growing seasons.[10] However, reverse osmosis is relatively expensive, and when deciding whether to use it, a typical producer will therefore weigh the additional cost against the expected increase in wine quality.

FERMENTATION

The next set of activities in the winemaking process are those related to transforming the grape must into wine. This stage of the wine-production process involves important decisions about fermentation vessel, yeast, and temperature, as well as post-alcoholic fermentation choices concerning extended maceration, malolactic fermentation, and lees contact. Decisions made in this stage will have a significant effect on wine style, quality, and cost.

Fermentation Vessel

A wine firm must decide on the type of vessel in which fermentation will take place. This container can be large or small, open or closed, and made from a variety of materials, such as wood, stainless steel, cement, glass, or plastic. Historically, most producers fermented wine in large, open, wood vats or smaller barrels, usually made of oak; today, the vast majority prefer stainless steel tanks. Stainless steel tanks have a number of advantages relative to oak vessels. They are less costly, easier to clean and sterilize, minimize the risk of harmful bacteria, and eliminate loss of wine from evaporation. Stainless steel tanks are also durable, do not require replacement at regular intervals, and can be readily modified to incorporate advanced winemaking technology, such as temperature controls, self-draining capability, rotofermenters, autovinifiers, and computer operation. It has been estimated that the cost of purchasing a single 12,000-gallon stainless steel tank is 75 to 90 percent less than two hundred new oak barrels with the same capacity.[11] In addition, it is much more costly to clean and maintain the oak barrels.

Given the advantages of stainless steel, why would any wine firm choose to ferment wine in wood vats or barrels? Oak vessels have the potential to increase quality by adding to the flavor and complexity of wine. Many winemakers believe that fermentation and maturation of wine in oak vessels is a better way to extract wood aroma and flavor compounds than oak maturation alone. For those wines that don't require oak treatment, stainless steel tanks are preferred, since they have no effect on wine flavor.

Yeast

Once a vessel is chosen, yeast are required to start fermentation. Yeast perform a very important role in wine production. Not only do they transform the sugar in grape juice into alcohol, but they also produce as much as half of the aroma and flavor compounds found in wine. One of the most important decisions a producer must make is whether to use natural or cultured yeast.

A variety of yeast strains exist naturally in the environment and on the skins of grapes. These yeasts will spontaneously start fermentation if allowed to do so. Many winemakers believe that natural yeasts produce a wine of higher quality, with more character, interesting flavors, complexity, and a better mouthfeel. Cost is minimized because no outlay is required. Others argue that natural yeasts are part of the location where the grapes are grown and contribute to the uniqueness and sense of place of a wine. But using natural yeast has several potential drawbacks. The winemaker has less control over the outcome of the fermentation process. It can take several days for fermentation to begin, and once it starts, it may stop before completion. Such a stuck fermentation poses a risk, since it may be difficult or impossible to restart. Delayed, stuck, or incomplete fermentation can be very costly. It is also possible that a particular strain of wild yeast can result in an off-taste and reduce wine quality. An example is the natural yeast strain *Brettanomyces*, which can give wine an aroma reminiscent of a barnyard.

Cultured yeasts are grown in a laboratory setting from various strains of carefully selected natural yeast. Use of cultured yeast eliminates the potential problems of stuck fermentation and undesirable yeast flavors and gives the winemaker more control over the outcome of the fermentation process. Specific strains of cultured yeast can be chosen to target a desired flavor profile and wine style. The major shortcoming of cultured yeast, some winemakers believe, is a wine of less complexity that lacks character and uniqueness.

Extraction and Fermentation Temperature

The main difference between producing white and red wine is that the former involves fermenting the juice and the latter the entire grape. The goal in making red wine is to extract color pigment, flavor compounds, and tannin from the grape skins. To accomplish this, the skins must be kept in contact with the juice from the crushed grapes while fermentation is taking place. During fermentation, yeasts produce both alcohol and carbon dioxide. Alcohol acts as a solvent to aid the extraction process, but carbon dioxide pushes the skins to the top of the fermentation vessel, where they form a cap. For extraction to take place efficiently, the cap must be pushed down at regular intervals so that the juice mixes with the skins. This is one of the most important activities involved in making red wine and is called "punching down." A number of punching-down techniques are available. It can be done manually with a wooden paddle or mechanically with a hydraulic ram, provided the fermentation vessel has an open top. Alternatively, a pump can be used to move liquid from the bottom to top of either an open or closed vessel. Another option is to use a stainless steel tank specifically designed to rotate or with an internal paddle to mix the skins and juice while fermentation takes place. Some small artisanal wineries that produce luxury wine use the labor-intensive manual punching-down technique; many believe this results in superior extraction and higher-quality wine. However, most larger volume producers opt for less gentle, labor-saving punching-down equipment.[12]

As yeast transform the grape sugar into alcohol and carbon dioxide, a large amount of heat is generated, and if no action is taken to control the temperature of the fermenting juice, it will naturally rise to 85 degrees Fahrenheit or higher. In these warm conditions, yeasts are very active, and fermentation occurs quickly and finishes within about five to ten days. A warm fermentation temperature is typically preferred for red wine, since it promotes the extraction of color pigment, flavor compounds, and tannin from skins. However, allowing fermentation to proceed at these high temperatures can have a detrimental effect on white wine by burning off primary aroma compounds that reside in the delicate juice, leaving the wine flavorless. To preserve its fruitiness, white wine is usually fermented at lower temperatures than red wine, typically within a range of 50 to 68° Fahrenheit. In these cooler conditions, yeasts are less active, and fermentation can take a month or longer to complete. The specific temperature at which white wine is fermented is an important determinant of its style. Fermentation at a temperature below 60°F tends to result in a crisp, fragrant wine with tropical fruit flavors, such as pineapple and banana, which can supplement, but often supplant, the natural flavors of a grape variety. At temperatures above 60 degrees, varietal flavors are dominant, but flavor intensity tends to diminish. Historically, the primary means of temperature control was to ferment white wine in small vessels in a cold cellar or add ice during the process of fermentation. Today, most wine firms use temperature-controlled, stainless steel fermentation tanks that allow for very precise temperature setting.

Malolactic Fermentation and Extended Maceration

After alcoholic fermentation, a secondary, nonalcoholic, malolactic fermentation may also take place. This involves the transformation of strong, green-apple-tasting malic acid into soft, buttery, lactic acid performed by lactic acid bacteria. A winemaker must decide whether to allow full, partial, or no malolactic fermentation to occur. Lactic acid bacteria exists naturally in most fermented grape must; if absent, they can be added to encourage malolactic fermentation. Alternatively, malolactic fermentation can be prevented or stopped before completion by adding sulfur dioxide and using filtration to inactivate and subsequently eliminate the lactic acid bacteria from the wine. Malolactic fermentation has an important influence on wine style and quality. Most winemakers choose to put red wine through full malolactic fermentation to soften the acid so that it better integrates with the tannin. Full or partial malolactic fermentation is also encouraged in some white wines, notably Chardonnay, to create a soft, round, buttery style that appeals to many consumers; however, it is usually prevented when a crisp, aromatic style is desired, which is typical of wines made from the Riesling and Sauvignon blanc grapes.

An important decision affecting wine style and quality is when to separate the wine from the skins and sediment. Winemakers who use high-quality grapes to make luxury wine often choose to let newly fermented red wine continue to soak in the skins for anywhere from a few days to a month or longer. This practice, called extended maceration, is used to extract additional tannin, color pigment, and flavor compounds, and it can result in a wine with softer tannin and more appealing mouthfeel that is capable of aging for a longer period of time. Once fermentation and maceration of red wine is completed, the liquid is separated from the skins to obtain free-run red wine. The skins are then pressed to obtain additional press wine, which is usually of lower quality and often sold under a separate label. Some wines, particularly those made from certain types of white grapes, such as Chardonnay, are allowed to remain in contact with the spent yeast cell portion of lees for a few weeks to a year. Lees contact is a winemaking technique used to add yeast-related flavor and smoother texture to wine to increase complexity and improve mouthfeel. This effect can be enhanced by regular stirring of the lees, a practice the French call *batonnage*.

MATURATION

After fermentation is completed, the wine is typically stored in a container for a certain period of time to let it mature. Maturing a wine allows it to stabilize, clarify, and more fully develop aromas and flavors. It can also be used to add oak flavors reminiscent of vanilla, cedar, coffee, and smoke to a wine. The maturation period can be as short as a few weeks or as long as several years or more. The decision about how long to mature a wine, and the type of vessel to use, are important factors affecting both wine style and cost.

Length of Maturation

In general, white wine is matured for a shorter period of time than red wine. Aromatic whites, such as Riesling and Pinot grigio, benefit little from oak treatment and maturation, and they therefore tend to be brought to market within a few months after fermentation. However, a fuller-bodied white wine like a Chardonnay made in a rich, oaky, style may require a year or longer in a wood container. A red wine made with the intention of being consumed young is often bottled and sold the spring or summer after the vintage. A high-quality red wine is typically matured for eighteen to twenty-four months. The longer a wine is matured, the higher the cost of producing it, because of both higher storage cost and revenue forgone from not bringing it to the market at an earlier date. The decision regarding how long to mature a wine can be driven as much by cash-flow considerations as desired wine style.

Oak Barrel Maturation

The two types of vessels most often used to mature wine are oak barrels and stainless steel tanks. Maturation in oak barrels has two potential effects on wine. Keeping wine in a wood barrel exposes it to a small amount of oxygen over time. Oxygen enters the barrel through the wood staves and around the stopper used to close the hole in the top of the barrel. Slow and steady oxidation allows the wine to breathe and improves mouthfeel by softening the wine and promoting the development of aromas and flavors. Wood barrels can also be used to influence the flavor of wine by subjecting it to oak treatment. Wine stored in an oak barrel absorbs flavor compounds and tannin from the wood. The nature and strength of the oak flavors depends upon the type, newness, and degree of charring of the oak, as well as the size of the barrel. The two major types of oak used to make wine are French and American. American oak tends to impart stronger flavors than French oak, often reminiscent of coconut and vanilla. The barrel-making process involves the application of heat that chars or "toasts" the wood. The degree to which a barrel is toasted—light, medium, or dark—can have a noticeable effect on wine flavor, resulting in aromas that may vary from toasty to smoky. New oak has a stronger effect on flavor than used oak. After about three or four years of use, an oak barrel becomes flavor neutral, but continues to allow for oxygen exposure. Therefore, a winemaker who wants to apply slow oxidation without oak treatment can do so by maturing wine in older oak barrels. Oak barrels also differ in size. The smaller the barrel, the more wood per unit of wine, and therefore the stronger the oak influence.

Maturation in oak barrels can contribute a significant amount to the cost of producing wine. The price of a new sixty-gallon oak barrel ranges from about $300 to more than $1,000. The typical price of a high-quality French oak barrel is $800 to $900; this may add $2 to $3 to the cost of a bottle of wine. The price of American oak is about 50 percent less. Another cost of barrel maturation involves the loss of wine from evaporation. The evaporation rate of wine stored in an oak barrel, and therefore the amount of revenue forgone, can be as much as 10 to 12 percent per year.[13]

Stainless Steel Tank Maturation

An alternative container used to mature wine is a stainless steel tank. Because stainless steel is an inert material, it prevents oxygen exposure and has no effect on wine flavor. Most white wine and some types of red wine is kept in stainless steel tanks for a relatively short period of time following fermentation to encourage clarification and stabilization, while protecting it from oxygen to preserve fresh fruit flavors.

Methods have also been developed that allow winemakers to provide oak treatment and controlled oxygen exposure to wine matured in stainless steel tanks. These techniques can be used to mimic maturation in oak barrels at much lower cost. They are primarily used for red wine and select white wines such as Chardonnay. To impart oak flavor, new oak staves can be used to line the inside of the tank. Alternatively, sacks of oak chips or dust can be placed in the maturing wine like tea bags. Using oak staves or chips can lower the cost of oak treatment by as much as 75 to 95 percent and reduce the amount of time required to mature a wine so that it can be brought to market sooner.[14] A technique called micro-oxygenation can be used to pump small amounts of oxygen into the tank to hasten the development of the wine, so that it is ready to drink at an earlier age.[15] A wine that requires one to two years in a barrel to fully develop its oak and fruit flavors may be ready for consumption in a couple of months when matured in a stainless steel tank with oak staves and micro-oxygenation.

If stainless steel tanks can be used to simulate the effects of oak barrels at a much lower cost, then why do many producers continue to mature wine in oak barrels? Many winemakers believe that maturation in oak barrels results in higher-quality wine with more complexity and age ability. If this is so, which is the subject of much debate within the wine industry, then using stainless steel tanks along with oak alternatives and micro-oxygenation involves trading off quality for cost savings, which may not be appropriate if the objective is to produce a premium or luxury wine. Even if the firm's objective is to maximize profit, the potential revenue forgone from the lower price consumers are willing to pay for non-barrel-matured wine of lower perceived quality may well exceed the reduction in cost. This may help to explain why producers that age wine in an oak barrel often make this explicit on the label, while those that use alternative methods of oaking simply allude to oak treatment without providing specific details.

CLARIFICATION AND STABILIZATION

Newly fermented wine is a cloudy, unattractive liquid that contains a variety of solid particles including bits and pieces of grape skins and pulp, dead yeast cells, proteins, live yeast, and bacteria. At this stage in the wine production process, its appearance is less than appealing to most consumers, and it is potentially unstable. To transform this liquid into a commercially viable product, it must be clarified and stabilized. Clarification involves removing larger visible particles, called lees, to make the wine clear and bright. Stabilization entails preventing microorganisms such as yeast and bacteria from initiating an undesirable secondary alcoholic or malolactic fermentation after the wine is bottled, or in some other way altering the wine so that it has an off-taste or unappealing appearance. Clarification and stabilization are usually achieved by using one or more of the following winemaking techniques: racking, fining, cold stabilization, and filtration. Each of these techniques has advantages and disadvantages related to wine quality and cost.

Racking and Fining

Racking involves a two-step process that is typically performed more than once while the wine is maturing. First, the wine is allowed to sit in a container long enough for solids to fall and collect on the bottom, which will occur naturally by the force of gravity. Next, the liquid is transferred or siphoned off to a new container, leaving these unwanted lees behind. Racking is the most natural and gentle way to clarify and stabilize wine, but it is a slow process that may take a year or longer and require wine to be transferred to a different oak barrel or stainless steel tank a number of times. The major advantage of racking is that it minimizes the risk of stripping flavor compounds and color pigments, and therefore may produce a wine with a better appearance and taste. However, because this process is relatively slow, the longer amount of time required to produce wine and bring it to market leads to higher cost. It may also result in noticeable sediment in the bottom of a bottle of finished wine, which most retailers and consumers dislike.

Most winemakers attempt to shorten the amount of time required for racking and more thoroughly clarify and stabilize a wine by applying a technique called fining.[16] This involves adding a substance to the wine that attracts solid particles and causes them to sink to the bottom of the container faster than they would otherwise have done, so that they can be racked off more quickly. The most popular fining agent is a type of clay called bentonite, which is particularly effective in absorbing particulate matter in wine. Other common fining agents include egg whites, gelatin, isinglass, and casein. The major advantage of fining is that it is minimally invasive, quality-friendly, and adds little to the cost of producing wine.

Cold Stabilization and Filtration

Wine that has been racked and fined may be clear when it is bottled but still unstable, because it has the potential to form tartrate crystals at a later date, after it is brought to the market. In red wine, these crystals are red or brown and look like sediment; in white wine, they are clear and have the appearance of small pieces of glass. While tartrate crystals are harmless and have no effect on wine flavor, a typical consumer dislikes this appearance and some even return the wine complaining it has a defect or contains shards of glass. As a result, most producers make an effort to ensure that tartrate crystals will not form after wine has been bottled. The most common way to do this is to use a technique called cold stabilization. Before wine is bottled, it is placed in a container, typically a stainless steel tank, and cooled at a temperature close to freezing for about a week. The cool temperature causes the formation of tartrate crystals, which are then removed by racking or filtering. This prevents these crystals from forming after wine is bottled and sold. While cold stabilization can increase the demand for wine by improving appearance, it requires specialized equipment and significant energy, which increase the cost of production.[17]

A very fast and effective but controversial way to clarify and stabilize wine is to use filtration. This involves running wine through a filtration pad after fermentation and before bottling. Depth filtration is used to remove large particles such as bits of grape skin and pulp to clarify the wine. This is typically done shortly after fermentation, when the wine is pumped into the maturation vessel. A second type of filtration, called sterile filtration, is used to remove microorganisms such as yeast and bacteria in order to stabilize wine, and is performed immediately before bottling. It can only be used if the wine is subjected to one or more depth filtrations to eliminate large particles that would plug the tiny holes of the sterile filtration pad. Filtration reduces production cost by shortening the time required to produce wine and minimizing the risk of spoilage. However, it requires an initial investment in relatively expensive filtration equipment.

The major drawback of filtration, and the crux of the filtration controversy, is that it may reduce quality by stripping a wine of flavor compounds and other substances that contribute to its complexity and uniqueness. Robert Parker and a number of other wine critics are vehemently opposed to filtration, particularly of premium wines, on these grounds. Yet many in the wine industry argue that filtration is not only innocuous, but often improves the taste of wine by removing impurities.[18] Larger commercial wine firms that produce a large volume of commodity wine invariably use filtration. Alternatively, many smaller wineries whose objective is to produce premium or luxury wine choose not to use filtration and typically indicate on the label that the wine is unfiltered. However, these producers run the risk that the wine will develop a significant amount of sediment in the bottle, compromising its appearance, and, even worse, an off-taste from inimical bacteria.

BLENDING

A pivotal activity in the production of wine is blending. This involves combining two or more separately fermented wines with different characteristics into a single finished wine. Almost all wines go through a blending process before they are bottled, even those that are sold as varietal wines. The component wines blended together can differ in multifarious ways, such as different grape varieties, different clones, different vineyards, different blocks within a vineyard, different vintages, different fermentation and maturation vessels, different fermentation temperatures, different yeasts, different malolactic fermentations, and different grape pressings. Blending can be used to achieve a particular wine style, improve wine quality, achieve vintage-to-vintage consistency, or lower production cost. Many wine professionals consider blending to be the true art of winemaking and the most valuable skill of a winemaker.

In the United States, wine regulations permit a wine to be labeled with a single grape name if it derives at least 75 percent of that grape. For instance, most wines labeled Cabernet Sauvignon are actually a blend of two or more grapes. To improve wine quality, many producers include Merlot to add softness to naturally tannic Cabernet Sauvignon, possibly some Cabernet Franc to enhance the aroma, and maybe even a small amount of Petite Sirah for a deeper, richer color. To lower cost, others may include a substantial amount of Zinfandel, whose price may be less than half the price of Cabernet Sauvignon.[19] Even wine made from Pinot noir or Chardonnay grapes, which typically do not blend well with other grape varieties, are often blends of different clones, vineyards, or blocks within a given vineyard. It is not uncommon for producers of Oregon Pinot noir to blend together more than thirty separately fermented wines made with Pinot noir grapes from different vineyards and clones. A 100 percent varietal Chardonnay wine is typically a blend of two or more Chardonnay wines that differ in terms of yeast, malolactic fermentation, or newness of oak barrels. For instance, Kendall Jackson Chardonnay, one of the best-selling Chardonnays in the United States, is a blend of Chardonnay grapes from about thirty different vineyards in four different California grape-growing regions, which allows the producer to achieve a particular style and avoid year-to-year variation.[20]

An increasingly common practice involves blending two wines with identical characteristics but different alcohol levels to achieve a desired alcohol content in the final wine. It is not uncommon for a rich, intensely flavored, finished wine to have too much alcohol relative to other taste components, so that it lacks balance. In this case, the winemaker may choose to reduce the alcohol level in the wine. Lowering the alcohol content to 14 percent or less has the additional advantage of reducing the excise tax that must be paid. The method most often used to accomplish this is reverse osmosis, the same technology used by some producers to remove excess water from grape must before fermentation. This technique involves taking a portion of the finished wine and feeding it into a reverse osmosis machine, which removes both water and alcohol. The water is added back to produce a wine with a lower alcohol content. This reduced alcohol version of the wine is then blended with the original higher alcohol version in a proportion necessary to achieve the desired level of alcohol in the final wine.

PACKAGING

The finished wine can be either packaged in small containers for sale to distributors, retailers, and consumers, or left unpackaged for sale as bulk wine.

Packaging Wine in a Bottle

Most wine is packaged in bottles. Bottling can take place at any time after a wine is deemed to be sufficiently mature, but not necessarily at the optimal time for consumption, because some wines improve with age in the bottle.[21] The main steps involved in bottling are filling, closing, and labeling. Some small wine producers bottle largely by hand with a manual filler and labeler, but most use a more sophisticated and efficient bottling line. A semi-automatic bottling line comprises separate filler, closure, and labeling machines, with bottles transferred among machines by hand, while an automatic line minimizes the amount of labor required by moving bottles from machine to machine by a conveyor belt. Some wineries, particularly those that produce wine containing residual sugar, attempt to minimize the risk of spoilage by using a sterilized bottling line. The bottling equipment is usually located in a special sanitized room. The wine is sterile- filtered immediately before being put into sanitized bottles. A bottling line can typically fill between 50 and 100 bottles per minute. After the wine is bottled, it is typically packaged in cardboard boxes, twelve bottles per box, which constitutes a case.

An important economic decision a wine producer must make is whether to invest in a bottling line or to contract with another firm to bottle its wine. Purchasing a bottling line requires a significant investment, from about $30,000 for the simplest technology to more than $500,000 for the most sophisticated equipment.[22] The biggest advantage of owing a bottling line is that it gives the winery more control over the bottling process so that wine can be packaged when it is ready, rather than when a contracted bottling line becomes available. About 95 percent of the wine produced in the United States is bottled in-house. This is because most large volume wine producers invest in their own bottling lines. The other 5 percent is bottled under contract with a winery that owns bottling equipment, a mobile bottling firm that specializes in providing bottling services via a truck or trailer, or through a bottling co-operative comprised of a small group of wineries that jointly own a mobile bottling line. Many smaller wineries that typically bottle their wine only a couple of weeks during the year choose to outsource bottling. Most lack the financial resources, winery space, and expertise to purchase, operate, and maintain their own bottling equipment.[23] Some large wine firms have separate bottling plants, and those that export wine have found that it is usually less costly to ship wine overseas in bulk containers and then bottle it in or near the foreign market where it is sold. For example, Diageo Chateau & Estate Wines, the eighth-largest wine producer in the United States, produces its popular Blossom Hill wine in a facility in California, ships it in bulk to its bottling plant in northern Italy, and then distributes the bottled wine to European countries such as the United Kingdom. The volume of Blossom Hill wine shipped for bottling is so large that it accounts for 33 percent of Italy's imported wine and 25 percent of Italy's exported wine to the United Kingdom.[24]

Bottle Closure

Another important decision that can affect both the quality and cost of wine concerns the type of closure used to seal the bottle. Until the 1990s, almost all wine bottles were sealed with a cork stopper. Cork was considered the ideal closure, since it is inexpensive, forms a tight seal, is easy to remove, and allows for a small amount of oxygen exposure, which many winemakers believe is beneficial. However, by the 1990s, it became generally recognized that corks frequently become contaminated with a chemical called TCA, which can ruin a wine by giving it a musty smell that many consumers describe as like wet cardboard or newspaper. It has been estimated that about 5 percent of wines closed with cork experience this type of cork taint.[25] Recent studies also find the quality of a given wine aged with a cork closure can vary significantly from bottle to bottle because of differences in rates of oxygen exposure among corks. On occasion, a cork will lose its seal altogether, and the wine is ruined from excessive oxidation. The problems of cork taint and bottle variation have resulted in the development of two popular alternative closures, the synthetic stopper and aluminum screw cap, which have experienced growing market shares over the last two decades.

Synthetic stoppers are made from either solid or extruded plastic, simulate cork, and do not develop cork taint. The higher-quality extruded plastic stopper is easy to extract and can be used for age-worthy wines. Recent estimates indicate that synthetic stoppers represent about 20 percent of closure sales and are used by half of the thirty best-selling wines in the United States.[26] The fastest-growing closure is the aluminum screw cap. It is the most popular type of bottle stopper in wine markets in New Zealand and Australia, and accounts for about 10 percent of closure sales in the United States. The screw cap eliminates the problems of cork taint and bottle variation, and hermetically seals wine to prevent oxygen exposure. Studies suggest that for purposes of aging wine, the screw cap may perform better than the cork at a lower cost than high-quality cork.[27] However, the screw cap is somewhat more costly than the cheapest cork and synthetic stoppers, and the cost of screw-cap bottling line equipment is about $30,000 more than that of these other stoppers.[28] Many retail establishments that sell wine are pressuring producers to bottle their wine with screw caps to minimize defective wines. This gives wineries an added incentive to choose this type of closure.

Bottle Label

Wine regulations in the United States require each bottle to have a front label that provides a minimum amount of information about the wine and its characteristics. Information required by law includes a brand name, wine type, liquid content, alcohol content, sulfite declaration, health-hazard warning, name and location of the firm that bottled the wine, and if produced outside the United States, the name and location of the importer.

The wine firm can choose any brand name it wants, provided it does not mislead the consumer. This may be a wine firm's legal name, trade name, or a name created for informational or marketing purposes. The firm that bottles the wine as indicated on the label is not necessarily the one that produced it. If the label states "bottled by," or "vinted and bottled by," or "bottled and cellared by," then the firm that bottled the wine may have purchased it on the bulk market from another producer and is selling it under its own brand name. Alternatively, if the label states "produced and bottled by," or "made and bottled by," then legally the firm must have fermented at least 75 percent of the wine; up to 25 percent can come from wine purchased on the bulk market and blended with its own fermented wine.

A wine firm is allowed to provide information on alcohol content in several alternative ways. If alcohol by volume is 14 percent or less, then the label may include either a numerical measure of the alcohol content or the phrase "Table Wine." If a numerical measure is reported, then a margin of error of plus or minus 1.5 percent is allowed provided the actual alcohol content does not exceed 14 percent. Any wine containing more than 14 percent alcohol must provide a numerical measure with a 1 percent allowable margin of error and a legal floor of 14 percent. For instance, a wine label that indicates an alcohol content of 13 percent may have an actual level of alcohol between 11.5 and 14 percent; one reporting alcohol of 14.5 percent may range from 14.1 to 15.5 percent.

A wine firm must also decide whether it wants to include additional information on the front label, and if it so chooses, an optional back label. Providing more information about the characteristics of a wine on the label may assist consumers in making informed buying decisions and may be used as an effective marketing device. Wine characteristics often printed on the label include American Viticultural Area, vintage, grape variety, vineyard, and a declaration the wine was estate bottled.

Like other wine-producing countries, the United States has a system for assigning official names to geographic locations where grapes are grown. Each named location is called an American Viticultural Area, or AVA. About 200 of these currently exist. An AVA can be as large as an entire state or as small as a tiny district. Examples of well-known AVAs are the Napa Valley in California, the Willamette Valley in Oregon, and the Columbia Valley in Washington State. If a wine firm chooses to include the name of an AVA on the label, federal regulations require that at least 85 percent of the grapes used to make the wine must come from that geographic location.[29] Vintage gives information on the year the grapes were harvested. If a vintage is printed on the label and the wine comes from an AVA, then at least 95 percent of the grapes used to make the wine must be harvested in that year.[30] If a wine is labeled as a varietal wine with the name of a specific grape, at least 75 percent of the wine must come from that grape variety. If the name of a vineyard is printed on the label, the wine is called a single vineyard wine, and 95 percent of the grapes must come from that particular vineyard. A firm can label a wine "estate bottled" only if it grows the grapes, and produces and bottles the wine itself. This informs the consumer that neither purchased grapes nor bulk wine were used to make it.

A host of other information about the characteristics of a wine can also be provided on the front or back label. This may include grape harvest date, grape yield, degree of filtering, fermentation and maturation vessel, and malolactic fermentation, as well as a number of other attributes.

It is clear that wine labels may provide less than complete information to consumers about the attributes of a wine, and might even be somewhat deceptive. For instance, a bottle labeled "2008 Sonoma County Chardonnay Produced and Bottled by Z Winery" may contain only 75 percent Sonoma County grapes, 85 percent of grapes harvested in 2008, and 75 percent fermented by Z Winery. This seemingly premium, single varietal Chardonnay may actually be 15 percent Chenin blanc purchased on the bulk wine market from grapes harvested in 2007 in California's San Joaquin Valley.

Packaging Wine in a Box

After the bottle, the most important wine container is the bag-in-box, a collapsible plastic bag of wine equipped with a tap, packaged in a cardboard box. About 25 percent of the wine sold in the United States comes in this type of container, which is designed for low-priced bulk wine intended to be consumed over a few weeks. One of the best-selling wines in the United States, Franzia Winetap wine, is sold in a box with a freshness date printed on it. The bag-in-box container is even more popular in countries such as Australia, where boxed wine accounts for more than half the wine consumed.[31]

7

Bulk Wine, Private-Label Wine, and Wine Alcohol

This chapter focuses on three important topics related to wine production: bulk wine, private-label wine, and wine alcohol. The bulk-wine market plays a little-known but important role in the economic organization of the wine industry. It allows for greater efficiency in resource use by producers and increased product choice for consumers. The characteristics of the bulk-wine market are described and a supply and demand framework is used to explain how wine firms interact in this market and factors that affect the price of bulk wine and the volume of transactions. Closely related to bulk wine is private-label wine, a proprietary product produced by a winery under contract for a client, typically a retail establishment. Private-label wine is the fastest-growing segment of the wine market and has the potential to significantly change the way wine firms produce and deliver products to consumers. The forces underlying the trend toward private-label wine and the implications for wine firms are discussed. Finally, alcohol content, an important and controversial characteristic of wine, is discussed. It is widely recognized that the alcoholic strength of wine has been rising over the past several decades. Moreover, recent studies suggest that wine firms make systematic errors when reporting alcohol content on wine labels. Is the high and rising alcohol content of wine the unintended outcome of global warming, or is it the result of rational decisions by winemakers and proprietors? What motivates wine firms to make systematic labeling errors? These questions are addressed in this chapter.

BULK WINE

Bulk wine is finished wine suitable for consumption but not yet packaged for sale. Most bulk wine is either transported in a tanker truck, railroad tanker car, or tanker ship to a different location by the same wine firm or sold on the bulk-wine market to another wine firm. The main reason a single wine firm transports bulk wine is to package it in close proximity to the location where it will be sold so as to reduce cost. It is less expensive to move wine over long distances in bulk rather than in bottles or boxes; this minimizes the weight and volume of a given amount of wine, which decreases transportation cost.[1] Recent advances in bulk-transportation technology that prevent deterioration in wine quality have provided an economic incentive for wine firms to produce wine in one country and package and sell it to consumers in another. For example, large wine firms that produce a significant amount of wine for export to foreign markets, such as Gallo and Bronco Wine Company, realize substantial cost savings by shipping wine in large containers with collapsible polyurethane bladders and bottling it close to the point of sale in countries like Italy, Great Britain, and Japan. This is particularly advantageous for lower-priced commodity wine products, for which transportation cost is proportionately higher than for higher-priced premium and luxury products.

A large amount of unpackaged wine is sold on the bulk-wine market. Although still largely unknown to most wine consumers, this is a very large and active market, in which a majority of wine firms participate as sellers or buyers, at least from time to time. The bulk-wine market has always played an important role in the U.S. wine industry. Prior to World War II, most California wineries specialized in producing bulk wine and sold it to firms throughout the United States that specialized in bottling wine. The bottlers would then sell it under their own brand names to local distributors. The bulk wine was typically transported across country in railroad tanker cars. Wineries that bottled and sold wine under their own brand names often purchased at least some of their wine from bulk producers.[2] During World War II, railroad tanker cars were used to transport wartime goods, which made it difficult for wineries to ship bulk wine. In addition, the system of price controls allowed higher prices for bottled wine and in-state sales of bulk wine. This provided an economic incentive for wineries to bottle and sell wine under their own labels or sell bulk wine to other wineries within the same state, rather than to independent bottlers located out of state.[3]

After World War II ended, the wine industry emerged with case-goods wineries that produced and bottled their own wine, bulk producers that specialized in selling unpackaged finished wine to other wineries, and wine firms that produced and sold both bulk wine and proprietary wine products. Today, an active bulk-wine market continues to exist, with a variety of participants that buy and sell finished unpackaged wine for a number of purposes. Estimates suggest that 10 to 15 percent of California wine produced in a given year is exchanged on the bulk market before it is finally packaged and sold.[4] Most wine firms don't like to talk about their bulk transactions, but in reality the unglamorous bulk market is an inextricable part of the wine business and increases the efficiency of wine firms and the range of products available to consumers.

The Characteristics of the Bulk-Wine Market

Bulk wine is exchanged on both a spot market for immediate delivery and on a long-term contract market with contracts that may have a duration of many years. Like the market for packaged wine, the bulk market can be separated into commodity and premium submarkets. Bulk wine traded on the commodity segment of the market is largely produced from grapes grown in high-yield vineyards in the Central Valley of California and countries such as Chile, Argentina, and Australia. Most premium bulk wine is the product of grapes grown in locations with a reputation for high quality such as Napa and Sonoma Counties in California, and highly regarded viticultural areas in the Willamette Valley in Oregon and the Columbia Valley in Washington State.

An ineluctable feature of the wine business is that in any given year, some wine firms will produce more wine than they plan to package and sell under their own labels, while others will produce less wine than the amount they desire for the products they wish to offer to consumers. There are many possible reasons for this. Some wine firms choose to specialize in producing bulk wine because they have a comparative advantage in this type of product. Others may find themselves with more wine in inventory than they are willing or able to package and sell. This may result from a variety of unanticipated events, such as an abundant grape harvest, incorrect wine demand forecast, insufficient tank and barrel capacity for a new vintage, excess blending components, or a batch of wine of lower than desired quality. This gives rise to a supply of bulk wine from specialized producers and other wine firms that desire to eliminate excess wine inventory. A demand for bulk wine arises from wine firms that desire to sell one or more wine products without under-taking the significant investment involved in growing grapes and pro-ducing wine. These firms may have a comparative advantage in market-ing or even blending wine, but not in producing it. Other wine firms may demand bulk wine as a blending component, or because of an unanticipated shortage of wine resulting from a poor grape harvest or surge in wine demand.

The market for bulk wine is organized as both a direct search and a brokered market. A majority of bulk market transactions involve poten-tial buyers and sellers searching the market for one another without the assistance of a third party intermediary. However, an increasing volume of transactions are taking place through bulk-wine brokers. The bro-kered market in California is largely organized by three brokerage firms: Ciatti, Turrentine, and Mancuso.[5] Ciatti and Turrentine also have offices in a number of foreign wine-producing countries. These brokers have relationships with a variety of wine firms that desire to sell bulk wine and are familiar with their products. They collect samples of the bulk wines offered for sale and make them available to wine firms that want to purchase bulk wine. This allows potential buyers to evaluate the quality of wine before making an offer to purchase it. The broker coordinates negotiations for the price, delivery date, and other terms of the transaction. For performing this intermediary function, the broker receives a commission, which can range from 2 to 10 percent of the value of the transaction. Some brokers also organize a market in "shin-ers." A shiner is a finished wine that has been bottled but does not have a label, and therefore has a shiny appearance. It can be thought of as bulk wine in a bottle that is not yet packaged for sale because it lacks a label identifying a brand name. A firm that buys shiners attaches its own label and sells the wine under its own brand name. The same shiner product may be purchased and sold by more than one wine firm under different brand names at different prices.

Suppliers of Bulk Wine

The major suppliers of bulk wine on the U.S. market are bulk produc-ers, case-goods producers, foreign wine producers, and grape growers.

A bulk producer is a firm that specializes in producing wine for sale on the bulk market. As part of its business strategy, it chooses to produce more wine than it plans to sell under its own label. Bulk producers vary in size from large corporations to small custom-crush proprietorships.

Large bulk producers include DFV Wines, Bronco Wine Company, Scheid Vineyards, and Golden State Vineyards, which is a wholly owned subsidiary of The Wine Group, the second-largest wine firm in the United States. These firms grow grapes on thousands of acres of self-owned vineyard land and have the capacity to produce millions of gallons of bulk wine per year at minimum cost in large, modern winemaking facilities, using technologically advanced methods of production and exploiting economies of scale.[6] For example, in 2010, DFV Wines sold 3.4 million cases of wine under its own label and the equivalent of 9 million cases on the bulk-wine market.[7] Almost all of the top twenty wine firms in the United States purchase some of their wine from these large bulk producers, either to blend with wine they produce in their own facilities or to bottle and sell under their own brand names. Large bulk producers often sell their wine under long-term contract.

Domestic case-goods producers are a second important supplier of bulk wine. A case-goods producer is a wine firm whose principal activity is producing, bottling, and labeling wine for retail sale under its own brand name. Most of these wineries use the bulk market to eliminate excess inventories of wine. There are a number of reasons why a case-goods producer might find itself with an unwanted wine surplus. An unexpectedly large grape harvest from either its own vineyards or those from which it buys grapes under long-term contract may result in a larger than anticipated supply of wine. It may be difficult to sell all of this through established distribution channels. Moreover, the producer may choose not to reduce price to adjust its inventory for fear of harming its brand image and establishing a new lower price point for the wine. A similar scenario may arise from an unexpected decrease in consumer demand. When sales decline, a wine firm may choose to sell some of its wine on the bulk market rather than bottle and store it. This reduces bottling and storage costs and generates revenue during a period when the wine firm likely needs cash flow to pay its bills. It may also be difficult to sell stored wine in a future year if consumers view it as an outdated vintage. From time to time, premium wine producers conclude that a particular batch of wine does not satisfy their quality standards and to protect their brand image therefore choose not to bottle and sell it under their own label. Selling this wine on the bulk market is preferable to discarding it. Some producers accumulate excess supplies of blending wines, while others may need barrel and tank space for a new vintage. In all of these situations, the bulk market serves as a potential outlet for the excess wine.

Foreign wine producers represent a third major source of bulk wine on the U.S. market. This includes both foreign bulk and case-goods producers that export surplus commodity wine. Imports are becoming a major source of bulk wine in the United States; in 2000, 4.5 million gallons were imported, representing 4 percent of all wine imports, but by 2010, this had grown to 50 million gallons, accounting for 20 percent of wine imports. The most important foreign suppliers of bulk wine to the United States are Australia, Chile, and Argentina. More than 40 percent of the wine exported by Australia and Chile is bulk wine.[8]

Smaller domestic grape growers are a fourth and increasingly important supplier of bulk wine. Periodically, independent vineyards accumulate excess supplies of grapes that are difficult to sell because of a bumper harvest or declining grape demand, particularly those without long-term contracts who sell their grapes on the spot market. In this situation, a growing number of vineyards are opting to contract with a winery to make the surplus grapes into wine and sell it on the bulk market, rather than accept a low price on the spot market or allow grapes to go unsold. Specialized bulk-marketing firms have arisen that assist growers in transforming their surplus grapes into bulk wine. Under one arrangement, the bulk-marketing firm purchases surplus grapes from growers at a discount, ferments the grapes into wine, and sells the wine on the bulk market through bulk-wine brokers. If the revenue from selling the bulk wine exceeds production and brokerage cost, the profit is shared by the grower and the marketing firm. However, if revenue falls short of cost, then the grower reimburses the marketing firm for the loss.[9]

Buyers of Bulk Wine

The major buyers of bulk wine are case-goods producers, negociants, and retailers that sell private-label wines.

Many case-goods producers use bulk wine as the source of one or more of their wine brands. Almost all large wine firms in the United States sell at least one brand made from bulk wine, and sometimes many. Often this wine is purchased from foreign producers at very low prices. For example, Franzia Chardonnay and Merlot, two best-selling bag-in-box wines marketed by The Wine Group, are produced with bulk wine sourced from Australia and Chile. Bulk wine from Italy is also used for Gallo's Turning Leaf Pinot noir and Constellation's Woodbridge Pinot grigio, to mention just a couple.[10] Without the bulk-wine market, many low-priced commodity wine brands sold in large quantities by big firms would not be economically feasible, and therefore unavailable to consumers. Often smaller wine firms that produce premium or luxury products will sell a lower-priced brand made from wine purchased on the bulk market. By using bulk wine for some of their products, wine firms can focus on marketing and selling additional brands or satisfy growing consumer demand without investing a substantial amount of money in new vineyards and winemaking equipment. Case-goods producers also use bulk wine as a blending component to reduce cost or improve wine quality. Many popular wine brands labeled "produced and sold by" large wine companies contain up to 25 percent bulk wine, primarily to minimize production cost and achieve wine consistency. The bulk market is also an important source of wine for wine firms that experience unexpected grape shortages as a result of weather conditions. Recently, wineries in Missouri and Texas that lost most of their grape crops to bad weather relied heavily on bulk-market purchases to satisfy demand for their wine brands and remain viable. Smaller premium wine producers may also purchase bulk wine for blending to improve quality by using it to compensate for winemaking mistakes or poor-quality grapes.

A significant amount of bulk wine is also purchased by firms called negociants, which typically bottle and sell wine under their own labels that they neither grow nor ferment, although they may blend and mature it.[11] An abundant global supply of wine and a large and growing bulk-wine market have resulted in a dramatic increase in the number of negociant firms in the U.S. wine market. These firms sell premium wine made with bulk wine sourced from small artisanal wineries, as well as commodity wine obtained from larger producers. They range in size from large wine companies down to one-person operations. Don Sebastiani & Sons, the fourteenth-largest wine company in the United States by volume with sales of 1.4 million cases in 2011, operates primarily as a negociant, purchasing wine on the bulk market and blending, bottling, and selling it under a variety of brand names such as Smoking Loon and Pepperwood Grove at a price point of around $10 per bottle.[12] Cameron Hughes Wine, a negociant firm with twenty-five employees, started in 2001, has annual sales of 400,000 cases of more than 100 wine products, sourced from ten different countries, that range in price from $5 to $28 per bottle.[13] Joseph Carr is essentially a one-person negociant operation that buys premium California bulk wine through a broker from locations like Napa and Sonoma Counties, blends the wine, contracts with a custom-crush facility to bottle it, and sells it under the Joseph Carr label.[14]

The new-style negociant in the U.S. wine industry is a contemporary version of a type of wine merchant that has a long history in Europe, particularly in France. Negociants are best known for the role they play in organizing and coordinating the production and sale of wine in the Bordeaux and Burgundy winegrowing regions of France. In Burgundy, French inheritance laws have resulted in a market with a large number of grape growers, each of whom owns little vineyard land and produces a relatively small output of grapes. Historically, it was not economically feasible for most of these growers either to invest in winemaking equipment and produce their own wine or to find potential buyers for the relatively little output they did produce. As a result, *négociant* vintners arose that specialized in purchasing grapes and wine from a number of individual growers, and then producing and blending the wine from the different growers into a single finished product. They would then sell the wine under their own labels.[15] Negociants performed a similar function in the Bordeaux region, where most of the châteaux fermented their wine and then sold it to negociants, who would age, bottle, and market it under the name of the individual château. Today, many of the 400 negociants doing business in Bordeaux function only as brokers, as most of the larger châteaux age and bottle their own wine. Also, many of the larger negociants of the 250 operating in Burgundy now own substantial amounts of vineyard land and produce and sell their own wines, as well as products using purchased grapes and wine.[16]

An increasing number of retailers also buy bulk wine for private-label wine products. A private-label wine is one sold exclusively by a store or restaurant, such as Costco, Safeway, or Lawry's Restaurants, that may have the retailer's name on the label, but may also have another name under which the retailer wishes to sell it. The most prominent example of a private-label wine is Charles Shaw wine, sold exclusively by Trader Joe's. It is often called Two Buck Chuck, since it is sold at a price of $1.99 in Trader Joe's supermarkets in California. The Charles Shaw brand is produced by the Bronco Wine Company. The original source of this product was large quantities of wine Bronco purchased on the bulk market and proceeded to bottle and label. Private-label wine is discussed in more detail below.

Factors Affecting the Price and Quantity of Bulk Wine

From an economic perspective, bulk wine is an intermediate product; that is, a good used as an input to produce packaged wine for final

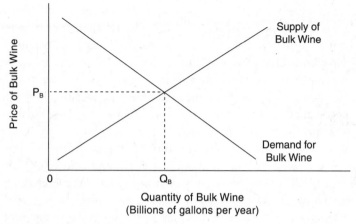

FIGURE 7. Market for bulk wine.

consumption. It may be blended with other wine to produce a final wine product or packaged and sold by itself. The price and quantity bought and sold of bulk wine is determined by the interaction of demand and supply. The bulk-wine market can be represented by a supply-and-demand graph, with price measured on the vertical axis and quantity on the horizontal axis. This is illustrated in figure 7.

As usual the supply curve slopes upward, illustrating that at higher prices, suppliers are willing and able to produce and sell more bulk wine, all else being equal. The higher price increases the profitability of selling bulk wine, and therefore gives suppliers an economic incentive to offer more on the market. For example, large bulk-wine producers who produce both bulk and proprietary wine may be induced to produce more bulk wine and less proprietary wine with their available resources. At the higher price, bulk producers that also grow their own grapes can afford to increase yield per acre by applying more fertilizer, water, and higher cost vineyard management practices. This results in more fruit for bulk production. As price rises, independent grape growers may be willing to use more of their grapes to produce bulk wine under contract with a custom-crush winery and sell fewer grapes on the spot market. Finally, some case-goods producers may be more inclined to sell some of their inventory of wine on the bulk market at the relatively higher price.

Consistent with the law of demand, the demand curve slopes downward, illustrating that at lower prices, bulk-wine buyers are willing and able to purchase larger amounts. As price falls, it is relatively cheaper for case-goods producers to use bulk wine as a blending component or package it as a wine brand, compared to the alternative of purchasing grapes and fermenting wine. Case-goods producers, negociants, and retailers who sell private-label brands have an economic incentive to purchase more, because they are able to obtain a larger quantity of bulk wine for their products at the same total cost. Finally, at the lower price, new negociants may enter the market and more retail establishments may offer private-label wines.

Given the supply and demand conditions in figure 7, the equilibrium price of bulk wine is P_B and quantity bought and sold is Q_B. This is where the two curves intersect, and quantity demanded therefore equals quantity supplied. When supply or demand conditions change, the supply or demand curve will shift and the equilibrium price and quantity of bulk wine will change.

The most important factor affecting the supply of bulk wine is the supply of grapes. Grape supply, in turn, depends upon the number of acres of vines cultivated and the yield per acre. An increase (decrease) in grape-bearing acreage or yield per acre increases (decreases) the supply of grapes, and therefore the supply of bulk wine. As a result, the supply curve for bulk wine shifts to the right (left), price decreases (increases), and quantity increases (decreases). A number of factors affect yield per acre, such as fertilizer, irrigation, and canopy management, but in any given year, the most important factor is unpredictable weather conditions. Good weather years result in higher yields and a greater supply of grapes. Bulk producers find themselves with more grapes to produce bulk wine. Case-goods producers that grow their own grapes or purchase them under long-term contract now have more grapes to ferment and a bigger wine inventory. Independent vineyards that sell grapes on the spot market may accumulate excess supplies and contract to ferment some of these grapes into bulk wine. As a result, at every possible price of bulk wine, quantity supplied increases, which forces the equilibrium price lower as a larger volume of bulk wine is traded. The opposite scenario occurs in bad weather years. As discussed in chapter 5, arguably the most important factor affecting vine-planting decisions is the expected future price of grapes. When grape supply is relatively low and price is high, growers expect the high price to prevail in the future and respond to this economic incentive by planting more acres. Several years later, when the new vines bear fruit, the supply of grapes and bulk wine increase and price falls. When grape supply is relatively high and price is low, the opposite occurs. As a result, the grape-supply cycle has a significant influence on the bulk-wine market. All else being equal, periods of overproduction and low prices in the grape market lead to lower bulk-wine prices and a larger quantity bought and sold. Periods of underproduction and high grape prices lead to higher bulk-wine prices and a smaller volume of bulk-market transactions.

As stated previously, foreign producers are an important source of bulk wine. Wineries in countries like Australia, Chile, and Argentina produce bulk wine for export to other countries such as the United States. The supply of wine offered by foreign producers depends on grape-bearing acreage and yield per acre in their home countries. Increased planting and favorable weather conditions in these countries result in an increase in the supply of imported bulk wine and lower prices in the United States. The supply of bulk wine from foreign producers also depends upon the currency exchange rate. An increase in the value of the dollar relative to the currencies of foreign producers provides an economic incentive for foreign wineries to offer more bulk wine for sale on the U.S. market; a declining dollar makes them less willing to supply bulk wine. For example, suppose the price per gallon of bulk wine in the United States is $10 and one dollar exchanges for 500 Chilean pesos on the foreign exchange market. After exchanging dollars for pesos, bulk-wine producers in Chile receive a price of 5,000 pesos for each gallon sold on the U.S. market. Now assume the dollar appreciates in value so that one dollar exchanges for 600 pesos. The increase in the value of the dollar increases the peso price of bulk wine to 6,000 pesos. Because it is now more profitable to sell bulk wine on the U.S. market, Chilean producers have an economic incentive to increase the amount supplied. All else being equal, this decreases the price and increases the quantity of bulk wine.

The demand for bulk wine is a derived demand; it is derived from the demand for the final packaged wine product. Anything that increases (decreases) the demand for packaged wine increases (decreases) the demand for bulk wine. This causes a rightward (leftward) shift of the demand curve for bulk wine, which results in a higher (lower) price and greater (smaller) quantity bought and sold. For example, in periods of economic expansion and rising personal income, the demand for packaged wine increases. This in turn increases the demand for bulk wine by case-goods producers, negociants, and retailers of private-label wine. The increased demand increases both the price and quantity bought and sold of bulk wine. The demand for bulk wine also depends on the prices of other inputs used in the production process. For example, many large wine firms view purchased grapes and bulk wine as substitute inputs in producing some of their commodity wine products. When grape prices increase, they have an economic incentive to substitute bulk wine for wine fermented from purchased fruit to minimize the cost of production. If the supply of bulk wine offered for sale by domestic suppliers is tight because of a relatively small grape harvest, it is often readily available from foreign producers in countries with surplus grapes and wine.

PRIVATE-LABEL WINE

The market for private-label wine is closely related to the bulk-wine market. A private-label wine is a proprietary wine produced by a winery under contract for a client. The winery either sources the grapes and ferments the wine or buys wine on the bulk market. It then bottles and labels the wine for the client. Private-label wine is the fastest-growing segment of the wine market in America. It has been estimated that these wines account for as much as 5 percent of wine sales in the United States, and 50 to 60 percent in the United Kingdom and Germany.[17]

Any winery can contract with a client to produce private-label wine. The major suppliers are large bulk-wine producers—such as DFV Wines, Scheid Vineyards, and Bronco Wine Company—and custom-crush wineries that specialize in providing grape-to-bottle winemaking services to clients. However, a growing number of case-goods producers are also making temporary or permanent arrangements with clients to provide private-label wines, particularly those with excess capacity or during periods of surplus wine. Some wineries that sell their own wine brand use the private-label market as a short-run adjustment mechanism providing private-label wine when they find themselves with excess inventory. Others are entering into long-term private-label partnerships to supplement their branded wine business. Many of these choose not to have their identity revealed on the label. An advantage of remaining anonymous is that the winery does not compete with its own wine brand, which typically has a higher price than the private-label product. Wineries with excess capacity have a strong economic incentive to produce private-label products. The cost of winemaking equipment required to produce its brand product such as fermentation and maturation tanks is a fixed one, which must be paid regardless of the amount of wine produced. Any revenue the winery generates from producing private-label wine, over and above the cost of grapes and other variable inputs, adds to its profit. Of course, the winery has no economic incentive to produce private-label wine if it cannot cover its variable cost.

The most important demanders of private-label wine are retailers, primarily supermarkets and restaurants. Some private-label wines are sold under the brand name of the retailer or a retailer's store brand name. Costco, a warehouse supermarket club that is the largest wine retailer in the United States, sells a number of private-label wines under its well-known Kirkland Signature name, which appears conspicuously on the label. It contracts with a variety of wineries in the United States and around the globe to produce a collection of limited production private-label wines. These private-label wines change over time as new products are added and existing products are sold out. The label indicates the geographic location where the grapes were grown, but may or may not reveal the producer. Producers of higher quality private-label products usually want their name concealed. Other private-label brands are owned by the wine producer and sold exclusively through a single retailer. The best example is the Bronco Wine Company's Charles Shaw brand, sold at Trader Joe's stores.[18] However, most private-label wine is sold under a brand name that differs from the retailer's name. For example, Wal-Mart sells its Oak Leaf and Lucky Duck brands; Safeway sells its Diablo Creek brand; and Target sells its Wine Cubes brand. Whole Foods sells as many as 100 private-label products in selected stores at any given time; most of these wines are not sold under its store brand name, 365.[19]

What is the economic incentive for a retailer to sell private-label wine? Today, retailers can source wine of acceptable quality at relatively low cost from grape-growing regions around the globe. During the overproduction phase of the U.S. wine-grape cycle, when grapes and bulk wine are plentiful, the wine for private-label products can be obtained in the United States, and when the cycle enters the underproduction phase and supplies tighten, it can be imported from other regions of the world. This strategy works well as long as the wine-grape cycles across countries are asynchronous, as they have been in the recent past. This enables retailers to offer private-label wines at lower prices than brand-name wines of equal quality. Not only does private-label wine have a higher profit margin, but the high quality-to-price ratio builds customer trust, loyalty, and repeat sales. For example, since it was introduced in 2002, Trader Joe's has sold well over 500 million bottles of Charles Shaw wine at a price as low as $1.99 per bottle. As for quality, Charles Shaw wine products have won a number of medals at wine competitions, including a double gold at the California State Fair in 2007.[20]

Some wine industry observers believe that large retail stores in the United States will eventually adopt a private-label wine strategy similar to the one used by the giant British supermarket chains Tesco and Sainsbury, and that private-label wines will account for as much as half of the U.S. market.[21] Tesco is the largest wine retailer in the United Kingdom and sells a wide variety of brand-name and private-label wines from all the world's major wine-producing countries. Private-label wines sold by Tesco and other food retailers account for more than 40 percent of wine sales in supermarkets in Britain.[22] Tesco competes with brand-name wines by its reputation for selling private-label wines of consistent quality at bargain prices. The Tesco name on the label informs consumers that the wine satisfies acceptable quality standards. This greatly simplifies the wine choice problem for consumers with limited information who must select a wine from the hundreds or thousands available in retail stores. Tesco uses a number of strategies to minimize wine cost, without sacrificing quality, to keep prices relatively low. It exploits its large size and market power to negotiate volume discounts from wine firms. It owns a bottling plant, imports bulk wine from other countries, and packages it in the United Kingdom. This reduces transportation costs. To ensure quality, Tesco blends purchased bulk wine like a negociant to make some of its private-label products. It also employs a team of winemaking consultants that monitor the winemaking activities of producers located around the world with whom it has contracts for quality-control purposes.[23]

If retailers in the United States are eventually successful in implementing a Tesco-like wine strategy, a significant part of the business of a typical wine firm will be private-label wine production.

WINE ALCOHOL

An important and controversial characteristic of wine is alcohol content. Unless the winemaker intervenes, the amount of alcohol in a wine product is primarily determined by the amount of sugar in the grape input. Grape sugar, in turn, depends upon grape ripeness. Riper grapes have a higher sugar content, which ferments into a more alcoholic wine. Grape ripeness is largely determined by the average temperature of the location where the grapes are grown and the length of time grapes are allowed to hang on the vine before they are harvested. All else being equal, warmer temperatures and longer hang times result in riper grapes. While the winemaker is able to influence grape ripeness, to the extent that he can choose when grapes are harvested, nature dictates the prevailing temperature across grape-growing locations and over time.

If the ripeness of the grapes predisposes a wine to have a nonoptimal amount of alcohol, the winemaker may choose to alter the alcohol content. A number of technologies are available to manipulate the level of alcohol in a wine. As discussed previously, alcohol can be increased by adding sugar or removing water from grape must. Water can be taken out of grape must by cryo-extraction, reverse osmosis, and other modern technologies. Alternatively, alcohol can be decreased by adding water to grape must, when state regulations do not prohibit it, or using modern technologies like reverse osmosis or a spinning cone to extract alcohol directly from a finished wine.[24] Several firms in California, including Vinovation, Wine Secrets, and ConeTech, specialize in providing such services to wineries.. Estimates suggest that as many as half of California wineries use reverse osmosis or spinning-cone machines to adjust the alcohol content of their wine, and ConeTech alone applies its alcohol reduction technology to about 3 percent of California's annual wine production.[25]

The Actual Alcohol Content of Wine

It is widely recognized that the alcohol content in wine varies across grape varieties and growing regions. Moreover, there is virtually unanimous agreement among wine professionals and aficionados that the alcoholic strength of wine worldwide has been trending up over the past several decades. The most comprehensive empirical study to provide quantitative estimates of the alcohol content of wine across geographic locations and over time is by Julian Alston et al. (2011a). This study analyzed data on 91,432 wine products from eleven wine-producing countries for the period 1992–2007.[26] The estimates reported indicate that red wine has more alcohol than white wine; wine from warmer growing regions has more alcohol than that from cooler regions; and wine produced in New World countries has more alcohol than that from Old World countries.[27] The most interesting finding relates to the trend in alcohol content over time. During the sixteen-year period studied, the average alcohol content of wine worldwide increased from about 12.7 to 13.7 percent. U.S. wine has the highest alcohol content of any country's, exceeding Italy's by about 1 percent, France's by 0.85 percent, and that of the closest country, Australia, by 0.20 percent.

Causes of the Rising Alcohol Content of Wine

The upward trend in the alcoholic strength of wine has been accompanied by a contemporaneous upward trend in grape ripeness at harvest. In a second study, Alston et al. (2011b) estimate that the sugar content of grapes harvested in California increased from 21.8 Brix in 1990 to 23.3 Brix in 2008. All else being equal, this 7 percent increase in grape sugar would result in a 7 percent increase in wine alcohol. For example, a wine that had an alcohol content of 13 percent in 1990 would have increased to 13.9 percent by 2008, assuming no winemaker intervention to manipulate the amount of alcohol in it. This same upward trend in grape-sugar content has been observed in wine-producing countries throughout the world. Many winemakers contend that harvesting riper grapes with more sugar and less acid is the unintended outcome of rising temperatures associated with global warming. An alternative explanation is that this phenomenon has little to do with constraints imposed by nature; rather, it is the outcome of rational decisions of winemakers and proprietors whose objective is to maximize utility or profit. Winemakers may increasingly demand overripe, physiologically mature grapes harvested later in the growing season to produce bigger, more intensely flavored wines that command higher prices and receive accolades from wine critics.

Alston et al. (2011a) analyzed the relationship between wine alcohol content and growing season temperature for grape-growing regions around the world. The researchers concluded that global warming accounts for little if any of the rise in wine alcohol. Their estimate of the effect of temperature on wine alcohol indicates that a 20°F increase in average growing season temperature would be required to increase the average alcohol content of wine by 1 percent. What is more, over the period 1992 to 2007, most grape-growing regions in the world had relatively little variation in growing season temperature. This includes the United States, which had the biggest increase in wine alcohol content. Alston et al. (2011b) examined the relationship between the sugar content of grapes in California and growing-season temperature for the period 1990 to 2008. The estimate produced in this study suggests that the observed increase in sugar content of 1.5 Brix over this period would have required an increase in average growing-season temperature of about 30°F. Global warming, to the extent that it may have occurred during this period, cannot explain the trend toward harvesting riper grapes in California. Together, these two studies support the hypothesis that choices by winemakers and proprietors, rather than global warming, explain the trend toward riper grapes at harvest and more alcoholic wines.

Labeled Alcohol Content of Wine

Alston et al. (2011a) also analyzed the relationship between actual alcohol content and that claimed on the label by wine producers for the 91,432 wine products sampled. Like the United States, most countries allow wine producers a margin of error in the alcohol content indicated on a wine label. The data revealed that 57 percent of the wines stated alcohol levels too low, 33 percent too high, and only 10 percent accurately. The countries with the biggest discrepancies were Chile, Argentina, and the United States. On average, wine products in the United States stated an alcohol content of 13.65 percent on the label compared to an actual alcohol content of 13.88 percent. The study also found evidence of systematic labeling errors. The alcohol content reported on the label of more alcoholic wines tends to be understated, while that of less alcoholic wines is overstated. This is consistent with a smaller study of wines sold in the United States. A publication called *Truth in Wine* tested twenty-seven best-selling wines and found that all of them overreported the alcohol content on their labels; actual alcohol content was below 14 percent.[28]

Why Higher Wine Alcohol and Systematic Labeling Errors?

What may motivate a wine firm to seek riper grapes and then underreport the alcohol content of the wine produced with these grapes? The following scenario provides one possible explanation of winemakers' and wine consumers' behavior based on the concepts of rational behavior and asymmetric information. Asymmetric information exists when buyers and sellers have different information about the characteristics of the product being exchanged in a market transaction.

Suppose a typical consumer of premium or luxury wine gets utility from two characteristics of a wine: flavor intensity and alcohol content. Flavor intensity is measured by wine critic scores, which either reflect or affect consumer preferences. Consumers are willing to pay a higher price for wines with more intense fruit flavors that receive higher scores from critics. People are concerned about the health effects of high-alcohol wine, and the price they are willing to pay for wine with a higher alcohol content is therefore less once the alcohol level exceeds a particular threshold, say, 14 percent.[29] Consumers are well informed about the flavor intensity of wine, but ignorant about the actual alcohol content of wine, and they therefore make buying decisions based on the alcohol content printed on the wine label. The actual alcohol content may legally differ from what is reported on the label by the allowable margin of error. A typical consumer is rationally ignorant about the actual alcohol content of wine, since this information is costly to acquire.[30] Time or money must be expended to learn the federal wine labeling laws and measure the actual level of alcohol in a wine. Because of this, many consumers are unaware that the actual alcohol content may legally deviate from the label content. Those who are informed about wine-labeling laws and desire to verify the veracity of the claim made on the label would incur the cost of performing a chemical analysis of the wine to determine the alcohol content.

Suppose a typical winemaker purchases grapes under contract at a fixed price per ton and can choose how long they are to be left on the vine. To produce a more intensely flavored wine, the winemaker must use riper grapes with a higher sugar content that are allowed to hang on the vine longer to achieve greater physiological maturity. Longer "hang time" reduces grape weight from dehydration, and therefore lowers grape cost. It is costly to reduce the higher alcohol content of wine produced with riper grapes using reverse osmosis or a spinning cone, and this technology may compromise quality. Producers are well informed about both the flavor intensity and the actual alcohol content of the wine they produce.

Under this scenario, winemakers have an economic incentive to demand riper grapes with longer hang times and legally distort the information they provide to consumers by underreporting the alcohol content on the label. All else being equal, riper grapes reduce grape cost and produce wine with more intense fruit flavor, which commands a higher price and receives high scores and accolades from critics. By exploiting their informational advantage and claiming a lower level of alcohol on the label, producers are able to command a higher price for wine with a perceived lower alcohol content without incurring the cost of alcohol reduction, which may also reduce wine quality.

To the extent that wine quality depends upon both flavor intensity and alcohol content, asymmetric information makes it difficult for consumers to assess quality differences among wine producers. By exploiting this informational advantage, a producer can charge a higher price for a wine of given quality and gain at the expense of consumers. If consumers come to believe it is in their own best interest to acquire and use information on the actual alcohol content of wine, this will result in a demand for this information. In response, market mechanisms will likely arise to minimize the informational advantage of producers. For example, some wine critics have started to publish information on the actual alcohol content of wines they evaluate. However, these sources will become available only to the extent that consumers demand and are willing to pay for the information provided.

Wine Distribution and Government Regulation

After a wine has been produced and packaged it must be distributed to consumers. The wine distribution system in the United States is very complex. Each state has its own regulations governing the distribution and sale of alcoholic beverages, which impose restrictions on the choices a wine firm has for delivering products to consumers. This chapter focuses on the three principal channels through which wine firms can sell their products to consumers and the regulatory constraints they confront when using each of these. It also examines the economic rationale for government regulation of wine distribution and sales, and whether these regulations serve the public interest or special interest.

WINE DISTRIBUTION CHANNELS

The three major avenues producers have for distributing wine to consumers are the three-tier, direct-to-retailer, and direct-to-consumer channels. Many wine firms use more than one of these.

The Three-Tier Distribution Channel

About 90 percent of wine in the United States is moved from producer to consumer through the three-tier channel.[1] This involves a producer selling wine to a distributor, who then sells it to a retailer, who finally sells it to a consumer. Related to each tier is a price markup that is compensation for the distribution activities performed. The difference between the winery and distributor wholesale prices is the distributor markup, usually in the neighborhood of 30 percent. Although this may appear to be substantial, distributors perform a number of important and costly distributional activities. They have trucks and warehouse facilities and use these to transport and store wine as it moves from producers to retailers. Distributors have sales forces that specialize in promoting and selling wines they hold in inventory. They perform administrative functions such as collecting state excise taxes and providing state governments with tax-related information, and often provide credit to retailers who purchase their wines.[2] Because distributors purchase wine from producers for their own inventory, they, not producers, assume the risk of selling it to retailers and collecting payment.

Retailers can be classified as off-premises and on-premises depending upon whether the wine is consumed away from or at the site where it is sold. Off-premises retailers include grocery stores, big-box stores, and wine shops; important on-premises retailers are restaurants, bars, and hotels. Retailers purchase wine at the distributor's wholesale price and resell it to consumers at the final consumer price. The difference between these two prices is the retail markup, typically around 30 percent for off-premises retailers and 200 percent or more for on-premises retailers like restaurants. Retailers provide a convenient outlet for consumers to purchase wine. This includes both "brick-and-mortar" locations and virtual wine store websites that take purchase orders on the Internet and deliver wine to consumers by package carrier. To perform this function, retailers acquire and store an inventory of wine and assume the risk of reselling it to consumers. Many also provide information about the characteristics of various types of wine products, enabling consumers to make better, more informed consumption decisions.

The Direct-to-Retailer Distribution Channel

To distribute wine through a direct-to-retailer channel, the producer sells wine directly to the retailer rather than a distributor. The retailer then sells it to the consumer. The obvious advantage to producers of using this sales channel is the potential to capture the markup that would have gone to the distributor. However, to do this the producer must organize and coordinate the activities performed by a distributor, such as transportation, storage, sales, and administrative functions, which may be very costly if the producer does not specialize and have a degree of expertise in these areas. Moreover, the producer, not the distributor, assumes the risk of finding retail establishments to sell the wine.

The Direct-to-Consumer Distribution Channel

The third major distribution avenue is the direct-to-consumer channel, in which the producer sells wine directly to the consumer without the assistance of a distributor or retailer. This typically involves selling wine to consumers at a winery tasting room and shipping wine to consumers who belong to a producer-sponsored wine club, those on a mailing list, or those who submit orders for wine over the telephone or on a producer website. About 59 percent of direct sales come from the tasting room, 16 percent from wine clubs, 8 percent from websites, and the rest from other types of direct sales.[3] Once again, the major advantage to producers of using this distribution channel is the potential to pocket the markup of both the distributor and retailer, which may be as much as 50 percent or more of the price paid by consumers. The disadvantage is that producers must organize and coordinate many of the costly activities typically performed by distributors and retailers who specialize in providing them. The direct-to-consumer channel is a particularly important distribution mechanism for smaller wine firms, which often have a difficult time finding distributors willing to carry their products. Direct sales may account for as much as 40 percent of revenues of wine firms that produce fewer than 5,000 cases per year.[4]

Brokers, Fulfillment Agents, and Importers

In addition to producers, distributors, and retailers, three other entities play an important role in the wine distribution system: brokers, fulfillment agents, and importers.

Wine brokers perform a search function and bring together producers, distributors, and retailers to make distribution-related transactions. Unlike distributors and retailers who purchase wine for their own inventories and hope to resell it at a higher price to make a profit, brokers never take ownership of wine and are paid a commission for the services they provide. They specialize in gathering information on the attributes of different types of wines available from producers and providing this information to retailers and distributors that demand wines with similar characteristics. This performs a valuable economic function in the U.S. wine market, with more than 7,000 wineries that produce more than 15,000 different wines and attempt to sell most of these products to consumers through hundreds of distributors and thousands of on-premises and off-premises retailers. Wine-broker services are of particular value to the large number of relatively small wine firms that lack the resources and expertise necessary to promote their wines and find distributors and retailers willing to purchase them.

Fulfillment agents perform a valuable function in the direct-to-consumer distribution channel. They specialize in the logistics of moving wine from the producer directly to the consumer by providing temporary storage, packaging, administration, and transportation services. This primarily involves fulfilling wine club and Internet orders for wine firms that sell directly to consumers, allowing wineries to devote their resources to the core activity of producing wine. These services are also provided to retailers that sell wine to consumers on the Internet. Like wine brokers, fulfillment agents never take ownership of the wine; rather, they earn a fee for the logistical activities they provide, which are similar to those performed by distributors.

Importers specialize in delivering U.S. wines to foreign markets and importing the wines of foreign producers. To distribute imported wines to U.S. consumers, the importer can sell wine to a distributor, who sells it to a retailer, who sells it to consumers. Alternatively, importers might sell directly to retailers or consumers. Some distributors and retailers also function as importers.

DISTRIBUTION AND WINE QUALITY

An important component of wine distribution is the logistics of transportation and storage. A number of factors related to shipping and storage can influence wine quality. These include movement, light exposure, vibration, and humidity, but temperature is by far the most important. Exposure to high temperature may cause wine to develop an off-taste or become flavorless. As a result, a given wine can vary in quality depending on how it is transported and stored after it is produced and before it is consumed.

Most wine is transported by truck or rail in uninsulated, insulated, or temperature-controlled containers. To assure wine quality, transportation by temperature-controlled truck or rail car is best, but this is expensive and can result in a significant increase in distribution cost and wine price. Transporting wine in uninsulated or even insulated vehicles, particularly over long distances in summer or winter under extremely high or low temperatures, can adversely affect wine quality. Wine may be stored for as little as a few days or as long as several years in a warehouse or store. Like transportation vehicles, warehouses may be uninsulated, insulated, or—best but most expensive—temperature-controlled. It is not unusual for wine to be stored without air conditioning on steel racks several stories high in a warehouse built of sheet metal. In some places, wine may well cook in summer or freeze during the winter under these conditions—particularly if stored near the roof. While some retailers keep at least part of their inventory of wine in a temperature-controlled storage facility, most do not because of space constraints and the cost of specialized storage facilities. Wine tends to be stored in retail establishments with significant light exposure at a comfortable room temperature, which is not necessarily favorable for wine quality.

GOVERNMENT REGULATION OF WINE DISTRIBUTION

A wine producer's choice of distribution channel is restricted by government regulation. In the absence of current regulatory constraints, the three-tier channel would likely function more efficiently, and significantly more wine would be distributed and sold through the direct-to-retailer and direct-to-consumer channels. Moreover, a greater degree of vertical integration of distribution channels would likely exist, with more producers owning and operating distributors and possibly retail stores.[5]

The Regulated Three-Tier Channel

The Twenty-First Amendment to the U.S. Constitution, passed in 1933, repealed Prohibition and granted each state the right to regulate the production, distribution, and sale of alcoholic beverages within its borders. Most states responded by requiring that alcoholic beverages be distributed and sold through a regulated three-tier channel. All alcoholic beverages produced in-state or out-of-state and shipped to the state must pass through a distributor and retailer before being sold to a consumer. The producer, distributor, and retailer must be separately owned entities and each one must be licensed by the state. In addition to a state license, producers, importers, and distributors must also obtain licenses from the federal government. A distributor or retailer can operate in more than one state, but must have a separate license for each state.

Some states do not grant distributor or retail licenses to private firms. In these states, called control states, the government acts as the distributor or retailer of some or all types of alcoholic beverages. For instance, the state of Pennsylvania is both the distributor and retailer of wine, beer, and spirits. New Hampshire acts as the distributor, but grants retail licenses to private firms to sell alcoholic beverages. In Utah, the state controls distribution and owns and operates retail stores, but also grants retail licenses to a limited number of private firms. The state of Alabama functions as distributor and retailer of spirits, but grants distribution and retail licenses to private firms for wine and beer.

Virtually all states impose additional restrictions on the choices of licensed producers, distributors, and retailers operating within the three-tier distribution channel. More than thirty states have franchise or territory laws that place restrictions on the relationship between producers and distributors.[6] Under some franchise laws, a producer that has contracted to sell wine through a particular distributor may not end the contractual arrangement without the distributor's consent. As a result, the producer is required to continue to sell wine through this distributor regardless of the quality of the service received. Other franchise laws require a producer to sell wine through a single distributor. Once this distributor is selected, the producer cannot change to another distributor. Territory laws require the producer to specify the geographic region within a state in which a distributor is allowed to sell its wine to retailers. Some states permit the producer to contract with more than one distributor to service the same geographic region or an overlapping region; others require the territory to be exclusive, giving a single distributor a monopoly in selling the producer's wine within that region.

Many states impose restrictions on the prices charged by producers, distributors, and retailers. These include post and hold, uniform pricing, minimum markup, and quantity-discount regulations. Post and hold regulations require producers, distributors, or both to post prices with the state at regular intervals, such as the beginning of each month, and to leave them unchanged between postings. This fixes wine prices over discrete intervals of time. Uniform pricing regulations require producers to sell to all distributors at the same price and distributors to sell to all retailers at the same price. Minimum markup regulations place a floor on the prices producers, distributors, and retailers can charge relative to cost of production or acquisition. For instance, until recently the state of Washington required producers to charge distributors a price at least 10 percent above cost of producing the wine. Distributors were required to charge retailers a price at least 10 percent above the producer's wholesale price. Ohio requires retailers to charge consumers a price at least 33 percent above the distributor's wholesale price. States argue that these price regulations help to prevent excessive alcohol consumption by keeping prices higher than those that would prevail in their absence. Quantity-discount restrictions prohibit producers from giving volume discounts to distributors and/or distributors from giving volume discounts to retailers.

A number of states prohibit credit transactions between producers, distributors, and retailers, mandating that all purchases be paid for in cash. Others impose warehousing restrictions that prevent retailers from owning warehouses or require the distributor to deliver wine to the retail premises where it will be sold. Also, it is not uncommon for states to prohibit retailers from selling alcohol on certain days, specific times of day, and in specified "dry" communities. Some states do not allow consumers to buy wine in grocery stores.

Distributing wine through the regulated three-tier channel can be difficult and costly for producers. No distributors are licensed in all fifty states and many operate in a few or even a single state. Some states require distributor owners to be residents. This makes it difficult for them to operate in multiple states. To sell wine in more than a few states, a producer may have to seek out and negotiate contracts with a relatively large number of distributors, which is time-consuming and costly.[7] Less than 20 percent of producers sell wine through distributors in all fifty states, and many small wineries do not use the three-tier channel at all. Moreover, franchise laws that limit producers' choice of distributors may result in a less than ideal relationship between a producer and distributor. Distributors may fail adequately to promote and market a producer's wine products, resulting in poor retail sales. Wine quality may suffer as it moves from distributor to retailer because of careless handling and poor storage conditions. Legally mandated price restrictions also increase the price consumers pay, resulting in lower wine sales.

The Regulated Direct-to-Consumer Channel

Almost all states have exceptions to their three-tier distribution requirement. One of these is to allow producers a limited opportunity to distribute wine through the direct-to-consumer channel. Most states allow licensed in-state producers to sell wine to consumers at the winery for off-premises consumption. They also license producers to operate an on-site and sometimes off-site tasting room where consumers can sample and purchase wine. In addition, a majority of states allow producers to take orders from consumers at the winery and tasting room, as well as by mail, phone, and Internet, and to ship wine directly to consumers.

Prior to 2005, a number of states allowed direct-to-consumer shipping for in-state producers but not out-of-state producers. So, for instance, a consumer who lived in Michigan could submit an order by phone or on the Internet for a case of wine to be delivered to his or her home from a Michigan winery, but not a California winery. Over the years numerous lawsuits were brought by consumers and wineries contending that laws prohibiting direct interstate shipping of wine to consumers violated the Commerce Clause of the Constitution. In May 2005 in the case of *Granholm v. Heald,* the Supreme Court ruled that states that permit direct-to-consumer shipping by in-state wineries must give the same right to out-of-state wineries. Failure to do so discriminates against out-of-state wineries, which is contrary to the Interstate Commerce Clause. The Supreme Court also held that states have the right to ban direct-to-consumer shipping of wine, but that if they exercise this right, they must apply the prohibition equally to both in-state and out-of-state wineries. Most states responded by modifying their regulations to allow some form of direct interstate shipment of wine to consumers. Today, thirty-nine states allow both in-state and out-of-state wineries to ship directly to consumers.

Most states impose additional regulatory restrictions on producers who choose to sell and ship wine directly to consumers.[8] Most states require producers to obtain a direct shipping license, with annual fees that range from $25 to more than $1,000. A few states also require consumers to purchase a license that allows them to receive wine shipments. Many states require quarterly or annual shipping, excise, or sales-tax reports. A producer that ships to all thirty-nine states permitting direct wine shipments may well have to submit more than 300 reports each year. Some states impose quantitative restrictions on the amount of wine that can be shipped to a single consumer or all consumers in a given state each year. Other restrictions imposed by various states include special packaging requirements and submission of a copy of photo identification of consumers to whom wine is shipped. These sorts of regulatory restrictions make it difficult and costly for producers to ship to consumers in many states. However, many fulfillment agents and compliance vendors now exist that specialize in assisting producers in complying with direct shipping rules and regulations.

The Regulated Direct-to-Retailer Channel

Some states also allow producers a limited opportunity to distribute wine through the direct-to-retailer channel. Prior to 2005, a number of states permitted in-state producers to sell wine directly to retailers such as grocery stores, wine shops, and restaurants; however, virtually all states prohibited this type of self-distribution for out-of-state wineries. Recently, a number of lawsuits have been filed arguing that the *Granholm v. Heald* decision applies to winery direct-to-retail sales as well as direct-to-consumer sales. In a few states, the courts have ruled it illegal to discriminate against out-of-state producers who desire to sell wine directly to retailers. Some states have responded to litigation by prohibiting all producers from self-distributing their wine. Others now allow self-distribution for in-state and out-of-state wineries, while imposing various restrictions such as production and shipment caps. An Internet-based e-market now exists to facilitate transactions between wineries and retailers. Grocery stores, wine shops, and restaurants can arrange to purchase wines directly from wineries that may not be available from distributors in states where direct-to-retail sales are permitted. Moreover, large wineries are increasingly marketing their wine directly to large retailers rather than through distributors. In this case, the only function performed by the distributor is transportation and delivery services, which results in a lower distributor markup.

ECONOMIC ANALYSIS OF GOVERNMENT REGULATION OF WINE DISTRIBUTION

Why do states choose to regulate the distribution and sale of wine? Why not allow wine firms, distributors, retailers, and consumers to interact in an unfettered market that does not constrain their choices and behavior? Why have states adopted varying laws governing the regulation of alcohol in general and wine in particular? What are the economic effects of wine distribution laws on consumers, wine firms, distributors, and retailers?

The Economic Rationale for Regulation

It would be difficult on economic grounds to justify regulating the behavior of participants who voluntarily choose to transact in the market for alcoholic beverages if it approximated an "ideal market." In such a setting, there would be a large number of producers, distributors, and retailers of roughly equal size, each of which would have a relatively small share of sales in the geographic market in which they operate. Competition would ensure that a variety of alcoholic beverages that satisfied consumers' wants would be produced and offered for sale at the lowest possible prices. Economic power would be equally dispersed among all participants so that no individual or group could manipulate others who chose to transact in the market. Consumers would make rational choices and be well informed about the characteristics of alcoholic beverages for sale, and the risks and implications of consuming these products. The choice by an individual to purchase and consume an alcoholic beverage would have no detrimental effect on others who did not voluntarily participate in the transaction. This type of ideal market environment would result in an efficient allocation of resources to alcoholic beverages; that is, just the right amount and mix of these products would be produced and consumed, not too much, not too little. The right amount is the quantity that maximizes the net benefits from alcoholic beverage production and consumption for the U.S. population. This, in turn, would enhance socioeconomic welfare in the United States.

Unfortunately, there are three major reasons why an unfettered market in alcoholic beverages may not conform to this type of ideal setting, and hence would not promote maximum socioeconomic welfare. These instances in which the market fails to achieve an efficient allocation of resources when left to its own devices provide an economic rationale for government intervention in the market.

Sometimes when consumers choose to purchase products from suppliers of alcoholic beverages, they impose a cost on others who were not involved in the transaction. Economists call this an external cost, because it is incurred by someone who is not a buyer or seller of alcoholic beverages. For example, consider an individual who consumes a bottle of wine at a restaurant. The benefit the individual receives from the voluntary purchase of the wine product is called a private benefit and is equal to the maximum amount he is willing to pay. Assume that when driving home, our wine consumer causes an accident because the alcohol impairs his motor skills. Any cost incurred by the other driver, such as auto repair and medical care expenses, is an external cost. Because of this external cost, the other driver is made worse off by the wine transaction. Since the wine consumer and auto accident victim are both members of society, the social benefit of the wine transaction is the private benefit minus the external cost. In this situation, the benefit to society of the wine transaction is less than the benefit to the individual who voluntarily purchased the wine.

From a societal perspective, the existence of external costs results in too much alcohol being produced and consumed. This is best explained with the aid of a supply-and-demand graph. Figure 8 illustrates the demand and supply curves for alcoholic beverages. The demand curve (D) reflects the maximum amount consumers are willing to pay for additional units. It is a marginal private benefit curve (MPB), since it captures the benefits that accrue directly to those who buy alcoholic beverages. The supply curve (S) reflects both the marginal private cost (MPC) and marginal social cost (MSC) of the inputs required to produce additional units. In an unfettered market, Q_2 alcohol is produced and consumed. If there are no external costs associated with the consumption of alcohol, then Q_2 maximizes the net benefits to society; that is, it maximizes the difference between the total benefit of consuming alcoholic beverages and the total opportunity cost of their production measured by the dollar value of other goods and services the nation forgoes. In this case, net private benefits equal net social benefits and are measured by the area under the demand curve above the supply curve to the left of Q_2. However, when there are external costs in the consumption of alcohol, the marginal social benefit curve (MSB) lies to the left of the marginal private benefit curve, and reflects both the benefit that accrues to those who purchase alcoholic beverages and the cost they impose on other members of society. The difference between the two benefit curves is the external cost. In this case, the smaller quantity Q_1 is the right amount of alcohol consumption from a societal perspective, because it maximizes net social benefits. However, buyers and sellers who transact in an unfettered market for alcoholic beverages will ignore the external cost they impose on others who are adversely affected by their choices, and too much will therefore be consumed, and the market will fail to achieve an efficient allocation of resources. The existence of external costs lowers the nation's economic welfare and provides a rationale for government to intervene in the market for alcoholic beverages and attempt to correct this market imperfection.

To make rational choices about the quantity and types of alcohol beverages to purchase, individuals must have an adequate amount of information about the characteristics of the products offered for sale. This includes the risks and behavioral implications of the amount of these products consumed. If consumers either lack information or the

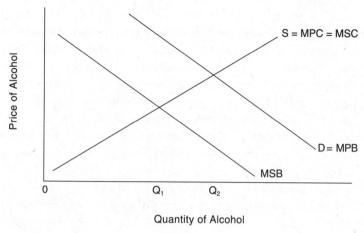

FIGURE 8. External cost of alcohol consumption.

ability to process available information, then they do not know the true costs and benefits and will not necessarily make rational alcohol consumption choices. In this case, an unfettered market in alcoholic beverages may fail to promote maximum social economic welfare. For example, suppose that a group of consumers are unaware of the long-term consequences of heavy drinking. If they had accurate information on the potential adverse health effects, they would demand less, because knowledge of this risk to their health reduces the benefits of alcohol consumption. Referring to figure 8, a market with poorly informed individuals has demand curve D = MPB and will consume Q_2 units. If consumers were well informed, the market demand curve would be MSB and only Q_1 units would be bought and sold. This latter outcome would maximize the true net benefits to society from alcohol consumption. This type of information problem, to the extent that it exists in the market for alcoholic beverages, provides a second economic rationale for government intervention.

The third justification for government involvement is to promote competition among producers, distributors, and retailers of alcoholic beverages, and prevent these suppliers from obtaining inordinate market power and engaging in business practices that adversely affect consumers, decrease efficiency, and lower socioeconomic welfare.

The government has two major tools at its disposal if it chooses to intervene in the market for alcoholic beverages in the event of external costs, inadequate information, and undue supplier market power. The first tool is taxes and subsidies that can be used to provide economic incentives to induce individuals or firms to change their behavior. For example, imposing an excise tax on alcoholic beverages increases price and gives individuals an economic incentive to consume less. Government can provide consumers with information on the consequences of heavy drinking or subsidize private organizations to do this. This reduces the cost of information acquisition and gives individuals an incentive to become more informed and make better choices. Taxes and subsidies influence behavior by altering the costs and benefits of choosing an alternative, but do not directly restrict the decisions of individuals. The second tool is regulation, where government restricts the choices of individuals or firms and directly attempts to control their behavior. For example, government can restrict where, when, and how alcoholic beverages can be sold, or even prohibit their sale altogether. It can control the quantity and types of alcoholic beverages that firms are allowed to produce as well as the price they can legally charge. Or the government itself can produce, distribute, or sell alcoholic beverages by owning and managing a public enterprise, and restrict or prohibit competition from private firms.

External costs, imperfect information, and market power may be used as economic arguments for government intervention; however, they do not necessarily explain why state governments choose to regulate the market for wine, why these regulations vary considerably across states, and why these regulations change over time. Two alternative theories have been proposed to explain government regulatory behavior: the public-interest and economic theories of regulation.

The Public-Interest View of Wine Regulation

One view is that state governments regulate the wine industry because it is in the public interest. The public recognizes that wine is an alcoholic beverage and that the consumption of alcoholic beverages has external costs. These include automobile accidents, violent crime, child abuse, disorderly conduct, and the lost productivity associated with heavy drinking. Moreover, suppliers can use their informational advantage or the market power they acquire to exploit consumers, especially individuals who lack information about product characteristics and health risks. As a result, the public demands regulations to correct these shortcomings of the market for wine and other alcoholic beverages. In response, state governments supply regulation to enhance socioeconomic welfare.

The public-interest theory may provide a reasonable explanation of why state regulations were originally instituted. After the repeal of Prohibition, each state was given the authority to decide how alcoholic beverages would be distributed and sold within its borders. While the public was in favor of ending Prohibition, there was broad support for regulating the consumption of alcoholic beverages because of concerns about excessive drinking. One can also argue that the public interest was served by preventing producers from monopolizing local markets by owning or controlling retailers (primarily saloons), which was a common practice before Prohibition, and eliminating from the industry the bootleggers and gangsters who were involved in the production and distribution of alcoholic beverages on the black market during Prohibition.

According to the public-interest theory, when Prohibition ended in 1933, states adopted a variety of regulatory controls to enhance socioeconomic welfare. Eighteen states chose to create public enterprises to distribute and sell alcoholic beverages within their borders. In these states, the government owns and manages the wholesale and retail business and prohibits competition from private firms. The state can exercise its monopoly power by acting as the sole purchaser of alcoholic beverages from producers and selling them exclusively in state-owned retail stores, or "outsourcing" some of its wholesale or retail activities for selected alcoholic beverages to private firms through a contracting or licensing arrangement. In principle, a state-run alcoholic beverage distribution and retail enterprise would appear to be a sensible choice. It eliminates the potential problems of private firms acquiring market power and criminal ownership of these firms. Managers could be instructed to make business decisions to maximize social welfare rather than profit. They could attempt to achieve the optimal consumption of alcoholic beverages (quantity Q_1 in figure 8) by choosing appropriate prices, product variety, number of retail stores, and days and hours of sale. But a state enterprise has potential problems of its own. Those who manage the state wholesale and retail operations may act in their own interest and not the public interest. Monitoring their performance is difficult, since social welfare, unlike profit, is difficult to measure. Providing appropriate economic incentives is equally challenging. Moreover, the state enterprise may provide poor services to consumers and not attempt to balance the benefits of wine consumption against the social cost.

Given the possible problems of operating a state-owned enterprise, the remaining states chose to license private firms to distribute and sell alcoholic beverages and regulate their behavior. Licensing requirements were used to exclude criminals and other undesirables from the distribution system. To prevent private firms from monopolizing the production and sale of alcoholic beverages, licensing states prohibited vertical integration by mandating a three-tier distribution system with separate ownership of manufacturers, wholesalers, and retailers. To restrict alcohol consumption, states promulgated multifarious regulations. These included restrictions on the number of licensed retail outlets, the types of retail establishments allowed to sell alcoholic beverages, days and hours of sale, price controls, labeling requirements, restrictions on non-price competition and advertising, and many more.

In addition to imposing a variety of regulations, states levied excise taxes on alcoholic beverages. Taxes on alcoholic beverages can be used by states as an alternative to direct controls to enhance socioeconomic welfare. Imposing a tax obliges consumers and producers to consider the external cost they impose on others when making production and consumption choices in the market for alcoholic beverages. An excise tax imposed per unit increases the cost to manufacturers of producing alcoholic beverages and gives them an economic incentive to supply less and ask for a higher price for any given amount they offer for sale to consumers. Referring to figure 8, the supply curve shifts to the left by the amount of the tax. At a higher price, consumers have an economic incentive to consume less alcohol. After the market adjusts to the tax, the price of alcohol is higher and the quantity produced and consumed is lower. From a social-welfare perspective, the optimal tax is equal to the external cost per unit of alcohol consumed. This reduces the consumption of alcohol from Q_2 to Q_1 and increases social welfare. With the imposition of an excise tax, when consumers choose to purchase alcoholic beverages, the higher price obliges them to bear the costs they impose on others. The excise tax makes the external social cost internal to private market transactions without mandating restrictions on the choices of producers and consumers. While a tax on alcoholic beverages has the potential to be an effective tool to discourage overconsumption of alcohol, states did not use it for this purpose; rather, it has been used primarily to raise revenue for other purposes.[9] A study by Manning et al. (1989) estimated the external cost of alcohol consumption at 48 cents per ounce of ethanol in 1989 dollars, about twice as high as the average tax. This suggests taxes are too low to achieve optimal alcohol consumption, and that those who transact in the market for alcoholic beverages do not bear the full external cost they impose on others.

Evidence of the Public-Interest Explanation of Wine Regulation

The manner in which state legislators and regulators have responded to the dramatic changes that have taken place in the U.S. wine industry over the past several decades provides little evidence in support of the public-interest theory. In the early 1960s, there were fewer than 400 wineries, close to 11,000 alcoholic beverage distributors, and thousands of retailers selling wine products in the United States.[10] Substantial competition existed among distributors, and it was relatively easy for most wine firms to find a wholesaler to deliver their products to retailers if they so desired. Beginning in the 1980s, the number of wine firms started to grow dramatically, along with wine consumption, and they today number over 7,000 in the country as a whole. Much of this growth is accounted for by relatively small wineries with an annual production of less than 5,000 cases. However, during the same period of time, there was a substantial decline in the number of distributors, because many wholesalers consolidated or exited the industry. Fewer than 700 distributors exist today and the largest 20 have a combined market share of about 75 percent. In some states, a handful of wholesalers dominate the distribution of wine products within the state's borders.[11] In addition, the retail tier has become more consolidated, since an increasingly larger share of wine is sold to consumers by large supermarket chains and big-box stores like Costco and Sam's Club. This has made it increasingly difficult for small producers to sell their products through the traditional three-tier system. Distributors and large retailers favor the high-volume brands of big wine firms. Many wholesalers will not carry the products of small wineries, and those that do often devote little effort to marketing these products. The development of the Internet has given rise to a number of web-based wine retailers that have the ability to offer consumers a wide variety of competitively priced wines, many of which are the products of boutique wineries and unavailable in most states through traditional distribution and sales channels. Wine consumption has become an increasingly important part of American culture. Much of the wine that is purchased is consumed in moderation with meals. Strong scientific evidence now exists that moderate wine consumption promotes good health.[12] A significant part of the increase in demand for wine over the past two decades has been attributed to people choosing to consume wine as part of a healthy lifestyle. It has become increasingly difficult for regulators to justify treating wine as just another alcoholic beverage like beer and spirits.

During the period of time these changes were taking place, states continued to restrict consumer access to wine by limiting the number of licenses granted to wine retailers. Eighteen states still prohibit grocery stores from selling wine, even though six of these allow food stores to sell beer.[13] Many states allow in-state retailers to ship wine directly to in-state consumers by package carrier or their own vehicle, but prohibit out-of-state retailers from doing so. Some states have also prohibited retailers from advertising alcoholic beverage prices.[14] There is no compelling evidence that limiting the number of retailers selling wine promotes social welfare by reducing excessive drinking, and prohibiting grocery stores from selling wine may reduce the likelihood that individuals will choose to consume wine with meals as part of a healthy lifestyle. It is also difficult to explain how restricting direct shipping of wine by out-of-state retailers, but giving this privilege to in-state retailers, serves the public interest. However, licensed retailers clearly benefit from restrictions on entry by new firms into wine retailing in their geographic market, which limits competition and results in increased prices. Bans on price advertising give retailers added information-based market power that enables them to charge higher wine prices. Consumers are clearly made worse off since they face higher prices and have a smaller variety of wine products from which to choose. The economic effect of these regulations is to transfer wealth from wine consumers to wine retailers.

As the number of wine firms was increasing and the number of distributors decreasing, many states passed franchise laws that increased the market power of wine distributors by making it difficult for a winery to terminate a relationship with a distributor regardless of the quality of the services provided by the distributor. In some states, wine firms are required to sell their products to only a single distributor in a given geographic area, essentially granting the distributor a local monopoly. In the U.S. wine industry where the vast majority of wine firms are small-scale producers and wine distribution is dominated by a relatively small number of large firms, it seems reasonable to question whether regulations that increase the market power of wine distributors promote the public interest or simply transfer wealth from producers and consumers to wholesalers.

Another reason to question the public-interest explanation of wine regulation involves restrictions that many states have imposed on interstate shipping of wine by producers directly to retailers and consumers. Before the 1980s, almost all states prohibited the direct shipment of wine to in-state consumers by out-of-state producers, while at the same

time permitting in-state producers to ship their products to in-state consumers.[15] State regulators have argued that this increases social welfare
by reducing the risk of underage drinking.[16] However, critics of these
regulations question whether teenagers would respond to direct wine
shipping by obtaining a credit card, ordering cases of fine wine from
out-of-state wineries, arranging to take delivery when their parents are
not home, and then secretly imbibing their purchases of Cabernet
Sauvignon or Merlot.[17] What is more, it is not clear why wine-drinking
youths would choose to actively seek out the wine products of out-of-
state wineries, but shun those of in-state producers that are allowed to
ship directly to consumers. To my knowledge, there is no evidence that
potential underage wine drinkers have discriminating wine preferences.

Legislation passed by California in 1986 led to the eventual negotia-
tion of reciprocity agreements by thirteen states. A reciprocity regulation allowed wine firms in Oregon, for instance, to ship products
directly to consumers in California only if Oregon allowed wineries in
California to ship wine directly to Oregon residents. By 2004, thirteen
additional states had modified their regulations to allow some form of
direct shipping from any state.[18] The remaining twenty-four states persisted with prohibition of direct shipping by out-of-state wineries, and
four of these made violation of this law a felony.[19] However, many of
these states, such as Michigan and New York, continued to allow direct
shipping by in-state wineries. A study by Gina Riekhof and Michael
Sykuta (2005) analyzed data for the period 1986 to 2001 related to
states decisions to adopt reciprocity regulations or allow direct shipping
from all states. They found no evidence to support the public-interest
explanation of state regulatory behavior related to direct shipping. For
example, their analysis indicated that states with a higher incidence of
arrests for driving under the influence of alcohol were actually more
likely to adopt laws allowing some type of direct shipping than states
with a lower DUI rate, all else being equal. On the other hand, states
with more distributors and a higher concentration of distributors were
more likely to prohibit any form of direct shipping, while states with a
more influential wine industry were more likely to pass laws favorable
to wine firms. These results are difficult to reconcile with a public-
interest motive by legislators; rather, direct-shipping regulations seem
to favor selected groups within a state, such as distributors that may
benefit financially from requiring all wine products to move through
the wholesaler tier, and wineries that may experience improved profitability from reciprocal direct shipping.

As noted previously, in 2005 in the case of *Granholm v. Heald*, the Supreme Court ruled that direct-shipment laws that discriminated against out-of-state wine producers violated the Commerce Clause, and states had to either allow or prohibit direct shipping by all wine firms. The court rejected the legal argument that prohibitions on interstate wine shipping were necessary to prevent underage drinking, and suggested that reciprocity laws were tantamount to instruments in a trade war states were waging against one another.[20] Thirteen states have responded to the Supreme Court decision by allowing direct shipments by out-of-state wineries; no state that previously allowed in-state producers to ship direct rescinded that right for all producers. However, a number of the thirty-nine states permitting direct wine shipments proceeded to impose new regulations governing this type of direct sale to consumers. Thirty-four states limit the amount of wine consumers are allowed to purchase via direct shipping. For example, Minnesota prohibits a single consumer from purchasing more than two cases per year. Michigan limits the total amount of wine a producer can ship to all consumers in the state to 1,500 cases per year. Several states have production caps that effectively prohibit direct shipping by large wineries. In Ohio, for instance, only wineries that produce less than 250,000 gallons per year (105,000 cases) are permitted to ship directly to consumers; Arizona has a production cap of only 20,000 gallons (8,400 cases).[21] States have also instituted a variety of other direct-shipping regulations, including special licensing requirements, licensing fees, and submission of periodic reports. Once again, it is difficult to explain how most of these direct-shipping regulations—which act as a barrier to interstate trade in wine and increase prices and limit product selection for wine consumers—are in the public interest. It is much easier to speculate about how they may benefit specific groups. Case limits on consumer purchases reduce the volume of direct shipping, which may result in more business and increased profits for distributors and wine retailers. Production caps may be set at the quantity produced by the largest in-state winery. This would allow all in-state wineries to ship direct, but prohibit larger out-of-state wineries from doing so, effectively decreasing competition from out-of-state producers.

Many argue that the *Granholm* decision also applies to direct shipping of wine by wineries to retailers and retailers to consumers. States continue to prohibit out-of-state wineries from shipping direct to retailers, even those who allow in-state wineries this privilege. Some states responded to the Supreme Court decision by allowing both out-of-state wineries and retailers to ship direct to consumers. Others have granted this privilege to in-state but not out-of-state retailers. Still others prohibit direct shipping by both in-state and out-of-state retailers. These laws are currently being challenged in the courts. The primary public-interest argument made by states for prohibiting direct shipment by retailers is prevention of underage drinking. However, the economic effect is to erect protective barriers for in-state wholesalers and retailers and slow the development of a national wine market where both brick-and-mortar and online wine retailers compete for wine consumers' business, resulting in lower prices and a greater variety of wine products available to consumers.

The Economic View of Wine Regulation

While the public-interest theory may be consistent with the original intent of government regulation of alcoholic beverages, it provides a tenuous explanation of much of the observed regulatory activity associated with the wine industry, particularly over the past fifty years. In many instances, states do not appear to have been pursuing the public interest in any systematic fashion. It is difficult to argue that many of the regulations states have instituted, modified, or refused to modify over time that apply to the wine industry have the intention of correcting potential market imperfections to enhance socioeconomic welfare. Instead, they often seem to be designed to benefit in-state wineries, distributors, or retailers at the expense of consumers and out-of-state suppliers by inhibiting competition and improving profitability. Over the years, the Supreme Court has invalidated a number of state laws that regulate price, advertising, and interstate shipping of wine, to mention a few, because these laws do not serve the public interest.[22]

An alternative explanation of wine-industry regulation is provided by the economic theory of regulation.[23] The economic theory views wine regulation itself as a good. The amount and types of wine regulations that exist are determined by the interaction of supply and demand. State legislators supply wine regulations. The objective of legislators is to maximize political support to increase the likelihood of being reelected. Interest groups demand wine regulations. Any group that is affected by wine legislation and whose members share a common interest is a potential demander. This may include wine firms, distributors, retailers, consumers, social conservatives, and religious groups. The objective of an interest group is to maximize the welfare of its members.

This typically, but not always, involves maximizing members' wealth. Legislators provide various "regulatory goods" to interest groups affiliated with the wine industry. For example, licensing requirements, direct-shipping laws, and production caps can be used by regulators to control entry of new firms into various segments of the wine market. This benefits producers, distributors, or retailers by restricting competition and enabling them to charge higher prices and make greater profits. Regulators can control wine markups and prices to benefit various groups such as different types of wine suppliers who receive higher prices or wine consumers who pay lower prices. Regulatory goods such as entry barriers and price controls redistribute wealth from the general public and members of other interest groups to the interest group that demands the regulation. To acquire these sorts of beneficial regulations, the demander must be willing and able to pay the political market price. This price is in the form of a block of votes, campaign contributions, and other types of political support that the interest group delivers to legislators in exchange for regulation.

The willingness and ability of an interest group to provide political support for or against a regulation depends upon the net benefit it bestows on its members. The most important factor affecting net benefit is the size of the interest group. To understand why, consider the following example. Suppose that a state has a million wine consumers who purchase ten million bottles of wine per year at an average price of $10 per bottle. Eight million bottles pass through ten large distributors who dominate the market and make a profit of 10 percent per bottle. The state currently allows producers to ship wine direct to consumers and bypass the distributor. Direct-to-consumer sales, mostly by out-of-state wineries, is the distribution channel through which the additional two million bottles are delivered to consumers. Suppose a law that prohibited direct shipping by out-of-state producers were to increase the price of a bottle of wine by 50 cents, to $10.50 per bottle. An additional two million bottles would pass through distributors, increasing their volume of business to ten million bottles per year. If state legislators passed this law, wine consumers would pay an extra $5 million per year for wine, or $5 per consumer. Distributors would make additional profits per year of $2.5 million or $250,000 per distributor. Although the total benefit of preventing the passage of the law for all consumers would be large, the benefit for a typical consumer would be small. As a result, individual consumers would be only weakly motivated to oppose the law. On the other hand, if the law passed, the benefit gleaned by each distributor would be large, even though the total benefit would be smaller than for consumers if they prevented its passage. As a result, individual distributors would have a relatively strong preference for this regulation.

In order to provide political support for or against the law, an interest group would have to be organized. The cost of organizing individual members into an interest group increases as the size of the group increases. It is easier for ten firms to organize a distributor interest group than it is for a million wine drinkers to form a consumer interest group. The cost of acquiring information about the effect of the direct-shipping law is likely to be lower for the members of the smaller distributor group than for wine consumers, many of whom are ignorant about the adverse effect the law would have on them. It is relatively easy for the distributors to form a trade association and monitor members to ensure that each contributes its fair share of political support. The trade association can effectively communicate the way in which distributors will support legislators, essentially conveying the "political price" they are willing to pay for the favorable regulation. The cost of organizing wine consumers into an interest group can be substantial because of the large size of the group. Someone must take the initiative and bear the start-up cost of forming the interest group. The economic incentive for an individual to undertake this is weak, since the benefit of saving $5 per year on wine purchases is small and the time and money cost of the required activities is relatively large. Moreover, in a large interest group, there is a strong incentive for individual consumers not to contribute their fair share of political support and attempt to "free-ride" on others who do. This free-rider problem makes it much more difficult for a large number of consumers to form a successful interest group than it is for a small number of distributors.

Because smaller interest groups tend to have a larger net benefit per member than larger interest groups, the former are more willing and able to provide political support for legislators in exchange for favorable regulations, and therefore will be more influential in affecting wine legislation.[24] The economic theory of regulation suggests that a number of interest groups related to the wine industry may arise to represent distributors, retailers, wine firms, and consumers, and compete against one another for favorable wine regulations. Smaller interest groups will tend to have more political power and influence than larger groups. Regulations will change over time as some interest groups become more influential and others lose political power. This could result from changes in wine-market conditions, new technologies, factors that affect the cost of organizing interest groups, and important judicial decisions.

The economic theory of regulation may explain why wine-industry regulations in a number of states appear to benefit distributors at the expense of other groups such as wine firms, retailers, and consumers. Prior to 1980, most states regulated the prices that distributors could charge retailers for alcoholic beverages, essentially prohibiting price competition among wholesalers. In 1980, the Supreme Court ruled that this type of price regulation violated the Sherman Antitrust Act. As price competition ensued, the number of wine wholesalers decreased, distribution became increasingly concentrated, and the market shares of large firms like Southern Wine and Spirits increased dramatically.[25] With fewer and larger distributors doing business in each state, it became less costly to organize effective wholesaler interest groups. Also, facing less competition, those distributors that survived were able to generate larger profits, which translated into more potential interest-group resources to provide political support, and therefore more power to influence wine regulations. The amount of political support that wholesalers have provided to state legislators, measured by campaign contributions alone, has been enormous. Between 2000 and 2006, distributors gave $50 million in campaign contributions to state legislators. Almost three-fourths of these contributions were provided by distributors in ten states. In Texas, where two large distributors have a market share in excess of 95 percent, state legislators received almost $7 million to help finance their campaigns. A single distributor, Southern Wine and Spirits, provided more than $2.5 million in campaign contributions in those states where it does business. During this period of time, states with powerful wholesaler interest groups that gave large campaign contributions to legislators passed laws beneficial to distributors, including prohibition of wine shipping by out-of-state retailers, restrictions on wine shipping by in-state retailers, and production and consumption caps on directly shipped out-of-state wine products.[26] These laws hinder wine products from bypassing the wholesale tier of the three-tier system and protect distributor sales and profits.

In 2008, Michigan legislators passed a law that prohibits all retailers from shipping wine direct to consumers. Ninety percent of Michigan legislators voted for the law; only ten percent were against it. The law was supported by Michigan distributors and opposed by interest groups representing out-of-state retailers, wine consumers, and Michigan restaurants. Prior to the adoption of this law, the Michigan Beer and Wine

Wholesalers Association, the trade organization representing the state's seventy-five distributors, provided substantial political support to the vast majority of Michigan legislators, both Democrats and Republicans. Between 2000 and 2006, it gave average campaign contributions of about $285,000 per year; in 2006 alone it contributed more than $700,000. In addition, it hosted numerous fundraisers for legislators in a reception room in its main building located across from the state capital. It also financed trips for a group of powerful lawmakers to attend wholesaler conventions in resort locations in Florida and the Caribbean.[27] Conversely, interest groups representing retailers, consumers, and restaurants provided little political support to Michigan legislators.

Studies of the Economic Effects of Wine-Distribution Regulations

Several recent empirical studies have estimated the economic effects of various wine-distribution regulations. A study by Bradley Rickard et al. (2011) analyzed the relationship between the availability of wine in grocery stores and total alcohol consumption, the types of alcoholic beverages consumed, the prices of these beverages, and traffic fatalities. Their analysis uses aggregate data on forty-eight states for the period 1982 to 2000. They find evidence that consumers in states allowing wine to be sold in grocery stores pay lower prices for wine and consume more than those in states with regulations prohibiting food-store wine sales. Their estimates suggest wine prices are about 7 percent lower in states that allow both wine and beer to be sold in grocery stores. In these states, consumers also spend less time and expense searching for wine products at retail outlets, which increases consumption by almost 50 percent. What is more, they find evidence that states whose residents consume more wine relative to beer and spirits have lower traffic fatality rates than those whose residents consume relatively more beer and spirits, all else being equal. This suggests that the external costs associated with wine consumption may be smaller than those of the consumption of other alcoholic beverages.

Two studies by Jerry Ellig and Alan Wiseman (2007, 2011) use data for the state of Virginia to analyze the effect on wine variety and prices of regulations that prohibit out-of-state retailers and wineries from direct shipment to in-state consumers, and production caps that prohibit these suppliers from shipping products of wineries that exceed a particular size. The researchers conclude that after 2003, when Virginia allowed direct shipping by both out-of-state wineries and virtual wine retailers, this enabled consumers to access many wine products at a lower price by ordering these products online. Moreover, entry of virtual wine retailers and wineries into the Virginia wine retail market induced in-state wine stores to lower prices on products in direct competition with these online suppliers. The difference between online and in-store prices fell by more than 25 percent, as in-state wine stores appeared to be setting their prices based on online prices and shipping costs borne by consumers. Most of the increased price competition came from virtual wine retailers, not wineries whose online prices were roughly equivalent to in-store prices. This suggests that consumers experience little benefit from lower wine prices in states that allow direct shipment from wineries, but not virtual retailers. However, consumers do benefit from a greater selection of wines available to them when wineries are allowed to directly ship their products. Finally, Ellig and Wiseman conclude that production caps have an adverse effect on both wine choice and prices. A relatively low production cap of 150,000 gallons may reduce the number of wine products available to consumers by more than 75 percent and increase prices of in-store offerings of products of wineries exceeding the cap. The most anticompetitive regulation is one that prohibits shipping by virtual wine retailers and allows only those wineries with an annual production of less than 150,000 gallons to ship direct to in-state consumers.

9

The Wine Firm

The principal decision-making unit in the wine industry is the wine firm. But what is a wine firm? Interestingly, this question does not have a simple and unequivocal answer. The term *firm* is commonly used to describe different types of organizations. The economics literature contains various definitions of a firm, each of which provides a somewhat different way to view this type of organization.[1] While several of these definitions are complementary, a consensus does not exist on the single best way to conceptualize a firm in all circumstances. With this in mind, the goal of this chapter is to propound a useful way to think about a wine firm, describe its salient characteristics, and discuss the choices it makes and the constraints it faces when making these choices.

WINE FIRM AND WINERY

Exactly what is a wine firm and how does it differ from a winery? Fundamentally, the distinction is one between a decision-making unit and a production facility.

Winery

A winery is a production plant in which wine production activities are performed. It is typically composed of a building that houses various types of winemaking equipment and a warehouse section for storing bulk or packaged wine. It may also have a visitor center or tasting room where wine is sold directly to consumers. Any wine firm that wants to operate a winery must first obtain a license from the U.S. Department of Treasury, Alcohol and Tobacco Tax and Trade Bureau (TTB). For legal purposes the TTB makes a distinction between three types of wineries: a bonded winery, an alternating-proprietor winery, and a custom-crush winery.[2]

A bonded winery is a production plant owned and operated by a single wine firm. To legally produce wine in such a facility, the firm must obtain a bonded-winery permit and a basic alcohol permit. The bonded-winery permit allows the firm to produce and store wine in the production plant. The basic alcohol permit provides the TTB information on the firm that owns the winery. The wine firm must also post a wine bond ensuring that it will pay the federal excise tax on the wine. As long as wine is stored in the area designated as the bonded portion of the winery, typically, the warehouse, no tax need be paid. However, once the wine is moved out of the bonded area, the firm must pay the tax. This applies even if the wine is moved from the warehouse portion of the winery to the visitor center or tasting room. Wine that is bottled in the bonded winery must have a label that is approved by the TTB.

An alternating-proprietor winery is a production plant that is shared by two or more wine firms. The firm that owns the production plant is called the host. The firms that share the facility are called alternators. The host typically charges rent to the alternators for use of space in the building and winemaking equipment. However, the TTB prohibits the alternators from contracting with the host for labor services, such as the services of the winemaker and other employees. All firms that produce wine in the alternating proprietor winery must have their own bonded winery and basic alcohol permits, and pay their own excise taxes.

A custom-crush winery is a production plant owned and operated by a single firm, called a custom producer, that performs wine-production activities under contract for one or more other firms. The custom wine producer must have bonded winery and basic alcohol permits. The firm that contracts for production activities is called the custom client. A number of alternative arrangements between the custom producer and client are possible. The client firm can enter into a contract with the custom producer to provide all wine-production activities: sourcing the grapes, producing the wine, maturing the wine, bottling the wine, and labeling the wine. Alternatively, the client firm may source its own grapes and contract with the custom producer to produce, mature, bottle, and label the wine. Under some arrangements the custom producer also sells the wine for the client, but typically the client takes delivery of the bottled wine and then sells it to distributors or possibly directly to consumers via the Internet. In this case, the client firm is not required to obtain bonded winery and basic alcohol permits, and the custom producer is responsible for the excise tax. If the client firm takes delivery of the packaged wine for resale, it must obtain a wholesale license from the TTB. However, it cannot sell wine directly to consumers at a tasting room.

In addition to these three types of wineries, the TTB also defines a facility called a bonded wine cellar. A bonded wine cellar blends, bottles, or stores wine on which the excise tax has not been paid. It differs from a winery in that grapes are not crushed and fermented. A firm that operates a bonded wine cellar must obtain a bonded warehouse permit. It is responsible for paying the federal excise tax when the wine is removed from the bonded area of the facility. Under one type of arrangement, a firm that operates a bonded wine cellar may purchase wine on the bulk market from several different suppliers, and then blend, bottle, label, and store the wine for future sale. Another possibility is for a firm to have a bonded wine cellar and stand-alone tasting room, and contract with a customer producer for finished bottled wine that it stores in the bonded warehouse and sells directly to consumers in the tasting room.[3]

The notion of a virtual winery is also becoming increasingly important in the wine industry. A virtual winery has been defined in various ways, but in general it refers to a situation where a firm produces one or more wine products without owning a winery. The label *virtual winery* is usually limited to firms that employ a winemaker or contract with a winemaking consultant to supervise and direct wine-production activities that are performed in a production plant owned by another firm. A virtual winery, therefore, is not a production plant per se; rather, it is a specific type of wine-related organization.

Wine Firm

A wine firm is a legal entity that organizes and coordinates the activities required to produce and sell wine to consumers. This includes all activities related to grape growing, wine production, and wine distribution. This entity is legally organized as a proprietorship, partnership, corporation, or limited liability company and can make binding contracts in its own name. It is owned by a single individual, group of individuals, or another firm. The owner may be motivated by profit or nonprofit objectives. To organize and coordinate the production and sale of wine, the firm either contracts for necessary activities with other firms in the marketplace or performs these activities itself by employing workers and other inputs. Any activity that is outsourced is either purchased on a spot market for immediate delivery or a long-term contract market where arrangements are made with another firm to perform the activity at regular intervals over an agreed-upon time period. To perform an activity internally, the firm enters relatively simple contracts with employees that allows it to direct, supervise, and monitor their performance as members of a team that works together to produce the activity.

Wine Brands and Products

A wine firm organizes and coordinates the production and sale of one or more wine products and brands. It is useful to make a distinction between a wine brand and a wine product. A wine brand is a name placed on a wine label that identifies one or more wine products. The TTB requires that a wine label have a brand name. This can be a wine firm's legal name, trade name, or any other name it desires, as long as it does not mislead the consumer.[4] It can identify a single wine product or more than one product that share the same brand name. Wine products differ in terms of grape variety, grape location, vintage, vinification methods, and wine style. Thus, for example, a wine firm that produces ten wine products can sell these under a single brand name or as many as ten separate brand names. It is common for two or more different varietal wine products to be sold under the same brand name.

Some Examples of Wine Firms

A variety of wine related organizations are consistent with the concept of a wine firm presented in this chapter. Some examples are provided in this section.[5]

E. & J. Gallo is the largest wine firm in the United States by quantity of wine sold, with estimated annual domestic sales of seventy-five million cases of sixty different wine brands. It also sells an additional five million cases per year in more than ninety countries. Gallo is legally organized as a family-owned private corporation. To organize and coordinate grape growing, wine production, and wine distribution, it employs about 5,000 workers. It also outsources many tasks through contracts with other firms. Gallo contracts with independent vineyards to source more than 90 percent of its grapes, estimated to be over a million tons annually, and satisfies the rest of its grape-input requirement from fruit harvested on about 15,000 acres of vineyards it owns. It produces a preponderance of its wine in seven of its own wineries, but also contracts with bulk wine producers for a substantial amount of wine that it bottles and sells under its own brand names. Its wineries are large-scale production plants; the facility in Modesto, California, has the appearance of a refinery and occupies more than sixty-five acres. Unlike most wine firms that contract with other firms for bottles and closures, Gallo undertakes this internally in its own bottle and closure plants. Gallo owns a trucking company that it uses to distribute wine directly to retailers in California, but has contracts with a large number of distributors to move wine to consumers in the other forty-nine states. It also sells wine directly to consumers by various means, including the Internet.

According to the wine industry publication *Wine Business Monthly,* Castle Rock Winery is the twenty-sixth largest wine company in the United States, with estimated annual sales in 2011 of 600,000 cases; however, it does not own a single vineyard or winery. To produce and sell more than fifty different wine products, it contracts with other firms to grow grapes and make and distribute the wine. Because it acts primarily as a contracting agent it has only eleven employees. Castle Rock has long-term contracts with a relatively large number of independent vineyards located in California, Oregon, and Washington State. It contracts with a number of different wineries in these states to produce wine from purchased grapes and employs a winemaker to oversee winemaking activities. It sells its wine through a large network of distributors in forty-eight states and directly to consumers over the Internet. Castle Rock is considered by many in the industry to be a virtual winery.

The Forman Vineyard wine firm, located in the Napa Valley near St. Helena, California, was founded in 1979. It produces three wine products, sells them under two brand names, and has annual sales of around 3,500 cases. As a legal entity, it is organized as a proprietorship; Rick Forman is the owner/proprietor. Grape growing and wine producing are done by the firm itself, largely by the proprietor and his son. Grapes are grown on three small vineyards, of 8.5, 20, and 60 acres. Two of these vineyards are owned by the proprietor and the other is co-owned with a partner. Vines are pruned and harvested by hand and hand-sorted. During the first few years of operation, wine was produced in an alternating-proprietor winery, but since 1985, it has been made in a relatively small Forman-owned bonded winery with modern equipment and stored in deep caves below the winery. Forman contracts with distributors to sell wine in twenty-five states and several foreign countries. Wine is also sold at an appointment-only tasting room at the winery.

Several additional examples illustrate the diverse manner in which firms choose to organize and coordinate the production and sale of wine products. The V. Sattui Winery, established in 1975, minimizes the outsourcing of tasks to other firms. It grows more than 75 percent of its grapes on hundreds of acres of vineyard land, produces about 40,000 cases of forty different wine products each year in its own production facility, and sells all of this output directly to consumers at its tasting room and by mail to 40,000 wine club members and consumers, who submit website orders. About 65 percent of the wine it produces is sold at its tasting room at St. Helena in the Napa Valley, and it has never contracted with a distributor or sold its wine directly to a retailer. The Kosta Browne Winery, founded in 2001 at Sebastopol, California, purchases all of its grapes from a variety of independent vineyards. It does not own a winery; ten different Pinot noir products are made in a leased production facility and sold under the Kosta Browne brand name. Its annual output is about 10,500 cases, and 85 percent of this is distributed directly to consumers who must sign up for a slot on a mailing list. In 2009, Kosta Browne was purchased by the Vincraft Group, a private equity firm, for an estimated $30 to $40 million. Because Kosta Browne owned neither vineyards nor a winery, the assets purchased were essentially the brand name, the wine inventory, the consumer mailing list, and the services of the former proprietors, who agreed to continue to produce and sell the wine.

The Number and Size of Firms in the Wine Industry

The wine industry is the collection of wine firms that participate in the wine market. Two important characteristics of the structure of a market are the number and size distribution of firms in the industry. These attributes of market structure are important because they affect firm behavior. For example, we would expect firms in an industry with 1,000 rivals to behave differently from firms in an industry with ten rivals. We would also expect firms in an industry made up of 1,000 rivals of equal size to behave differently from firms in an industry in which three large firms have 90 percent of the market and 997 the remaining 10 percent.

To measure the number of firms in the wine industry and their size distribution, it is necessary to choose a specific definition of a wine firm. A wine firm has been defined as a proprietorship, partnership, limited liability company, or corporation that organizes and coordinates the activities required to produce and sell wine to consumers. However, this concept does not necessarily provide a clear line of demarcation between an organization that is and is not a wine firm. To a degree, drawing a boundary is a matter of judgment. For instance, consider the following wine-related organizations, which are becoming increasingly prevalent:

- A negociant that neither grows grapes nor ferments wine. It buys wine on the bulk market and blends, bottles, and sells this wine under its own label, or sells finished wine under its own label that is made and bottled by another producer under contract.

- A custom-crush winery that provides winemaking services to other organizations under contract, but does not produce and sell wine under its own label.

- A custom-crush client that contracts with a custom producer to source grapes and produce and sell wine under its own client label.

- A custom client that takes delivery of bottled wine and resells it.

- A commercial vineyard that sources its own grapes but contracts with a custom producer to make bulk wine, which it then sells on the bulk market to another firm.

- A retail store, such as Whole Foods Market, Costco, or Trader Joe's, that contracts with a winery to produce a private-label wine.

Which of these wine-related organizations are wine firms and which are not? One might argue that a firm that operates a custom-crush winery that does not sell wine under its own label is not a wine firm because it organizes wine production but not sales. Alternatively, an argument can be made that it is a wine firm if it arranges for the sale of a custom client's wine product, even though it is not the firm's own brand. One may even argue that Whole Foods Market is a wine firm. It organizes and coordinates the production and sale of wine by contracting with a number of different wine producers for as many as 100 different private-label wines, which it sells to consumers in its retail stores across the nation. Two Whole Foods wine buyers are actively involved in directing the winemaking activities for these products through specification of the desired wine style and even blending the final wine.[6] This is consistent with the concept of a virtual winery like Castle Rock Winery, which most industry observers would consider a wine firm. While private label wine products represent a relatively small proportion of revenues for Whole Foods, the same can be said of large wine and beverage companies like Diageo, which generates only 6 percent of its revenue from wine sales. Similar arguments can also be made for and against including the other wine-related organizations under the group of wine firms. While my definition provides a useful conceptual way to think about a wine firm and illustrates the inherent fuzziness of its boundaries, it does require a degree of judgment in deciding specifically what organizations will be included in the group of firms that make up the industry.

Many wine market analysts prefer to view the winery, rather than the wine firm, as the fundamental unit in the wine industry, and therefore attempt to measure the number of wineries. However, this approach also requires a specific definition of exactly what qualifies as a winery and presents its own problems in drawing boundaries. A winery has been defined as a plant in which wine production activities are performed. These activities include crushing, fermenting, maturing, clarifying and stabilizing, blending, and packaging wine. How many of these activities must be performed in a facility for it to qualify as a winery? In some facilities, only a subset of these activities are performed. For instance, one type of facility may blend, mature, and package wine without fermenting it. Another type of facility may bottle and store wine. Each of these types of facilities must have a license from the TTB to engage in these activities for commercial purposes. If all of these facilities are included in the definition of a winery, then the number of wineries in the United States can be approximated by the number of licenses issued by the TTB. Using this broad definition of a winery, there were 7,626 wineries in the United States in 2010.[7]

Defining a winery as a production plant is not very informative in understanding the behavior of wineries in the industry that supply wine to consumers. As a result, to measure the number of wineries, some definitions incorporate specific types of wine-related organizations as well as a more restricted notion of a production plant. Perhaps the most widely cited of these is provided by *Wine Business Monthly*. Included in this definition and measure are two types of wineries: bonded wineries and virtual wineries. A bonded winery is described as a facility that is managed by an organization composed of one or more individuals that has a bonded winery permit from the TTB, or two or more facilities that have separate bonded winery permits but are managed by the same organization. Thus, if the same organization manages three separate bonded facilities, this is counted as a single bonded winery. If three independently managed organizations share the same facility and have separate bonded winery permits, this is counted as three separate wineries. An example would be an alternating-proprietor winery with a host and two alternators. A virtual winery is described as an organization with its own management and winemaker, but without a bonded facility, that produces and bottles at least one wine brand using the services of a bonded facility of another organization.[8] Using this definition and measure of a winery, there were 7,116 wineries in the United States in 2011. Of these 6,027 were bonded wineries and 1,089 were virtual wineries. All fifty states have wineries, ranging from 3,458 in California down to two each in Wyoming and Mississippi. Fourteen states have more than seventy wineries apiece.[9]

The *Wine Business Monthly* definition and measure of a winery is closely related to the concept of a wine firm as an organizational decision-making unit rather than a production facility. The collection of bonded and virtual wineries included in this measure may well correspond to a group of legal entities that organize and coordinate the activities required to produce and sell wine to consumers, and that most analysts would include as firms in the wine industry. However, it does not resolve the problem of drawing boundaries between wine firms, or even wineries, and other wine-related organizations. A cogent argument can be made that some types of bonded wineries are not wine firms. Judgment is also required in applying the definition of a virtual winery to certain types of organizations to determine if they qualify. Notwithstanding these considerations, the *Wine Business Monthly* measure is a reasonable approximation to the number of wine firms in the U.S. wine industry.

The most widely used measure of the size distribution of firms in an industry is the concentration ratio. Firms in an industry are ranked from largest to smallest by a proportional measure of size, such as percentage of sales. If n represents the number of firms selected, the sales percentages for the largest n firms are then summed to obtain the concentration ratio for the industry. In 2009, the four-firm concentration ratio in the U.S. wine industry measured by annual sales volume was 56 percent.[10] The top two wine firms, Gallo and The Wine Group, produced 137 million cases in 2011, accounting for roughly 40 percent of all domestic wine sales.[11] The twenty-firm concentration ratio was close to 90 percent, so that the remaining 7,000 + wine firms together accounted for only 10 percent of case-goods sales. About 70 percent of wine firms sell less than 5,000 cases per year.[12] However, this picture of the wine industry as dominated by a handful of large firms is somewhat deceptive. Large firms tend to sell a preponderance of the wine they produce in the lower-priced commodity segment of the market for everyday consumption. Smaller firms concentrate in the higher-priced premium and luxury segments, which supply higher-quality wines to consumers. The market environment at the low end, where a firm has few large rivals, is significantly different from that at the high end, where a firm has many relatively small rivals. As a result, firms may behave much differently in these segments of the market.

THE WINE FIRM AS A LEGAL ENTITY

For a wine firm to exist as a legal entity, the owner must choose a legal form of organization. Once the firm is a legal entity, it can then enter into contracts. These contracts play an important role in the organization and coordination of the activities required to produce and sell wine to consumers. This section focuses on the different ways in which a wine firm can be legally organized, the types of contracts it can enter into, and some economic implications of the different organizational forms and contractual arrangements.

Legal Forms of Wine-Firm Organization

As a legal entity, a wine firm can be organized in four major ways: as a proprietorship, a partnership, a corporation, or a limited liability company. The legal organization of a wine firm has important implications for the ownership, control, and financing of the firm.

A proprietorship is a wine firm owned by an individual or family, called the proprietor. The proprietor has complete control of the firm and the power to make all decisions. He can enter contracts in the name of the firm, but is personally liable for the firm's obligations and other legal matters. This means that if the wine firm cannot pay its debts or is successfully sued, the proprietor's house, car, bank accounts, or other personal assets can be seized. Small wine firms are typically organized as proprietorships. Even if the proprietor wishes to increase the size of the firm, this type of legal organization is not conducive to obtaining the financing necessary to do so, since most of the money available to the firm is provided by the proprietor and limited bank borrowing. Some wine firms start as proprietorships and then change their legal structure to expand, but many continue as proprietorships over their lifetimes.

A partnership is a wine firm owned by two or more individuals, called partners. A general partnership shares many characteristics of a proprietorship. The partners share control, profits, and losses of the firm, and all partners have unlimited liability for the obligations of the firm. Each partner has the legal right to enter into contracts for the firm, and all partners bear responsibility for the decisions made by each one individually. However, partners can pool their financial resources to potentially obtain more money for the firm, which is an advantage relative to a proprietorship.[13]

Unlike a proprietorship or partnership, a corporation is a legal entity that is separate from the individuals who own it, called stockholders. As a "legal person," a corporation can enter into contracts, own assets, and incur liabilities independent of its owners. The owners have limited liability. If the corporation fails to pay its debts or is sued, the maximum amount owners can lose is limited to their investment in the firm; their other personal assets cannot be seized. Limited liability makes ownership in the firm more attractive and facilitates selling ownership shares to a large number of individuals. This makes it easier for a wine firm to obtain the money it needs to expand. As a result, large wine firms tend to be organized as corporations. It is not always clear exactly who controls a wine firm when it is organized as a corporation. Stockholders elect a board of directors who have the legal authority to make decisions for the wine firm. These decisions are often delegated to managers. Directors and managers may or may not also be owners, and if they are, their ownership shares may be large or small.[14]

A limited liability company (LLC) is a wine firm owned by one or more members. Members can be individuals, corporations, or other LLCs. An LLC has legal attributes of both a partnership and a corporation. While it has the tax advantages of a partnership, it is a legal entity distinct from its owners like a corporation.[15] An LLC can enter into contracts, own assets, borrow money, and sue and be sued, but the assets of owners are protected by limited liability. Because a wine firm organized as an LLC can have from one to a large number of owners and many different types of operating agreements, it is not always clear who controls and makes decisions for the firm. But an LLC with relatively few members is likely controlled in a manner similar to a typical partnership or proprietorship.

The Distribution of Legal Wine Firms

While it is not possible to obtain the information necessary to construct the exact distribution of legal wine firms, I estimate that less than 5 percent are organized as corporations.[16] If this estimate is a reasonable approximation, then corporate representation is much smaller in the wine industry than the economy as a whole; 18.5 percent of firms in the United States operate under the corporate form of organization. Only six wine firms are organized as public corporations; the rest are private corporations. Three of the public corporations are involved exclusively in the wine industry, and the other three are wholly owned subsidiaries of public corporations that have operations outside the wine industry. The public corporations are owned by a large number of stockholders. Most of the private corporations are owned by a single family or a relatively small group of unrelated investors. The remaining 95+ percent wine firms are organized as proprietorships, partnerships, and limited liability companies. A preponderance of these noncorporate wine firms are family owned and operated.

The choice of legal organization is related to wine-firm size. The largest wine firms are organized as corporations; the smallest are overwhelmingly proprietorships. This is largely because limited liability offered by the corporate form of organization is an essential feature in raising the large amount of money necessary to finance a large wine firm. Of the largest ten wine firms in the United States in 2011 measured in terms of annual case sales, five are private corporations, three are subsidiaries of public corporations, one is an autonomous public corporation, and one is a limited liability company. These firms have annual sales ranging from 4.5 to 75 million cases (mc) and account for more than 80 percent of domestic wine industry sales volume.[17] The largest private corporation is Gallo (75 mc), followed by Trinchero Family Estates (16.5 mc), Bronco Wine Company (12 mc), Jackson Family Wines (5.5 mc), and DFV Wines (4.5 mc). All of these private corporations are owned and controlled by family members. The largest public subsidiary wine firm is Constellation Wines U.S. (47 mc) followed by Ste. Michelle Wine Estates (7.3 mc), and Diageo Chateau & Estate Wines (6 mc). Constellation Wines U.S. generates the largest portion of the parent firm's revenue (75 percent); Diageo Chateau &

Estate Wines contributes the smallest (6 percent).[18] The parent firms of Constellation and Diageo are alcoholic beverage conglomerates that also sell spirits or beer. Ste. Michelle is owned by the Altria Group Inc., which has tobacco and smokeless tobacco company subsidiaries. The stocks of the parent firms are widely traded on national stock exchanges. The second-largest wine firm in the United States, The Wine Group (62 mc), is legally organized as a limited liability company and owned by a small group of individuals. Treasury Wine Estates (18 mc), the fourth-largest wine firm, is a public corporation that resulted from a spin-off of the wine division of the Fosters Group in 2011.[19]

Contracts and Transactions

To organize and coordinate the activities required to produce and sell wine, a wine firm engages in transactions. A transaction involves an agreement between two parties to exchange a good or service for money. The terms of the agreement is called a contract. The contract may be formal or informal, written or verbal, or unstated but implied. For example, a wine firm makes a transaction with a commercial vineyard when it agrees to exchange $800 for a ton of grapes. The terms of the agreement that specify the price, quantity, grape variety, delivery date, mode of delivery, and so on, constitute the contract. A survey of California grape growers estimated that about 20 percent of growers with long-term grape contracts have verbal contracts.[20]

A wine firm can enter into a variety of different types of contracts. A legal contract is a written, oral, or implied transaction agreement between two parties that is enforceable by law.[21] Certain types of transactions may require a written contract to be enforceable, and implicit agreements are the least likely type of contract to have legal status. For example, a verbal agreement by a wine firm to purchase grapes may be enforceable, but not one to buy a vineyard. If a wine firm has a legal contract with another party and this party breaches the contract by not honoring the terms, enforcement may involve requiring the party either to carry out the terms of the contract or to compensate the wine firm by making payment of a specific amount of money.[22] However, even if a contract is not legally enforceable, the market may provide an enforcement mechanism. A wine firm that breaches legally unenforceable but legitimate verbal or implicit contracts may develop a dubious reputation and have a difficult time finding grape growers, custom-crush producers, distributors, and so on, with whom to transact, which may be very costly or possibly prevent it from conducting business at all.

Contracts and Transaction Costs

Any cost incurred in making a transaction—other than the good, service, or money payment being transferred—is called a transaction cost. A distinction can be made between two types of transaction costs: search cost and contracting cost. Search costs are the costs of acquiring information about transaction opportunities that may exist. These costs include the time and money spent collecting information about parties with whom to transact, their locations, and the prices and characteristics of the goods they are willing to exchange. For example, if a wine firm wishes to purchase Cabernet Sauvignon grapes, it must devote time and money to obtaining information on vineyards that grow this grape variety and offer it for sale, their geographic location, the attributes of the grapes, and the prices at which these growers are willing to sell.

Contracting costs are the costs of negotiating and enforcing a transaction agreement. For example, once a wine firm finds a grape grower with whom to transact, it incurs initial costs in arriving at an acceptable agreement and describing the terms in a written or verbal contract. A wine firm also incurs the ongoing costs of making sure the grower abides by the terms of the contract and taking necessary action if the agreement is violated. Contracting costs include all opportunity costs, both explicit and implicit. Explicit costs are money payments for resources like legal services used in negotiating and writing contracts and money outlays related to litigation or arbitration, if these enforcement mechanisms are used. Implicit costs do not entail explicit money outlays; rather, they are benefits forgone from not using time and other resources in their next best alternative use when these resources are devoted to negotiating and enforcing an agreement.

Spot and Long-Term Contracts

It is useful to make a distinction between a spot contract and a long-term contract. A spot contract is an agreement between a wine firm and another party to exchange money for a good or service at the same point in time. This type of transaction takes place on the spot market, sometimes called the market for immediate delivery. For example, after sampling the Merlot bulk wine of a custom-crush producer to assess quality, a wine firm might agree to take delivery of 1,000 gallons in five days at its bonded winery facility at a price of $10 per gallon in exchange for a payment of $10,000 when delivery is made. This type of spot contract is relatively easy to negotiate and enforce, since the exchange of bulk wine for money takes place simultaneously, and the transaction is completed quickly.

A long-term contract involves a transaction that extends over time where a wine firm and another party agree to exchange money for a good or service at different points in time. For example, a wine firm may contract with a custom producer today to deliver Merlot bulk wine on a specific date each year for the next three years in exchange for a money payment upon delivery. This type of transaction is more complex than the relatively simple spot-market transaction, and therefore is more difficult to negotiate and enforce. The wine firm and custom producer would likely attempt to negotiate a contract that specifies the quantity, quality, and price of the bulk wine to be exchanged. However, when negotiating these terms, both parties have imperfect information about events that may occur during the contract period, such as changes in the demand for wine and the cost of grapes, as well as a host of other contingencies. Faced with this uncertainty, the wine firm and custom producer must decide whether quantity and price will be fixed over the duration of the contract or allowed to vary from year to year. If allowed to vary, what particular formula will be used? Should the price of bulk wine be tied to the spot-market price or some index of cost? Even if both parties reach an agreement on a specific formula, chances are that it will not adequately account for all possible contingencies. An agreement regarding quality may be even more difficult to negotiate. When making a bulk wine transaction on the spot market, the wine firm can evaluate quality by sampling the wine before entering the contract. However, under a long-term contract, this type of quality evaluation can take place only after the custom producer has completed its side of the agreement by producing and delivering the wine. What, if any, criteria will be established to determine acceptable wine quality? Should the wine satisfy specific measures of alcohol, acidity, and residual sugar, or should it exhibit certain sensory characteristics, such as balance, flavor intensity, and an adequate finish? Who is responsible for taking those measurements or deciding if the wine has these characteristics, the wine firm, the custom producer, or a third party? If the wine fails to satisfy the quality criteria, to what compensation is the wine firm entitled? What if the wine firm insists that the wine be unfiltered, and as a result it develops an off-taste, or inclement weather beyond the control of the custom producer reduces both grape and wine quality? Because the wine firm and custom producer do not have perfect foresight, they cannot possibly account for every possible contingency related to quantity, quality, and price when writing a contract. Even if they could, it would be too costly to specify all of these as terms of the contract. As a result, most long-term contracts are incomplete.[23] An incomplete contract may lead to a dispute between the wine firm and custom producer, and eventual litigation. However, enforcement by the courts may be difficult, particularly if it involves a gap in the contract or unclear and vague terms.

Incomplete Contracts and Opportunistic Behavior

The Nobel laureate economist Oliver Williamson argues that incomplete contracts may result in opportunistic behavior defined as "self-interest seeking with guile."[24] Extending the above example, suppose the bulk-wine contract excludes quality criteria, or those criteria are ambiguous. An unexpected decrease in wine demand may induce the wine firm to renege on the contract by refusing to make payment when the bulk wine is delivered. It may claim that the wine does not satisfy the implicit or explicit quality standards of the contract, and that it is therefore invoking the terms of the agreement. The nebulous terms of the contract would make it difficult or costly for the custom producer to establish for a court or an arbitrator that the wine firm's behavior is inappropriate. As a result, the incomplete nature of the contract creates an economic incentive for the wine firm to exploit the custom producer.

A recent example of an incomplete contract resulting in a highly visible dispute and possible opportunistic behavior involves wine firms and grape growers in California. Most grape contracts specify the price a wine firm will pay for each ton of grapes purchased, but do not specify a harvest date. Growers have publicly complained that wine firms have insisted that they harvest fruit later in the growing season, when grapes have a lower water content and weigh less, reducing their revenue by as much as 30 percent. They argue that wine firms' motivation for late harvest is the desire to minimize grape input cost, since water lost to overripeness can be added back during the wine-making process at little cost. Wine firms have responded that picking grapes later is necessary to achieve physiological maturity, enabling them to satisfy consumer demand for intensely flavored wines.[25]

Contracts and Information Asymmetry

When the parties to a transaction have different information about the good or service being exchanged, an *information asymmetry* is said to exist. If one party has information unknown to the other about the characteristics of the good or service prior to the exchange, this type of information asymmetry is called *adverse selection*. If one party has better information about implementation of the terms of the exchange, this type of information asymmetry is called *moral hazard*. In both instances, one party may engage in opportunistic behavior and attempt to use its informational advantage to benefit at the expense of the other. Provisions to minimize the negative effects of adverse selection and moral hazard may therefore be included in a contract.

Consider, for example, a wine firm that desires to purchase high-quality grapes from a commercial vineyard. Suppose vineyards differ in their ability to grow quality grapes, and this is known to the grower but not to the wine firm. The wine firm is faced with the adverse selection problem of not knowing if it is contracting with a grower capable of producing grapes with the desired characteristics. It may contract with a vineyard that delivers grapes of lower than expected quality. The grower benefits at the expense of the wine firm, because it receives a price commensurate with higher-quality grapes. Even if the wine firm knows the vineyard's ability to produce quality grapes, after it makes the contractual agreement, it may face a moral hazard. It may lack information on the effort put forth by the commercial vineyard in growing and harvesting the grapes during the period of contract implementation. This information asymmetry may allow the grower to benefit at the expense of the wine firm by shirking on the use of costly, quality-enhancing vineyard practices such as canopy management, cluster thinning, and spraying. When the grapes are delivered, the grower can claim that the amount of effort expended, cost incurred, and the quality of fruit produced are commensurate with the agreed upon price, whereas in reality this is not true.[26]

To minimize the negative effects of adverse selection and moral hazard, the wine firm may include provisions in the contract designed to change the behavior of the commercial vineyard and nullify its informational advantage. These provisions typically affect grape price or viticultural practices of the grower. For instance, a long-term contract negotiated before a new vineyard is planted may require the grower to use a certain clone, rootstock, trellis system, or irrigation technology to achieve a particular level of grape quality. The wine firm may include a provision in the contract of an existing vineyard that allows it to be involved in making management decisions regarding tasks such as pruning, spraying, and harvesting. Another possibility is to include financial incentives in the form of bonuses or penalties for achieving or not achieving measurable characteristics of quality such as sugar and acid levels. In addition to these sorts of provisions that directly affect viticultural practices, the wine firm may include price incentives to indirectly mitigate moral hazard. For instance, the contract may contain a price formula with a component tied to the price of the wine produced from the grapes. This gives the grower a financial incentive to provide maximum effort to produce high-quality grapes to maximize wine quality and price.[27]

When a wine firm grows its own grapes and hires a vineyard worker to prune grapevines, it may have an informational disadvantage. Adverse selection exists if the worker's ability to prune vines is unknown to the wine firm. Moral hazard exists if the worker's output is difficult to observe, and he shirks and puts forth less effort than he is supposed to under the employment contract. The worker's effort may be difficult to observe if he is a member of a pruning team and his output cannot be easily distinguished from that of other members of the team. One way for the wine firm to deal with the moral hazard is to write an employment contract that pays the worker a piece rate rather than a fixed hourly wage. Piece-rate compensation gives the worker a financial incentive to maximize work effort. One study estimated that pruning an acre of vines took a typical hourly wage worker twenty-six hours, but a piece-rate worker only nineteen hours, with no significant difference in pruning quality.[28]

THE WINE FIRM AS AN ECONOMIC ENTITY

A wine firm exists as an economic entity when it makes decisions related to wine production and sales. These decisions concern the organization and coordination of grape growing, wine production, and wine distribution; the types of wine products to offer consumers; and the quantities, qualities, and prices of those products. In making these choices, a wine firm must decide which tasks to outsource and which to perform within the firm. When activities are performed in-house, it must choose the amounts of labor services, capital equipment, and other inputs to use, and how to direct, supervise, and monitor the performance of hired employees so that the tasks are carried out in the desired manner. The decisions a wine firm makes as an economic entity depend in large part on whether the owner is motivated by the goal of maximizing profits, the extent to which the owner has nonprofit objectives, the constraints imposed by government regulation, the current state of technology, and the market environment.

Objectives

A standard assumption in economics is that the primary objective of a firm is to maximize profit. Profit is the amount of sales revenue a firm receives over and above all costs. So why does a particular wine firm choose to grow organic grapes, harvest them by hand, ferment the must in a stainless steel vessel, mature the wine for two years in oak barrels, bottle the wine on a semi-automatic bottling line, and sell 1,000 cases of the wine to consumers through three different distributors in ten states at a price of $20 per bottle? The motivation for each of these decisions is to maximize the difference between the revenue the firm receives from selling this wine and the cost of producing and distributing it.

A cogent argument can be made that profit maximization is a reasonable approximation of the objective of a large wine firm that is legally organized as a public corporation, such as Constellation, Treasury Wine Estates, and Diageo. The owners of a large public corporation are tens of thousands of stockholders. In its fiduciary role, the board of directors hires managers to make decisions in the best interest of the stockholders. To do this, managers should make choices that maximize stockholders' utility. Because utility depends indirectly on wealth, managers can act in the best interest of stockholders by making decisions that maximize profit.[29]

As discussed previously, all but six firms in the U.S. wine industry are privately owned and legally organized as proprietorships, partnerships, limited liability companies, and private corporations. In the vast majority of these wine firms, the owners are also active managers who make most or all of the significant decisions for the firm. This facet of the internal organization of a private firm is fundamentally different from that of a public corporation, where the owners delegate decision-making authority to professional managers, separating those who own the firm from those who control its operations. Is profit maximization a reasonable approximation of the objective of privately owned wine firms in which the same individuals or family members both own and control the firm?

At first glance, it would appear that privately owned wine firms have a stronger motivation to maximize profit than public corporations. It is reasonable to assume that the owners of a private wine firm want to maximize utility. Suppose all goods that yield utility to the owner as a consumer can be purchased in the marketplace. Because profits from the wine firm contribute directly to the owner's income, or possibly constitute his entire income, to maximize utility, he must in that case maximize profit. However, suppose the owner derives utility from a good for which a market does not exist; it can only be obtained by owning a wine firm. The enjoyment from this type of nonmarket good can be sourced within the firm by an owner who is willing to sacrifice profit. In this case, the assumption of profit maximization may not be a reasonable approximation of the objective of the wine firm; the wine firm may well have nonprofit objectives related to the owner's desire to obtain utility from one or more goods that cannot be purchased in the marketplace.

An example will help to clarify the idea of a nonmarket good. Assume a wine firm owner has a preference for employing family members at the winery that is separate from their contribution to profit. Let us call this nonmarket good *nepotism*. Suppose nepotism were offered for sale on a market at a price of $100 per week. To maximize utility, the owner would maximize profits from the wine firm and use this money to purchase the utility-maximizing amount of nepotism and other market goods. However, because a market does not exist for nepotism, the owner must source it within the firm. Assume that the owner can employ either a family member or a non-family-member for a particular wine-making task. Suppose that the family member would contribute $500 per week to profit; the non-family-member would make a larger weekly contribution of $600. If the owner chooses to employ the family member, then he sacrifices $100 per week in profit for the utility derived from nepotism. Conceptually, there is no difference between making the profit-maximizing choice of hiring the more productive non-family-member and using the extra $100 in profit to buy nepotism on a market, if one existed, and "purchasing" nepotism within the firm by employing the less productive family member and sacrificing $100 of profit.

Anecdotal evidence and surveys of the attitudes of owners of private wine firms suggest that a number of nonmarket goods that may give rise to nonprofit objectives. Many wine firm owners appear to derive substantial utility from the quality of their wine independent of the effect of wine quality on profit. Some owners may view winemaking as an artistic expression, and therefore value the process of producing a high-quality wine that is tantamount to a beautiful painting. Stories of such artisanal wineries abound in the wine media. Others may seek the status and prestige a high-quality wine affords them among their peers, wine critics, or wine aficionados, even if it comes at the expense of personal wealth. Numerous stories appear in the wine press on a regular basis of the latest rich lawyer, venture capitalist, wealthy investor, or real estate magnate who paid an exorbitant price for vineyard land to start a boutique winery with the goal of producing the next "cult wine" that receives high scores from wine critics and accolades from the wine community.[30] Making money from the winery seems to be inconsequential to these owners. Many of the choices made by wine firms related to the trade-off between quality and cost discussed in chapters 4 and 6, such as cluster trimming, manual pruning and harvesting, and preferring oak barrels to cheaper alternative oak treatments, are consistent with a willingness to trade-off profit for quality. The prevailing evidence suggests that for many of these choices, the increase in quality may well come at the expense of making less money. For some owners, winemaking philosophy and wine style may be a source of utility. A proprietor may have a strong preference for making wine in an Old World style with subtle nonfruit flavors that reflect the location where the grapes are grown, even though he could make more money offering generic, New World, international-style wine products characterized by intense fruit and oak flavors for which there is greater consumer demand. Another potential nonmarket good that has received much attention involves the lifestyle of a wine proprietor. Many proprietors seem to get much enjoyment from owning an idyllic winery overlooking a beautiful vineyard and participating in tending the land and making the wine, even though they could generate greater profit by purchasing grapes from an independent grower and contracting with a custom-crush producer to make wine, or investing their resources in a different line of business. Other aspects of lifestyle that proprietors may value include socializing with others who share a love of wine, living a rural lifestyle, being one's own boss, and favoring family members and relatives.

A survey of 184 California wine firms provides some empirical support for the existence of nonprofit motives in the wine industry.[31] Almost 80 percent of owners surveyed indicated they would be unlikely to sell their wineries if they could make more money by investing the proceeds in the stock market. About 40 percent said they would be willing to lose money to improve the quality of their wine products. More than half stated that love of wine and the winemaker's lifestyle were a motivation for owning a wine firm. Almost all of these owners said they wanted to cover their costs and earn some profit. Together these survey responses suggest that while almost all owners want to make some profit, they are not necessarily motivated by earning maximum profit. Many are willing to trade off a certain amount of profit for other sources of utility that can only be obtained through ownership of a wine firm.

Given the above arguments, anecdotal evidence, and survey evidence, it seems reasonable to conclude that the wine industry consists of a mix of both profit-maximizing firms whose primary objective is to make as much money as they can for the owners, and firms with nonprofit objectives whose owners willingly sacrifice profit for firm-specific nonmarket goods such as wine quality and lifestyle. However, is profit-maximizing behavior necessary for long-run survival in a competitive environment like the wine industry, with over 7,000 firms? Are firms with owners who have nonprofit motives jettisoned from the market over time?

Consider the standard "survival of the fittest" argument, which has a long history in economics. Economists distinguish between accounting profit, normal profit, and economic profit. Accounting profit is the difference between a firm's sales revenue and business expenses. Normal profit is the amount of money the owners of a firm could make if they used the resources currently invested in the firm in their next best areas of employment. Economic profit is the difference between accounting profit and normal profit.[32] Positive economic profit provides an economic incentive for new firms to enter an industry. Negative economic profit is an incentive for firms to leave an industry. In the long run, the forces of competition eliminate economic profit. The only firms that can survive in an industry are those that make a normal profit. Because profit-maximizing firms are more efficient and produce output at a lower cost than firms with nonprofit motives, only profit-maximizing firms can earn a normal profit and remain viable.

A simple example will help to clarify the logic of the survival argument and allow us to assess whether it is applicable to the wine industry. Consider two wine firms: a profit-maximizing firm (P), and a non-profit-maximizing firm (N) that sacrifices profit to nepotism. To keep the example free of cumbersome detail, assume that the only resource the owner provides to the firm is his own time. Normal profit is then the amount of money the owner could make if he shut down the firm and devoted his time to the next best employment opportunity. Assume that this opportunity is working for another winery as a cellar manager earning $1,000 per week. According to the survival of the fittest argument, if a firm does not earn an accounting profit of at least $1,000, the owner will choose to leave the industry and take the more lucrative employment opportunity. Now assume that P hires more productive nonfamily labor; N engages in nepotism and employs less-productive family members. As a result, the cost of producing wine is $100 per week higher for N than for P, and P therefore earns an accounting profit of $1,000, while N's accounting profit is only $900. P is making a normal profit and hence will choose to remain in the industry. On the other hand, N will choose to exit the industry because accounting profit is less than normal profit and the owner can make more money working as a cellar manager.

Why might this survival of the fittest argument not apply to the wine industry? It assumes that markets exist for all goods that provide utility to the owner as a consumer, including nonmarket goods such as nepotism. However, because a market does not exist for nepotism, the owner of N can and will choose to remain in the wine industry and sacrifice $100 of accounting profit for the enjoyment of employing less-productive family members, even though he is earning less than a normal profit and could make $100 more by opting to work as a cellar manager. Clearly N is able to incur the higher cost of nepotism and survive competition from lower-cost P, because N still covers all business expenses of producing wine and makes an accounting profit of $900. The owner of N maximizes his utility by giving up $100 of accounting profit to purchase nepotism and using the $900 of accounting profit to purchase market goods in his role as a consumer. Nevertheless, N faces a cash-flow constraint. If accounting profit is negative, then N does not generate enough sales revenue to cover business expenses, and the owner must therefore either make up the shortfall from other sources, such as personal wealth, or declare bankruptcy and be forced to leave the industry.

To conclude, the survival of the fittest argument is not applicable to the wine industry. Wine firms with both profit and nonprofit motives can survive and thrive in the long run. While it is not possible to directly observe owner and manager motives, I speculate that profit maximization is a reasonable approximation for the relatively small number of large wine firms organized as public corporations, private corporations, and limited liability companies that account for 80 to 90 percent of the wine produced in the United States, even though a number of these, such as Gallo, are owned, controlled, and managed by family members. I also conjecture that a large proportion of the 7,000+ smaller wine firms, many of which are legally organized as proprietorships and partnerships, have nonprofit motives that may have a significant effect on their production and sales decisions and induce them to behave differently from profit maximizers.

When making decisions, the set of alternatives from which all wine firms are able to choose regardless of their objectives is limited by available grape-growing, winemaking, and wine-distribution technology; the characteristics of the market environment in which they operate; and regulatory restrictions imposed by government. The next three subsections discuss these constraints and how they circumscribe wine firms' choices.

Technology

Wine technology is the current state of knowledge about how to grow grapes, and produce and distribute wine. This knowledge is often embodied in capital equipment such as mechanical harvesters and pruners, rotofermenters, pneumatic grape presses, and temperature-controlled trucks and ships for transporting bulk and packaged wine. However, technology is also embodied in individuals who grow grapes and make wine in the form of human capital from scientific knowledge, much of which has been produced and disseminated by universities. The current state of technology determines the methods of production that are available to a wine firm to grow grapes, produce wine, and distribute wine.[33] Technology is a constraint on the decisions of a wine firm because it limits the feasible methods of production from which it is able to choose.

Technology is an important determinant of a wine firm's cost of production. The cost of producing a given level of output depends upon the technologically feasible methods of production available to a wine firm and the prices it must pay for inputs. A wine firm whose objective is to maximize profit will always choose the least-cost method of producing its desired quantity and quality of output since this is a necessary condition for maximizing the difference between revenue and cost. However, a utility-maximizing wine firm whose owner derives enjoyment from some aspect of the production process will not necessarily choose the cost-minimizing method of production. For example, an owner who derives utility from vineyard land may choose a feasible method of production that has more than the cost-minimizing amount of this input. An owner that experiences utility from a deeply rooted winemaking tradition may choose a method of production that does not minimize the cost of producing wine. In these instances, the utility the owner derives from the higher-cost method of production comes at the expense of profit the wine firm could have made.

In most industries, advances in technology allow firms to produce more output with the same amounts of inputs, or the same level of output employing fewer inputs. These are called cost-decreasing technological advancements, since they result in an increase in technical efficiency and productivity, and therefore lower the cost of producing a given amount of output. However, some types of advances in technology may introduce feasible methods of production that reduce cost, but also lower grape or wine quality. Exactly which technologies and methods of production fall into this category is often the subject of vociferous debate among wine professionals. This is because it is typically much easier to measure the effect of a new technology on cost than on quality. The owner of a utility-maximizing wine firm that cares about wine quality may choose not to adopt a cost-saving technology if he believes that this entails trading off quality and personal satisfaction for the increased profit the new technology will bring. The owner of a profit-maximizing wine firm will adopt the new technology if he believes the reduction in cost exceeds the loss of revenue from selling lower-quality products.

Market Environment

Technology limits input and production choices. The economic environment in which a wine firm operates constrains its output, price, quality, and selling decisions. Economists call this environment market structure. This section discusses some important characteristics of the structure of the wine industry and how this environment constrains firms' choices. These attributes include the number and size distribution of domestic wine firms and buyers, import competition, the nature of the wine product, barriers to the entry of new wine firms, and the presence of conglomerate wine firms.

The number and size distribution of firms in an industry affects the competitive structure of a market. A characteristic of a competitive industry is the existence of a large number of firms of roughly equal size. A wine firm that operates in a highly competitive market has little discretion in choosing the price of its wine products and is compelled to accept the going market price. While the wine industry has more than 7,000 firms, they range in size from gigantic Gallo with a market share exceeding 20 percent to small boutique producers with market shares less than one one-thousandth of one percent. Because the four largest domestic producers account for more than half of case sales, many would describe this market environment as a highly concentrated oligopoly. However, it is more appropriate to view the wine industry as composed of several different segments occupied by firms producing commodity, premium, and luxury wine products that differ in terms of perceived quality and price. The lower-quality commodity segment is dominated by a handful of the largest firms like Gallo, The Wine Group, Bronco Wine Company, and Constellation; a relatively large number of small boutique firms compete in the high-quality luxury segment. The premium segment is populated by many medium-sized firms, a substantial number of small firms, and relatively few large firms. The environment that characterizes each of these segments imposes different constraints on price, output, quality, and selling decisions.

Closely related to the number of firms in the domestic industry is the extent of import competition. Imported wine products account for about one-third of wine sales in the United States. In addition, in 2010, domestic producers imported fifty million gallons of bulk wine to bottle and sell under their own brand names and use as a blending component in other brands.[34] The choices that domestic wine firms are able to make in the commodity, premium, and luxury segments of the market may be limited by import competition. However, availability of imported wine may also expand opportunities for new wine brand offerings, as well as the characteristics of existing brands. The Wine Group's Franzia brand Chardonnay and Merlot wine products, two of the largest bag-in-box wines sold in the United States, are produced with bulk wine imported from abroad. Today, many domestic wine firms view purchased grapes and imported bulk wine as close substitutes when producing specific products, which increases their winemaking choices. When domestic grape prices increase, wine firms can readily substitute relatively less expensive imported bulk wine for wine produced from purchased fruit in making blended wine products.

The number and size distribution of buyers is also an important characteristic of market structure. From a wine firm's perspective, it is useful to identify three types of wine buyers: consumers, retailers, and distributors. Wine firms sell their products to about 100 million consumers in the United States. Ninety percent of this wine is sold through distributors; only 10 percent is sold directly to consumers and retailers. Since the 1990s, the number of wine firms has more than doubled, while the number of distributors has declined by more than 80 percent. Today over 7,000 wine firms produce more than 15,000 wine products each year, but must compete to sell them through fewer than 700 distributors. The largest twenty distributors have a combined market share of over 75 percent, and the top five account for more than 50 percent of purchases from wine firms. As the distributor segment of the wine market continues to become more concentrated, it is increasingly difficult for many firms, particularly smaller ones, to find wholesalers willing to carry and promote their products. To increase profit margins, many distributors have eliminated brands of medium-sized and small wineries with slow inventory turnover rates in favor of the high-volume brands of large producers such as Gallo, Kendall-Jackson, and Ste. Michelle Wine Estates. Others have limited the marketing support they provide for many of the wines they carry. This places constraints on the selling choices of wine firms and compels many to promote and market their wines themselves, or distribute their products directly to consumers.

A third prominent characteristic of industry structure is the nature of the good sold on the market. Firms in an industry may produce either identical or differentiated products. In some markets, such as agricultural goods and steel, buyers perceive the products of different firms to be perfect substitutes. In this type of market environment, all firms receive the same price for their products, and branding a product is not a viable option. However, in the wine industry, consumers perceive the products of different wine firms to be imperfect substitutes and develop a preference for the products of certain firms. As a result, if a firm increases the price of a wine product it sells above that of its competitors, it may lose some but not all of its customers; some of its customers still prefer the particular characteristics of the wine product it is selling. This significantly increases the range of choices open to a wine firm. It has more leeway in setting price and can respond to changing market conditions by altering the characteristics and quality of its product. Branding its product through advertising and other promotional activities is also an option.

Consumers may perceive that the sensory characteristics of wine products differ across firms. However, wine products may also be differentiated in ways not related to their sensory characteristics. Many wine firms attempt to create a brand image so that consumers think its products are different from those of other firms, even if this difference is imagined rather than real. They may do this by choice of brand name, bottle and label design, advertising, and the types of retail outlets where they choose to sell their products. A wine firm may choose to undertake promotional activities to brand a product as a luxury wine, even though it has the sensory characteristics of a premium wine, to create a perception of cachet among consumers. A prestigious brand image can give a wine firm significant freedom to charge a high price without sacrificing the amount of the product it sells. A status conscious consumer may well be willing to pay $1,000 for a bottle of 2009 Screaming Eagle Cabernet Sauvignon, even if wine critics conclude that a $70 bottle of 2009 Pride Cabernet Sauvignon has more favorable sensory characteristics, because Screaming Eagle has higher "cachet value." Another way products are often differentiated is by wine-related services provided by a wine firm. Most wine firms have tasting rooms and sell their wine products to wine-club members and others who submit orders by phone or on a winery website. Some wine firms have well-trained staffs and provide excellent service to consumers in the tasting room and to those who purchase wine by mail.

Barriers to entry are a fourth important characteristic of industry structure. An entry barrier is anything that makes it difficult or impossible for a new firm to enter an industry. All else being equal, the lower the barriers to entry, the greater the number of firms we would expect to find in the industry, and therefore the more competitive the market. Several types of entry barriers exist that affect the ability of new firms to enter the commodity, premium, and luxury segments of the wine market. The commodity segment is characterized by economies of large-scale production. To achieve low unit costs of producing commodity wine, a firm must produce a large volume of it. It would be difficult for a new wine firm to compete with the few existing large producers in this segment of the market, like Gallo, The Wine Group, and Bronco Wine Company, which produce millions of cases per year and thus enjoy low unit costs. This is because the new firm must either enter the commodity segment as a small-scale, high-cost producer, or raise the large amount of money necessary to enter at the efficient scale. It has been estimated that the investment required for a winery with the capacity to produce 500,000 cases per year, which does not fully realize all economies of scale, is about $35 million. Even if the new firm raised this large amount of money and entered at an efficient scale, the consequent substantial increase in the supply of wine would lower price and likely result in losses for both the incumbents and the entrant. The premium and luxury segments of the wine market achieve low unit costs with a smaller output, and they therefore have lower entry barriers. Estimates suggest that the investment required here for a 2,000-case wine facility is about $600,000.[35] These costs can largely be avoided by entering as a virtual wine firm and contracting with a custom-crush producer. In fact, this is the strategy that many entrants choose to enter the premium and luxury segments of the market.

A second type of entry barrier germane to the wine industry concerns the absolute cost disadvantage of an entrant that results from the limited amount of vineyard land capable of growing high-quality grapes. To enter the luxury segment of the wine market and successfully compete with incumbent producers, an entrant may require high-quality grapes. Vineyard land capable of producing these grapes is in relatively fixed supply and has increased dramatically in price over the past decade. For instance, in Napa Valley, California the highest-quality vineyard land costs as much as $300,000 per acre, and grapes sourced from these vineyards can command prices of as high as $25,000 per ton. Luxury wine producers who already own high-quality vineyard land have a significant absolute cost advantage over potential entrants, which may preclude new firms from entering the luxury segment of the wine market.

A third type of entry barrier involves product differentiation. Wine firms in the commodity segment of the market have established brand names that many consumers associate with availability, consistency, and low price point quality. They spend a large amount of money on advertising and other promotional activities to maintain their brand images and loyalty. A new entrant is at a disadvantage because it must somehow persuade consumers that the new wine it brings to the market is preferable to existing commodity wines. To induce consumers to try its product, it may have to charge a lower price than incumbent firms and make substantial advertising and promotional expenditures. This may be a consideration that dissuades new firms from attempting to enter the commodity segment of the wine market. However, product differentiation may work to the advantage of firms attempting to enter the premium or luxury segments of the market. By making a wine with slightly different sensory characteristics than existing firms and promoting this product with an interesting story that catches the attention of consumers, the owner may be able to find a niche in the market and operate a small-scale winery.

The size distribution of firms in an industry can be easily quantified by gathering available data and calculating a concentration ratio. The existence and height of entry barriers for the different segments of the wine market is much more difficult to measure. However casual observation suggests that entry barriers are very high for the commodity wine segment and much lower for the premium and luxury wine segments. During the past decade very few firms have entered the commodity segment, while a large number of new firms have entered (and exited) the premium and luxury segments of the market.

The final characteristic of market structure that is relevant to the wine industry involves the existence of large conglomerate firms. A wine conglomerate is defined as a large corporation that produces and sells products in the market for wine as well as one or more other product markets. Under this definition, four large conglomerate firms currently have a presence in the U.S. wine market and account for about 30 percent of case sales.[36] In terms of revenue, Diageo is the largest conglomerate, followed by the Altria Group, Constellation Brands, and Brown-Forman Corporation. These conglomerates have annual revenues ranging from about $3 to $16 billion. Constellation began as a wine producer and diversified into the spirits and beer markets; Diageo and Brown-Forman originally produced spirits and extended their activities into wine during the decade of the 1990s.[37] The Altria Group, a large producer of tobacco products, entered the wine market in 2009 when it acquired UST, a manufacturer of smokeless tobacco products that owned Ste. Michele Wine Estates. Constellation is the only conglomerate for which wine is the most important source of sales revenue. The presence of conglomerates can affect competition in the wine market independent of the number and size distributions of firms in the industry. These firms might use profits obtained from products other than wine to gain a competitive advantage in the wine market by charging lower prices for wine products than rivals, some of whom may then be forced from the market. Economies of scale and scope gleaned by large conglomerates may also place smaller, undiversified wine firms at a disadvantage. Large distributors, most of whom deal in spirits as well as wine products, may give priority to the products of diversified wine and spirits conglomerates, making it more difficult for other wine producers to market and sell their products.

Government Regulation

Wine firm choices are also constrained by the system of federal, state, and local laws and regulations that apply to the production and sale of wine. Compared to other countries, wine laws in the United States place relatively few restrictions on grape growing and wine production, but significantly more restrictions on wine distribution.

In European nations such as France, Germany, and Italy, wine laws and regulations often impose substantial restrictions on grape growers' choices in the form of permissible grape varieties, maximum grape yield, and viticultural practices, such as allowable pruning techniques and trellis systems. Wine producers typically face legal restrictions on their choice of grape varieties, alcohol level, acid, sugar, fining agents, maturation time, and in some regions the earliest date at which a wine can be sold. Most European wine regulations apply to quality wines, as opposed to ordinary table wines, and compel wine firms to make choices that are consistent with traditional winegrowing methods and techniques. Grape growers and wine producers in the United States have much more freedom when making these sorts of choices. Regulatory constraints on growers are typically in the form of land-use regulations and laws governing water quality, waste management, and endangered species. While some states have laws that prohibit adding sugar or acid to wine, and federal regulations specify maximum permissible sulfite levels, relatively few regulations govern the production of wine, and those that exist are typically nonbinding. As discussed in chapter 8, the most substantial legal constraints on wine firms' choices are state laws and regulations governing the distribution and sale of wine.

Wine-Firm Behavior

A wine firm is a legal entity that organizes and coordinates the production and sale of wine. To do this, it must make a number of economic decisions that are limited by available technology, market environment, and government regulations. Collectively, these constrained decisions determine how a wine firm will behave. The focus of this chapter is on two facets of wine-firm behavior. The first involves wine quality and price. How do wine firms choose the price and quality of their products and convey information about quality to consumers? The second is the sourcing decision. How do wine firms choose which tasks to perform within the firm and which to contract to other firms in the marketplace? What do these price, quality, and sourcing decisions imply about wine-firm behavior? Before proceeding, a caveat is in order. The literature on decision making by firms contains a number of alternative theories and perspectives, so providing an explanation of wine-firm behavior is not a simple matter. The goal of this chapter is to draw from different strains of the literature to provide some perspective on why wine firms may behave the way they do in organizing and coordinating the tasks required to produce and sell wine to consumers and choosing the price and quality of their wine products.[1]

ASYMMETRIC INFORMATION AND WINE-FIRM QUALITY BEHAVIOR

Wine firms have better information than consumers about the characteristics of the wine they sell. Because consumers cannot assess the quality of wine before they consume it, the decision to purchase a particular wine involves uncertainty and risk. If wine firms cannot find a way to convey quality information to consumers, then low-quality products may come to dominate the wine market. This outcome is predicted by the Nobel laureate George Akerlof's adverse-selection "lemons theory." The word *lemon* refers to defective automobiles sold on the used car market, which Akerlof used to illustrate his theory.[2]

Used Cars and Wine Products

Following Akerlof, consider the market for used cars. Suppose owners of used cars offer two types of automobiles for sale: good cars and lemons. Assume individuals who desire to buy a used car would be willing to pay $12,000 for a good car, but only $6,000 for a lemon. However, only the sellers know whether the cars offered for sale are reliable or unreliable. Because buyers lack information on quality, they know the cars they are purchasing may be lemons. Suppose they believe that there is a 50 percent chance of getting an unreliable car. Given the uncertain quality of used cars, they are only willing to pay $9,000, which reflects the risk of purchasing a lemon. Lemon owners are happy to get $9,000 for an unsatisfactory car worth much less. Owners planning to sell good cars are frustrated because the price they can get is below their true value. This discourages owners of good cars and encourages owners of lemons to offer them for sale. As a result, fewer reliable automobiles and more lemons are supplied on the used car market. Over time, the price and volume of used car transactions fall, because a larger proportion are unreliable. When this dynamic process ends, most of the small number of used cars bought and sold will be relatively low-priced lemons.

Given that producers have much better information than consumers about the quality of the wine they offer for sale, why isn't the wine market a relatively small market dominated by wine products that are "lemons"? Why are consumers willing to pay a relatively high price for a variety of wine products of uncertain quality? Wine firms that produce higher-quality products have an economic incentive to convey this information to consumers. The perceived risk of buying a "good wine" of uncertain quality decreases as the amount of information that consumers find useful in evaluating the quality of the wine increases. But how do wine firms convey information that consumers would find valuable in assessing wine quality? They do this by building a reputation for producing wine of a given quality and providing signals or indicators to consumers to communicate this information. By behaving this way, wine firms that produce higher-quality products can distinguish them from lower-quality products and sell them at a higher price. Wine critics also have an economic incentive to specialize in evaluating the quality of wine products and providing this information to consumers, often in the form of wine scores. Consumers are willing to pay for information provided by credible wine critics to reduce the uncertainty of wine buying. In this way, the wine market is separated into commodity, premium, and luxury segments by quality and price. Wine firms then direct signals about their products to the appropriate segment of the market.

Wine-Firm Quality Signals

Wine firms can use several types of signals to indicate quality. One form of signaling involves reputation. To establish a reputation, a wine firm can take necessary actions to produce a wine of above average or superior quality from vintage to vintage. Consumers who initially buy this wine and discover that it is good make repeat purchases. Information on the quality of the wine spreads as these individuals and retailers recommend it to others. The wine firm's reputation builds gradually as more and more consumers learn about its product by word of mouth.

A potential shortcoming of relying exclusively on reputation based on the firm's past performance to signal quality is that it may be a slow process and take many years. This is particularly true in the wine market, where consumers have thousands of wine products from which to choose. A more efficient way to build a reputation and signal quality may be to establish a brand name. A wine firm can invest in brand-name reputation by advertising, label and bottle design, newsletters, websites, and other tasks. By doing this, it makes a commitment to produce wine products of a given quality. If the wine firm does not deliver on the quality promise, then consumers will not make repeat purchases, and its investment in the brand name will be a waste of money. If the wine firm does honor its quality commitment, then consumers will associate the brand name with the promised level of quality and price.

Many wine drinkers come to rely heavily on established brand names that honor their quality commitment. As a result, brand name itself is an intangible asset with market value. In some cases, the market value of a brand name may even exceed the value of the real assets a wine firm owns, such as the winery production plant and vineyards. Today, wine firms regularly buy and sell wine brands as a stand-alone asset, independent of wineries, the services of winemaking personnel, or vineyards. A recent transaction provides an example. Prior to 2007, the Davis Bynum wine firm produced five single-varietal wine products—Pinot noir, Chardonnay, Zinfandel, Sauvignon blanc, and Merlot—and sold them under the Davis Bynum brand name. About 8,000 cases of these products were produced each year in a Davis Bynum–owned winery from both purchased grapes and grapes grown in a Davis Bynum–owned vineyard. In 2007, the Rodney Strong wine firm purchased the Davis Bynum wine brand and the existing inventory of five wine products, but not the winery or vineyard. Rodney Strong now produces the Davis Bynum Pinot noir and Chardonnay wines in its own production facility and sells them under the Davis Bynum brand name.[3] The value of the Davis Bynum brand name depends in large part on the degree to which Rodney Strong can maintain the quality and reputation of the two wines formerly produced in another winery by another winemaker with grapes possibly sourced from different vineyards.

A wine firm can also signal the quality of its products by sending a sample to a publication such as *The Wine Spectator* or *The Wine Advocate* to be evaluated and scored. The score given by a prominent critic can be a very powerful signal of wine quality and help to establish the reputation of a product very quickly. The risk is that the wine may receive a score below the actual quality level and adversely affect the firm's reputation and brand name. Anecdotes abound of how the critic Robert Parker has made a wine firm's reputation overnight. For instance, Elin McCoy, in her book *The Emperor of Wine*, tells the story of Sine Qua Non, a small startup winery whose products were virtually unknown to consumers. It was producing about 100 cases of wine per year in a rented warehouse in Southern California when the proprietor sent a bottle of its wine to Robert Parker who gave it a score of 95. The day after the next issue of Parker's newsletter *The Wine Advocate* was distributed, which included a description and score of the wine product, Sine Qua Non received a plethora of telephone orders from consumers worldwide. Subsequent high scores and consumer demand firmly established the quality reputation of this previously unknown winery, and allowed it to charge high prices for its high-quality products.[4]

Other quality signals a wine firm may use include wine tourism and information provided on a wine label. Wine tourism brings consumers to a winery tasting room to sample its products and evaluate quality. Consumers may make repeat purchases of products whose quality is commensurate with price and spread the word to others, which helps to build a wine firm's reputation. A variety of information related to wine quality can be given on the label. This includes a description of the smell and taste of the wine, the location where the grapes were grown, and winemaking techniques. For example, grapes sourced from a location with a reputation for high quality, such as the To Kalon vineyard in Napa Valley, and maturation of the wine in costly new French oak barrels may signal a high-quality wine product to consumers.

MARKET STRUCTURE AND WINE-FIRM PRICE AND QUALITY BEHAVIOR

The prices and qualities a wine firm chooses for its products depend upon the objectives of the owners or managers and the market environment in which it operates. As discussed previously, the wine industry can be separated into commodity, premium, and luxury segments. These submarkets have different structural characteristics and are populated by wine firms with different objectives.

Price and Quality Behavior in the Commodity-Wine Submarket

The commodity segment of the wine industry resembles an oligopoly dominated by a small number of large producers such as Gallo, The Wine Group, Constellation, Trinchero Family Estates, and the Bronco Wine Company, which sell well-known wine brands like Carolo Rossi, Franzia, Taylor California Cellars, Sutter Home, and Charles Shaw. These firms take full advantage of economies of scale, have established brand names, and spend a large amount of money to maintain their brand images. Economies of large-scale production and brand loyalty serve as barriers that make it very difficult for new wine firms to enter the commodity submarket. It is reasonable to assume that the large firms occupying this segment of the market maximize profit. Each firm is acutely aware that if it changes the price or characteristics of its commodity-wine products, this will affect its rivals, which may respond by altering their own price and quality decisions. As a result, when choosing the profit-maximizing price and qualities for a commodity wine, each firm must predict how other firms will react.

In this environment, characterized by a high degree of perceived mutual interdependence, firms may exhibit a wide range of behavior, and a large number of economic theories have therefore been developed to explain how firms make price and quality choices. While the data and studies necessary to determine which of these theories offers the best explanation of firm behavior in the commodity submarket do not currently exist, a few observations related to price and quality decisions are germane.

To maximize profit, firms would seem to have a strong economic incentive to cooperate in setting the prices of their commodity wines. By cooperating and avoiding potentially mutually destructive price competition, they can act as joint monopolists, charge higher prices, share the commodity market, and make greater profits than they would if they behaved as rivals. The most effective way to cooperate is to make a formal agreement as a cartel. However, a cartel agreement is not legally enforceable and even worse is illegal under the Sherman Antitrust Act of 1890. Any such agreement must be surreptitious. While firms in many oligopolistic industries do attempt to make and enforce secret cartel agreements from time to time, the Justice Department has never brought a price-fixing case against firms in the wine industry and there is no anecdotal evidence that large wine firms have ever attempted to collude to fix prices. A more subtle and legal way for wine firms to cooperate is by engaging in tacit collusion. This involves coordinating firms' behavior by developing a method to indirectly communicate pricing decisions to one another. A common type of tacit collusion observed from time to time by firms in the automobile, steel, airline, cigarette, beer, and breakfast-cereal industries is price leadership. One firm emerges as the price leader, such as Anheuser-Busch, and makes pricing decisions for all firms in the industry. Other firms implicitly concur by setting their prices in line with the price leader, without making a formal agreement to do so. By behaving this way, firms can avoid price competition. In this type of tacit agreement, the price leader is typically the largest firm in the industry or the one that has been in business the longest. In the wine industry, this role could be performed by Gallo. However, once again there is no compelling evidence that large wine firms tacitly consent to a price-leadership arrangement.

Why don't wine firms in the commodity submarket attempt to explicitly or tacitly collude in making pricing decisions? One possible explanation is that the economic incentive to do so is not sufficiently strong. Large wine producers sell a variety of differentiated wine products on the commodity submarket. If one firm, such as Gallo, drops price, this may not have a big effect on the market shares of other firms, such as The Wine Group and Constellation, that sell products consumers perceive as imperfect substitutes. Differentiated products reduce the degree of interdependence among the pricing decisions of different firms, and therefore the perceived benefit of taking actions to coordinate these decisions. What is more, finding a mutually agreeable price structure for a variety of differentiated products is complex and difficult, and it may therefore not be worth it to large wine firms to attempt to coordinate pricing decisions.

Even though large wine firms do not appear to attempt to coordinate pricing decisions through a surreptitious cartel agreement or a tacit price-leadership arrangement, commodity-wine prices are relatively rigid, suggesting that these firms avoid significant price competition. Each firm likely recognizes that attempting to increase market share by aggressively cutting the prices of its commodity products would likely be ineffective, inasmuch as this would elicit quick matching price reductions by rivals. Moreover, this type of pricing behavior might well degenerate into a price war and substantially reduce profits for all the firms. Large wine firms are more inclined to compete by introducing new commodity wines or brands at a given price point with characteristics that better satisfy consumer wants than those currently on the market, and building the reputation of existing brands. This type of nonprice competition is not as easily matched by rivals as a price cut. Introduction of a successful new brand or an improvement in the image of an existing brand can result in a substantial increase in profits. For example, Constellation introduced twenty new wine products in 2011, with several brands such as Simply Naked and Primal Roots selling at a price point of less than $10 per 750 ml bottle. The Simply Naked brand, which attempts to satisfy consumer preferences for crisp, fruit-forward, unoaked wine, sold about 180,000 cases during the first six months after its debut.[5]

Price and Quality Behavior in the Premium and Luxury Wine Submarket

The premium and luxury submarket more closely approximates a market environment called monopolistic competition, with characteristics of both a competitive and monopolistic industry. As in a competitive market, there are thousands of firms, most of which are small or medium-sized. Entry barriers are low, and it is relatively easy for new firms to enter this submarket as either a bricks-and-mortar or virtual wine producer. However, because firms sell wine products that have different perceived characteristics, consumers make buying decisions by comparing the qualities of products as well as price, so each firm has a degree of monopoly power in setting its price. Wine firms that sell products in this submarket act independently and may have either profit or nonprofit objectives.

A study by Fiona Scott Morton and Joel Podolny (2002) analyzes the price and quality behavior of wine firms that choose to operate in the premium and luxury submarket. To do this, they formulate a theory of wine-firm behavior and test the predictions it yields with empirical data. Their theory allows the premium and luxury submarket to be inhabited by both profit-maximizing and utility-maximizing wine firms. Profit-maximizing owners care only about making money. Utility-maximizing owners are assumed to derive utility from making good wine as well as profit. They may also derive utility from other types of nonmarket goods, such as those related to wine lifestyle and personal involvement in the winemaking process. All wine-firm owners are rational and increase wine quality as long as marginal benefit exceeds marginal cost. For profit-maximizing owners, the marginal benefit is the contribution to revenue a higher-quality wine will generate. The marginal benefit for a utility-maximizing firm includes the enjoyment the owner experiences from improving wine quality in addition to the increment in revenue. Those utility-maximizing proprietors who derive satisfaction from nonmarket goods that can only be obtained by owning a wine firm increase their consumption as long as the marginal benefit, measured by the additional enjoyment these tasks bring, exceeds the marginal cost resulting from the concomitant reduction in winemaking efficiency. Wine firms produce differentiated products, and therefore face a downward-sloping demand curve. Further, it is assumed that the ability to produce wine differs among owners when they initially enter the wine industry, which results in differences in the marginal cost of wine production. However, the more experience an owner has, the more he or she learns about efficient winemaking techniques.

The theory yields three important predictions. First, utility-maximizing proprietors are willing to trade off profit for the opportunity to produce high-quality wine, and therefore need to make less money than profit-maximizing proprietors. To enter the wine industry and remain viable, profit-maximizing owners must make an accounting profit at least as large as the money payments forgone from not using their resources in the next best area of employment. Utility-maximizing owners are willing to accept less than a normal profit, and some may choose to enter the wine industry even if they expect to make little or no accounting profit, provided they can afford to subsidize any losses they might incur. Because they require less profit and care about making high-quality wine, more utility-maximizing firms than profit-maximizing firms will inhabit the upper end of the premium segment and the luxury segment of the market and will drive some profit-maximizers out of the wine market altogether. The profit-maximizing wine firms that remain in the market will tend to produce products at the lower end of the premium segment.

The second prediction is that utility-maximizing wine firms will have lower average ability and higher marginal costs than profit-maximizing wine firms and charge higher prices for their products. They have lower average ability since they require less profit to enter the industry. They have higher marginal cost for two reasons: first, they have lower average winemaking ability, and second some are willing to accept higher cost in return for the utility of nonmarket goods associated with grape growing and wine producing. Finally, because they have higher marginal cost and face a downward-sloping demand curve for their wine, they will charge higher prices.

The third prediction is that the marginal cost of producing wine will decrease the longer a proprietor operates in the industry. The more experience an owner has making wine, the more he or she learns about the winemaking process. This results in increased efficiency and lower costs.

To test these predictions, Scott Morton and Podolny use data on a sample of 184 California wine firms for the period 1980 to 1990. Based on answers to a number of survey questions, they construct variables that measure the strength of firm owners' nonprofit and profit objectives. They proceed to analyze the relationship between these variables and measures of wine quality and price, controlling for potential confounding factors. Their results suggest that proprietors with stronger nonprofit motives produce higher-quality wine and tend to operate exclusively in the luxury segment of the market. These proprietors are typically unwilling to include lower-quality premium wine in the portfolio of products they sell. Proprietors motivated by profit produce predominately lower-quality premium products. Those who also produce some luxury wines often don't make money on these products, but this helps to build a reputation for quality that allows them to charge higher prices for their premium wines. Wine firms whose owners are motivated by nonprofit objectives also tend to charge a higher price for a wine product of given quality than firms whose goal is to make money. This is consistent with the theoretical prediction that utility-maximizing proprietors have higher marginal costs than profit-maximizers. All wine firms lower the prices they charge for wine products of a given quality the longer the owners are in business, but the reduction in price is more rapid for utility-maximizers than for profit-maximizers. This is predicted by the theory of wine-firm behavior and reflects learning by doing and higher initial costs for utility-maximizers who enter the industry with lower average winemaking ability.

The theory and empirical findings of Scott Morton and Podolny imply that the luxury segment of the wine market will be largely populated by utility-maximizing wine firms that enjoy producing high-quality wine and are willing to trade off profits for the opportunity to do so. Relatively inexperienced utility-maximizing proprietors will charge higher prices for products of equal quality than the few profit-maximizing competitors who produce luxury wines, but this price difference will disappear over time as utility-maximizers gain more wine-making experience that results in increased efficiency and lower cost. Even though they are able to produce luxury wine at a lower marginal cost, most profit-maximizing firms choose not to sell these products. Utility-maximizing firms that are willing to accept less than a normal profit and may even use personal wealth to subsidize grape-growing and winemaking operations are willing to pay inordinately high prices for the best vineyard land, highest-quality grapes, most talented wine-making consultants, and other inputs used to produce luxury wines. This makes it unprofitable for most profit-maximizing wine firms to operate in the luxury segment, and they therefore tend to populate the premium segment. The existence of utility-maximizing proprietors who get personal satisfaction from producing high-quality wine suggests the types of luxury wine products offered for sale by these firms depend upon the tastes and preferences of proprietors as well as consumers.

SOURCING BEHAVIOR

The wine firm's sourcing decision refers to the choice of insourcing or outsourcing a task related to grape growing, wine production, or wine distribution. To insource a task is to perform it within the firm. To outsource a task is to contract with another firm in the marketplace to perform it.

To analyze the sourcing decision, it is assumed that the wine firm may have either profit or nonprofit objectives. The owners or managers make rational decisions, weigh the benefit and cost of insourcing or outsourcing a task, and choose the alternative for which the benefit exceeds the cost. The benefit and cost of insourcing or outsourcing a task are reciprocal: the benefit of insourcing is the opportunity cost of outsourcing; the opportunity cost of insourcing is the benefit of outsourcing. For example, suppose the search and contracting cost a wine firm would incur if it purchased grapes from an independent vineyard is $20,000. This transaction cost is a cost of outsourcing grape production. If the wine firm performs this task internally and grows its own grapes, it can save $20,000 in transaction costs. This is a benefit of insourcing. Continuing this example, suppose the cost of producing grapes within the firm is $75,000 and the price of purchasing the same amount of grapes from the independent vineyard is $50,000. The $25,000 difference between the internal production cost and external acquisition price is a cost of insourcing and a benefit of outsourcing. If transaction and production costs are the only two factors that affect the benefit and cost of sourcing grapes, the wine firm will choose to outsource this task, because the benefit of insourcing the grape input ($20,000) is less than the cost ($25,000), or alternatively the benefit of outsourcing the grape input ($25,000) exceeds the cost ($20,000).

A useful way to think about the sourcing decision is in terms of the following conceptual framework. Suppose that twenty-five technically separable tasks are required to produce and sell wine. A rational wine firm would evaluate the benefit and cost of performing each of these tasks within the firm. It would then order these twenty-five tasks in terms of their net benefits and internalize all of those with positive net benefits, starting with the highest and proceeding down to the lowest. Tasks with negative insourcing net benefits, and therefore positive outsourcing net benefits, would be contracted out to other firms in the marketplace. The benefits and costs of insourcing differ across firms, and wine firms will therefore differ in terms of their sourcing decisions. Factors affecting benefits and costs may also change over time and induce a wine firm to outsource tasks previously insourced or insource tasks heretofore outsourced.

As noted previously, a typical wine firm produces two or more wine products and sells them under one or more brand names. The wine firm must make sourcing decisions about the tasks required for each product. Given its evaluation of benefits and costs, it may choose to insource a task for one product and outsource the same task for another product. For example, a wine firm may choose to insource grape growing and wine production for a luxury wine, while at the same time outsource these tasks for a premium or commodity wine. This gives rise to the possibility that some tasks may simultaneously be insourced and outsourced.

Four important factors affect the benefits and costs of insourcing and outsourcing, and therefore provide a wine firm with economic incentives to organize and coordinate wine production and distribution tasks in a particular manner. These are transaction costs, production costs, product quality, and nonmarket goods.

Transaction Costs

As discussed in the previous chapter, transaction costs are the costs of searching for a party with which to make an exchange in the marketplace, and negotiating and enforcing the contract that specifies the terms of the exchange. The higher the transaction costs of a task, the greater the benefit (cost) of insourcing (outsourcing) it, and therefore the stronger the financial incentive for the firm to perform the task itself. Two important attributes of a market exchange that affect transaction costs are uncertainty and asset specificity. Transactions involving more specialized assets and more uncertain conditions have higher contracting and transaction costs largely because of the potential for opportunistic behavior.[6]

Uncertainty, or imperfect information, is a characteristic of all transactions. No contract between a wine firm and another party, such as a grape grower, a custom-crush producer, or a distributor, can specify every possible contingency related to a market transaction. The more contingencies associated with a transaction, the higher the contracting costs. This is because more contingencies make a contract more difficult and costly to negotiate and enforce. Much time and money is spent attempting to identify various contingencies that may arise and describe how they are to be resolved. Contingencies not specified in the contract may occur that result in opportunistic behavior and high enforcement costs, or lead the wine firm and the other party to engage in a costly renegotiation of the contract, possibly a number of times over its life. Another type of uncertainty involves measuring and evaluating the good or service being exchanged in the transaction, such as grapes or bulk wine. The more difficult it is to assess the characteristics of a good or service, the more difficult and costly it is to negotiate price and other terms of an agreement and enforce a contract should disputes arise. This is particularly important in wine market transactions since the quality of the grape input and wine product may be difficult to measure and evaluate. As discussed in the previous chapter, the party with whom a wine firm transacts to outsource a task may have better information about the quality of the good or service it is providing and the effort put forth in carrying out the agreement resulting in potential adverse selection and moral-hazard problems. To minimize this type of opportunistic behavior, complex and costly contracts may be necessary. Too many contingencies might even make it impossible for a wine firm to negotiate an agreement with another party to outsource a task, and handling it within the firm may therefore be the only viable option.

Transaction costs of outsourcing grape growing and wine production tasks stem largely from uncertainty and asymmetric information, and may be substantial. Grape quality can be difficult to assess. It depends upon measurable characteristics like sugar and acidity, and nonmeasurable characteristics related to physiological maturity and other flavor-related considerations. Growers generally have better information than wine firms on their ability to produce quality grapes and the effort they expend to do so. The quality of grapes used to produce lower-priced commodity wines is adequately measured by sugar content at harvest time.[7] As a result, relatively simple contracts can be written that include penalties or bonuses for sugar content to ensure the desired level of quality and minimize adverse selection and moral-hazard problems. These contracts are relatively easy to negotiate and enforce and the transaction costs of outsourcing grapes for commodity wines is therefore relatively low. However, measuring the quality of grapes used in the production of premium and luxury wines is much more difficult, since physiological and flavor-related characteristics desired by wine firms are difficult to measure at harvest. To ensure quality and minimize problems of adverse selection and moral hazard, relatively sophisticated contracts that account for more contingencies are required. They may include a number of viticultural provisions and monitoring devices that are more difficult to negotiate and enforce. Contingencies not covered by the contract can result in costly disputes and contract renegotiation. As a result, the transaction costs of outsourcing grapes for premium and luxury wines can be relatively high giving a wine firm a financial incentive to insource these grapes.

Outsourcing wine production also entails considerable uncertainty and asymmetric information. Wine quality is uncertain and imperfectly measured. A finished wine product deemed adequate by a custom producer may not satisfy the quality standards of the contracting wine firm. The wine firm and custom producer must agree on what characteristics measure quality and who determines if these characteristics are satisfied. Failure to do so may open the door to a serious dispute. Other contingencies may also occur. For instance, wine quality may be compromised by a poor vintage or other factors beyond the control of the custom producer. Disputes may arise if these issues are not resolved. Moreover, a wine firm cannot perfectly observe the effort put forth by custom producers, many of which also make their own wine products. These custom producers may take better care of their own products than those of their clients, and custom contractors whose effort cannot be measured may shirk and produce a wine of lower than expected quality. Custom producers may not adequately implement the client's winemaking instructions, and therefore fail to achieve the desired wine style. Contracts that do not address these sorts of contingencies may result in irreconcilable disputes and costly litigation. Writing contracts that cover many of these contingencies can be difficult, and they can be costly to negotiate and enforce. Because of this, outsourcing wine production tasks may entail relatively high transaction costs, particularly for higher-quality premium and luxury wines.

Most transactions between a wine firm and another party involve one or more assets that are required to carry out the exchange. For example, a transaction between a wine firm and a custom-crush producer to exchange money for a wine product requires the use of the plant and equipment assets of the custom producer. A transaction between a wine firm and a grape grower to exchange money for grapes involves the assets used to produce grapes, such as vineyard land, trellises, an irrigation system, and so on. A transaction between a wine firm and a winemaking consultant to exchange money for winemaking services includes the knowledge of the winemaker needed to make the wine, which is called a human-capital asset. When a wine firm or another party invests in an asset that is specialized to a transaction, this is called asset specificity. The degree of asset specificity can be measured by the difference between the cost of investing in the asset for this particular transaction and its value in its next best alternative use: the greater this difference, the more specific the asset is to this transaction.

As an example, consider the following transaction. A manufacturer invests $1 million in equipment designed to produce wine bottles with a unique shape and size for a wine firm. Because this equipment is used to make a highly specialized product that only this wine firm needs, it cannot be used to produce bottles for any other firm, and the next best use of the equipment is therefore as scrap metal with a value of $10,000.

The substantial difference between the value of the equipment in its current use and its value in its next best alternative use indicates that this asset has a high degree of specificity. The higher the degree of asset specificity involved in a transaction, the higher the contract and transaction costs. Why? Continuing the previous example, once the contract is signed and the investment is made in the bottling equipment, the manufacturer and wine firm have limited alternatives. The manufacturer is the only producer of the unique bottle design for the wine firm. The wine firm is the only demander of this particular type of bottle from the manufacturer. This creates an incentive for opportunistic behavior by both the wine firm and manufacturer. The wine firm may renege on the contract and try to use its position as the only potential source of demand for the bottles to negotiate a lower price than the one it originally agreed to pay. The bottle manufacturer may renege on the contract and try to use its status as the only source of supply to negotiate a higher price. To protect each party from opportunistic behavior by the other, the contract must have complex terms that are very costly to negotiate and enforce, resulting in high transaction costs.

Asset specificity may help to explain why Gallo produces its own wine bottles. Gallo has manufactured wine bottles since 1957. It currently produces 2.5 million bottles per day with an assortment of molds capable of producing over 100 different bottle design and color combinations.[8] If outsourced, the specialized assets required for the variety of bottle designs that Gallo desires would likely entail high transaction costs, which is reduced by internalizing bottle production. Asset specificity may also provide an incentive for wine firms to produce high-quality grapes for luxury wine products from estate-grown grapes, but contract with independent vineyards for grapes of lesser quality for premium or commodity wines. High-quality grapes with a specific bundle of characteristics that a wine firm desires to make a luxury wine may necessitate an investment in a specific type of vineyard land and equipment, giving rise to relatively high transaction costs. Lower transaction costs are incurred when contracting with an independent vineyard that uses less specialized assets to produce grapes with acceptable characteristics for lower-quality wines.

Production Costs

The costs of performing a task are termed *production costs*. When the cost of performing a given task within a firm is lower (higher) than the cost of contracting in the marketplace to have it done externally, this results in an insourcing benefit (cost) and an outsourcing cost (benefit). The greater the benefit (cost) of relatively lower (higher) production cost within the firm, the stronger the financial incentive for the firm to insource (outsource) the task. The most important factors affecting relative production costs are economies and diseconomies of scale and scope and wine-firm capabilities.

It is typically the case that when the scale of production increases, the average (unit) cost of output declines, at least up to a point. This phenomenon, called *economies of scale,* is an important factor affecting the cost of performing tasks. Economies of scale in the wine industry can occur either at the winery plant or firm level, and may characterize some tasks a firm performs but not others. For example, it has been estimated that the average cost of producing premium wine in a single winery production plant falls as output increases up to and beyond 500,000 cases per year. The estimates indicate the unit cost of producing a case of wine decreases by 40 percent as the scale of production increases from a relatively small plant capable of producing 10,000 cases per year to a much larger plant with a 500,000-case production capacity.[9]

There are technological, specialization, and financial reasons for economies of scale. To undertake a task, a firm must typically invest in certain types of assets. The cost of these assets does not vary with the amount of the activity produced. This results in a reduction in unit cost as output expands. For example, to produce wine, a firm typically purchases a building and the equipment it needs to crush, press, ferment, mature, bottle, and store wine. It has been estimated that the initial cost of plant and equipment for a winery with an annual production capacity of 10,000 cases of wine is about $1.6 million, with annual fixed costs of $230,000.[10] Suppose the average cost of grapes, labor services, and other variable inputs required to vary output in this winery is $40 per case. If this plant produces 2,000 cases per year, then average fixed cost is $115, average variable cost is $40, and unit cost is $155. If annual production is increased to 4,000 cases, then average fixed cost is $57.50, average variable cost is $40, and unit cost is $97.50. The more cases of wine produced in this building with this equipment, the lower the average cost per case as these large fixed costs are spread over more cases. Also, for technical reasons, the initial cost of purchasing the building and equipment for a larger winemaking plant is proportionately less than for a smaller plant. The investment required for a winery capable of producing 50,000 cases of wine per year is not five times as much as one that has an annual capacity of 10,000 cases, since it does not require five times as much building space, and so on. It has been estimated that the setup cost for a 50,000-case winery of $4.9 million is only three times as much as the $1.6 million investment requirement for a 10,000-case winery, resulting in a lower unit cost for the larger plant. Growing grapes also involves an initial investment in such assets as land, trellises, an irrigation system, tractors, pruners, and a harvester, and a larger vineyard operation can therefore reduce unit cost by spreading overhead and benefiting from the proportionately lower investment cost of a larger scale of production.

A second reason for economies of scale involves specialization of labor. By expanding the scale of a task, workers can specialize and develop an expertise in performing different tasks. As a result, worker productivity rises and unit cost falls. For example, in a small winery with an annual production of 1,000 cases, two or three workers may be required to divide their time among a variety of wine production tasks. In a large winery, workers can specialize in different areas of the production process, such as sorting and crushing grapes, fermenting the must, blending the wine, chemical analysis of the wine, and wine bottling. Specialized workers develop a high degree of proficiency in different tasks. This increases productivity and lowers unit cost. Increased efficiency from specialization also occurs in grape growing and wine distribution.

Performing a task at a larger scale of production may also allow a firm to use specialized equipment that would not be feasible at a smaller scale. This equipment enables the production process to be more highly automated, which increases labor productivity and lowers unit cost. For instance, the Trinchero Family Estates wine firm recently invested $200 million in a new winery near Lodi, California, with the capacity to produce more than six million cases of wine per year. The large scale of this winery allowed Trinchero to install specialized equipment to automate the production process and minimize the amount of labor required. The facility has a test station that automatically takes samples of grape juice to measure sugar content. Grapes are pressed by eighteen machines with automatic grape-filling capacity. Red grapes are fermented in self-cleaning, computerized, stainless steel tanks with a 175-ton capacity and automatic "cap punching" technology. The winemaker is able to program the fermenter to achieve the desired wine style. The plant has the capacity to store more than 30 million gallons of wine in 391 temperature-controlled stainless-steel tanks of varied size, some holding as much as 360,000 gallons. Juice, must, and wine are automatically moved from station to station through conveyor and pump-driven stainless-steel pipes. This minimizes the amount of labor required to perform this function.[11] These sorts of productivity-enhancing machines and technologies, which lower the unit cost of producing wine, would not be feasible in a small or medium-sized plant. Large-scale commercial vineyards can also reduce the unit cost of grape production by taking advantage of specialized equipment. For example Beckstoffer Vineyards, the largest commercial grape grower in Northern California, with more than 3,000 acres of vineyard land, employs productivity-enhancing equipment such as automated irrigation systems, machine harvesters, weather-monitoring equipment, computer technology that monitors grape maturity and harvest, and specialized software that measures labor productivity.[12] This type of equipment is not feasible for the small-scale vineyards with 5 to 10 acres of vineyard land that comprise more than 50 percent of grape growers in the United States.

Organizing a task on a larger scale can also result in cost savings from lower input prices. A firm may be able to obtain quantity discounts if it purchases large amounts of material inputs. For example, when the 43-million case producer Constellation Wines U.S. purchased the 400,000-case Blackstone winery, it reduced Blackstone's annual bottle cost by $800,000.[13]

Economies of scope occurs when two or more products can be produced at a lower cost by a single plant or firm than if each of these products were produced by a separate plant or firm. The most important reason for economies of scope is that the different products employ common inputs. For example, suppose two vineyards grow different grape varieties, one Chardonnay and the other Cabernet Sauvignon. Each vineyard can be harvested with the same mechanical grape picker. The cost of harvesting the two vineyards for a single firm that owns a mechanical harvester is less than cost of two separate firms harvesting these vineyards, each with its own mechanical grape picker. This is because a single firm can spread the fixed cost of the grape harvester over the two grape products. Economies of scope often arise in the production and distribution of different wine products and products related to wine, such as spirits and beer. Here a variety of common inputs may exist. The same plant and equipment can be used to produce different wine brands and products. A winery with excess capacity can produce multiple wine brands at a lower cost than if each brand were produced with the same equipment in a different winery, possibly by a different wine firm. A sales force that sells wine, spirits, and beer may have a lower cost than if each of these products were sold by a separate sales force. The same salesperson can sell more than one wine brand or alcoholic beverage to a distributor or retailer. Distributors and retailers may prefer to deal with one wine firm for all of their wine needs, rather than multiple firms, if the single firm has a wide variety of wines. The input that is shared among different products does not have to be a physical asset; it can also be a knowledge input. Information about one wine brand might help to reduce the cost or improve the quality of another brand. A wine firm that produces multiple products can share grape-growing and winemaking information and expertise across all of these products. Having an expertise in selling spirits may enable a firm to market wine more efficiently. In these situations, it is more costly to produce and sell products separately, because the knowledge input would need to be duplicated for each product.

Economies of scale and scope are not mutually exclusive. A firm that sells many wine products can specialize tasks by plant, such as bottling and blending, to achieve cost savings from economies of scale, while at the same time spreading the cost of common inputs like sales force, knowledge, and shared information across products.

It is possible to glean the benefit of lower production cost from economies of scale and scope by either insourcing or outsourcing a task. For instance, as we have seen, estimates suggest that a wine firm can decrease the unit cost of producing wine by 40 percent if it increases the size of its winery from a plant producing 10,000 to one producing 500,000 cases per year. This cost savings a wine firm would realize is a benefit of becoming larger and insourcing more wine. But what if the demand for its product does not justify this larger scale of operation or it faces constraints in distributing a greater volume of wine? A custom-crush producer that specializes in producing wine products for a number of client firms can enjoy the same economies of scale, and the relatively low unit cost of production can be passed on to client firms in the form of a lower price. As a result, the acquisition price of purchasing 10,000 cases of wine from the custom producer may be lower than producing this wine internally. If so, then the wine firm would have an economic incentive to outsource production. The custom producer might also enjoy additional cost savings from economies of scope that are reflected in price. The custom producer's facility and equipment can be used to produce multiple wine brands for clients and fully utilize plant capacity. The specialized knowledge of the custom producer in sourcing grapes, producing wine, and possibly marketing wine can be spread over multiple products and clients.

A supplier that specializes in performing grape-growing, wine-production, or wine-distribution tasks for a number of smaller wine firms may be able to operate on a larger scale or scope than each individual wine firm performing these tasks internally. If the cost savings to the supplier firm from economies of scale or scope translate into a lower acquisition price for a wine firm than the unit cost of performing a task in-house, this gives the wine firm an economic incentive to outsource the task. However, if only one or a few large specialized firms perform task, such a supplier may use its monopoly power to charge a relatively high price. This may weaken or eliminate the incentive for a wine firm to outsource.

Large wine firms often realize substantial cost savings from economies of scale and scope by performing tasks in-house, while smaller firms exploit these cost savings through outsourcing. Large firms like Gallo, Constellation, Bronco Wine Company, and Trinchero Family Estates realize economies of scale in grape growing, wine production, and wine distribution from ownership of thousands of acres of vineyards; large-scale or multiple wineries that produce millions of cases of wine each year; specialization of tasks such as blending, bottling, and, for Gallo, bottle production; large volume purchases of equipment, grapes, packaging materials, and other inputs; and large sales forces. These large producers also achieve economies of scope by producing a large number of wine products, with several selling fifty or more different wine brands. Some large wine firms are organized as wine groups. They own a diversified portfolio of wineries that produce different wine brands and sell products in different segments of the market at different price points. Each winery is allowed to act as an independent entity in making product and production choices. Cost savings from economies of scale are obtained through centralized input purchasing, and economies of scope from marketing and selling the firm's portfolio of products. The firm can offer large distributors and retailers a variety of wine products, which reduces marketing cost and allows smaller volume brands to compete for retail shelf space and expand sales. Distributors and retailers benefit from the ability to purchase many of their wine products from a single wine firm rather than multiple firms.

Many small wine firms achieve the benefits of economies of scale and scope by outsourcing wine production to custom-crush producers. Twenty years ago, there were relatively few of these and most were wine firms willing to contract out production only in periods when they developed excess capacity. Today, a relatively large number of specialized custom producers exist. Many of these have fifty or more clients. Small wine firms that contract with custom producers are able to realize economies of scale and scope indirectly by paying a lower price for a wine than the cost of producing it in their own winery. The custom producer is often able to benefit from volume discounts on inputs that can be passed on to clients. The cost of expensive equipment and technology such as sorting tables, crushers, fermentation tanks, filtration systems, and bottling lines is spread across a number of client firms. For some small wine firms, purchasing this equipment would be prohibitively expensive. A wine firm can use the knowledge of the custom producer and information shared by other clients when producing its product. Some small wine firms realize cost savings from economies of scope by producing their wines in an alternating-proprietor winery. This allows them to spread the fixed costs of the building and equipment over several wine firms, which share the facility and fully utilize the winery.

Small wine firms can also indirectly exploit the cost advantages of economies of scale and scope in grape growing by contracting with a large commercial vineyard. For example, the large independent grape grower Beckstoffer Vineyards sells grapes under contract to more than fifty small-to-medium-sized wine firms. Grapes are grown on different blocks of vineyard land for different wine firms. The fixed cost of productivity-enhancing high-tech equipment such as automated irrigation systems, mechanical harvesters and pruners, weather-monitoring equipment, and GPS technology is spread over the large number of contracting wine firms. These firms would experience high average fixed costs and therefore units costs, or not be able to afford to invest in this type of equipment at all, if they produced grapes in-house in a vineyard the size of their Beckstoffer block. Beckstoffer's expertise in growing high-quality grapes cost-effectively is shared by the contracting wine firms, allowing them indirectly to realize economies of scope from this information input.

When the scale of a plant or firm that performs a task or set of tasks continues to grow and surpasses some particularly size, average cost may rise with greater production. This phenomenon is called *diseconomies of scale*. The major reason for diseconomies of scale is the difficulty of efficiently managing a large-scale operation. For example, in a small winery, the winemaker is also the cellar master, who oversees relatively few cellar workers and makes all the important decisions about wine production. It is easy for the winemaker to obtain the information he or she needs by directly observing winemaking tasks and communicating with workers. This permits implementation of effective, efficient decisions. Also, in a small winery cellar workers may be more committed to their job, and it is easier to monitor their performance to minimize shirking and maximize productivity. As the scale of the winery operation increases, the head winemaker has to delegate responsibility and authority to lower level employees. A medium-sized or large winery typically has one or more assistant winemakers involved in implementing the wine production plan, and cellar masters who supervise and manage a relatively large group of cellar workers and lab assistants. Because of the different levels of management and employees, the head winemaker is farther removed from the actual winemaking process. Information must be transmitted among cellar workers, cellar masters, assistant winemakers, and the head winemaker. Problems with communication may result in inaccurate information and misunderstood instructions. Decision-making at different levels makes it more difficult to coordinate wine production. Red tape and paperwork increase. Cellar workers may feel less committed to the winemaking process and, because they are a members of a large team, take the opportunity to shirk, provide less work effort, and take on-the-job leisure. As a result, more supervisors may be needed to monitor workers and maintain productivity. Management and supervision problems of this type contribute to increasing average cost when the scale of a task becomes too large to control and coordinate in an efficient manner. These sorts of management difficulties may well be amplified in a large wine firm that does much of its own grape growing, wine production, and wine distribution. Top management must control and coordinate a wide variety of tasks. As more tasks are carried out internally, planning, coordination, and administration within the firm become increasingly complex and difficult, and the marginal cost of insourcing additional tasks therefore rises. This provides the wine firm with an increasingly stronger incentive to outsource tasks.

Large wine firms may be motivated to outsource grape and wine production to avoid rising costs associated with diseconomies of scale. None of the largest wine firms in the United States grow all of their own grapes or produce all of their own wine. For example, it has been estimated that Gallo produces about 10 percent of its annual million-ton grape input requirement internally on 15,000 acres of vineyard land that it owns and contracts with independent growers for the remaining

90 percent. One possible explanation is that by contracting with a number of grape growers, each of which is big enough to achieve economies of scale, it can indirectly enjoy the cost savings that grape-growing scale brings and avoid the managerial inefficiencies and higher production cost of growing most or all of the grapes it needs in its own mammoth vineyard operation.

The wine firm's capabilities are another factor affecting production cost. Wine firms and the suppliers with which they might potentially contract may differ in their ability to perform various tasks cost-effectively. This may result in differences in the cost of performing a given task, and therefore motivate the sourcing decision.[14] The benefit of insourcing a task is higher for those that a firm is capable of performing more efficiently or for some other reason at a relatively lower cost. Firm capabilities may differ because of different endowments of resources such as the knowledge and skills of owners and employees, capital equipment, and land. Individuals within a wine firm may have knowledge and skills that are specific to producing and selling wine. For example, by reason of experience, education, or natural ability, an owner may be particularly competent in growing grapes, producing wine, or marketing and distributing it. This expertise may be based on tacit knowledge acquired from observation and practice, as in blending wine, and thus not be easily transferrable to other individuals.[15] In any case, it may enable the firm to perform specific tasks efficiently and provide an incentive to insource them. Finally, ownership of the capital equipment or land necessary to perform a given task cost-effectively clearly also increases the benefit of insourcing and the cost of outsourcing it.

Consider the following example. Two wine firms desire to produce 10,000 cases of premium wine per year. The investment required to build and equip a winery with this capacity is $1.6 million.[16] The proprietor of Firm A inherited a winemaking facility with the capacity to produce this quantity of wine. He also gained significant winemaking experience, knowledge, and skill from being raised in a family that owned a wine firm. The proprietor of Firm B does not own the plant and equipment necessary to produce wine. Having worked for marketing firms, he has expertise in selling wine, but he knows relatively little about winemaking. If Firm A chooses to insource wine production, it will have a variable cost of $544,000 plus an annual fixed cost of $16,000 for property taxes, insurance, and maintenance, making its total cost $560,000, or $56 per case. Variable cost reflects the price of grapes, packaging, utilities, and other variable inputs, and the ability of the proprietor to use efficient winemaking techniques. For Firm B, the annual fixed cost of producing 10,000 cases of wine is substantially higher. Like Firm A, it must spend $16,000 per year on insurance, property taxes, and maintenance, but it must also raise $1.6 million to purchase a winery. This adds an additional $207,000 to its fixed cost. The annual fixed cost for Firm B would therefore be $223,000. Given Firm B's lack of expertise in cost-effective winemaking, it would have a higher variable cost of $600,000, reflecting the use of less-efficient methods of production. The total cost of internal wine production for Firm B of $823,000, or $82.23 per case, reflects its higher fixed and variable costs. The production cost advantage Firm A enjoys is the result of its endowment of capital equipment and the winemaking knowledge and skills of the proprietor. Now, suppose that both firms are able to contract with a custom-crush producer who charges $70 per case of wine. Firm A would get a production cost benefit from insourcing and Firm B from outsourcing wine production. Firm B may also get an additional benefit from outsourcing production, because it enables the owner to forgo the task of raising $1.6 million to build a winery. For many would-be winemakers, obtaining the large amount of money required to purchase a winery may be difficult or prohibitively expensive. However, because Firm B is endowed with knowledge and skills in marketing and distributing wine, it has an incentive to perform sales tasks internally. Firm A has an incentive to outsource marketing and sales, since it has no specialized knowledge or skills in that area and therefore gets a production cost benefit by contracting those tasks out.

Firm capabilities may be an important factor influencing the sourcing decisions of a variety of wine firms. Several examples help to illustrate this notion. The Teatown wine firm, located in Hudson, New York, calls itself a virtual winery and sells several different wine products in more than fifteen states. It owns neither vineyards nor a winery. Before starting the firm, the proprietor had more than fifteen years of experience as a restaurant wine buyer and working for wine distributors. This prior experience, along with relationships he developed with grape growers, winemakers, and wine firms, provided him with expertise in purchasing bulk and finished wine and marketing it to distributors and restaurants. Based on the proprietor's knowledge, these tasks are thus performed within the firm. Grape growing and wine production, areas in which the proprietor lacks knowledge, skills, and capital equipment, are outsourced to California wine firms, and the products are sold as Napa Valley Chardonnay and Merlot wine.[17]

Cameron Hughes is described by many as a negociant. When he was growing up, his father worked in wine sales. He spent several years as a wine broker, acquired substantial knowledge about the bulk wine market, and made the connections necessary to make cost-effective transactions in bulk and surplus bottled wine. Hughes eventually started the Cameron Hughes Wine firm, which draws on his knowledge of the bulk-wine market and sales, along with the skills of the winemaker Sam Spencer, who has expertise in tasting and blending wines, to purchase high-quality bulk and surplus bottled wine at low cost and sell it under the Cameron Hughes label at bargain prices. Cameron Hughes Wine sells its products on a website and through large retailers nationwide like Costco, Sam's Club, Kroger, and Safeway.[18]

The wine critic Robert Parker calls David Abreu a "superstar viticulturist" with extraordinary grape- growing knowledge and skills. He owns the David Abreu Vineyard Management Company and manages vineyards under contract for many well-known wine firms in California whose wines consistently receive high scores from the critics. The high quality of these wines is often attributed to Abreu's expertise in growing high-quality fruit. Abreu also grows grapes on about seventy acres of vineyard land he owns and uses some of this fruit to produce wine that he sells under his own Abreu label. As the proprietor of a wine firm, Abreu uses his expertise in vineyard management to produce his own grapes, but outsources the production and distribution of his annual output of about 500 cases of wine.[19]

Large wine firms like Gallo and Castle Rock Winery also have particular capabilities that affect the benefits and costs of the sourcing decision. In addition to Gallo's large endowment of winemaking plant and equipment, it has an expertise in the application of advanced cost-reducing technology that yields large benefits. Gallo has implemented technology to automate its bottle-manufacturing facility to minimize production costs. The Gallo Wine Manager System provides its winemaking team with information on the cost of producing wines of varying styles. Gallo's regional distribution centers are equipped with a recently installed innovative and efficient inventory management system that has doubled warehouse productivity. It has sophisticated software that provides distributors and retailers with information on Gallo products and their availability. The Gallo Technology Center continues to develop and apply new cost-minimizing technologies on an ongoing basis.[20] As noted previously, the Castle Rock Winery is the twenty-sixth largest wine firm in the United States, but contracts out all grape growing and wine production. Marketing, sales, and development tasks are performed within the firm by a relatively small number of individuals who have expertise in these areas.

Product Quality

The discussion so far has focused on the effect of cost on the sourcing decision. All else being equal, the higher the transaction cost and the lower internal production cost, the stronger the incentive is to perform a task within the firm. However, in the wine industry, product quality is also an important factor affecting the benefits and costs of sourcing. Maintaining consistent wine quality may be instrumental in building or protecting a wine firm's reputation and brand loyalty for its products, so that customers are less likely to switch to products of other firms. Improving wine quality may allow a firm to charge a higher price, generate more revenue, and increase prestige, all of which may benefit the owners through either greater profit, increased utility, or both. The quality of wine products depends upon grape growing and winemaking, which can be performed either within the firm or outsourced. When the contribution to wine quality of a task performed within the firm is greater (smaller) than when it is outsourced, this results in an insourcing benefit (cost) and an outsourcing cost (benefit).

One possible factor contributing to wine quality is the degree of control a wine firm has over a task. Industry participants often maintain that an important benefit from insourcing grape growing and winemaking tasks is that a wine firm has maximum control of them. This ensures the supply of important inputs and allows it to make decisions necessary to protect or improve wine quality. Purchasing grapes from independent vineyards on the spot market may be unreliable. The availability and quality of fruit may be uncertain and may vary from vineyard to vineyard and from one year to the next. A wine firm and grower must carefully coordinate the timing of the harvesting and delivery of grapes, because they are perishable, and failure to do so can have an adverse effect on wine quality. A wine firm can gain more control over the outsourcing of grapes by entering into a long-term contract with a grower. However, as discussed previously, a contract cannot specify all possible contingencies, and adverse selection and moral-hazard problems may preclude it from achieving the desired level of input quality. Some commercial vineyards allow contracting wine firms to opt for greater control over grape-growing decisions by paying per acre of land farmed, rather than per ton of grapes produced, and be actively involved in managing their vineyard blocks. However, by producing grapes in its own vineyards, a wine firm achieves maximum control and is assured of a timely supply of grapes that are more likely to have attributes that satisfy its quality standards.

Lack of control when outsourcing winemaking tasks may also compromise wine quality. In a typical custom-crush arrangement, the contracting wine firm specifies a wine style and possibly winemaking instructions. The custom producer uses its own judgment to achieve the desired wine style, and in so doing may make inappropriate decisions because of lack of communication or moral-hazard problems. Many custom producers have hundreds of clients and high staff turnover, which can result in winemaking chaos. To increase quality control, many wine firms have their own winemakers or contract with a winemaking consultant to oversee the winemaking process. Some custom producers encourage or even require this practice, while others prohibit it. Producing wine internally allows a wine firm to avoid these problems and gives it more control over quality.

Firm capabilities may also have a significant effect on wine quality and therefore the sourcing decision. The benefit of insourcing is higher for those tasks for which a wine firm is capable of making a greater contribution to wine quality. Wine firms and suppliers may differ in their ability to deliver quality because of differences in resource endowments. Arguably, the most important resources affecting wine quality are the quality of vineyard land and the skills of the vineyard manager and winemaker. Vineyard land with climate, soil, and landscape characteristics capable of producing high-quality grapes is in relatively fixed supply, and much of this land has been owned by the same wine firms and independent growers for decades. Firms with an endowment of high-quality land have a stronger incentive to insource grape growing than those who do not. For example, the To Kalon vineyard in Napa Valley, California, originally planted in 1868, is part-owned by Constellation's Robert Mondavi Winery and part-owned by the independent grape grower Beckstoffer Vineyards. It is acknowledged by many to yield the best red wine grapes in the United States. Constellation insources most of the grapes for its Mondavi Cabernet Sauvignon from its To Kalon acreage. Other producers of high-quality wines that do not have an endowment of vineyard land of comparable quality, such as Schrader Cellars, outsource grapes from To Kalon by contracting with Beckstoffer.

A wine firm that desires to produce high-quality wine and has a highly skilled winemaker realizes greater benefits from producing wine in-house than contracting out for winemaking services, while one with a winemaker of average skill may be motivated to outsource some of its wine products or contract with a winemaking consultant. Today, an active market exists in winemaking consulting. Many of these consultants, such as Helen Turley, Heidi Barrett Peterson, Michel Rolland, Paul Hobbs, and Philippe Melka, are considered to be superstar winemakers of exceptional ability. They have been instrumental in greatly enhancing the reputation of many wine firms that produce high-quality wine. Many of the top winemakers produce wine under their own label and provide consulting services to other wine firms. Some of these, called flying winemakers, provide global consulting services. The French winemaker and enologist Michel Rolland works as a consultant for more than 100 wine firms in the United States, France, Chile, Argentina, and a number of other countries.[21] A similarly active market exists in vineyard management and consulting services with superstar grape growers like David Abreu.

Nonmarket Goods

The higher the transaction cost, the lower the internal production cost, and the greater the contribution to quality of performing a task in-house, the more likely a profit-maximizing wine firm is to realize net benefits from insourcing it. This is because net benefits for a profit-maximizing wine firm are measured by the difference between the marginal revenue and marginal cost of a task. Performing tasks within the firm that increase revenue by enhancing quality and reducing cost by not outsourcing contribute to the goal of making as much money as possible for the owners. However, for a utility-maximizing wine firm, the cost-benefit calculus of sourcing includes an additional consideration: the value to the owners of an activity related to a nonmarket good such as wine quality, lifestyle, or nepotism. An owner may derive an insourcing benefit from growing grapes in a self-owned vineyard or producing wine in a self-owned winery because he derives utility from the contribution these activities make to his desired lifestyle. Conversely, he may derive an outsourcing benefit from contracting with a superstar winemaking consultant to assist with or make winemaking decisions because he derives utility from the contribution this makes to his goal of producing a high-quality wine, independent of the effect on wine-firm revenue.

The Wine Consumer and Demand

According to the Wine Market Council, there are one hundred million wine consumers in the United States. About eleven million of these drink wine every day, another forty-five million consume wine at least once a week, and the rest typically imbibe a couple of times a month. A typical American wine consumer drinks about thirty-five bottles of wine per year or three and one-half five-ounce glasses per week. In the aggregate, wine consumers in the United States drink the equivalent of 295 million cases of wine per year, the largest total consumption of any nation in the world, but per capita consumption is still much less than in many other countries, such as France, Italy, Spain, and the United Kingdom.[1] This chapter begins by describing the characteristics of these wine consumers and trends and patterns of wine consumption in the United States. Economic concepts are then used to shed light on wine consumers' behavior and to analyze important factors that affect wine consumption.

CHARACTERISTICS OF WINE CONSUMERS

Sixty-six percent of American adults aged twenty-one or older choose to consume alcoholic beverages.[2] Forty-four percent drink wine; some of these also consume beer or spirits. A typical wine consumer tends to be an affluent, college-educated, middle-aged, married, homeowner in a technical, professional, or proprietary occupation, and enjoys cultural events and participating in sports or exercise-related activities. A majority of wine drinkers have household incomes in excess of $100,000, about half have college degrees, more than one-third have graduate degrees, and almost nine out of ten own their own homes. About half of all wine drinkers are between the ages of thirty-five and fifty-five, and more women consume wine than men. Wine is the preferred alcoholic beverage of women aged thirty and older, and the proportion who choose wine over beer and spirits increases with age. While more than half of all American women older than thirty prefer to drink wine, more than 80 percent of men of all ages prefer beer or spirits. However, men tend to drink more of any type of alcoholic beverage than women.

Most wine is consumed by a relatively small segment of the U.S. population. Frequent wine consumers, those who drink wine at least once a week, represent 25 percent of the adult population, but account for 93 percent of the wine consumed. About 20 percent of these drink wine every day. Consumption of wine on a daily basis increases with age. Only 6 percent of Americans aged from twenty-one to thirty-four drink wine each day, while 12 percent of those sixty-five or older do so daily. Infrequent wine consumers, those who drink wine at least once a month, constitute 19 percent of the adult population and account for only 7 percent of the quantity of wine consumed. A typical infrequent consumer drinks wine two to three times a month.

A large study by Constellation Brands, called Project Genome, suggests that there are significant individual differences among U.S. consumers in their attitudes to wine. The largest segment, 23 percent, report being overwhelmed when making wine-buying decisions. This is largely the result of the vast number of wines from which they must choose and lack of information about the relevant characteristics of these products. The second-largest segment, comprising 20 percent of wine consumers, see wine as a status symbol and believe that price is a good index of quality. A typical wine "image seeker" tends to be a male in his mid-thirties. Another 16 percent of wine consumers have a strong preference for well-known, national brands and tend to be loyal to a particular brand. Fourteen percent of wine consumers are relatively uninformed about wine and tend to have a few favorite wine brands that they purchase on a regular basis. The smallest segment of wine consumers, 12 percent of the wine-drinking population, are very enthusiastic and knowledgeable about wine and keep abreast of critics' evaluations and quality ratings. About half of all wine expenditures are made by wine enthusiasts or status-conscious individuals, accounting for one-third of all U.S. wine consumers.

TRENDS AND PATTERNS IN WINE CONSUMPTION

This section discusses some notable trends and patterns in wine consumption in the United States. The focus is on aggregate sales and expenditures, quantity consumed, and price. Some information on the types of wine and share of wine consumed in different price segments is also provided.

Wine Sales and Expenditures

To describe the behavior of aggregate wine sales data, it is useful to begin with the accounting identity S = PQ. S is the dollar value of wine sales during a given period of time or equivalent dollar value of consumer wine expenditures. P is the average price per unit of wine for the time period. It is sometimes called the nominal price, because it is an absolute measure of price in current dollars. Q is the number of units of wine purchased by consumers during the given period. Units of wine are typically measured in gallons, 750 ml bottles, or twelve-bottle cases. This identity informs us that consumer spending on wine can increase (decrease) if consumers pay a higher (lower) price for the same quantity of wine, purchase a larger (smaller) quantity of wine at the same price, or some combination of these. An increase (decrease) in the average price of wine can result from an increase (decrease) in the general level of prices in the economy or inflation (deflation), an increase (decrease) in the price of wine relative to the prices of other goods and services, an improvement in wine quality, or consumers substituting higher-priced (lower-priced) wine products for lower-priced (higher-priced) ones. For example, if the inflation rate for a given year is 5 percent and the average price of wine increases by 7 percent, the relative price of wine has increased by 2 percent. This 2 percent increase in relative price can be the result of an increase in demand for wine relative to supply or a manifestation of consumers' willingness to pay a higher price for higher-quality wine, which may result from either a general improvement in the quality of wine products or consumers substituting higher-priced premium wine for lower-priced commodity wine.

Table 1 provides data on several alternative measures of annual sales of wine in the United States over the twenty-year period 1991 through

TABLE I   U.S. ANNUAL WINE SALES, 1991–2010

Year	Nominal sales (billions of $$)	Real sales (billions of 2010 $$)	Real sales per capita (2010 $$)	Sales as a proportion of disposable income
2010	30	30	97	0.26
2009	28.7	29.2	95	0.26
2008	30	30.4	100	0.27
2007	30.4	32	106	0.29
2006	27.8	30.1	100	0.28
2005	25.8	28.8	97	0.28
2004	24	27.7	94	0.27
2003	22.3	26.4	91	0.27
2002	21.8	26.4	96	0.27
2001	20.3	25	88	0.27
2000	19.2	24.3	86	0.26
1999	18.1	23.7	88	0.27
1998	17	22.7	84	0.26
1997	16.1	21.9	82	0.27
1996	14.3	19.9	75	0.25
1995	12.2	17.5	67	0.22
1994	11.5	16.9	65	0.22
1993	11	16.6	64	0.22
1992	11.4	17.7	70	0.24
1991	10.9	17.4	69	0.25

SOURCES: Data for wine consumption from the Wine Institute, www.wineinstitute
.org; data for disposable income from the Bureau of Economic Analysis, www.bea
.gov; all-item consumer price index (CPI), used to adjust nominal sales from the
Bureau of Labor Statistics, www.bls.gov.

2010, for which reliable sales data are available. Current dollar (nominal) expenditures on wine grew from $10.9 billion in 1991 to $30 billion in 2010, an increase of 175 percent. Aggregate spending on wine increased each year between 1994 and 2007, before declining in both 2008 and 2009. Part of the increase in wine expenditures during this period is the result of an increase in the average level of prices of all goods, as well as an increase in the population of potential wine consumers. Column 3 of table 1 adjusts nominal spending for inflation and provides a measure of real wine sales in year 2010 dollars. The pattern in real spending mirrors that of nominal spending; however, after accounting for inflation, real spending for the period 1991 to 2010 increased by only 72 percent. Column 4 makes an additional adjustment for population growth and measures real spending on a per capita basis. In 1991, spending per U.S. resident on wine measured in 2010 dollars was $69. By 2010, it had grown to $97, an increase of 41 percent. This indicates that the pattern of rising expenditures persisted even after accounting for population growth and inflation. The last column in table 1 gives a measure of wine expenditures as a percentage of consumer disposable income. During this twenty-year period consumers devoted roughly the same proportion of disposable income to wine. In 1991, a typical consumer spent 0.25 percent of after-tax income on wine. By 2010, this had increased slightly to 0.26 percent.

The pattern of rapidly rising nominal and real spending on wine occurred during a period of economic expansion and rising disposable income, and persisted during a brief, mild recession from March to November 2001. However, this trend was interrupted shortly after the onset of the major economic recession in December 2007. Not only did consumers reduce total spending on wine, but they also devoted a smaller portion of their reduced disposable income to wine. This recession, which was the biggest economic contraction in sixty-five years, officially ended in June 2009. It appears that the upward trend in wine expenditures may have once again returned as consumers increased spending on wine in 2010.

The data on the year-to-year behavior of wine expenditures masks the seasonal pattern that occurs with regularity within any given year. In a typical year, monthly wine sales display relatively little variation between January and October. However consumer spending on wine increases dramatically during the months of November and December, largely because of the holiday season that includes Thanksgiving, Christmas, and New Year. For example, in 2011, monthly off-premises wine sales varied within a range of $675 to $750 million during the first ten months of the year, but exceeded $900 million for November and December.

Quantity of Wine Consumed

Table 2 presents annual data on the quantity of wine consumed per capita in the United States, measured in gallons, for the period 1951 to 2010. Between 1952 and 1962, the amount of wine consumed per capita was flat, varying within a range of 0.88 to 0.94 gallons. Beginning in 1963, per capita consumption rose continuously for two decades, reaching a peak of 2.43 gallons in 1986. The quantity of wine consumed per resident during this twenty-three-year period increased at an annual

TABLE 2   U.S. WINE CONSUMPTION PER CAPITA, 1951–2010 (GALLONS)

Year	Wine	Year	Wine	Year	Wine	Year	Wine	Year	Wine
2010	2.54	2000	2.01	1990	2.05	1980	2.11	1970	1.31	1960	0.91
2009	2.50	1999	2.02	1989	2.11	1979	1.98	1969	1.17	1959	0.89
2008	2.48	1998	1.95	1988	2.24	1978	1.96	1968	1.07	1958	0.89
2007	2.47	1997	1.94	1987	2.39	1977	1.82	1967	1.03	1957	0.89
2006	2.39	1996	1.89	1986	2.43	1976	1.73	1966	0.98	1956	0.90
2005	2.33	1995	1.77	1985	2.43	1975	1.71	1965	0.98	1955	0.88
2004	2.26	1994	1.77	1984	2.34	1974	1.64	1964	0.97	1954	0.88
2003	2.20	1993	1.74	1983	2.25	1973	1.64	1963	0.93	1953	0.89
2002	2.14	1992	1.87	1982	2.22	1972	1.61	1962	0.90	1952	0.88
2001	2.01	1991	1.85	1981	2.20	1971	1.48	1961	0.94	1951	0.83

SOURCE: Wine Institute, www.wineinstitute.org.

average rate of 7.4 percent and was 2.7 times higher in 1986 than 1963. However, per capita consumption then proceeded to decline each year until it hit a low of 1.74 gallons in 1993, the same quantity of wine a typical member of the U.S. population had consumed in 1976. In 1994, per capita consumption started to rise once again, and it increased each year, with the exception of 2000, achieving an historic high of 2.54 gallons per resident in 2010.

For the most part, per capita wine consumption has been resistant to economic downturns. During this fifty-year year period, the economy experienced ten economic recessions with declining aggregate output and income. However, the quantity of wine consumed per resident fell during only two of these contractions in economic activity. During the 1973–75 recession, when oil prices skyrocketed, inflation continued unabated, and the stock market fell precipitously, wine consumption per capita increased by 12 percent. Even during the recent severe recession of 2007–9, per capita consumption rose by a healthy 1.2 percent. However, during this same recessionary period, nominal wine expenditures decreased from $106 to $95 per capita, a decline of about 10.4 percent. The contemporaneous increase in the quantity of wine consumed and decrease in spending on a per capita basis indicates that consumers were paying a lower average price for the wine they purchased. The evidence suggests that the average price of a bottle of wine fell for two reasons. First, many wine firms lowered prices in response to the poor economic environment in order to sell their wine. Second, a number of consumers maintained or increased their consumption of wine, but substituted lower-priced commodity and premium wines for the higher-priced luxury wines they were consuming prior to the downturn, when they had higher incomes and there was less uncertainty about their employment status.

Even though wine consumption per capita is at an historic high in the United States, we still consume significantly less wine per resident than many other nations, such as France (12 gal.), Italy (11 gal.), Spain (7 gal.), Australia (6.6 gal.), Argentina (6.3 gal.), the United Kingdom (5.7 gal.), and Canada (2.6 gal.), to name just a few of the thirty-two countries that consume more wine per resident than the United States.[3]

Wine Prices

Table 3 reports several alternative measures of the average price of a bottle of wine in the United States for the period 1991 to 2010. To

TABLE 3 U.S. ANNUAL AVERAGE PRICE OF WINE PER
750 ML BOTTLE, 1991–2010

Year	Nominal Price (U.S.$$)	Real Price (2010 $$)*	Relative Price (2010 $$)**
2010	7.58	7.58	7.58
2009	7.41	7.54	7.48
2008	7.89	8.00	8.12
2007	8.08	8.50	8.69
2006	7.68	8.31	8.56
2005	7.39	8.25	8.43
2004	7.15	8.26	8.27
2003	6.91	8.20	8.22
2002	7.00	8.49	8.49
2001	7.01	8.63	8.68
2000	6.70	8.48	8.51
1999	6.60	8.65	8.62
1998	6.40	8.57	8.59
1997	6.15	8.35	8.40
1996	5.67	7.88	7.92
1995	5.21	7.46	7.54
1994	4.96	7.31	7.33
1993	4.85	7.33	7.24
1992	4.75	7.38	7.18
1991	4.63	7.42	7.22

SOURCES: Data for wine consumption and sales used to calculate average price of wine from Wine Institute, www.wineinstitute.org; all-item consumer price index (CPI) and alcoholic beverage component of the CPI from Bureau of Labor Statistics, www.bls.gov.
*Nominal price adjusted for changes in the average level of prices of goods and services based on the CPI.
**Price relative to the prices of all alcoholic beverages based on the alcoholic beverage component of the CPI.

calculate the nominal price shown in column 2 of the table, I use the accounting identity, $S = PQ$, and the available data on aggregate nominal wine sales (S) and total gallons consumed (Q). Gallons are converted to 750 ml bottles and price is expressed as dollars per bottle. This measure of price will change if either the prices of wine products change or the distribution of wine purchases at various price points change. For instance, the average price of wine will decrease if the prices of all wine products remain unchanged, but consumers purchase more lower-priced and fewer higher-priced products.

During this twenty-year period, the nominal price of wine increased in sixteen years and fell in only four. In 2010, the average price of a bottle of wine at $7.58 was 64 percent higher than in 1991, when consumers paid $4.63. However, we would like to know whether wine prices have been rising more or less rapidly than the prices of other goods and services in general, and the prices of alcoholic beverages in particular. Column 3 of Table 3 reports a measure of the real price of wine expressed in year 2010 dollars, which adjusts the nominal price for changes in the average level of prices of goods and services using the all-item consumer price index (CPI). The real price of wine rose in ten and declined in ten years. After adjusting for inflation, the price of wine increased by a mere 2.2 percent over this twenty-year period, indicating that almost all of the increase in nominal price can be attributed to inflation. Moreover, it is generally recognized that significant improvements were made in wine quality during this period, so one may easily argue that after adjusting for the higher quality of wine products, wine has become a "better bargain" relative to many other goods and services.

For many consumers, beer and spirits substitute for wine. When the price of wine changes relative to the price of these substitute alcoholic beverages, some consumers are induced to purchase more of the beverage whose price is relatively lower and less of the one whose price is comparatively higher. Column 4 reports a measure of the price of wine relative to the prices of all alcoholic beverages using the alcoholic beverage component of the CPI. Once again this relative price is in 2010 dollars. The behavior of relative price shows that the price of wine increased relative to the price of all alcoholic beverages in thirteen years and decreased in seven. By 2010, the price of wine was 5 percent higher than prices of other alcohol beverages relative to 1991. Once again, one can argue that consumers were more than compensated for this rather small increase in relative price because of the bigger improvement in wine quality compared to beverages like beer and spirits.

The thousands of wine products brought to the market each year vary in quality and are sold at a wide variety of prices. Because wine products range in price from $2.00 to more than $2,000 a bottle, the behavior of average price fails to tell the entire price story. Table 4 presents data on the market shares of wine products purchased from off-premises retailers for six different price segments for several time periods. Off-premises retailers, such as grocery and liquor stores, account for about 80 percent of the wine sold at retail establishments; the residual 20 percent is purchased primarily at restaurants and bars. Price is measured as dollars per 750 ml bottle or equivalent. Wine products priced below $3 a bottle are usually referred to as value or jug wines. Most of these are generic wines without varietal labels sold in containers larger than 750 ml. Wines in the $3 to $6 range are often called "fighting varietals." These are low-priced varietal wines, such as Chardonnay and Merlot, made from grapes grown in high-yield vineyards, often from the Central Valley of California. Producers of these wine products attempt to mimic higher-priced varietal wines by using modern winemaking techniques, such as oak alternatives. Wine products priced above $6 are typically considered premium wines. This segment spans a relatively large range of prices from lower- to higher-end premium products. At the top of the price point scale are the luxury wines. These wines are typically made from low-yield, high-quality grapes, often from a single vineyard, and employ relatively high cost winemaking techniques like oak barrel maturation.

Columns 2 and 3 of table 4 report market shares by wine quantity for six price segments for two one-year periods: November 2005–November 2006 and July 2007–July 2008. The quantity of wine purchased falls at higher price points. For example, the fighting varietals priced between $3 and $6 account for about 30 percent of the off-premises market; the mid-priced $6 to $9 premium wines have about 19 percent of the market; the high-end premium and luxury wines priced above $15 have a relatively small market share of around 3 percent. During this three-year period, premium and luxury wines priced above $12 gained market share, while the market share of value wines below $3 declined. This phenomenon of substituting higher-priced wines for lower-priced wines is called "trading-up" in the wine industry. It is interesting to note that trading-up occurred even though real disposable income was falling, suggesting the possibility of a shift in tastes and preferences toward higher-quality wine products during this period. Columns 4 through 6 report market shares based on the dollar value of sales. Like quantity, fighting varietals also have the largest market share of sales accounting for almost 30 percent of off-premise wine expenditures in the most recent period. Sales shares tend to fall at higher price points with the exception of wines priced below $3.00. While these value wines account for about 30 percent of the quantity of wine sold, they generate less than 10 percent of the dollar value of sales. The sales-share data suggest that trading down occurred during 2009–10 as consumers spent more on fighting varietals and less on higher-end premium and luxury wines. This trading-down behavior occurred during a period of severe economic downturn with high unemployment and falling housing prices.

TABLE 4   MARKET SHARE BY PRICE SEGMENT

Price Segment ($$ per 750 ml bottle or equivalent)	Quantity Shares (%)		Sales Shares (%)		
	Nov. 2005– Nov. 2006	July 2007– July 2008	Nov. 2005– Nov. 2006	July 2007– July 2008	Oct. 2009– Oct. 2010
< $3	32.4	29.8	12.0	10.6	8.6
$3–$5.99	30.7	31.5	25.1	24.7	29.3
$6–$8.99	19.4	19.3	24.6	23.0	20.6
$9–$11.99	11.2	11.0	19.9	19.2	20.4
$12–$14.99	3.1	4.9	7.3	10.9	10.0
≥ $15	3.1	3.4	10.8	11.5	11.0

SOURCES: Nielson Company data from Tinney 2007 and 2008b; "Off Premise Wine Sales Increase in October," *Wine Business Monthly*, January 2011.

Types of Wine Products Consumed

The five largest selling varietal wines in the United States are Chardonnay, Cabernet Sauvignon, Merlot, Pinot grigio/gris, and Pinot noir. Together they accounted for 51 percent of the dollar value of wine sales in off-premises retail stores between March 2011–12. Of these, Chardonnay and Cabernet Sauvignon are easily the two most important, with market shares of 21 and 15 percent respectively. To satisfy consumer tastes and preferences and generate adequate cash flow, the vast majority of wine firms include one or both of these in their product line. Consumers spend 13 percent more on red wine than white wine, and eight times more on varietal than generic wine. Imported wine accounts for 28 percent of retail store wine sales, with Italian wine the most popular (8.5 percent) followed by Australian (7.5 percent), Argentinian (2.5 percent), Chilean (2.4 percent), and French (2.3 percent).[4]

FACTORS AFFECTING WINE CONSUMPTION

The economic theory of consumer choice presented in chapter 1 implies that the amount of wine a typical individual is willing and able to purchase depends upon the price of wine, income, prices of goods related to wine, and tastes and preferences. The remainder of this chapter provides a detailed discussion of these factors and summarizes results from empirical studies that attempt to quantify and test their effects on wine consumption.

The Price of Wine

The price of wine is an important factor affecting wine consumption. The relationship between the quantity demanded and price of wine is illustrated graphically by a demand curve, such as the one in figure 1 in chapter 1, and represents either an individual's demand for wine or the aggregate demand of all consumers collectively in a wine market. The negative slope of the demand curve reflects the law of demand. This is the commonsense notion that at lower prices, people want to buy more wine, and at higher prices, less, if other factors affecting wine demand such as tastes and preferences, income, prices of related goods, and wine quality remain unchanged. It also follows logically from rational decision making and the law of diminishing marginal utility. This section focuses on demand curves that aggregate over consumers. An aggregate demand curve exists for a single wine, such as Kendall-Jackson Chardonnay, or for a collection of wine products. The collection can be a particular wine brand composed of multiple products, red-wine products, white-wine products, varietal products, imported wine products, and other possibilities. Each of these can be viewed as a market demand curve for a different segment of the wine market. The highest level of aggregation is a demand curve for the entire wine market encompassing all wine products. It should be noted that at levels of aggregation above a single wine product, the notion of a demand curve becomes less precise, because it represents a collection of differentiated products, and the market price is an average of the product prices.

A common argument is that wine is different from a typical good or service, and that many individuals therefore violate the law of demand when making consumption decisions. Some individuals fail to respond to price changes because of brand loyalty and habitual behavior. Others, often referred to as wine snobs, derive more utility from the prestige a wine confers than from the enjoyment they get from actually drinking it. A prestigious wine is valued primarily because it is scarce and drunk by relatively few consumers. An increase in supply that reduces price and increases availability lowers the prestige value of the wine, and a wine snob will therefore buy less at the lower price. Alternatively, a higher price that reflects greater scarcity and lower consumption by others induces a wine snob to buy more. There are also other individuals in addition to wine snobs who engage in conspicuous wine consumption. These derive utility from the impression a wine makes on others about their economic or social standing. Because the price of a wine product conveys their socioeconomic status, the utility they derive from it depends on both its sensory characteristics and the price they pay for it. A higher price may induce these people to buy more, and a lower price, less. Finally, several studies suggest that many wine consumers use price to assess the quality of a wine. As a result, it is possible that some of these consumers will be induced to buy more at a higher price, and less at a lower price, even if the inherent quality of the wine, as reflected by its sensory characteristics, is unchanged.

The law of demand may be observed for a collection of consumers in a wine market even if this market includes individuals who are brand-loyal, wine snobs, habitual consumers, conspicuous consumers, or equate price with quality. First, consider the case of a market with unresponsive consumers. For example, suppose the market for Turning Leaf Chardonnay has a core of brand-loyal and habitual consumers, many of whom drink a glass each evening with dinner. It also has a fringe of consumers without these traits. If Gallo lowers its price, these core consumers may choose not to purchase more; however, some individuals currently drinking other wines or alcoholic beverages may enter the Turning Leaf market and buy this wine. In like manner, if Gallo raises its price, many habitual, loyal Turning Leaf drinkers may maintain their current consumption, but those fringe consumers who are less enthusiastic about this brand, or wine in general, may exit the Turning Leaf market and purchase a substitute wine, or beer, or spirits. At the market level, therefore, the law of demand may be largely a manifestation of new wine consumers entering as price falls and the less loyal consumers exiting as price rises.

As a second possibility, consider the market for a luxury wine like Screaming Eagle. Suppose some consumers in this market behave as wine snobs and others do not. If price falls, existing non-snobs may be inclined to consume more, new non-snobs will enter the market, and total consumption will rise. Increased consumption reduces the prestige value of Screaming Eagle for wine snobs, so some will leave the market. As they exit total consumption falls. However, the negative snob effect on total consumption must be smaller than the positive non-snob effect, and the market demand curve for Screaming Eagle will therefore be downward-sloping. If not, a reduction in price would result in a decrease in total consumption, which would increase prestige and induce wine snobs to purchase more.

Lastly, consider a wine market with conspicuous consumers or individuals who judge wine quality solely on the basis of price. If a sufficiently large number of these consumers exist in the market, then the aggregate demand curve for the wine or collection of wines may be upward-sloping. In this case, consumption would rise as price rises, at least up to some point. While theoretically possible, this violation of the law of demand seems unlikely, with the possible exception of a few very high-end luxury wines.[5]

Surveys of wine consumers and empirical studies of the wine market provide evidence in support of the law of demand. A 2006 survey by the Wine Market Council reported that more than 20 percent of wine consumers would drink wine more often at a lower price. More than 30 percent would consume more wine in restaurants if prices were reduced. Empirical studies consistently find that the demand curve for individual wines, different segments of the wine market, and the entire wine market slope downward. The following section discusses some of the findings of these empirical studies and their implications.

Empirical Studies

Empirical studies of the effect of price on wine consumption typically address three questions. First, does price have an effect on the amount of wine consumed? If it does, this is necessary but not sufficient evidence in support of the law of demand. Second, what is the direction of the effect? Does wine consumption rise or fall at higher prices? Verification of the law of demand requires evidence of a negative relationship between price and consumption. Third, what is the size of the effect? How responsive are consumers to a price change? Do consumers respond by altering their wine consumption by a relatively small or large amount?

To isolate the effect of price on wine consumption and draw valid conclusions, empirical studies use statistical methods to account for confounding factors, reverse causation, and chance. Failure to account for these potential problems, if they exist, may invalidate the conclusions of a study. A confounding factor is a variable that affects wine consumption and is correlated with wine price. For example, income is likely to influence the quantity of wine consumed. Suppose consumers with higher incomes tend to live in locations with higher wine prices than those with lower incomes. If income is not statistically controlled, then the estimate of the effect of price on wine consumption may also include the effect of income. Because these two effects are "confounded," it is difficult to draw conclusions about the impact of wine price alone. Reverse causation occurs if price affects wine consumption and wine consumption affects price. Failure to control for the latter effect will result in a biased estimate of the effect of price on wine consumption, since this estimate will capture both the direct and reverse effects. At the market level, reverse causation is always a potential problem, because price and quantity consumed are determined simultaneously by the interaction of market demand and supply. Lastly, the effect of price on wine consumption observed in a sample of wine consumers may be either a real effect or a fluke that results from chance. To account for chance, most studies report a statistic called a p-value. The p-value is the probability that the observed effect is due to chance. For example, if the estimate of the effect of price on wine consumption has a p-value of 0.10, this indicates a 10 percent likelihood that the effect observed in the sample is the result of chance, and a 90 percent likelihood that it is a real effect. The smaller the p-value, the stronger the evidence that an observed effect is real and not a fluke.

To measure the size of the effect of price on wine consumption, most economic studies use the concept of price elasticity of demand. This is defined as the ratio of the percentage change in quantity of wine demanded to the percentage change in price. Because the changes in wine consumption and price are percentages, it is a unit-free measure of size. The estimate of price elasticity will be the same regardless of whether wine consumption is measured in gallons, bottles, cases, or any other meaningful unit. Moreover, a direct comparison can be made between the magnitudes of elasticity estimates of different wine products, wine and beer, wine and spirits, or wine and any other good or service, and determine for which good price has the biggest effect on consumers' buying decisions. An elasticity of one serves as a useful benchmark. If the absolute value of price elasticity of wine is greater (less) than one, and the proportional change in consumption is therefore greater (less) than the proportional change in price, the demand for wine is elastic (inelastic) and consumers' buying decisions are relatively responsive (unresponsive) to price changes. If the proportional change in the quantity consumed is equal to the proportional change in price, demand is unit-elastic and equal to one.

More than one hundred studies have analyzed the aggregate demand for alcoholic beverages in a wide variety of countries. These studies focus on the national market for wine, beer, and spirits. Wine consumption is typically measured as the quantity consumed per capita and encompasses the thousands of differentiated wine products purchased by consumers. An index of wine prices is used to measure the average price of wine. Together, these studies provide strong evidence in support of the law of demand for the aggregate consumption of alcoholic beverages in general and wine in particular. For the United States, studies report a wide range of price-elasticity estimates for wine, with an average estimate of -0.55. This indicates that a 10 percent reduction in the average price of wine products would increase consumption by 5.5 percent. The comparable estimates for beer and spirits are -0.52 and -0.60.[6] These estimates suggest that consumers' buying decisions are least responsive to changes in the price of beer and most sensitive for spirits. U.S. consumers tend to be somewhat more responsive to wine prices than consumers in other countries. The average elasticity estimate for eighteen other wine-consuming nations is -0.48.

The most important determinant of price elasticity is availability of close substitute products. If consumers can easily substitute another desirable beverage for wine—possibly beer, spirits, soda, or bottled water—then an increase in the price of wine will provide an incentive for them to switch and consume more of this other beverage in its place. The elasticity estimates suggest that for a typical consumer, beer has fewer desirable substitutes than wine, and spirits more. Another potentially important determinant of elasticity is the amount of time consumers have to adjust to a price change. Many may be in the habit of consuming wine, possibly as part of their lifestyles. A sharp rise in wine prices may have relatively little effect on their wine consumption in the short run. However, over time, they may decide to sample other beverages, such as beer and spirits, and eventually develop a taste for them. As a result, the longer these higher wine prices persist, the more willing they are to substitute other beverages for wine. Tsolakis, Riethmuller, and Watts (1983), a study using aggregate data for Australian wine consumers, estimated short-run and long-run price elasticities for wine in Australia and concluded that the demand for wine was inelastic in the short run, but elastic in the long run: the long-run elasticity estimate of -1.35 was more than three times as large as the short-run estimate of -0.43. The extent to which this behavior generalizes to U.S. wine consumers is unknown.

While a large number of studies have estimated the effect of price on wine consumption for the general U.S. wine market, relatively few have provided estimates for different segments of the market or individual wine products. A study by Stephen Cuellar and Ryan Huffman (2008) focuses on the off-premises retail segment and analyzes the behavior of consumers that purchase wine products from establishments such as grocery stores and wine shops. This excludes wine purchased at restaurants and bars, and directly from wine firms at tasting rooms, wine clubs, and over the Internet. In addition, they analyze consumer behavior in different segments of the off-premises market, including red, white, and varietal wines, as well as various price categories.

Cuellar and Huffman conclude that the demand for all types of off-premises retail wine products is elastic, with a price elasticity estimate of −1.23. This suggests that the demand for off-premises wine products is more elastic than overall wine demand, for which price elasticity is −0.55. We would expect consumers' buying decisions to be more sensitive to changes in the prices of off-premises retail wine products, since there are more available close substitutes than for all wine products in general. If the prices of off-premises products increase, consumers can switch to products sold directly by wine firms and those available at restaurants and bars. To avoid an increase in the prices of all wine products, consumers would have to switch to beer, spirits, or nonalcoholic beverages, which many may view as poor substitutes.

Within the off-premises segment of the market, consumers are more responsive to changes in the prices of red wines than those of white wines. The demand for white wine is approximately unit elastic; the elasticity estimate for red wine is −1.23. Within each of these color segments, consumers are more price-responsive to changes in higher- than lower-priced red wines, but the opposite is true for white wines. A 10 percent increase in wine priced above $10 results in a 11.5 percent decrease in quantity demanded of reds; for whites, the quantity purchase falls by only 6.9 percent. For wine priced under $10, consumers are equally responsive to the prices of red and white wines, with an elasticity of about −1.10. One possible explanation is that consumers believe that there are fewer available close substitutes for higher-priced, higher-quality white wines than red wines. Alternatively, the average price of reds above $10 may be significantly higher than that of whites, and therefore absorb a larger fraction of consumer income. For example, suppose the average price of higher-end red wine is $40 per bottle, but only $25 for white wine. A 10 percent price increase in the former of $4 takes a larger fraction of income than a $2.50 increase in the latter. Because a given percentage increase in higher-priced whites results is a smaller income drain than reds, consumers are less sensitive to changes in white-wine prices.

Lastly, Cuellar and Huffman disaggregate the off-premises sector of the wine market into varietal segments and analyze the individual demands for six red and six white wines: Cabernet Sauvignon, Merlot, Pinot noir, Syrah, Zinfandel, Malbec, Chardonnay, Sauvignon blanc, Pinot grigio, Riesling, Chenin blanc, and White Zinfandel. All varietal products have downward-sloping demand curves, with estimated elasticities between -0.49 and -2.56. Once again this confirms the general applicability of the law of demand. Demand is elastic for ten of the twelve varietal products. Consumers are least responsive to price changes for Malbec and White Zinfandel, with elasticity estimates less than 1; they are most responsive for Chenin blanc and Riesling with estimates exceeding 2. Price elasticity of demand for the two most popular varietals, Chardonnay and Cabernet Sauvignon, are very similar. A 10 percent increase in price results in a 11 percent reduction in the quantity of Cabernet Sauvignon consumed and a somewhat larger 11.4 percent reduction in Chardonnay.

In another study, Cuellar, Lucey, and Ammen (2006) use data on off-premises retail sales to analyze the demand for a representative fighting varietal wine product: Gallo Turning Leaf Merlot. They report a price elasticity estimate of -5.7, indicating that a 10 percent increase in price will reduce quantity consumed by 57 percent. It is instructive to note that price elasticity for this individual red wine is more than five times larger than the elasticity for all reds priced at $10 or less. This is easily explained by availability of a large number of close substitutes. There are numerous substitutes for Turning Leaf Merlot in the low-price segment of the red wine market. These include Yellow Tail, Woodbridge, Bogel, Smoking Loon, Red Diamond, and Pepper Grove Merlot, as well as many more. Even a small increase in the price of Turning Leaf Merlot will induce large numbers of consumers to switch to a relatively less expensive substitute.

The Implications of Price-Elasticity Estimates

An important relationship exists between the price elasticity of demand for wine and consumer expenditures on wine. An understanding of this relationship is particularly useful for wine firms; consumers' wine expenditures are wine firms' sales receipts. If consumers' buying decisions are quite responsive to a price change, and demand is thus elastic, a price reduction will result in an increase in consumer spending on wine and more revenue for wine firms. This is because the revenue loss from the lower price is more than offset by the revenue gain from proportionately more bottles sold. However, if demand is inelastic, a reduction in price will result in a decrease in consumer spending and wine-firm revenue. In this case, when consumers' buying decisions are not very sensitive to a price change, the revenue gain from selling relatively few additional bottles is more than offset by the revenue loss from the lower price per bottle. On the other hand, if the price increases, expenditures and revenue fall when demand is elastic and rise when demand is inelastic.[7]

Cuellar and Huffman (2008) estimate that the price elasticity of demand for all types of off-premises retail wine products is −1.23. This implies that a 10 percent decrease in the price of wines sold in grocery and liquor stores will result in a 12.3 percent increase in the number of bottles sold, and therefore an increase in wine-firm revenue. This is indeed true if wine firms can sell their products directly to consumers at the retail price. However, wine firms in the aggregate sell about 90 percent of their wine to distributors at the wholesale price. Distributors then resell this wine to retailers, who receive the retail price. The price elasticity of demand for a product that a wine firm distributes through the three-tier channel may differ from the elasticity for the same product when sold at the retail level. To see why this is, consider the following example. Suppose a wine firm sells a product at a wholesale price of $10. After distributor and retailer markups, this wine is sold in off-premises retail establishments at a price of $20. Now, suppose the wine firm reduces the wholesale price by $1 to $9, and as a result retailers lower the retail price by $1 to $19. The 10 percent reduction in wholesale price lowers the retail price by only 5 percent. Given the retail price elasticity of −1.23, consumers will respond to the 5 percent reduction in retail price by purchasing 6.15 percent more. As a result, the wholesale price elasticity is 0.615. Even though demand is elastic at the retail level, it is inelastic from the perspective of the wine firm. As a general rule, the retail elasticity will be an accurate measure of the firm-level elasticity only if the distributor and retail margin as a percentage of the retail price is invariant to changes in the wine firm's wholesale price. If this margin increases when the wholesale price changes, as in this example, then the demand curve for wine at the firm level will be less elastic than at the retail level. The opposite will be true if the distributor and retail margin declines.

If the objective of a wine firm is to maximize profit and the demand for its wine is inelastic, it will be motivated to charge a higher price. By increasing price, it will generate more revenue, even though consumers purchase fewer bottles of wine. Because it has to produce less wine to satisfy the lower level of consumption, its production cost will fall at the same time as revenue rises. However, at higher prices, consumers typically become increasingly responsive to additional price hikes, and eventually demand will become elastic.[8] At this point, further price increases reduce both revenue and cost, and profit will therefore rise only if the revenue loss is less than the reduction in cost. This suggests that a profit-maximizing wine firm will prefer to operate in the elastic portion of its demand curve. Cuellar and Huffman estimate that the demand for Malbec and White Zinfandel are inelastic. This implies that producers of these two varietal wines could generate greater profits by raising prices. However, most Malbec sold in the United States is imported from Argentina. It may be that Argentinian producers are pricing their products at less than the market would bear to gain a foothold in the U.S. market. Most White Zinfandel is sold at a price below $10 in a segment of the market where a number of producers offer similar White Zinfandel products. While the demand for White Zinfandel as a whole is inelastic, the demand for the product of each producer is likely highly elastic. Short of colluding to set price, wine firms in this competitive segment of the market have little incentive to raise prices, since by doing so they might lose large numbers of consumers of their products to competitors.

Finally, if U.S. consumers tend to adjust their wine purchases slowly in response to changes in wine prices, as Tsolakis, Riethmuller, and Watts (1983) found for Australian consumers, demand may be inelastic in the short run and elastic in the long run. This implies that a strategy of short-term price discounting by wine firms to stimulate sales during an economic downturn may actually reduce both revenue and profit. Revenue will rise only if these price reductions are allowed to persist for a sufficiently long period of time for consumers to adjust their wine consumption behavior.

Income

A second important factor affecting wine consumption is income. Income determines an individual's ability to purchase wine products. Consumers with higher incomes are able to buy more and higher-quality wine products if they so choose. The manner in which wine-buying decisions respond to a change in income depends upon the nature of the wine and consumers' preference for it; this determines whether an economist classifies it as a normal or inferior good.

To illustrate the distinction between a normal and an inferior good, and how a consumer may respond to a change in income, consider the following example. Suppose that over the course of a year, Joe Oenophile consumes a mix of commodity, premium, and luxury wine products.

Now, assume that his income increases, and that as a result, he buys more premium and luxury wine. Economists call these types of wines normal goods: as Joe's income rises, he is willing and able to buy more, and as his income falls, less. For a normal wine product, Joe's demand curve shifts to the right when his income increases: at the prevailing price of wine, whatever it is, Joe wants to purchase more. When Joe's income decreases, his demand curve shifts to the left, and he demands less at any given price. However, the responsiveness of Joe's buying decisions may differ for different normal wine products. For example, suppose that prior to the rise in income, he purchased eight bottles of premium and two bottles of luxury wine per year. He enjoys both types of wine, but each is subject to the law of diminishing marginal utility: the more he consumes during the year, the less utility he derives from each additional bottle. Because he consumes only two bottles of the luxury wine, he gets a relatively large amount of satisfaction from the consumption of an additional bottle. Also, given its high quality, the marginal utility of the luxury wine declines slowly as his annual consumption increases. An additional bottle of the premium wine yields him less utility, since he already consumes eight bottles per year, and declines more quickly as the number of bottles purchased increases. Because of these differences in the marginal utility of the two products, after Joe's income rises, he will purchase more additional bottles of the luxury wine than the premium wine.

Suppose that after his income rises, Joe responds by buying less commodity wine. Economists call this an inferior good. At a higher level of income, Joe is able to buy more but willing to buy less, and his demand therefore decreases. Conversely, when Joe's income falls, he is able to buy less but willing to buy more and his demand increases. Why would having a greater ability to buy a good induce a consumer like Joe to purchase less? Suppose that before he experienced the increase in income, the bulk of his annual wine consumption, say twenty bottles, was low-priced commodity wine. He would have much preferred to consume more premium and luxury wine but could not afford to do so. With a higher level of income, he is now able to replace some of the lower-quality wine with wine of higher quality.

Because goods can be either normal or inferior, there does not exist a "law of demand" for the relationship between income and the quantity of wine consumed. An increase in income may result in either an increase or decrease in the demand for a wine depending upon whether consumers perceive it as normal or inferior. The concept of an inferior good provides one possible explanation of the much discussed phenomenon of "trading up" and "trading down" in the wine market. In periods of rapid income growth, such as the late 1990s and the period from 2002 to 2007, trading-up occurs as the demand for higher-end premium and luxury wines rises and the demand for lower-end premium and commodity wines falls. In periods of falling income, such as 2008–9, trading down occurs as consumers substitute lower-priced commodity and premium wines for those at higher price points. This suggests that many consumers view generic wines and "fighting varietals" as inferior goods. They are not inferior because their absolute level of quality is low, but only because consumers prefer to consume less when they have more money to spend and more when they have less to spend.

Empirical Studies and Implications

To measure the size of the effect of income on wine consumption, most economic studies use the concept of income elasticity of demand.[9] The income elasticity of total wine demand has important implications for the wine industry. Long-term income growth of the economy potentially affects the total amount and composition of wine products consumed in the United States. Rising per capita income enables consumers to buy more and higher-quality wine. A total income elasticity close to zero would suggest either that there is little difference in wine consumption across the income distribution of consumers or that the vast majority of consumers respond to rising income by substituting higher- for lower-quality wine products, with little net effect on overall consumption. A relatively large positive income elasticity indicates that rising income lifts total wine consumption, as well as possibly altering the composition of products purchased. A total income elasticity of less than zero has several alternative interpretations. It may indicate that wine is an inferior good for a typical individual; as income rises, a preponderance of consumers switch to other alcoholic or nonalcoholic beverages, which now become increasingly affordable. However, a more plausible interpretation may be that as income rises, a typical consumer drinks less wine, but wine of higher quality.

A total income elasticity of demand of greater than one implies that consumers spend a rising proportion of their incomes on wine as the economy expands, and therefore that the wine industry may well prosper with economic growth in the long run. However, it also suggests that economic recessions may have a relatively large negative impact on wine sales and profits as consumers respond to lower incomes in periods of economic contraction by sharply cutting back on wine consumption. Alternatively, an income elasticity of less than one suggests that the wine industry is less affected by the business cycle, but may have poor prospects for future growth. Of course, it is possible that the effect of income growth or decline could be offset by changes in wine prices, prices of other goods, and consumer tastes and preferences. It should be kept in mind that most studies use statistical methods to control for these influences, and therefore measure the change in wine consumption that results from a change in income, holding other factors constant.

Of the twenty-three studies undertaken to estimate the income elasticity of total U.S. wine demand, only one concludes that wine is an inferior good with an income elasticity of –0.58. Twelve studies find evidence that the demand for wine is income-elastic; eleven produce income-inelastic estimates. The average elasticity estimate of all twenty-three studies is 1.30, suggesting that the demand for wine is income elastic and that in the aggregate, consumers' wine-buying decisions are quite responsive to changes in income and the business cycle. This is considerably larger than the average income elasticity estimate for beer and spirits of 0.45 and 0.87 and of 0.84 for the wine consumption of fifteen other countries.[10] An income-elastic total demand for wine seems at odds with the prior observation that over the past sixty years, per capita wine consumption has been largely impervious to economic recessions, falling in only two of the ten downturns when aggregate output and income declined. A possible explanation for this is that the reduction in consumption resulting from falling income was countervailed by lower wine prices and a trend toward a stronger preference for wine. For instance, per capita wine consumption fell in the recession of 1953–54, in a decade when wine consumption was flat, and again in 1990–91, during a period when wine consumption had been trending down for the prior five years. It may be that during these recessions, the decrease in consumption resulting from declining income was not offset, and that in the recession of 1990–91, it was reinforced by an ongoing shift in preferences away from wine. During the other ten recessions, wine consumption was either flat or increased. These downturns occurred during periods when per capita consumption was trending up, possibly in large part because of more favorable preferences for wine. Moreover, during the recession of 2007–09, wine prices fell dramatically in both nominal and real terms, and relative to other alcoholic beverages. This may have helped to stem the fall in wine consumption.

Estimates of income elasticity of demand for different segments of the U.S. wine market and individual wine products are scant. One of the few studies to produce such estimates is the one by Cuellar and Huffman (2008) discussed previously, which analyzed wine demand for a number of different segments of the off-premises retail wine market. Its estimated income elasticity of 1.51 for all off-premises wine products indicates that a 10 percent increase in income will result in a 15.1 percent increase in demand for wine sold in grocery stores and wine shops. Products in the red, white, and all but one varietal segments of the off-premises market are normal goods, but income-elasticity estimates vary widely in size.[11] For example, the estimate for white wine products of 2.35 is more than two times larger than the 0.89 estimate for reds. This suggests that the demand for whites is much more sensitive to cyclical ups and downs in economic activity than that for reds. Estimates of different price segments suggest this difference is largely explained by a low income elasticity of demand for red wines priced below $10. Income-elasticity estimates for varietal products vary from −0.43 for Merlot to 4.99 for Pinot noir. However, most of the estimates for varietals, including the negative income-elasticity estimate for Merlot, identifying it as an inferior good, are imprecisely measured, so it is difficult to draw conclusions with an acceptable degree of confidence.

Cuellar, Lucey, and Ammen (2006) reports elasticity estimates for two individual wine products: Turning Leaf Merlot, a lower-priced fighting varietal wine, and Sterling Merlot, a higher-priced premium wine. The estimate of −3.57 indicates that Turning Leaf is an inferior good: a 10 percent increase in income will induce a 35.7 percent decrease in quantity consumed. However, Sterling Merlot is a normal good, with an income elasticity of 1.76, indicating that a 10 percent increase in income will result in a 17.6 percent rise in consumption.

The Prices of Goods Related to Wine

Related goods are products that tend to be consumed either together or in place of one another. If an individual is inclined to consume wine with another product, such as steak, then the two are called *complementary goods* or *complements*. On the other hand, if an individual is willing to replace the consumption of wine with another product, such as beer, then the two are *substitute goods* or *substitutes*.

The price of goods related to wine is an important factor affecting wine consumption. An increase in the price of a complementary good such as steak induces an individual to consume less steak and less wine. This is because he or she prefers to drink wine when eating steak and consumes less steak at the higher price. This increase in the price of a complementary good is illustrated by a leftward shift of the demand curve as demand for wine decreases. An increase in the price of a substitute good, such as beer, provides an economic incentive for an individual to drink less beer and more wine. This is because he or she enjoys both of these beverages and is willing to consume more wine at the relatively lower price. As a result, the demand curve shifts to the right, and demand for wine increases. The opposite will occur when the price of a complementary or substitute good falls.

When analyzing the demand for wine, it is important to understand that the particular goods an individual perceives as substitutes and complements for wine depend upon his or her subjective tastes and preferences and may differ for different consumers. At the market level, substitutes and complements are determined by consumers' buying decisions in the aggregate and apply to an average or typical wine consumer in the market. A good example of this is the relationship between wine and food. A common practice of professional wine writers is to mandate a web of rules that define which wine goes with which food. Cabernet Sauvignon, it is said, can only be consumed with beef, never with fish. Chardonnay is permissible with fish, seafood, and poultry, with the exception of oily fish. And the list goes on. These rules would seem to suggest, for example, that red wine and beef are complements and red wine and fish are unrelated. From an economic perspective, this is true only if it is consistent with the choices made by an average consumer in the marketplace. If a carefully performed empirical study finds that the demand for red wine increases when the price of fish falls, all else being equal, an economist would conclude that red wine and fish are complementary goods, regardless of how appalling this may be to wine professionals. Some prominent members of the wine community have in fact argued that esoteric "wine rules" such as these have adversely affected consumers' preferences and demand for wine. The late Robert Mondovi, wine proprietor extraordinaire, once stated that when inundated with all of these rules a typical consumer says, "to hell with it; give me a beer, a scotch, a cup of coffee."[12]

Empirical Studies and Implications

To determine whether a particular good is related to wine, and if so the size of the effect of the price of the good on wine consumption, economic studies use the concept of cross-price elasticity of demand.[13]

Cross-price elasticity of demand provides important information to wine firms. If two wines sold by different firms have a positive cross-price elasticity, then consumers view them as substitutes, and they therefore compete in the marketplace. The larger the cross-price elasticity, the greater the competition. If the two wines have a low cross-price elasticity, a firm has a greater ability to raise its price without losing many customers to its competitor. Conversely, a high-cross price elasticity informs a firm that even a relatively small price increase will induce a large number of its customers to switch to the other firm's wine. Cross-price elasticity of demand, therefore, provides valuable information to a wine firm about the market in which it sells its wine and is a valuable tool in making pricing decisions.

Relatively few studies have been performed to estimate cross-price elasticities between wine and other products. Most of these focus on the total demand for wine, beer, and spirits, and use data on countries other than the United States. The results of these studies are mixed; some conclude that beer and spirits are a substitute for wine; others find evidence of a complementary relationship; still others suggest wine consumption is unrelated to that of beer or spirits. A study of U.S. consumers by Dale Heien and Greg Pompelli (1989) estimating cross-price elasticities for wine and other beverages found wine, beer, and spirits to be complementary, and wine, soft drinks, and juice to be substitutes. The sizes of the estimates are relatively small, suggesting that these beverages are weak complements and substitutes for wine. For example, the cross-price elasticity of wine and beer is –0.21. This implies that a 10 percent decrease in the price of beer results in a 2.1 percent increase in wine consumption. The estimate for wine and soda of 0.02 indicates that a 10 percent decrease in the price of soda will decrease wine consumption by a mere 0.2 percent. Heien and Pompelli conclude that the complementary relationship between wine, beer, and spirits can be explained by the effect of a change in the prices of these beverages on consumer real income. To elaborate, suppose that during the course of a month, Joe Oenophile consumes a certain amount of wine and beer. Given his preferences, he views wine and beer as beverages that can be consumed in place of each other. Assume that the price of beer decreases. Beer is now relatively less expensive than wine, so Joe is willing to drink more beer and less wine. However, the reduction in the price of beer gives Joe the ability to buy more of both beverages. This is because the purchasing power of his monthly income is higher, since he now pays a lower price for the beer he consumes. Assuming that beer and wine are normal goods, he is willing to buy more of each. If the income effect of the fall in the price of beer on Joe's buying decisions is greater than the price effect that makes wine relatively more expensive, he will purchase more wine and beer, even though he does not prefer to consume the two together.

A study by Steven Buccola and Loren VanderZanden (1997) analyzed the demand for wine sold in retail stores in Portland, Oregon. Wine products were aggregated into four separate groups according to the region where the wines were produced: Oregon reds, California reds, Oregon whites, and California whites.[14] The researchers were interested in whether a typical consumer in Portland views these types of wine products as substitutes or complements, and how strongly they are related. They conclude that Oregon and California reds are substitutes, and Oregon and California whites are substitutes. The demand for Oregon wines is highly sensitive to a change in the price of California wines. A 10 percent reduction in the price of California reds (whites) decreases the consumption of Oregon reds (whites) by 19.8 (11.9) percent. However, the demand for California wines is much less responsive to a change in the price of Oregon wines. A 10 decrease in the price of Oregon reds (whites) reduces the consumption of California reds (whites) by a much smaller 3.7 (6.5) percent. This suggests that if California wine firms lower prices in the Portland market by say 10 percent, a large number of Portlanders will quickly switch to these wines, and Oregon producers will lose significant market share. To prevent these consumers from switching to California wines, Oregon wine firms would have to respond by reducing the prices of their reds by 53 percent and their whites 18 percent. Conversely, if California producers increase prices, Oregon wine firms can gain substantial market share by keeping their prices constant, because many Portlanders will switch to the relatively lower-priced Oregon Pinot noir, Chardonnay, and Pinot gris to avoid paying relatively higher prices for California wines. Buccola and VanderZanden also find evidence that a typical Portlander views red and white wines as complements. When the price of red wine falls, the consumption of white wine increases. The same is true of red wine consumption when the price of white wine decreases. One possible explanation is that a typical Portlander consumes both red and white wines. The particular wine selected depends upon how well it pairs with the food consumed at a meal.

Cuellar, Lucey, and Ammen (2006) estimates the cross-price elasticity of demand for three Merlots in the fighting varietal segment of the market, Turning Leaf, Woodbridge, and Sutter Home. While all three pairs of these wines have large positive cross-price elasticity estimates, the closest substitutes are Turning Leaf and Woodbridge, with an estimate of 5.76. These estimates provide empirical evidence of the highly competitive nature of the market for fighting varietal wines.

Tastes and Preferences for Wine

The economic theory of consumer choice implies that tastes and preferences are potentially an important factor affecting wine consumption. A favorable change in consumers' preferences for wine will result in an increase in demand and shift the demand curve to the right. An unfavorable alteration in tastes will have the opposite effect. Unfortunately, economic theory provides little guidance on what factors determine tastes and preferences, and why these factors might change. There is no economic theory of preference determination. Economists recognize that individuals' preferences differ and can change over time. However, economic theory typically assumes that preferences are stable during the period of time under consideration. The theory is then used to predict how consumers will respond to changes in prices and income. This permits the economist to attribute a change in consumption to a change in preferences only after a careful consideration of other factors. Playing by these rules minimizes the temptation to rely too heavily on the amorphous notion of tastes to explain changes in consumption. When performing empirical studies of consumer behavior, most economists attempt to account for tastes and preferences either by assuming they are an unobservable random variable or by including variables they believe may be correlated with preferences. This section begins by discussing a number of factors that economists and wine professionals speculate may influence consumers' tastes and preferences for wine. It then discusses the findings of some empirical studies that have attempted to analyze patterns and changes in wine consumption associated with tastes and preferences.

Copious factors may affect consumers' preferences for wine. Most of these fall under one of four general categories: demographic characteristics, knowledge and information, cultural influences, and health considerations. Demographic characteristics include variables such as age, education, gender, race, marital status, occupation, family size and composition, and geographic location. The argument is that these sorts of personal characteristics and social factors help to shape tastes for wine and may explain wine consumption patterns independent of prices and income.

Preferences may also be influenced by wine knowledge and available information. One source of information about wine is advertising. There is an ongoing debate in economics about whether advertising is primarily persuasive or informational. Advertising that provides consumers with information about wine characteristics and prices may reduce their cost of obtaining this information when making buying decisions without altering preferences. Advertising designed to persuade consumers to drink a particular wine product or wine in general may change preferences and shift the wine demand curve. Some industry observers have argued that much of the downward trend in per capita wine consumption that occurred from 1986 to 1995 can be explained by a decrease in wine industry advertising that caused a shift in consumers' preferences towards other beverages. In 1991, the wine industry spent $92 million on advertising. By 1995, this had fallen to $60 million in inflation-adjusted dollars. During this same year, Anheuser-Bush devoted $577 million to advertising its beer products, while Coors spent $205 million. Pepsico spent $1.3 billion on advertising soda, more than twenty times as much as the entire wine industry. Dairy, pork, and egg producers have successfully increased the demand for their products by undertaking industrywide advertising campaigns with slogans like "Got milk?" "the other white meat," and "the incredible edible egg."[15]

Much attention has also been given to the role of wine critics in shaping the preferences of consumers. Most critics use the 100-point rating scale instituted by Robert Parker in the 1980s to evaluate the quality of thousands of different wine products. Some wine professionals maintain that critics' scores provide valuable information to consumers without influencing their preferences. Given the thousands of different wine on the market, consumers cannot typically taste a wine to evaluate its characteristics before making a purchase. As a result, wine critics' scores provide consumers with useful information. Most of their advocates acknowledge that wine scores depend largely upon the subjective tastes of critics, and different critics often assign different scores to the same wine. However, they maintain that consumers learn which critics have preferences similar to their own, and that if they purchase a highly scored wine that does not agree with their taste, they will not buy another bottle. Like the advertising controversy, other wine professionals argue that consumers' preferences are significantly influenced by critics' scores. They contend that many consumers believe that these scores are a better measure of wine quality than their own preferences. Critics, through their scores, essentially teach consumers to enjoy certain wine styles, and by doing so reshape consumers' preferences to match their own tastes. Regardless of whether wine critics' scores affect or reflect consumer's preferences, almost all agree that they have a significant effect on wine demand and the wine industry. Producers, distributors, and retailers use these numbers as an important marketing tool. Many consumers buy wines based on the scores they receive from critics, which are often posted in retail stores and provided on restaurant wine lists. Many retailers report that products receiving a score of 90 points or above are in great demand and sell out quickly; those with a score below 90 quite often suffer the opposite fate. It is argued that wine scores also affect the types of products wine firms produce. The bold, intensely flavored, fruit-forward style favored by a majority of wine firms today is often attributed to Robert Parker, who has a strong preference for this style and rewards wine products that possess these sensory characteristics with high scores.

Wine preferences may also be influenced by a consumer's level of wine education. Many consumers perceive wine as a complex product. Those who are less educated and informed about the intricacies of wine and how it pairs with food may be inclined to purchase less or prefer other beverages, such as beer or spirits, that are less confusing and intimidating. Many argue that the wine industry fostered a mysterious, formal, and elitist image of wine for years, which had a negative effect on demand. However, more recently this has changed, since consumers have become more educated about wine. Knowledgeable consumers, it is argued, have a more favorable preference for wine, leading to increased demand.

Cultural heritage and social tradition have long been recognized as factors influencing wine preferences. In many European nations, drinking wine with meals is a venerable tradition. If more consumers in the United States incorporated this routine into their lifestyles, the resulting shift in preferences would likely have a large impact on wine demand. Popular culture may also influence the taste for wine. After the hit movie *Sideways* disparaged Merlot and extolled Pinot noir, sales of Merlot slowed and Pinot noir rose, particularly for wines costing $20 per bottle or more (it had a relatively small negative effect on the consumption of Merlot priced below $10 per bottle).[16]

In the past, the Wine Market Council, a leading trade organization for the wine industry, has argued that the most important factor affecting wine consumption is consumers' perception of wine's health effects. This conclusion has been supported by Wine Market Council research and anecdotal evidence. In 1991, for example, the widely watched television news show *60 Minutes* aired a segment on the so-called French paradox, looking into why the French have a much lower incidence of heart disease than Americans, even though they consume a high-fat diet, many smoke, and relatively few exercise. Medical research suggested that this might be the result of regular French consumption of red wine, *60 Minutes* asserted, and the show summarized a growing body of evidence of the positive health effects of moderate alcohol consumption. Within the next couple of months, U.S. red wine sales increased by 30 percent.[17] As additional medical studies were published on the positive health effects of wine, demand continued to grow. Many wine industry professionals maintain that a shift in preferences resulting from the perception of wine as a healthful beverage has been a key factor in the inexorable growth of per capita U.S. wine consumption since the early 1990s.

Empirical Studies

Most empirical studies that analyze the effect of factors related to tastes and preferences on wine consumption focus on consumers' demographic characteristics. As stated previously, surveys indicate that a majority of U.S. wine drinkers are highly educated, middle-aged, married professionals. However, this may not necessarily reflect preferences for wine. Individuals with these characteristics also tend to have higher incomes than others. When drawing conclusions about the effect of demographic characteristics on wine demand, empirical studies attempt to control for income and other potential confounding variables. This is necessary to isolate the independent effect of various demographic factors on wine demand that may be related to wine preferences.

The empirical findings for age, marital status, and occupation are consistent with the descriptive characteristics of wine drinkers. Controlling for other factors, married individuals consume more wine than those who are single, widowed, or divorced; the middle-aged consume more wine than those who are younger and older; and professionals consume more wine than non-professionals. The results for education are mixed and inconclusive. This may suggest that individuals with more education tend to consume more wine because of their higher incomes, rather than having a stronger preference for wine than those with less education. These studies also find evidence of greater than average wine consumption by urban white Californians knowledgeable about wine with few or no children.[18]

Wine Quality

The final important factor affecting wine consumption is wine quality. If it is assumed that a rational individual prefers higher-quality to lower-quality wine, the maximum amount he or she is willing to pay for a given quantity of wine will increase with quality. Equivalently, at a given price, the amount of wine purchased will increase with quality. As a result, higher wine quality increases demand and shifts the demand curve to the right; lower wine quality has the opposite effect. Economists have developed a theoretical framework that can be used to analyze and measure quality and its effect on wine demand and prices. This is the topic of chapter 12.

12

The Wine Consumer, Quality, and Price

As discussed in chapter 2, wine quality refers to the bundle of common sensory and nonsensory characteristics that wine products possess. All wines have a particular appearance, smell, and taste that result largely from grape variety, vineyard location, viticultural practices, winemaking techniques, and vintage. Differences in quality result from differences in the amounts of these characteristics embodied in different wines. To assess quality, it is necessary to determine the value consumers place on additional units of wine characteristics. Once the value of these characteristics is measured, they can be related to wine demand and price. The greater the value of characteristics embodied in a wine, the greater the demand for it, and, all else being equal, the higher the price. This chapter focuses on how economists measure the value consumers place on wine characteristics and analyze the effect of those characteristics on wine price.

Hedonic price theory is used to guide quality measurement and analyze the relationship between wine characteristics and price. According to this theory, competitive markets exist for wine qualities.[1] Consumers' preferences determine the demand for these characteristics. Consumers prefer wine that has a better appearance, smell, and taste, but like other goods, these characteristics are subject to the law of diminishing marginal utility. The attributes wine firms supply depend upon the cost of providing products with these characteristics. As discussed in chapters 4 and 6, producing more aromatic and brilliant, better-tasting wine entails higher costs, and cost therefore rises as a larger amount of each of these qualities is incorporated. The bundle of characteristics embodied in a wine and its price are determined by the interaction of supply and demand. The observed market price of a wine depends upon the unobserved implicit prices of each of its characteristics.[2] Each implicit price reflects consumer willingness to pay for an attribute and the cost to the wine firm of providing it. Most studies of wine quality and price focus on the demand side of this market and use statistical methods to measure consumers' marginal willingness to pay for each characteristic. The estimated implicit prices, which reflect consumer's preferences, are then used to analyze the effect of wine characteristics, and therefore quality, on wine price.

THE LOGIC OF CONSUMERS' CHOICE OF WINE QUALITY

Hedonic theory assumes that consumers spend their limited income on wine and other goods in such a way as to maximize utility. The utility a consumer experiences from a wine depends upon the utility derived from each of its sensory characteristics. In selecting for quality, consumers behave as if they are rational and compare the marginal benefit of an additional unit of a sensory characteristic to its marginal cost. They will choose a wine of higher quality as long as the benefit of enjoying more of a particular characteristic, measured by the maximum amount they are willing to pay, exceeds the cost measured by the higher price they have to pay for a wine of higher quality. To maximize utility, a consumer will purchase the wine product for which the amount he or she is willing to pay for an additional unit of each characteristic is equal to the amount an extra unit of that attribute contributes to price. This marginal contribution to the price of a wine product is called the implicit price of a characteristic. Hedonic price theory implies that an implicit price measures the amount consumers are willing to pay for one more unit of an attribute. The more a typical consumer is willing to pay for an extra unit of a characteristic, the higher the implicit price, and therefore the higher the observed market price.

The price a rational consumer is willing to pay for a wine product depends upon subjective evaluation of its appearance, smell, and taste. However, a typical consumer has relatively few opportunities to sample a wine to learn about its sensory characteristics before making a first-time buying decision. Consumers are clearly better informed in making repeat purchases of the same wine, but the appearance, smell, and taste of a wine may nonetheless vary with bottle age, the condition of the closure, and vintage.

Because of this inability to taste a wine before it is purchased and the bottle is uncorked, a typical consumer makes buying decisions under conditions of uncertainty and imperfect information about sensory characteristics. Buying decisions may, of course, be guided by wine experts. To guide buying decisions, he or she may use quality indicators. Publications like the *Wine Advocate, Wine Spectator,* and *Wine Enthusiast* typically provide a description of appearance, smell, and taste, as well as a score that aims to quantify wine quality. Other quality indicators are grape variety and location where it was grown, brand name, and vintage, which are typically given on the label. Grapes grown in more favorable locations, such as Napa Valley, may signal higher-quality grapes and wine. Wine firms located in a particular geographic region may develop a collective reputation, and individual firms and brands a specific reputation, that provides information to consumers about winemaking techniques and wine quality. Vintage informs consumers of a wine's age and possibly about growing-season weather conditions that may affect its sensory characteristics. Finally, recommendations from friends and wine-shop personnel may guide buying decisions, as may the number of cases of a wine produced, and possibly wine price.

When making buying decisions, a rational consumer will continue to gather information from these sources as long as the marginal benefit of additional information exceeds the marginal cost. The benefit is the higher probability of buying a wine with the desired sensory characteristics and quality; the cost is the time and money required to acquire the information. Since information is costly to acquire, a typical consumer has incomplete information when buying wine products; however, because of differences in benefits and costs of information acquisition some consumers will make more informed buying decisions than others. Data obtained from a study called Project Genome sponsored by Constellation Brands, which attempted to measure wine consumers' attitudes suggests that about 40 percent of wine consumers, who account for approximately 30 percent of wine purchases, make wine-buying decisions based on information that is readily available at the point of purchase. The remaining 60 percent of consumers, who purchase most of the wine they drink in retail stores and restaurants, use information obtained from other sources, which may include wine publications, websites, and critics' ratings and reviews.[3]

CLASSIFICATION OF WINE MARKETS AND PURCHASES

In thinking about how wine consumers make buying decisions, it is useful to distinguish between the primary and secondary markets for wine products, and first-time and repeat wine purchases. The primary market is the market for newly released wine products. However, if a consumer believes that a particular wine is age-worthy and may develop a more pleasing aroma and flavor over time, he or she may store it with the intention of consuming it at a much later date or reselling it to someone else. If this previously released wine is sold to another party, this transaction takes place on what is called the *secondary market*. Most wine bought and sold on the secondary market is luxury wine. This typically includes the products of winemakers like Château Lafite Rothschild and Château Cheval Blanc in the Bordeaux region of France; Romanée-Conti and Domaine Leroy Chambertin in Burgundy, France; Tenuta San Guido Sassicaia in Tuscany, Italy; and Screaming Eagle Winery and the Bryant Family Vineyard in Napa County, California. The salient characteristic of these sorts of age-worthy wines is that their quality tends to increase as they age in the bottle for ten to twenty years or longer. They are often purchased as investments by individuals who expect to resell them at a higher price for a profit. Investment-grade wine may sell at prices that some would consider exorbitant. For instance, in 2007, forty-two bottles of Screaming Eagle commanded a price of $3,117 each.[4] The secondary market is largely organized as an auction market. Well-known auction houses such as Christie's and Sotheby's hold large wine auctions several times a year. Smaller wine auctions are also held by a number of lesser-known auction houses and wine stores in many different parts of the United States. Wine auctions on the Internet now occur with regularity and have contributed to the significant growth of the secondary market.[5]

Many wine writers have argued that modern winemaking techniques and winemaker skill have minimized year to year variation in the sensory quality of wine.[6] This contention has been supported by blind wine-tasting experiments that find a typical wine consumer cannot detect a difference in the quality of wine products of different vintages, even when wine critics rate one vintage high and the other low.[7] A recent research project that surveyed wine consumers in the United States and a number of other nations concluded that both for U.S. and foreign consumers, the most important criterion for choosing a wine is prior experience in tasting the wine.[8]

Hedonic wine studies do not distinguish between first-time and repeat wine purchases. Most of these studies explicitly or implicitly assume that all wine-buying decisions involve first-time purchases, and therefore that a consumer's prior tasting experience plays no role in making these decisions. This may not be a reasonable approximation of the information used by a typical wine consumer in the United States. As discussed in chapter 11, the Wine Market Council estimates that frequent wine consumers—those who drink wine at least once a week—account for 93 percent of wine consumption. Given total U.S. wine sales, this implies that a typical frequent wine consumer purchases 59 bottles per year, or about 5 bottles per month. It is doubtful that all or even a majority of these are first-time purchases. Given the potential importance of repeat purchases, it is difficult to imagine that frequent consumers ignore their prior tasting experience when making choices. This is an important consideration in the interpretation of estimates from hedonic wine studies.

THE METHODOLOGY OF STUDIES OF WINE QUALITY AND PRICE

Hedonic wine studies use data to analyze the relationship between the price and characteristics of a wine. The objective of such a study is either to explain how each characteristic affects price, or to predict future prices based on the relationship. Studies that have an explanatory goal typically address two questions. Does a wine characteristic have an effect on price? The effect of interest is usually an independent causal effect. If it does not have an effect, the implicit price of the characteristic is zero. In this case, a typical consumer does not value the attribute and is thus not willing to pay for it. To decide if a characteristic has an effect, a p-value is calculated and compared to a predetermined decision criterion, typically a value of 0.05.[9] If the calculated p-value is less than or equal to 0.05, then the study concludes that the characteristic has an effect. This means that the probability that the estimated effect is the result of chance is 5 percent or less, and we can therefore be at least 95 percent certain that we have observed a real effect in the sample. If a study concludes that a characteristic has an effect, a second question is then addressed: What is the size of the effect? Size is measured as either the percentage or dollar effect of a one-unit or 1 percent change in the characteristic on price. For example, if the characteristic is an expert wine rating measured on a 100-point scale, three alternative measures of size may be reported: the dollar change in price from a one-point change in score; the percentage change in price from a one-point change in score; and the percentage change in price from a 1 percent change in score. The advantage of the last measure is that it is an elasticity and can be used to directly compare the size of the effects of two or more characteristics measured in different units.

To address these questions, a sample of data is used to estimate an equation of the general form $P = \beta_1 x_1 + \beta_2 x_2 + \ldots + \beta_k x_k$, where $x_1, x_2 \ldots x_k$ are the amounts of k wine characteristics, and $\beta_1, \beta_2, \ldots \beta_k$ are the parameters attached to the characteristics.[10] These parameters are interpreted as marginal implicit prices and measure the effect of a one-unit change in an attribute on wine price holding all other attributes constant. A p-value is calculated for each estimated implicit price. The numerical value of the parameter estimate is a measure of size. If price and characteristics are measured in their original units, an implicit price measures the effect of a one-unit change in a characteristic on the dollar price of wine. If price is measured in logarithmic form, the parameter measures the effect of a one-unit change in a characteristic on the approximate proportional change in price. If both price and characteristics are measured in logarithmic form, the parameter is an elasticity. For example, suppose x_1 is an expert wine rating and $\beta_1 = 0.10$. A one-point increase in score increases price by 10 cents if price is measured in dollars per bottle, or by 10 percent if price is the logarithm of dollars per bottle. If both price and rating are measured in logarithmic form, then a 1 percent increase in score results in a 0.10 percent increase in price. Some studies report more than one of these measures of effect size.

To interpret the parameter estimates as independent causal effects of characteristics on consumer willingness to pay for quality, a study must account for confounding factors and reverse causation, and address what is called the identification problem. As discussed in chapter 11, variables that are correlated with a characteristic and affect wine price must be statistically controlled. If this is not done, the estimate does not measure the independent effect, since it may also include the influence of the confounding variable. For example, suppose we wish to estimate the effect on wine price of the geographic location where grapes are grown. If different locations tend to specialize in growing different grape varieties, and if grape variety affects wine price, then grape variety is a potential confounding variable that should be controlled for. As an example of reverse causation, suppose critics use price as an indicator of quality when tasting and scoring wine products. To interpret the estimate of the implicit price of rating as a measure of the causal effect of this quality score on price, the study must purge the reverse effect of price on score.

Finally, economic theory tells us that the implicit prices of the wine product characteristics are determined by the interaction of supply and demand. To interpret the estimate of an implicit price as a measure of willingness to pay reflecting consumers' preferences rather than wine firms' costs, demand must be separated from supply. Various arguments and approaches have been used to obtain identification by researchers who wish to give their estimates a causal interpretation. The potential problems of confounding factors, reverse causation, and identification can be ignored for the most part if the objective of the study is simply to describe the relationship between wine price and characteristics or use it to generate predictions.

The remainder of this chapter discusses the results of hedonic wine studies that have used data to analyze the relationship between price and a variety of wine attributes. These studies have been performed for wine sold in a number of countries, including the United States, Australia, France, Spain, New Zealand, and Sweden. Wine quality and price as they relate to U.S. wine consumers are of primary interest. However, applicable information will also be drawn from hedonic studies involving wine products and consumers in foreign markets, as well as nonhedonic studies related to wine quality.

SENSORY CHARACTERISTICS

To study the relationship between sensory quality and price, it is necessary to measure the appearance, smell, and taste of wine and determine the value consumers place on these characteristics. The more consumers value these attributes, the more they are willing to pay for a wine that embodies them, and the higher therefore the price it can command. Three alternative approaches that have been used to determine the value consumers place on wine sensory characteristics are the consumer-trained panel approach, the contingent valuation approach, and the hedonic price approach. While the first two approaches may provide useful information on consumers' preferences for specific sensory characteristics, the hedonic price approach is the only one capable of analyzing the relationship between sensory quality and wine price.

The Consumer-Trained Panel Approach

The consumer-trained panel (CTP) approach assumes that consumers have preferences for wine products that possess different bundles of sensory characteristics and are able to express these preferences in terms of how much they like or dislike these products. However they are unable to describe the value they attach to specific attributes related to appearance, smell, and taste in a coherent manner. A typical consumer may say that he or she likes a given Cabernet Sauvignon very much, for example, but have difficulty articulating that this is because it has an intense aroma of blackcurrant, concentrated fruit, a moderate amount of oak flavor, and a nice mouthfeel from the ripe tannin and viscous alcohol. Most consumers do not have the background or training to convey information about their preferences for these sorts of characteristics. As a result, to determine the attributes consumers prefer in wine, the CTP approach uses a trained panel of consumers to measure the amounts of various sensory characteristics embodied in different wine products and relates these data to how much a group of untrained consumers like or dislike the same products. Sensory characteristics are typically measured by intensity ratings. Intensity measures may be provided for such attributes as color, hotness, acidity, tannin, sweetness, vanilla, smoke, apple, pineapple, blackcurrant, red berry, and others. How much a consumer likes or dislikes a wine is measured by a hedonic rating. A typical rating device is a nine-point Likert scale that assigns a value of 1 for "dislike extremely," 9 for "like extremely," and seven intermediate values for gradations between these two end points. By using a group of trained consumers to objectively measure sensory characteristics embodied in wine products and a second group of untrained consumers to express their preferences for these products, the CTP approach attempts to determine the attributes of appearance, smell, and taste that consumers prefer.

To my knowledge, relatively few CTP studies have been performed. One such study by researchers at the Australian Wine Research Institute analyzed the preferences of 203 consumers for twelve different Cabernet Sauvignon and Shiraz wines with different sensory characteristics. This study suggests that the wines Australian consumers like most have a higher intensity of dark fruit, red berry, floral, vanilla, and caramel flavor, while those least liked have a hotter, more bitter mouthfeel, and a greater intensity of aromas and flavors of smoke, pepper, herbaceousness, and barnyard. While consumers do not have homogeneous tastes for wine, they can be placed in four separate groups with similar preferences. These groups do not differ in terms of education, gender, age, marital status, and other demographic characteristics, but do differ in wine-drinking experience. Perhaps, the most interesting finding is that winemakers and various other wine professionals have significantly different wine preferences from consumers, leading the researchers to conclude that consumers and winemakers have different notions of quality.[11]

While the CTP approach may provide insight into the attributes of wine appearance, smell, and taste that consumers like and dislike, it does not provide an estimate of the economic value consumers place on these characteristics. In economics, value is measured by consumers' willingness to pay. The contingent valuation approach fills this void by providing information about the amount wine consumers are willing to pay for sensory characteristics.

The Contingent Valuation Approach

The contingent valuation (CV) approach measures the economic value of an option by asking individuals how much they would be willing to pay for it in a hypothetical situation. This information is usually obtained by having them complete a questionnaire that describes the circumstances involving a particular option of interest to the researcher. CV is typically used by economists to estimate the value of goods that are not traded on markets. Examples include public goods like parks and endangered species, and different types of health-care programs. One way to estimate the value consumers place on sensory characteristics of wine would be to survey a sample of consumers and ask them how much they would be willing to pay for wine products that differ in terms of color and clarity, complexity and intensity of aroma and flavor, sweetness, and mouthfeel. However, eliciting information about willingness to pay for sensory characteristics from a questionnaire based on this sort of hypothetical wine-tasting scenario would not be very useful. A more fruitful application of CV would be to ask consumers how much they are willing to pay for different wine products they sample in a blind tasting. This measure of willingness to pay could then be related to the sensory characteristics embodied in the wine to analyze the value consumers place on these attributes. This is the approach taken in a study of wine consumers in Washington State by Yang et al. (2009).

The objective of the Washington State study was to analyze consumers' willingness to pay for three red wines with different sensory characteristics. After blind tasting each of the three wines, sixty individuals were asked to fill out a questionnaire indicating if they would be willing to pay several alternative dollar amounts for the wine by answering "yes" or "no." These same sixty consumers were also asked to indicate how much they liked or disliked the aroma, flavor, and mouthfeel of the wine using a nine-point Likert scale, and the intensity of each of these sensory characteristics using a nine-point intensity-rating scale. Mouthfeel was measured by consumer ratings for astringency (related to tannin) and bitterness (related to acidity). No information was obtained for the appearance of the wines, which was concealed by using red lights to illuminate the tasting room. The researchers also used two other methods to measure sensory characteristics. A separate trained panel of consumers was asked to provide an objective measure of the mouthfeel characteristics of the wine—astringency and bitterness—using an intensity-rating scale. Like the CTP approach, this consumer panel was used as a measurement device only. An objective chemical measure of mouthfeel was also taken by measuring the amount of tannin in each wine.

The researchers used statistical methods to estimate the effect on willingness to pay of consumers' preferences and intensity assessment of aroma, flavor, and mouthfeel. The statistical analysis also controlled for gender, age, and frequency of wine consumption. As expected, a typical consumer is willing to pay more for wine with an aroma, flavor, and mouthfeel he or she likes more as measured by the Likert scale. The results also suggest that a typical consumer is willing to pay more for wine with more intense flavor and less for wine with a more bitter mouthfeel. Age is the only control variable that affects willingness to pay. A younger consumer is willing to pay more than an older consumer for a wine that possesses the same bundle of characteristics. The researchers also estimated the effect of objective measures of mouthfeel on willingness to pay, but not of aroma or flavor. Measures of both astringency and bitterness provided by the trained panel have an effect on untrained consumers' willingness to pay; the effect of astringency is positive, and that of bitterness is negative. The chemical measure of tannin has a nonlinear effect on willingness to pay, suggesting that the value a consumer places on additional units of tannin increases at a diminishing rate. After assessing the ability of the consumer, trained panel, and chemical measures of sensory characteristics to predict the amount a consumer will pay for a particular wine, the researchers concluded that all of these measures produce relatively accurate predictions. This suggests that objective trained panel and chemical measures may capture consumers' preferences for sensory characteristics reasonably well.

The major criticism of the CV approach is that we cannot be sure that individuals will pay the amount they report on a questionnaire when they make actual wine purchases as consumers in the marketplace. Most economists prefer to use data on what consumers actually do rather than what they say they will do. Moreover, while the CV approach may provide some insight into the value consumers place on sensory characteristics of wine, it does not yield estimates of the effect of these attributes on wine price. The hedonic price approach has the potential to rectify both of these shortcomings by using market data to estimate the effect of sensory characteristics on both consumers' willingness to pay and wine price.

The Hedonic Price Approach

A number of studies have employed the hedonic price approach to estimate the effect of sensory characteristics on wine price using market data. The objective of almost all of these studies is to analyze the causal effect of sensory attributes on price and make inferences about consumer willingness to pay for wine quality. To give the estimates a causal interpretation, hedonic theory requires sensory characteristics to be measured objectively. When making buying decisions, all consumers must know and have the same perception of the number of units of appearance, smell, and taste embodied in a wine, whatever those units are. Hedonic theory does allow individual consumers to place different subjective values on those objectively measured attributes.[12] For example, if the taste characteristic "body" is measured as light, medium, and full, then all consumers must have the same perception of these three levels of the weight or fullness of a wine and know whether a particular product is a light-, medium- or full-bodied wine when making buying decisions; however, one consumer may place a higher value on, say, a full-bodied wine than another consumer. To my knowledge, all studies that have attempted to estimate the effect of objectively measured sensory characteristics on wine price have involved consumers in foreign wine markets including France, Sweden, and Norway. It should be kept in mind that the results from these studies may or may not generalize to the population of interest to us here, which is U.S. wine consumers.

Hedonic wine studies have used two approaches in an attempt to obtain objective measures of wine sensory characteristics. The first identifies characteristics related to appearance, smell, and taste, and measures the chemical content of these attributes in wines. Examples of chemical measures that have been used are alcohol, residual sugar, acidity, tannin, and extract. While a measure of alcohol can easily be obtained from the wine label, it is typically subject to a plus and minus 0.5 to 1.5 percent legal margin of error, depending on the specific country in which the wine is produced. Other chemical measures are much more costly to obtain. Because of this, relatively few studies have adopted the chemical approach. Those studies that have been done use data on wines sold in Sweden and Norway where the state has a wine monopoly and uses chemical analysis as a source of information when choosing wines to offer for sale to consumers. The second approach obtains measures of sensory characteristics from a panel of experts, who conduct a blind tasting to evaluate the appearance, smell, and taste of a collection of wines. This is similar to the CTP approach, in that the panel of wine experts essentially plays the same role as the panel of trained consumers and is used as a measurement device only. However, the hedonic price approach relates the sensory data provided by the panel of experts to market data on the prices that consumers pay for wines.

Two hedonic price studies have used chemical measures of sensory characteristics. Both of these also include sensory attributes measured by a panel of experts as well as additional control variables. A study by Marc Nerlove (1995) suggests that Swedish consumers value wine with more acidity and less color intensity; however, there is no compelling evidence of effects of fifteen other chemical and expert measures of sensory characteristics. This implies that Swedish consumers value few sensory attributes of wine products. A descriptive study of Norwegian consumers by Christer Thrane (2004) found evidence that sugar, alcohol, body, and fruit flavor all have positive effects on the prices of French red wines. No attempt was made to give the results a causal interpretation, and no conclusions can therefore be drawn about consumers' willingness to pay for wine quality. Four additional studies involving French wines and consumers using sensory measures obtained from expert panels suggest that a typical French wine drinker considers relatively few attributes related to the appearance, smell, and taste of wine when making wine-buying decisions, and that sensory qualities therefore have little effect on wine price.[13] When researchers include an overall quality rating by the same expert panel, this measure has a positive effect, suggesting that French consumers are willing to pay a higher price for wines that receive a higher score from expert tasters, but the magnitude of the effect is relatively small. Moreover, these studies find evidence that nonsensory characteristics and wine-firm classified-growth rank, information that appears on a typical wine label, play a more important role in guiding consumer buying decisions and influencing wine prices.

There are several possible explanations for the finding that sensory characteristics generally have little if any effect on consumers' willingness to pay and wine prices. First, it may be that sensory quality does not matter to consumers when making wine purchases. That is, a typical consumer just doesn't care how a wine looks, smells, and tastes. While this is one possible interpretation of the study results, it seems very unlikely. A second explanation is that a typical consumer does not make buying decisions by considering chemical attributes or criteria that are used by experts when these experts perform a sensory evaluation of wine. For instance, in all but one of the French studies, sensory characteristics were measured by professional wine-tasting quality criteria that included balance, complexity, concentration, finish, intensity, tannin, acidity, firmness, suppleness, and others. If consumers either do not perceive these characteristics or perceive them differently from experts, they will not evaluate them when making buying decisions. In this case, it is not surprising that most of these sensory characteristics have no effect on price and are not valued by consumers, since they do not reflect consumers' preferences. It is more plausible that a typical consumer evaluates a wine by determining how much he likes the way it looks, smells, and tastes. The one French study that included measures of smell and taste (poor, medium, good) as sensory characteristics reported that these more general attributes have an effect on wine price. Moreover, expert overall quality ratings have an effect on wine price in all of these studies. Some researchers argue that using a single score that measures appearance, smell, and taste as an index of sensory quality may better reflect consumers' preferences than a number of specific quality characteristics that have little or no meaning to most individuals who purchase wine. A third explanation is that when purchasing wine, consumers typically do not have the opportunity to evaluate the appearance, smell, and taste of a wine product personally, and must therefore rely on quality indicators that provide indirect information on sensory characteristics. This may explain why a typical French wine drinker values nonsensory characteristics more than sensory attributes.

Because of the questionable relevance of chemical attributes and expert criteria as measures of sensory characteristics and the incomplete information that confronts most consumers when making first-time purchases, many studies have used wine critics' scores as either a quality index that reflects consumers' preferences or a quality indicator used by consumers as a source of information about uncertain sensory characteristics when making wine-buying decisions. Perhaps the major reason most hedonic wine studies have used critics' scores is their ready availability and relatively low cost.

WINE SCORES

A large number of publications and websites worldwide evaluate and rate the quality of tens of thousands of wine products produced each year by wine firms in a variety of countries. Some of these use a qualitative rating system with stars or some other symbol to indicate the level of quality of a wine product. By far the most popular rating system is Robert Parker's quantitative 100-point quality scale. Since it was first published, U.S. wine consumers have been attracted to this rating system because it is easy to interpret and analogous to the 100-point grading scale used by most American schools. A wine that receives a score of 95 is clearly superior; one that receives a grade of 85 is likely to be above average; and one with a score of 65 has obviously failed the quality test. Consumers in other countries have also developed a strong preference for wine scores as a measure of quality. Because a wine score is a quantitative measure that can be given a useful interpretation, it has been incorporated into hedonic price models to quantify and measure different aspects of sensory quality potentially related to wine price, including the current or expected future quality of a single wine, the quality reputation of a single producer or collection of wine firms, and the overall quality of a vintage. The vast majority of hedonic wine studies use scores published by Robert Parker and a handful of editors employed by the *Wine Spectator*. Not only do these sources report wine scores, they also provide information on retail prices, number of cases produced, and other characteristics of wine products. To my knowledge, all hedonic price studies of the U.S. wine market and consumers have used *Wine Spectator* scores as a quality index or indicator. Most studies that have analyzed age-worthy Bordeaux wines purchased by U.S. and foreign consumers have used Robert Parker scores, sometimes called "Parker points." As a result, it is useful to discuss in more detail these two sources of wine ratings and some potential problems with wine scores as a measure of sensory quality.

Critics and Scores

The role of a wine critic is to perform a sensory evaluation of wine products to determine their quality. The wines are usually, but not always, tasted blind, so that the critic doesn't know what wine he is sampling. After tasting the wine, he typically writes a description of the appearance, smell, and taste, and gives it a score that summarizes over-all quality. The scores assigned by both Robert Parker and *Wine Specta-tor* range between 50 and 100 points and a standard grading scale is used: A, 90–100; B, 80–89; C, 70–79; D, 60–69; F, 50–59. Letter grades are not actually assigned; rather, wines that fall in the A range are labeled extraordinary, classic, or outstanding; those in the B range, above average or very good; those in the C range, average or mediocre; those in the D range, below average or not recommended; and those in the F range, unacceptable or not recommended. Parker uses specific criteria for assigning points: five points for appearance; fifteen points for smell; twenty points for taste and finish; and ten points for overall quality and aging potential. *Wine Spectator* does not state publicly how points are awarded, and the weights given to appearance, smell, and taste are therefore unknown. A *Wine Spectator* critic typically tastes between 20 and 60 wines per day; Robert Parker may taste 80 to 130 in the course of a day. The same wine product is typically never tasted more than twice. Collectively, *Wine Spectator* critics evaluate more than 15,000 wines annually; Parker alone has tasted as many as 10,000 wines in a given year.

Scores reported for individual wine products in *Wine Spectator* and Parker's newsletter, the *Wine Advocate,* are almost always assigned by a single critic, rather than an average rating of a panel of two or more critics. For *Wine Spectator,* the vast majority of wines are rated by six critics, each of whom is responsible for wines produced in one or more geographic regions. For instance, California wines are rated by James Laube, who has assigned scores since 1983. Oregon, Washington, Australia, and New Zealand wines are rated by Harvey Steiman, who has assigned scores since 1984. Until 2003, Parker himself rated all wines that appeared in the *Wine Advocate,* which included products from California, France, Italy, and Australia. Since 2003, he has put together a team of critics to extend the geographic coverage of wines evaluated. By 2011, Parker himself was rating French wine products only; wines from the United States and other countries are now evalu-ated by his associates, each of whom specializes in specific geographic regions, similarly to the approach used by *Wine Spectator.*

Hedonic wine studies that include wine scores as a measure of sen-sory quality explicitly or implicitly assume that they are either a quality index that reflects the preferences of an average consumer or a quality indicator that a typical consumer uses as a source of information when making wine-buying decisions. As a quality indicator, wines scores may either reflect or affect consumers' preferences. On the one hand, they may simply provide consumers with information about the qualities of the variety of wines available in the marketplace and reduce the search cost of finding those that are consistent with their tastes. Alternatively, wine scores may persuade consumers to purchase wines with particular characteristics, and therefore influence and shape their preferences. As a result, it would be of interest to know how well wine scores assigned by an individual critic reflect consumers' preferences, and the similarity of the sensory evaluations of different critics. For instance, a hedonic study that uses *Wine Spectator* scores as a quality index for wine products sold in the United States implicitly assumes that wine scores of different critics are assigned in a similar manner, if more than one critic is performing the sensory evaluation, and that these scores are an accurate and reliable measure of the tastes of a typical wine consumer in the United States. *Wine Spectator* scores would be biased and inaccurate if they were systematically different from the average score that all consumers would assign in a blind tasting if consumer rating of wine products were feasible. One possible source of bias is that wine critics may not like the same types of wine products as a typical consumer. Another possibility is that scores may be assigned for financial gain, for example, to generate advertising revenue. *Wine Spectator* scores would be unreliable if the same critic, or multiple critics, assigned inconsistent scores to wine products with the same sensory characteristics.

While the accuracy and reliability of the scores awarded by *Wine Spectator* and Robert Parker have not been subjected to formal study, a few studies have been done related to the similarity of the preferences of wine professionals and consumers, and the reliability of the experts who judge wine competitions. The study by the Australian Wine Research Institute discussed previously (Lattey et al. 2007) compared the measure of how much consumers liked the twelve Cabernet Sauvignon and Shiraz wines to the quality scores of a sample of winemakers, wine educators, and sommeliers obtained from a blind tasting. The researchers reported that the wines most liked by consumers received relatively low scores by wine professionals; in general, the measure of consumers' preferences and the professional wine score were uncorrelated. A study by Robin Goldstein et al. (2008) used data obtained from seventeen blind tastings involving 506 consumers and experts in various locations around the United States to analyze the relationship between wine enjoyment and price when participants did not know the price of the wine they tasted. Their results suggest that an average consumer tends to like less expensive wines better than more expensive wines, while a typical expert prefers higher-priced wines to those with a lower price. The size of the estimate of the effect of wine price on the quality scores assigned by consumers and experts is easily grasped by way of an example. Suppose the price of a bottle of a Napa Valley Cabernet Sauvignon is $150 and the price of a Cabernet Sauvignon from the Central Coast region of California is $15. On a 100-point scale like the one used by *Wine Spectator*, a typical consumer will award a score of four points lower for the Napa Cabernet than the Central Coast Cabernet; an average expert, on the other hand, will assign a score of seven points higher to the Napa Cabernet than to that from the Central Coast. This suggests that the preferences and sensory quality rating of a typical consumer are significantly different from those of a typical wine expert.

Matt Kramer argues that the scores assigned by wine critics when doing blind tastings of a large number of wine products are biased by a "low-cut dress syndrome." When blind tasting forty or fifty different wines in a single session, wine critics award the highest scores to the biggest, richest, oakiest, deepest-colored ones, which stick out the most, just as a typical male in a room with a number of beautiful women is visually drawn to the one with the lowest-cut dress.[14]

Two studies of U.S. wine competitions by Robert Hodgson (2008, 2009) conclude that a typical expert judge is neither consistent in the quality scores he assigns to the same wine products nor consistent with other judges in the rating he awards to identical products. For instance, the results of Hodgson's first study suggest that on an 80- to 100-point quality-rating scale, the score a typical judge awarded the same wine varied by plus or minus four points from one blind tasting to the next. So, for example, a judge who assigned a score of 90 on the first tasting might well assign 86 on a second tasting and 94 on a third. The results of the other study (Hodgson 2009) suggest that receiving a quality rating high enough to earn a gold medal in multiple wine competitions is the result of chance. This impugns the ability of different judges to award similar scores to the same wine. Together, these studies cast doubt on the accuracy and reliability of wine experts in rating the sensory quality of wines, and by extension wine critic scores. Moreover, a study that compared the ratings published by *Wine Spectator* and the *Wine Advocate* in the year 2000 reported a relatively low correlation coefficient of 0.49.[15]

Wine Spectator generates revenue from newsstand sales, subscribers, and advertisers. It rates the quality of products of wine firms that do and do not choose to place advertisements in the magazine. This has raised the question of whether advertising is a source of bias in the scores awarded. It would seem that *Wine Spectator* has a strong financial incentive to give favorable ratings to wine firms that advertise in it, since this would induce more of them to place ads in the magazine and increase advertising revenue. However, if *Wine Spectator* develops a reputation for publishing biased ratings, this may result in fewer magazine sales and less revenue. Therefore, it is not clear whether *Wine Spectator* would benefit financially from giving systematically higher scores to advertisers. A recent study by Jonathan Reuter (2009) estimated that *Wine Spectator* awards scores to the products of wine firms who advertise that are about one point higher than those producers who choose not to place ads in the magazine. About half of this difference can be explained by selectively tasting wines of advertisers twice and adjusting the score upward on the second tasting. The other half of the difference may reflect either unexplained bias or higher average quality of the advertisers' wines. This study suggests that the evidence that *Wine Spectator* favors its advertisers is weak, and that if it does, the bias is relatively small.

Studies of the U.S. Retail Wine Market

Hedonic price studies have used wine scores as a measure of the sensory qualities of wines. These scores have also been used to construct measures of the quality reputation of the firm that produced a wine, the quality reputation of the collection of wine firms located in the region where a product was produced, and the overall quality of all wine products produced in a particular vintage. This section discusses results from studies that have used wine scores to measure current sensory quality. Some of these studies also include wine score measures of individual wine-firm and collective-reputation variables. The estimates and interpretation of these reputational wine-score measures will be discussed in later sections in this chapter.

A number of studies have used *Wine Spectator* scores to analyze the relationship between the sensory qualities and prices of wines in the U.S. retail wine market. Different studies focus on different segments of the market, including Bordeaux wines, Argentinian wines, California wines, Oregon wines, New World wines, and wine products from all regions and countries sold in the United States. They also differ in terms of the wine types included, ranging from Pinot noir to all grape varieties and blends. All of these studies control for a number of potential confounding variables that may be correlated with wine scores and have an effect on price in an attempt to isolate the independent effect of sensory quality on wine price. These variables typically include wine type, wine age, vintage, producer reputation, and the region where the grapes are grown or the wineries are located. The estimates of the effects of these characteristics on wine prices are also of interest and will be discussed later in this chapter.[16]

A study by John Haeger and Karl Storchmann (2006) analyzing the effect of wine scores, climate, and winemaker characteristics on the price of California and Oregon Pinot noir estimated that a one-point increase in score results in a 4.2 percent increase in the price of a typical North American Pinot noir. Their results suggest that grape-growing climate and winemakers' skills are relatively more important in explaining wine prices than critics' scores. Studies by Guillermo San Martin et al. (2008) of Argentinian wines and Helene Bombrun and Daniel Sumner (2003) of California wines report estimates similar to those of Haeger and Storchmann (2006). These studies find that a one-point increase in score leads to a 4.5 percent increase in the price of Argentine wine sold in the United States and a 4.9 percent increase in Cabernet Sauvignon, Merlot, Pinot noir, Red Zinfandel, and Chardonnay produced in California. Focusing on the red Bordeaux segment of the U.S. wine market, Stuart Landon and Constance Smith (1998) also found strong evidence that wine score influences price; however, the size of the effect is very small. A one-point increase in score increases the price of an average bottle of red Bordeaux in the United States by less than 1 percent. Landon and Smith conclude that the individual and collective reputation of Bordeaux wines have a much larger effect on price than sensory quality. This suggests, at least for the red Bordeaux segment of the U.S. wine market, that a typical consumer makes buying decisions with incomplete information about sensory quality and therefore relies heavily on reputational quality indicators. Finally, two studies by Günter Schamel (2000, 2009) estimate unit-free wine-score elasticities. The first study includes all types of wine products sold in the United States, both domestic and imported. In the most comprehensive wine-product price analysis to date, Schamel estimates that a 1 percent increase in wine score results in a 3.83 percent increase in price.[17] This implies that an increase in score of one point from a rating of 90 to 91 raises price by roughly 4.2 percent. In the second study, Schamel focuses on Cabernet Sauvignon and Chardonnay from the United States, Australia, Chile, and South Africa and reports that a 1 percent increase in wine score leads to a 2.9 higher price.

To conclude, studies of U.S. consumers find strong evidence of a positive relationship between *Wine Spectator* scores and wine prices for a variety of wine products produced in a number of different regions within the United States and foreign countries. With the exception of red Bordeaux wines, the sizes of the estimated effects of wine score on price reported by the different studies are similar and suggest that a one-point increase in critics' score results in an increase in price in the neighborhood of 4 percent. For example, suppose that the *Wine* Spectator score of a $30 bottle of wine increases from 90 to 91. This would lead to an increase in price of $1.20 to $31.20 per bottle. In the context of hedonic price theory, the estimate of the implicit price of the wine rating tells us that a typical consumer is willing to pay a 4 percent higher price for each one-point increase in the *Wine Spectator* score assigned to a wine. But why is this? One interpretation of this estimate is that it measures the value consumers place on an additional unit of sensory quality. For this interpretation to be tenable, two conditions must be satisfied. First, consumers must have complete information about the appearance, smell, and taste of wine when making buying decisions. Second, *Wine Spectator* scores must accurately reflect the taste of the average consumer. Under these conditions, wine scores capture consumers' preferences for sensory characteristics even if consumers do not use these scores to make buying decisions. However, this would apply only to those who have already drunk a wine, ascertained its quality, and are making a decision about whether to purchase it again. When a consumer is making a buying decision about a wine not previously consumed he is uncertain about its sensory characteristics, and therefore may use wine scores as one possible source of information to form expectations about its actual but unknown quality. Because first-time wine-buying decisions are based on expected quality, wine scores affect consumers' willingness to pay and wine price via the information they provide about sensory characteristics. As a result, a second interpretation of the implicit price of the wine rating is that it measures the value consumers place on the expected increase in wine quality from the information contained in a one-point increase in the score *Wine Spectator* assigns to a wine. If consumers believe that wine scores tell them something useful about sensory quality, these will have an effect on wine demand and price.

When consumers use wine scores as a source of information to guide their buying decisions, these scores may either reflect or affect consumers' preferences. One possibility is that consumers have preferences about wine sensory characteristics independent of critics' ratings and use wine scores to reduce the cost of finding wine products they like. However, in this case *Wine Spectator* scores are only of value to those who have preferences similar to the critic who assigns the rating. For example, *Wine Spectator* scores of California wine products would not be useful to consumers whose taste for wine is significantly different from James Laube's. A second possibility is that the information content in wine scores influences wine demand and price by affecting and shaping consumers' preferences. Wine ratings may persuade consumers to purchase wines with particular sensory characteristics. By doing so, wine scores essentially coax or teach consumers to acquire a taste for wine styles and products preferred by the critics. Most researchers argue that wine scores influence willingness to pay and price by providing consumers with information about potential wine quality, but don't address the question of whether these scores reflect or affect consumers' preferences.

It is likely that the estimate of the implicit price of the *Wine Spectator* quality rating captures the net effect on wine price of the decisions of well-informed consumers making repeat purchases with tastes similar to those of the critics and less informed consumers making first-time purchases, some of whom use these scores to guide them to wine products consistent with their own preferences, and others who are persuaded to buy products based on the preferences of wine critics. Of course, it is also conceivable that some individuals are willing to pay more for wine products with higher *Wine Spectator* scores because of the utility they derive from the prestige value of these highly rated wines.

Studies of the Futures and Auction Markets for Bordeaux Wine

Robert Parker is considered to be the most influential wine critic in the world. It is often maintained by many in the wine industry that the scores he assigns to wines have a large impact on consumer demand and the prices wine firms receive. A number of studies have attempted to formally test whether Parker ratings have an effect on wine price and assess the size of the effect if one exists. Most of this research has been directed at the prices of age-worthy French Bordeaux wines sold on the primary futures market and the secondary auction market for these products. Since consumers in the United States purchase wine products on these markets, this section will provide a brief description of the market for Bordeaux wine and the results of a few of these studies.

Most Bordeaux wine firms, or *châteaux*, that produce age-worthy wine sell between 50 and 90 percent of their newly produced wine each year on the futures market. The futures market for Bordeaux wine is similar to the futures market for commodities such as corn, wheat, and soybeans. The concept of a futures transaction is best explained by an example. In early summer 2012 a château agrees to sell a buyer a specific number of cases of newly fermented vintage 2011 wine at a specific price, and to deliver the finished wine in spring 2014, after it has been barrel-aged for from eighteen to twenty-four months and bottled. The buyer signs a futures contract that requires him to pay a predetermined price today even though he will not actually take delivery of the wine for two years. The château benefits from this futures transaction, because it receives money today rather than waiting until the wine is eventually bottled and ready to be released. The buyer benefits because he can lock in a price and guaranteed amount of Bordeaux wine today rather than waiting several years, searching the market for the desired wine, and paying the release price, which is typically higher than the futures price. However, when purchasing Bordeaux wine on the futures market, the buyer takes a risk, since the future quality of the wine is uncertain and will not be known for many years, until after it has been bottled and has had sufficient time to age. As a result, when deciding how much he is willing to pay for the futures contract, the buyer may use information provided by Robert Parker, who tastes Bordeaux wines shortly after they are fermented and are maturing in the barrel, and assigns scores that reflect his sensory evaluation and prediction of the future quality of the wine. Many in the wine industry believe that these scores have a big impact on futures market prices.

Extending the above example, Bordeaux grapes for the vintage 2011 wine are harvested in fall and fermented shortly thereafter. The wine is then placed in barrels to be matured. In March 2012, Robert Parker and other wine critics arrive in Bordeaux on their annual trip to taste and evaluate the *en primeur* wine. This is the name given to wine that is still maturing in the barrel and not yet bottled. Parker publishes his scores at the end of April in his annual Bordeaux issue of the *Wine Advocate*. Châteaux then sell futures contracts during the months of May, June, and July, after Parker scores are publicly available. Many wine professionals argue that the châteaux use Parker scores in setting their futures prices. A higher Parker score indicates that consumers will be willing to pay a higher price for the wine product. As a result, the château is able to set a higher futures price. Once the châteaux have set prices, brokers arrange to sell the futures contracts to French merchants called *negociants,* who keep a certain number of contracts for themselves and sell the rest to retailers. Retailers, in turn, may retain some and sell the rest to consumers. Most consumers in the United States buy Bordeaux futures contracts from large retailers and websites that specialize in selling them. The retailer is responsible for eventually delivering the Bordeaux wine to the consumers who have purchased the futures contracts.[18]

Once the age-worthy vintage 2011 Bordeaux wines are bottled and delivered in 2014, retailers typically will sell their stock on the retail market. Most consumers will store the wines for future consumption or sale, since they usually are not ready to drink for at least five years and may continue to increase in quality for twenty years or longer. As these wines age, some are consumed and some are resold on the secondary auction market. Parker typically re-tastes the Bordeaux wines and assigns revised scores once or several times after they have been bottled, released, and are aging. Many wine professionals maintain that these scores have a big effect on consumer willingness to pay and on prices on the secondary auction market.

A study by Pierre Dubois and Céline Nauges (2007) analyzing the effect of Parker scores on Bordeaux futures prices argues that the futures price a château sets for the wine it produces in a given vintage depends upon its own evaluation of the expected future quality of the wine, its past quality reputation, and Parker's quality prediction, summarized by the score he awards the wine during his annual barrel tasting. The château has better information about the true quality of the wine than consumers, since it is more knowledgeable about the growing conditions and winemaking techniques that produced the wine. When deciding how much they are willing to pay for a wine product on the futures market, consumers rely primarily on the château's reputation and Parker score. Consumers are willing to pay a higher futures price for a wine with a higher Parker score and one that is sold by a château with a reputation for producing higher-quality wine in past vintages. A château will charge a higher futures price for a wine it believes has a higher future quality. It will also set a higher price if the wine is awarded a higher Parker score. This is because the château believes that consumers are willing to pay more for wine Parker predicts will achieve a higher future quality, irrespective of its own quality evaluation of the vintage. After analyzing data on 108 châteaux for the period 1994–98, the researchers conclude that Parker scores have an effect on the futures price independent of a château's own assessment of wine quality, but that the size of the effect is relatively small. They estimate that a one-point increase in score leads to a 1.38 percent increase in price.

A study by Gregory Jones and Karl Storchmann (2001) found evidence of a much larger "Parker score effect" on age-worthy Bordeaux wine products traded on the secondary auction market. The researchers analyzed data on 1996–97 worldwide auction prices for the wine products of twenty-one top-ranked châteaux for the vintages 1980 to 1994. Their sample included Lafite Rothschild, Latour, Margaux, Mouton Rothschild, Haute Brion, Petrus, and Cheval Blanc, as well as others with reputations for producing long-lived, high-quality wine. To isolate the influence of Parker's quality evaluation on auction prices, the study accounted for wine age, scarcity, and measures of grape ripeness (sugar and acid levels) determined by weather conditions that prevailed during the growing season in which a particular wine was produced. Jones and Storchmann report that a one-point increase in Parker score results in a 7 percent increase in the average auction price of the wine products of the twenty-one châteaux. The size of the effect of Parker scores on price varies widely across the châteaux, ranging from 1 to 12.5 percent. For example, a one-point increase in score leads to a 11.6 percent increase in price for a wine product produced by Château Margaux, but a much smaller 4.7 percent increase for Château Lafite Rothschild. What is more, Parker's ratings have a bigger influence on the price of wine products of smaller châteaux and those that have received higher scores for wine produced in previous vintages. Finally, the size of the effect of a one-point-higher Parker score increases as the total score increases. For example, a one-point increase in score from 91 to 92 has a larger effect on price than an equivalent one-point increase from 90 to 91.

GRAPE VARIETY

Wine can be made from a single variety or a blend of two or more varieties. The variety or varieties selected as the grape input predisposes a wine product to a particular taste profile with a distinguishable flavor and mouthfeel. Some grape varieties and blends may have a reputation among consumers for producing higher-quality wine. Consumers may also differ in their tastes and preferences for different varieties. As a result, almost all hedonic price studies include measures to capture the effect of grape variety on price and determine whether consumers place a higher value on some varieties and blends than others.

In general, the results of hedonic price studies suggest that American consumers are willing to pay a higher price for red wine than for white wine all else being equal. Among red wines, consumers place the highest value on Pinot noir and the lowest on Sangiovese. One study estimated that a typical consumer is willing to pay 42 percent less for Sangiovese than for Pinot noir.[19] Another reported that consumers are willing to pay 10 percent more for California Pinot noir than for California Cabernet Sauvignon, Merlot, red Zinfandel, or Chardonnay.[20] Among white wines, consumers place the highest value on Viognier, and prefer Chardonnay and Pinot gris to Sauvignon blanc.[21] For imported products, U.S. consumers place the highest value on Bordeaux blends that contain a higher proportion of Cabernet Franc.[22] The highest-valued Australian variety is Grenache, while the lowest-valued is Semillon.[23] Consumers are willing to pay more for Argentinian blended wines than for varietal wines, including the signature Malbec variety. Highly valued blended wines include products that contain a mix of Cabernet Sauvignon, Malbec, and Merlot.[24]

GRAPE LOCATION

Many wine-industry professionals maintain the most important determinant of the sensory quality of wine is the quality of the grapes. High-quality grapes result in high-quality wine; in essence, wine is grown, not made. What is more, many of these same professionals, particularly those who subscribe to the Old World winemaking philosophy, argue that the most important determinant of grape quality is the location where the grapes are grown. The best grapes come from locations with favorable climate, soil, and landscape characteristics. If this argument is valid, consumers should be willing to pay more for wines that source grapes from locations conducive to growing high-quality grapes, and these products should therefore command higher prices in the marketplace. Almost all hedonic wine studies analyze the relationship between grape location and wine price to determine if the prices of wines differ across growing regions after controlling for other factors that may affect price.

Two alternative approaches have been used to analyze the effect of location on price. One approach attempts to measure environmental attributes of different grape-growing regions—such as temperature, rainfall, and soil composition—and relate these to the prices of wines from vineyards in these locations. The second approach argues that the location where grapes are grown affects wine prices largely through its reputation. If this argument is valid, then the price of a wine product will depend upon the reputation of the vineyard or region from which the grapes are sourced.

The most comprehensive study of the relationship between grape-growing location and wine price in the United States is Haeger and Storchmann (2006), which analyzes data on 451 Pinot noirs sold during the period 1998 to 2003 by firms that sourced grapes from nineteen different regions in California and Oregon. The influence of climate is captured by regional measures of temperature and precipitation. The researchers hypothesize that warmer growing season temperatures increase grape quality and wine price at a diminishing rate, because of the adverse effects on grape ripening of temperatures that are both too low and too high. Higher-quality wines are expected to come from locations that have abundant rainfall during the winter when vines are dormant, but that are relatively dry in summer and fall as harvest approaches. In addition to climate measures, the analysis includes variables that indicate the specific region from which the grapes were sourced and whether a wine was produced from grapes grown in a single vineyard or a blend of grapes from two or more vineyards within that region. Wine labels with a single vineyard designation may indicate quality-enhancing soil and landscape characteristics, or simply be a marketing strategy. Regional variables may also capture climate, soil, and landscape attributes of a location other than temperature and precipitation. Alternatively, they may reflect the reputation of wine firms that source grapes from different locations. To analyze the effect of location variables on price, the researchers control for the influence of *Wine Spectator* scores, wine age, the number of cases of the wine produced, and the wine firm that produced the product. The results indicate that Pinot noir prices are significantly influenced by the characteristics of the location where the grapes are grown. There is strong evidence that temperature affects grape quality and wine price. The highest-priced wines come from locations that have a temperature close to that of a high-quality Pinot noir vintage in Burgundy. Precipitation appears to have little or no influence. One possible explanation for this result is the widespread use of irrigation, which reduces the importance of annual rainfall. Consumers are willing to pay a price premium of

8 percent for Pinot noir made from grapes from a single vineyard, and a premium of 22 to 25 percent for Pinot noir from the Carneros or Russian River Valley regions of California. It may be that consumers believe higher-quality grapes come from a single vineyard within a growing region and from these two locations. However, the higher price may also reflect wine-firm reputation and a marketing strategy that uses vineyard designation to successfully differentiate a wine.

Two additional studies of highly regarded Bordeaux wine find evidence of an effect on quality and price of climate, but little or no influence of soil and landscape. Jones and Storchmann 2001, discussed earlier in this chapter, analyzes the mechanism by which temperature and precipitation affects the auction prices of the wines produced by twenty-one top-ranked châteaux. This study concludes that locations with warm weather and relatively little rain during the growing season produce riper grapes with more sugar and less acid. Grapes with a higher sugar-to-acid ratio result in higher-quality long-lived wines that command higher prices on the secondary auction market. The quality and price of Bordeaux wines that are primarily Merlot blends are more sensitive to climatic conditions than those which consist mostly of Cabernet Sauvignon. Thus a cooler, wetter growing season lowers the price of Château Cheval Blanc's non–Cabernet Sauvignon wine by about four times as much as that of Château Mouton Rothschild's Cabernet Sauvignon–dominated blend.

A study by Olivier Gergaud and Victor Ginsburgh (2010) examines the influence of soil and landscape characteristics, and viticultural and winemaking techniques on wine quality and auction prices of 102 châteaux located in the Médoc *appellation* of the Bordeaux region, which has a reputation for producing some of the best wines in the world. Many French vintners argue the most important factor influencing wine quality is the soil in which vines are planted. Grapes that produce high-quality wine able to command high prices in the marketplace come from vineyards characterized by soil with good drainage and heat absorption and relatively poor fertility. These desirable attributes of soil are amplified in vineyards planted on a sloped hillside. However, after analyzing the data, Gergaud and Ginsburgh conclude that soil and landscape characteristics have a negligible effect; viticultural and winemaking technology are much more important factors influencing wine quality and price.

Landon and Smith (1998) study the effect of reputation on wine price. They argue that the prices of Bordeaux wines sold on the U.S. retail market depend upon both actual and expected sensory quality. The expected quality of a product, measured by the consumer's prediction of its *Wine Spectator* score, depends on the collective reputation of all vineyards and wine firms in the location where the grapes are grown and the wine is produced. Their analysis includes ten official Bordeaux appellations including Pauillac, Pomerol, Margaux, Saint-Émilion, Saint-Estèphe, and Saint-Julien. They find strong evidence that location is an important source of information used by a typical consumer to form quality expectations. These quality expectations have an important effect on the consumer's willingness to pay for Bordeaux wine. For example, a typical consumer is willing to pay almost $10 more, in 1985 dollars, for a wine from Pomerol than one from Margaux, all else being equal.

More recent studies of the effect of reputation on wine price also find evidence that grape-growing location has a significant and sizable effect on consumers' willingness to pay for wine. Schamel (2009) studies the effect on the U.S. retail wine price of wine products from twenty-seven locations in the United States and other wine-producing nations, including France, Italy, Spain, Germany, Austria, Australia, New Zealand, Chile, Argentina, and South Africa. After controlling for *Wine Spectator* score, brand reputation, wine type, and wine age, his results suggest that consumers are willing to pay the highest prices for wines from Burgundy, France, Napa, California, and Tuscany, Italy, while wines from Languedoc-Roussillon, France, Chile, and Argentina command the lowest. Bombrun and Sumner (2003) included indicator variables for 126 different California grape-growing locations and found that Napa Valley, Oakville, and Sonoma Mountain wines fetched the state's highest prices.

VINTAGE

Vintage is the year in which grapes are harvested. A vintage wine is one that is made from grapes harvested in a single year. A non-vintage wine is a blend of wines made from grapes harvested in two or more different years. About two-thirds of the wine sold in the United States is vintage wine, with the year printed on the label.[25] There are two reasons why vintage may be related to wine quality. First, the vintage year determines the age of a wine. The appearance, smell, and taste of wine change with time in the bottle. Most wines achieve their peak sensory quality shortly after they are released, and if not consumed at a young age, they may start to deteriorate. However, a relatively small subset of wines have the potential to improve with age and reach maximum quality a number of years or even decades after they are released. Among the most age-worthy are a select group of red Bordeaux, Napa Valley Cabernet Sauvignon, and Australian Shiraz wines. They tend to have a significant amount of harsh, bitter tannin when young that softens with time in the bottle as they develop complex and interesting aromas and flavors. These wines are often bought and sold on the secondary auction market as they age. The second reason vintage may be related to wine quality is that it captures the grape-growing and winemaking aspects of wine produced in a particular year. For individual wines, this may include changes in viticultural and vinification techniques, a new winemaker, or a revised wine style. However, most year-to-year variation in wine quality is attributed to variation in grape quality resulting from weather conditions, which may differ from one growing season to the next. Vintage-related weather is likely to have the biggest effect on the quality of wines intended for aging that are heavily dependent on grape quality for their character, complexity, and ability to age. These grapes often come from a single vineyard in a particular location and require propitious weather conditions to realize their full potential. Firms that produce wines with a consistent but less complex aroma and flavor that are intended to be drunk young may be more effective in minimizing year-to-year variation in weather by employing modern winemaking technology and blending wine from different geographic locations, and in the case of nonvintage wines, from different years.

Several hedonic wine studies have analyzed the effect of vintage on the secondary market auction prices of age-worthy red Bordeaux and Australian Shiraz wine. Orley Ashenfelter et al. (1995), the first to study the relationship between vintage-related weather, wine age, and auction prices, assume that the quality of long-lived red Bordeaux wine produced by the top châteaux is measured by the price consumers are willing to pay on the secondary auction market after it has aged ten to twenty years or longer and is fully mature. While there is uncertainty about the future quality of this wine when it is young, after it reaches the stage of maturity, auction market participants are well informed about its sensory characteristics, whose value is reflected in the price. Higher auction prices reflect higher-quality wine. A salient feature of the auction market for mature Bordeaux wine is the large variation in price between different vintages of the same wine, produced by the same château from grapes grown in the same vineyard, and vinified by the same winemaker. For example, 1964, 1965, and 1966 Château

Lafite Rothschild wines sold for $649, $190, and $1,274 a case respectively at auction in London in 1990–91. Ashenfelter et al. hypothesize that the age of the wine and weather conditions during the year when the grapes were grown and harvested explain the variation in the price and quality of mature wines of different vintages. As a Bordeaux wine ages, the amount that is available to be sold on the secondary market decreases as more is consumed over time, and this greater scarcity value of the wine is reflected in a higher price. Moreover, the longer a wine is stored, the higher the opportunity cost of not investing the money tied up in the wine in an alternative asset, and the pleasure forgone in not drinking the wine. As a result, the seller will demand a higher price to compensate for this cost. Variation in wine sensory quality from one vintage to the next results primarily from differences in growing-season temperature and rainfall that affects grape quality. To test their hypothesis, the researchers constructed an index of the 1990–91 London auction prices of twenty-seven vintages from thirteen châteaux prior to 1981. These data are used to estimate a "Bordeaux equation" that describes the relationship between the average price of a vintage, wine age, and weather-related variables. The results provide strong evidence that both wine age and weather have an effect on the quality of a vintage as measured by the vintage price index. Eighty-three percent of the variation in price is explained by age and weather; age accounts for 21 percent and weather for the rest. This suggests that the quality and price of wine of a given vintage are largely explained by the weather conditions that prevailed when the grapes were grown and harvested. The weather variables that affect sensory quality are the average temperature during the growing season, the amount of rain in August and September, and the amount of rain during the winter months. Vintages with higher prices are associated with higher growing-season temperatures, less rainfall in the months prior to harvest and more rain during the winter, when the vines are dormant. This suggests that years with warm, dry growing seasons and wet winters produce the best vintage wines, while those with cool, wet growing seasons and dry winters result in vintages of relatively low quality.

The estimated Bordeaux equation is used to predict the price of mature vintages and assess the efficiency of the auction market for vintages that have not reached the stage of maturity, so that their quality is unknown. The market for immature Bordeaux wine is said to be efficient if the price of a vintage reflects all publicly available information about factors that determine the true quality of the vintage. In this case, the auction price is an unbiased estimate of unknown quality and should be a good predictor of the price of the vintage when it matures. On the other hand, the market for immature wine is said to be inefficient if consumers and investors waste information by ignoring predictors of future quality when making buying and selling decisions. In this case, the price of an immature vintage is a biased estimate of true quality and will systematically overestimate or underestimate the price of the vintage at maturity. Analysis of the data shows that the Bordeaux equation provides much more accurate predictions of the price of mature vintages than the price of these vintages when they are first traded on the auction market. This suggests that the market for immature wine is inefficient because consumers and investors ignore the information on the weather conditions of the vintage when determining how much they are willing to pay for a young vintage. Moreover, the evidence suggests that market participants tend to overestimate the quality of Bordeaux vintages when they are first sold at auction, and therefore pay prices that are too high relative to sensory quality and price of the vintage when it matures. It often takes ten years or longer for the auction market to process publicly available information about wine quality efficiently, and for price to reflect the weather that prevailed during the year that produced the vintage.

Ashenfelter has used the Bordeaux equation to forecast the future quality of vintages shortly after the grapes are harvested and weather information is available, and before wine critics like Robert Parker taste the *en primeur* wine and assign scores. These predictions used to be published in Ashenfelter's newsletter *Liquid Assets*. While many wine professionals have derided Ashenfelter for using statistical methods rather than wine tasting to predict the future quality of a vintage, many of his predictions have been more accurate than those of the wine critics.[26] Unfortunately, no formal study has been done to compare the predictions of the Bordeaux equation with those of the critics to determine which are more accurate.

Two additional studies have used an approach similar to the Bordeaux equation to analyze the relationship between vintage and the auction prices of age-worthy Australian wine products. R.P. Byron and Ashenfelter (1995) study the effects of age and weather variables on the quality and price of a single wine product, Penfolds's Grange, which many consider to be Australia's premier age-worthy wine. They find that vintage-related age, temperature, and rain explain 86 percent of the variation in the auction price. Weather conditions during the growing season have a smaller effect on quality than in Bordeaux: 73 percent of the variation in the auction price is attributed to wine age. This may be the result of less variation in climatic conditions in Australia than in the Bordeaux region. As in Bordeaux, warmer weather during the growing season and less rain in the months before harvest are associated with a higher price. The positive influence of temperature on quality diminishes, with an average growing-season temperature of 66°F producing the best wine. Unlike in the case of Bordeaux, rainfall during the period when vines are dormant has no effect, while less temperature variability is conducive to higher-quality wine. Once again the researchers found evidence that market participants did not use information about weather conditions when pricing young, immature Grange wine; however, this information was eventually reflected in the auction price of the mature wine.

A study by Danielle Wood and Kym Anderson (2006) extends the work of Byron and Ashenfelter by analyzing the influence of vintage-related advances in grape growing and winemaking techniques, as well as age and weather, on the auction prices of three highly regarded, age-worthy Australian wines: Penfolds Grange, Penfolds St. Henri, and Henschke's Hill of Grace. They find evidence that consumers were willing to pay higher auction prices for vintages of Hill of Grace after a change in family proprietors and after the installation of an advanced new trellis system. This suggests that new management and viticultural techniques improve wine quality of subsequent vintages. As in prior studies, age has an effect on price, but the relationship is nonlinear for two of the three wine products. Auction prices for St. Henri and Hill of Grace increase at a diminishing rate until they reach about twenty years of age, flatten out for a period of years, and then once again rise. The researchers suggest that these wine products may reach their peak sensory quality during the plateau phase when price stabilizes. Eventually, price begins to rise again, even though sensory quality diminishes, as the wines become old and extremely scarce, and wine collectors are willing to pay an increasing amount to own such a rare wine. The importance of vintage-related weather in determining auction prices is also confirmed. In addition to temperature and rainfall prior to harvest, windiness also influences quality, with an optimal wind speed of 7 to 11 mph.

Less than 1 percent of all wines have the ability to improve with age beyond five years, and 90 percent are vulnerable to a decline in sensory quality if not consumed within the first year after they are released on the market.[27] Many wine professionals argue that for a typical wine, the potential adverse effect on quality of a poor-weather vintage can be nullified by modern grape-growing and winemaking technology. Moreover, 90 percent of the wine produced in the United States is made from grapes grown in California, which has a favorable grape-growing climate and relatively little year-to-year variation in temperature and rainfall during the growing season. Many wine professionals maintain that this minimizes the influence of vintage-related weather conditions on wine quality and price. To test these assertions, a recent study by Carlos Ramirez (2008) uses data on the prices and *Wine Spectator* scores of 1,635 Napa Valley Cabernet Sauvignons and weather variables for the period 1970 to 2004. The objective of this study is to determine if vintage-related temperature and rainfall affect the retail price and quality of a typical Napa Valley Cabernet Sauvignon. His data set includes wines that vary in price from $4 to $500 per bottle. He finds evidence that more rain in the winter months of January and February and less rain and higher temperatures during the growing-season months of April through September are associated with higher retail prices. What is more, weather conditions and a variable that captures trend influences explain 70 percent of the variation in the retail prices of Napa Valley Cabernet Sauvignon during the period studied. Because consumers who buy wine on the retail market are not necessarily well informed about the sensory characteristics of first-time Cabernet Sauvignon purchases, and retail prices are set by wine firms rather than in an auction market, it is not assumed that price measures wine quality. To analyze the effect of weather variables on sensory quality, *Wine Spectator* scores are used as a measure of quality. The results indicate that only 3 percent of the variation in *Wine Spectator* scores over the period 1970 to 2004 can be explained by temperature and rainfall. There is thus no convincing evidence that weather conditions are an important determinant of wine quality measured by *Wine Spectator* scores. One possible explanation for the different results for price and quality is that consumers and producers use information on vintage-related weather conditions when making buying and selling decisions, and this information is therefore incorporated into retail prices. *Wine Spectator* critics, on the other hand, may ignore weather-related information and instead rely on their own tastes and preferences and possibly other subjective considerations when assigning scores. Regardless, economic studies of the influence of vintage find compelling evidence that wet winters and warm, dry growing seasons are associated with higher auction prices of mature, age-worthy Bordeaux and Australian wines, and higher retail prices of

California Cabernet Sauvignon wines that tend to be consumed at a relatively young age.

VITICULTURE AND VINIFICATION

Wine professionals concur that viticultural practices and winemaking techniques affect wine quality, but often differ in their opinions about the specific methods that are most beneficial and the degree to which they lead to quality improvements. As discussed in chapter 4, many argue that the viticultural practice of restricting grape yield is required to produce high-quality wine, even if this necessitates the use of cluster pruning to remove grape bunches and reduce vine output. Others maintain that higher-quality grapes and wine result from high-density vineyards, canopy management, organic farming, manual harvesting, and various other practices. New World winemaking philosophy emphasizes the importance of vinification techniques in producing quality wine. Winemakers who subscribe to this philosophy attempt to achieve a predetermined appearance, smell, and taste profile in the wine they produce through the application of modern technology. This may include micro-oxygenation, reverse osmosis, computerized fermentation tanks, and color and flavor additives like Mega Purple grape concentrate. Alternatively, winemakers who adhere to the Old World philosophy are less inclined to intervene actively in the winemaking process, particularly if they have high-quality grape inputs, instead preferring to allow nature to take its course.

Few hedonic wine studies have analyzed the impact of viticultural practices and winemaking techniques on wine quality and price, and none have involved wine firms in the United States. This is likely the result of the difficulty in obtaining data on these characteristics. However, several studies have examined the influence of individual or collective wine-firm reputation on consumers' wine-buying decisions. Measures of reputation may well capture winemaking techniques and viticultural practices of the wine firm or the vineyards from which it purchases grapes. Moreover, consumers may be willing to pay a higher price for products of wine firms that choose grape-growing and winemaking techniques that result in a reputation for consistently producing high-quality wine, particularly if they have incomplete information about the quality of a newly released wine.

The seminal study of the effect of wine-firm reputation on price is Landon and Smith 1998, which assumes that in making buying decisions, a typical consumer may have incomplete information on the actual quality of Bordeaux wine sold on the U.S. retail market, and may therefore form an expectation of the quality of a newly released product based on the reputation of the wine firm. The amount a consumer is willing to pay for a Bordeaux wine depends on both actual and expected quality. Information on actual quality can be costly to acquire, and the consumer may therefore rely on expected quality when making purchasing decisions. The expected quality of a wine depends upon the producer's short-term and long-term quality reputation, as well as the collective reputation of the group of Bordeaux wine firms with which it is identified. *Wine Spectator* scores for the prior two vintages measure the quality of a firm's products in the recent past, and therefore its short-term reputation. The long-run reputation of the producer is captured by Robert Parker's ranking of the thirty-year quality performance of Bordeaux châteaux. Collective reputation indicators are the official government and industry quality classifications, including the well-known 1855 classification, and the region within Bordeaux where the wine firm is located. After analyzing data on 151 Bordeaux wines for the vintages 1989 and 1990 sold on the U.S. retail market, Landon and Smith find strong evidence that individual and collective reputation of Bordeaux wine firms have a sizable effect on wine price through their influence on expected quality. The marginal effect of expected quality on price is seventeen times bigger than the impact of actual quality. Expected quality is more heavily influenced by a wine firm's long-term reputation for producing quality wine than the quality of its recent products over the preceding few years. The evidence also indicates that consumers view government and industry quality classifications as good predictors of wine quality, and are therefore willing to pay a premium for wine products of more highly ranked châteaux. For example, the wine of a top-ranked "first-growth château" has a price premium that is three times larger than that of a still highly ranked "second-growth château."

Günter Schamel (2009) studied the influence of critics' wine scores on producers' reputations and product prices in the U.S. retail wine market. He argues that a typical consumer learns about a wine firm's reputation for quality from information provided by the scores critics award to its products for the prior four vintages. Because consumers have a limited ability to process the large amount of information contained in the scores of thousands of wine products, they focus their attention on those firms that make an indelible impression by receiving critics' ratings that are substantially higher or lower than those of other producers located in the same region. It is assumed that the top 20 percent of wine firms develop a reputation for producing high-quality products, while the bottom 20 percent stand out as low-quality producers. The empirical results indicate that U.S. consumers are willing to pay a 28 to 31 percent higher price for the products of firms with a reputation for high-quality wine and a 10 to 12 percent lower price for products of firms with a reputation for low-quality wine, relative to firms without a quality reputation.

In their study of factors that determine Pinot noir prices in the United States, Haeger and Storchmann (2006) include indicator variables for ninety-three wine firms. After controlling for *Wine Spectator* score, growing region temperature and rainfall, wine age, and cases produced, they find that consumers are still willing to pay substantially higher prices for the wines of certain producers and lower prices for those of other producers. They suggest these firm-specific price differences may reflect differences in winemaking skills, reputation, or marketing.

13

The Globalization of Wine

Historically, most of the wine consumed in the United States was produced by domestic wine firms that exported little of their output for sale abroad. Foreign wine firms and their products were a relatively insignificant component of the U.S. wine industry. Wine markets in other nations were also characterized by local production and consumption. The exception was France and Italy, which consumed mostly domestic wine, but also exported a substantial amount of wine to other European countries. Over the past several decades, world wine markets have become increasingly integrated. Retail store shelves in the United States and other nations are now filled with wine products from all over the world. Large multinational firms that source grapes and produce wine in a variety of countries have become important players in world wine markets. Joint ventures between wine firms in different countries are proliferating. Winemaking consultants, called flying winemakers, assist in directing wine producing across the globe, spreading innovative new vinification techniques and advances in technology. Australia, Chile, Argentina, South Africa, and New Zealand have emerged as new suppliers and formidable competitors in the United States and other wine-consuming countries, exporting much of what they produce. The demand for wine is increasing dramatically in Asian nations, creating large new potential wine markets. Countries like China and Japan are becoming major consumers of luxury wine products.

To what extent and why are world wine markets becoming globalized? What are the salient characteristics of the structure of the global wine industry? To what degree does the United States participate in the global wine market? These questions are the focus of this chapter.

INDICATORS AND CAUSES OF WINE GLOBALIZATION

A number of indicators suggest that over the past few decades the production and consumption of wine has rapidly transformed from a local to a global industry. From the late 1980s to 2009, the proportion of the world's wine produced in one country but exported and sold in others increased from 15 to 32 percent.[1] Today, about one of every three bottles of wine consumed in the world is an imported product. These products include a number of international brands made from wine produced in a variety of countries and sold by multinational wine firms. For example, prior to 1990 Blue Nun was a popular German white wine product made from grapes grown in Germany. Today, Blue Nun is a wine brand comprising twenty separate products, including Cabernet Sauvignon, Merlot, Shiraz, Zinfandel, and Chardonnay made from bulk wine produced in a variety of countries, France, Australia, Spain, and the United States among them.[2] The German wine firm Langguth sells an estimated 500,000 cases of Blue Nun each year in more than 100 countries.[3] The Blossom Hill wine brand is produced in California, bottled in Italy, and sold primarily in European countries by the London-based conglomerate Diageo. Most consumers purchase Blue Nun, Blossom Hill, and other high-volume international wine brands like Franzia and Lindemans based on their quality-to-price reputation and consistent style, and neither know nor care in which country the grapes were grown and the wine was produced, or even the name of the firm that produced it.

Also indicative of wine globalization is the emergence of what is sometimes called an international wine style. Historically, different regions and countries were known for wine products with unique sensory characteristics that reflected differences in natural environment, grape varieties, winemaking technology, and winegrowing tradition. French wines, Italian wines, Spanish wines, and the wine products of other countries had manifestly different styles. More recently, there has been an evident trend toward a uniform style of wine that lacks a regional identity and could come from anyplace in the world. Many of the international commodity brands share a similar fresh, fruity, slightly sweet style that appeals to casual wine consumers in a variety of countries. The most successful expression of this style is the Yellow Tail brand identified by the distinctive wallaby on the label and produced by the Australian firm Casella Wines. Yellow Tail was originally created for the U.S. market and made its debut in 2001. Wine industry analysts maintain that Casella's objective was to produce wine products that appealed to the potentially large population of nontraditional U.S. wine consumers who were accustomed to consuming soft drinks and shunned wine because they believed it was too tannic, acidic, dry, or oaky, characteristics traditional wine drinkers often prefer. Casella initially offered two Yellow Tail products, a Chardonnay and a Shiraz, with prominent fruit flavors, some sweetness, a trace of oak, and a soft mouthfeel at a price of $5.99 per 750 ml bottle. When Yellow Tail was launched in 2001, 225,000 cases were purchased. By 2006, it was the largest imported wine brand in the United States, with annual sales of 8.1 million cases.[4] Most of this growth was attributed to word-of-mouth promotion by satisfied consumers, rather than a large advertising campaign or high scores from wine critics. By 2009 sales of Yellow Tail in the United States exceeded the combined sales of all imported French wines.[5] Today, more than twenty Yellow Tail products are sold in fifty countries, with annual sales exceeding 10 million cases.[6] Many wine firms have responded to the huge commercial success of Yellow Tail by producing competing commodity brands that have a similar style and flavor profile. An increasing number of wine firms that produce premium and luxury wines are also opting for an international style of wine directed at what they believe are the tastes of a more sophisticated wine consumer in the global market. This is a rich, intense, fruit-driven style complemented by oak flavors of vanilla and toast, with soft tannins and relatively high alcohol. It is criticized by some wine professionals for being a generic style of wine that can come from any wine-producing region in the world, and lacks a unique character or personality that reflects the location where the grapes are grown and the wine is made.

The development of an international wine style coincides with, and may largely result from, another globalization indicator: the growing influence of international winemaking consultants, called flying winemakers, and foreign direct investment in domestic vineyards and wineries. Prior to the 1980s, grape growing and winemaking ideas and technology spread slowly from one country to another country, primarily by written communication or winemaking internship abroad. At the end of the 1980s, European merchants began to contract with Australian winemakers to travel to Europe and perform winemaking tasks during the months of September to November, a period when they had no winemaking responsibilities at home because of differences in the grape-growing season between the Northern and Southern Hemispheres. Australian winemakers were preferred because Australia was at the forefront of developing innovative new winemaking techniques. The Australian winemakers were successful at using their advanced technology to transform cheap grapes into wine of acceptable quality. Eventually, winemakers from other countries, including France, Italy, New Zealand, and the United States, started to provide consulting services to wineries in a variety of wine-producing countries around the world. Highly regarded consultants like Michel Rolland of France, Alberto Antonini of Italy, and Paul Hobbs of the United States each advise as many as 100 wineries worldwide. This has resulted in the rapid dissemination of cutting-edge winemaking techniques and technology, and has certainly contributed to the development of an international wine style directed at the satisfaction of consumers' preferences, supplanting the variety of wine styles based on winemaking tradition and geographic location.

Also contributing to the spread of winegrowing technology and a more uniform style of wine is the enormous investment wine firms located in one country have made in the wine industries of other countries during the past couple of decades. These investments have transformed many wine firms that previously operated in a single country into multinational enterprises. Investments in vineyards and wineries have taken several forms, including joint ventures, acquisitions, and the establishment of new wine firms. One of the first major joint ventures was the Opus One winery located in Napa Valley, California, launched in 1979 and co-owned by the U.S. winemaker Robert Mondavi and France's Château Mouton Rothschild. It was designed to produce a single luxury wine product using both American and French grape-growing and winemaking know-how. Today, such joint ventures are commonplace in wine-producing countries around the world. U.S., French, and Spanish wine firms have invested millions of dollars to acquire or establish wine firms in countries like Chile and Argentina. In the process, they have provided capital for the modernization and expansion of the wine industry in these countries and have introduced new technologies such as canopy management, vertical trellis systems, stainless steel vessels, and sorting tables. Today, all major wine-producing countries are populated by multinational wine firms. To a degree, the international wine style may reflect foreign investment and improved grape-growing and winemaking techniques spread around the globe by flying winemakers that have eliminated wine flaws associated with traditional viticultural and vinification techniques.

A final important indicator of globalization is the entry of new suppliers into the export market. Prior to 1990, the international wine market was dominated by "Old World" European producers from France, Italy, Spain, and Germany. In the late 1980s, non-European wine-producing countries accounted for only 3 percent of the volume of world wine exports. By 2009, non-European producers—led by Australia, New Zealand, Chile, Argentina, South Africa, and the United States—had increased their share of the global export market to 37 percent.[7] Today, wine firms located in these New World countries are formidable competitors in the global market.

A number of factors have contributed to the globalization of the wine industry. Many countries have negotiated free-trade agreements that reduce tariffs and other barriers to trade, allowing foreign wine firms to better compete with domestic firms and gain access to markets. In countries with growing wine demand where tariffs on wine are still high, foreign wine firms have an economic incentive to set up joint ventures with domestic firms. Often this involves a foreign producer shipping bulk wine to a domestic market, where it is then blended, bottled, and sold by a domestic partner to circumvent the high tariff.

Argentina, Chile, and South Africa have ideal natural environments for growing wine grapes and a long history of producing wine for domestic consumption. However, prior to the 1990s, political instability and unfavorable economic policies precluded them from participating in the global wine market. Economic policy provided incentives for the wine industry to produce large quantities of low-quality wine for domestic consumption and protected the industry from foreign competition. As a result, there was little demand for their wine on the export market. The inimical economic environment along with political uncertainty was a disincentive for foreign wine firms to invest in the domestic wine industry in these countries, even though they had low land and labor costs and a propitious winegrowing climate. However, these conditions started to change in the 1990s with the return of democracy to Chile, the end of apartheid in South Africa, an improvement in the political climate in Argentina, and economic reforms favorable to foreign investment and wine exports.[8]

Industry initiatives have also fostered wine globalization. In Australia, the wine industry, dominated by a handful of large firms operating in a domestic wine market limited by a small population, formulated a strategy in the 1990s to grow by exporting substantially more wine on the global market. The plan, called *Strategy 2025*, resulted in more than a doubling of vineyard acreage and economic policies that have led to a dramatic increase in wine exports. More recently, Argentina developed a strategic plan similar to Australia's to provide economic incentives for strong export growth, and South Africa promotes exports through the Wine Industry Trust created in 1999. Producers in the highly concentrated Chilean wine industry also recognize that the only way to grow is through exports, given Chile's small population and domestic market, and have acted accordingly.

A shift in wine consumption from traditional to nontraditional wine-consuming countries has opened up new export markets for wine producers worldwide. France, Italy, Spain, Portugal, and Argentina, historically some of the world's largest wine-drinking countries, have experienced an ongoing decline in per capita wine consumption as demand has shifted away from wine to beer, spirits, and nonalcoholic beverages. Conversely, as wine becomes an increasingly important part of lifestyles, per capita wine consumption has been steadily rising in North America, northern Europe, Asia, and Russia. Many countries in these regions of the world have limited or no capability to produce wine, and must therefore rely heavily on imports to satisfy growing wine demand. The biggest potential future export market is China, where grape-wine consumption grew at a rate of 13 percent per year from 2000 to 2009. The only other countries with a larger annual rate of increase during this period were India (32 percent), Mexico (25 percent), Turkey (16 percent), and Korea (15 percent); however, China's aggregate wine consumption is 17 to 113 times bigger than that of those countries.[9]

A final important factor contributing to wine globalization has been advances in transportation and information technology. As discussed previously, the development of large cargo containers with collapsible polyurethane bladders allows firms to produce wine in one country, ship it in bulk, and bottle it in (or near) the country where it is sold, without compromising quality. This has made it much easier and less costly to produce large quantities of wine for export. In 2009, bulk wine accounted for 37 percent of the volume of world wine exports.[10] Advances in information technology have reduced the cost to wine consumers of acquiring information and increased the global influence of the growing number of wine critics. Many of these critics, like Robert Parker, have promoted an international wine style consistent with consumer tastes rather than producer preferences based on regional characteristics and winemaking tradition.

THE STRUCTURE OF THE GLOBAL WINE MARKET

Countries

The global wine market is composed of all those countries that produce and consume wine. There are approximately 63 wine-producing and 213 wine-consuming countries worldwide.[11] A major reason a large proportion of these produce little or no wine domestically is because they are located in the Northern or Southern Hemisphere outside of the temperate climate zone between 30 and 50 degrees latitude, which is necessary for wine grape production. While a large number of countries participate in the global wine market, a preponderance of production and consumption is accounted for by relatively few of these.

Table 5 provides data on the top ten wine-producing countries (column 1) ranked by world share of wine-production volume (column 2) for year 2009. Columns 3 through 5 give data on percentage of global export volume, percentage of global export value, and exports as a percentage of domestic wine-production volume, with world rank in parentheses. Table 6 presents analogous data for the top wine-consuming nations. The ten largest winemaking countries produce 81 percent of total world output and account for 86 percent of world wine exports by volume and 84 percent by value. The world's top three producers are Italy, France, and Spain. These three Old World winemaking countries, along with Germany, account for about 50 percent of global wine output, 56 percent of exports by volume, and 62 percent of exports by value. On average, 36 percent of the volume of wine they produce domestically is exported and sold to consumers in other countries. However, over time these traditional wine-producing nations have become relatively less important players in the global industry, as evidenced by declining market shares in both production and exports. In the late 1980s, they produced a significantly larger 58 percent of the world's wine and accounted for 75 percent of exports by volume and 83 percent by value.

The five largest New World producers are the United States, Argentina, Australia, South Africa, and Chile. Together they account for 26 percent of world production, up from 18 percent in the late 1980s. They have also captured a much larger share of the world export market,

TABLE 5   NATIONAL SHARES OF WINE PRODUCTION BY TOTAL VOLUME, VOLUME
OF EXPORTS, AND VALUE OF EXPORTS, 2009

Country	Share of world volume (%)	Share of world export volume (% with world rank)	Share of world export value (% with world rank)	Domestic volume exported (% with world rank)
Italy	18.5	22.4 (1)	19.3 (2)	38.7 (7)
France	16.8	14.5 (3)	30.5 (1)	27.5 (11)
Spain	12.0	14.9 (2)	8.6 (3)	39.7 (6)
United States	9.9	4.6 (7)	3.5 (7)	14.8 (19)
Argentina	4.5	3.4 (9)	2.5 (11)	24.0 (13)
Australia	4.4	8.9 (4)	7.1 (4)	65.5 (3)
South Africa	3.9	5.0 (6)	2.8 (9)	40.9 (5)
Chile	3.7	8.0 (5)	5.4 (5)	70.1 (1)
China	3.6	0.0 (>20)	0.0 (>20)	0.7 (>20)
Germany	3.5	4.0 (8)	4.0 (6)	36.8 (9)
Total	80.8	85.7	83.7	

SOURCE: Anderson and Nelgen 2011, tables 185, 192, 194, 198, 204, 206, 243.

TABLE 6   NATIONAL SHARES OF WINE CONSUMPTION BY TOTAL VOLUME,
VOLUME OF IMPORTS, AND VALUE OF IMPORTS, 2009

Country	Share of world volume (%)	Share of world import volume (% with world rank)	Share of world import value (% with world rank)	Domestic volume imported (% with world rank)
United States	11.6	10.8 (3)	15.4 (2)	34.0 (15)
Italy	11.1	1.7 (15)	1.3 (16)	6.0 (>20)
France	10.4	6.7 (5)	2.7 (9)	23.5 (18)
Germany	9.2	16.4 (1)	10.2 (3)	65.2 (12)
United Kingdom	5.8	14.8 (2)	15.7 (1)	93.1 (5)
China	4.8	2.0 (>20)	1.7 (14)	15.0 (>20)
Russia	4.7	4.2 (6)	2.2 (12)	32.8 (16)
Spain	4.4	0.3 (>20)	0.6 (>20)	3.0 (>20)
Argentina	4.4	0.1 (>20)	0.0 (>20)	1.0 (>20)
Belgium and Luxembourg	2.6	7.7 (4)	10.2 (4)	110.5 (1)
Total	69.0	64.7	60	

SOURCE: Anderson and Nelgen 2011, tables 186, 195, 198, 199, 204, 206, 243.

increasing their share from about 2 percent to 30 percent by volume, but a smaller 21 percent by value, suggesting that growth in exports of higher-priced premium and luxury wine have lagged behind lower-priced bulk commodity wine. While the United States is the biggest New World wine producer, the most important exporter by volume is Australia with a 8.9 percent share, followed by Chile (8 percent), South Africa (5 percent), United States (4.6 percent), and Argentina (3.4 percent). On average, 43 percent of the wine produced by these five New World countries is exported; if the United States is excluded, this rises to 50 percent. The wine industries in Chile and Australia, two countries with relatively small domestic wine markets, are highly dependent on sales abroad: Chile exports 70 percent of the wine it produces and Australia 66 percent. Even though these New World countries are gaining a larger share of the world export market, the top three wine exporters are Italy (22.4 percent), Spain (14.9 percent), and France (14.5 percent). France continues to dominate the global market for premium and luxury wine, with a substantial 30 percent export share by value. This exceeds the value of exports of the five largest New World countries, which collectively account for only 21 percent.

China has a long history of making wine, but much of what was produced until recently was made from rice and millet, not grapes. In the 1980s, the Chinese wine industry started to shift its resources to traditional grape-wine production. To obtain the capital, winemaking know-how, and technology necessary to expand the industry and increase wine quality, many Chinese producers have set up joint ventures with wine firms from France, Italy, and Australia. China has also been a popular destination for flying winemakers. The Chinese wine industry is presently undergoing rapid growth, and China is the ninth-largest wine producer in the world. During this development phase, the focus has been on making wine for domestic consumption, and exports account for less than 1 percent of production. However, many analysts predict that China will eventually be a formidable competitor in the global wine marketplace.[12]

Turning to the demand side of the global wine market, table 6 reveals that wine consumption is somewhat less concentrated than production. The top ten countries consume 69 percent of the world's wine, importing 65 percent of it by volume and 60 percent by value. Seven of the ten largest wine-producing countries are also top consumers, with the United Kingdom, Russia, and Belgium and Luxembourg replacing Australia, South Africa, and Chile. While the United States, Italy, and France are the three largest wine consumers in the world, Germany is the top wine importer by volume, and the United Kingdom by value: 93 percent of the wine consumed in the United Kingdom and 65 percent of the wine drunk in Germany is imported. On the other hand, in Spain and Argentina, imported wine accounts for 3 percent or less of consumption, and these countries have tiny global import shares. Italy, the world's second-largest consumer, accounts for less than 2 percent of world import volume, and much of the wine it does import is bulk wine that is bottled in Italy and then exported to other countries.

Even though the United Kingdom produces little wine domestically, it plays an important role in the global wine market as both a consumer and market leader. Many big wine-producing countries are highly dependent on the large and growing British market for export sales and compete vigorously in it for market share. Australia, New Zealand, and South Africa sell more than 30 percent of their exports in the United Kingdom, the United States about 25 percent, and Chile, France, Italy, and Germany between 15 and 20 percent each.[13] The United Kingdom has a number of prominent wine critics and highly regarded wine publications, which affect wine sales worldwide. It has sophisticated wine consumers and an active auction market for age-worthy wines. Finally, it has been at the forefront of the global trend of increased wine sales in supermarkets.[14] Many large retailers like the U.S.-based chain Costco, the U.K.-based chain Tesco, and the German-based chain Aldi now operate in a variety of countries and sell large quantities of both brand-name and private-label wine on the global retail market. Today, large supermarkets dominate the retail wine market in many countries.

China is the world's sixth-largest wine consumer, and wine sales are rising rapidly there. The Chinese government has promoted increased wine consumption as a way to reduce the incidence of alcoholism and has provided consumers an economic incentive to substitute wine for spirits by significantly reducing taxes on both domestic and imported wine.[15] Imported wine accounts for 15 percent of domestic consumption and includes imported bottled wine, bulk wine bottled in China and sold under a foreign label, and bulk wine blended with domestic wine and sold under a Chinese label. Chinese consumers also purchase a significant amount of imported luxury wine, particularly Bordeaux and Burgundy from France. Hong Kong has one of the most active wine auction markets in the world. Because of China's large population and low per capita wine consumption, it has the potential eventually to become the world's largest wine consumer and import market.

U.S. Participation in the Global Wine Market

By any measure, the United States is an important participant in the global wine market. It is the world's largest consumer of wine and has the second-largest import market by value and third-largest by volume. A large population and relatively small but increasing per capita consumption of wine each year for almost two decades suggests there is plenty of room for the market to grow in the future. It has one of the lowest levels of trade barriers on imported wine of any nation in the world and an economic environment conducive to foreign investment. Because of these attributes, the U.S. market is attractive to foreign wine firms that want to expand their business on a global scale. For several decades, foreign wine firms have entered the U.S. market through both exports and direct investment in the U.S. wine industry. Between 1990 and 2009, imported wine continuously increased its share of the U.S. market. During this period, the volume of imported wine increased at an average annual rate of about 8 percent. Between 2005 and 2009, on average, about one-third of the wine consumed in the United States was imported.[16] Italy sells the most wine in the United States, followed by Australia, Chile, Argentina, and France. In 2009, U.S. consumers purchased 31 percent of Australian exports, 28 percent of Argentine exports, and 20 percent of Chilean exports, suggesting that these countries are highly dependent on the U.S. market for their global wine sales.

A large number of foreign wine firms have also entered the U.S. market by setting up joint ventures with some U.S. wine firms, acquiring others, and starting new wineries. Foreign investment in the U.S. wine industry began in earnest in the 1980s when a number of French Champagne producers purchased vineyards and constructed wineries in California to satisfy the growing demand for sparkling wine. Foreign wine firms specializing in still wines from France, Spain, Germany, and Italy soon followed, with some establishing new wineries and others purchasing existing wine firms.[17] By 2011, five of the thirty largest wine producers in the United States were owned by firms variously based in Australia, Chile, France, and the United Kingdom, which penetrated the U.S. market mostly through acquisition of U.S. wineries. Recently, Chinese investors have started to purchase vineyards and wineries in the United States.

On the supply side, the United States is the world's fourth-largest producer and seventh-largest exporter of wine. In 2009, it produced 10 percent of the world's wine, sold almost 15 percent of the wine it made to foreign consumers, and had a 4.6 percent share of the global export market. Prior to the 1990s, U.S. wine firms demonstrated little interest in selling their wine outside of the domestic market. During the 1980s, annual U.S. wine exports accounted for a paltry 2 percent of wine production. In 1985, Congress passed legislation that provided subsidies to wine firms to promote exports.[18] This gave producers a financial incentive to pursue opportunities to sell their products in foreign markets, and initiated a quarter-century effort to increase wine exports. By the late 1990s, wine firms were exporting almost 10 percent of their production, and by 2009, this had reached 15 percent.[19] Wine exports have continued to grow, and by 2011, they accounted for about 20 percent of the value of wine sales by U.S. wine firms. The twenty-seven member nations of the European Union account for more than one-half the volume of U.S. exports and one-third of the value; within the European Union, the United Kingdom is the biggest market for U.S. wine. Canada is the second-largest export market, followed by Hong Kong, Japan, China, Switzerland, and Vietnam.[20] U.S. wine firms have also made significant investments in foreign wine industries. Some of the first to establish operations abroad were Gallo in Italy, Robert Mondavi in France, and Kendall-Jackson in Italy, Argentina, and Chile. Today, large U.S.-based wine firms like Constellation own wineries in a number of different countries throughout the world.

THE STRUCTURE OF THE GLOBAL WINE MARKET: FIRMS

The total number and size distribution of the firms that constitute it are important aspects of the global wine industry. Economic theory suggests that competition among firms in an industry will be more vigorous and market power more dispersed the larger the number of firms and the smaller the disparity in their size. Table 7 provides estimates of the number of wine firms in each of the ten largest wine-producing countries for the most recent year for which data could be obtained, and gives a rough idea of the approximate number of producers in the global wine industry. Market shares of the largest two and four firms in the domestic industry measured by the volume of wine sold for year 2009 are also given. Table 8 presents estimates of the global market shares of the largest two, four, twenty, and thirty wine firms for years 2003, 2006, and 2009. These estimates are useful in drawing some generalizations about differences in the structure of wine industries across countries and trends in the global wine market.

Table 7 reveals that the global wine industry has over 128,000 firms supplying wine to domestic markets, with a fraction of these also producing wine for export to foreign markets. Table 8 shows that the world's four largest wine firms accounted for less than 9 percent of the volume of world wine sales in 2009, and the largest thirty firms for just over 23 percent. No single firm dominates the world market. The largest producer, U.S.-based Gallo, has a market share of less than 3 percent and sells about 95 percent of the wine it produces in its home market. By way of comparison, the world's largest beer producer, the Belgian-Brazilian multinational AB InBev, has a global market share of 20 percent, and the top three beer and spirits firms have shares of 35 and 42 percent respectively.[21] While concentration in the global wine industry is low, it has been trending up over time. The share of world wine sales of the four largest firms rose from 6.8 percent in 2003 to 8.5 percent in 2009. The ten-firm concentration ratio increased from 11.4 to 14.3 percent, and the thirty-firm share from 18.2 to 23.2 percent. A decade ago, a number of analysts predicted that the wine industry today would be dominated by ten or fifteen large multinational conglomerates, which would continue to grow through mergers and acquisitions and capture the lion's share of global wine sales. While global wine production has become more concentrated, however, it is still a long way from being dominated by a small group of conglomerates like other beverage industries.

From a global perspective, the number and size distribution of wine firms suggests that producers may have relatively little power in the world market and face substantial competition. However, there are significant differences in the structure of national wine industries. In general, concentration of wine production is higher in New World than Old World countries. France, Italy, Spain, and Germany collectively have more than 100,000 wine producers, and the market shares of the four largest firms are between 3.8 and 21 percent, with an average of 14 percent. Moreover, producers in France and Germany face substantial competition from foreign firms, with wine imports accounting for 34 percent of sales in France and 65 percent in Germany. The most dominant producer in the domestic industries of these European countries is García Carrión, with an 11.5 percent share in its home market in Spain. Together, the five New World countries listed in table 7—Australia, Chile, Argentina, South Africa, and the United States—have fewer than 12,000 wine firms with an average four-firm concentration ratio of 59 percent. With the exception of the United States, producers

TABLE 7   NUMBER AND SIZE DISTRIBUTION OF WINE FIRMS BY NATION

Country	Number of firms	2009 share of the two largest firms (%)	2009 share of the four largest firms (%)
France	36,440	14.3	15.9
Italy	43,000	8.0	9.7
Spain	6,355	15.5	21.0
United States	7,116	37.6	56.0
Argentina	1,275	42.8	60.5
Australia	2,320	41.4	62.3
Chile	300	59.8	>80.0
South Africa	560	35.4	37.1
China	500	19.4	28.0
Germany	30,470	2.3	3.8
Total	128,336		

SOURCES: Estimates of number of U.S. firms from *Wine Business Monthly*, February 2012; for China, Jenster et al. 2008, 66; for all other countries, Lewin 2010, 234. Market share data from Anderson and Nelgen 2011, table 33.

TABLE 8   WORLD PERCENTAGE SHARES OF THE LARGEST WINE FIRMS

Year	Share of the two largest firms (%)	Share of the four largest firms (%)	Share of the ten largest firms (%)	Share of the twenty largest firms (%)	Share of the thirty largest firms (%)
2003	4.7	6.8	11.4	16.8	18.2
2006	5.8	8.4	13.8	19.2	21.9
2009	5.6	8.5	14.3	19.8	23.2

SOURCE: Anderson and Nelgen 2011, table 35.

in these countries face little competition from imported wine products. Imports account for about 1 percent of domestic consumption in Argentina, Chile, and South Africa, and only 12 percent in Australia. The Chilean wine industry has the least competitive structure of any in the world; the four largest firms have a combined market share of more than 80 percent. The two largest producers, Concha y Toro and Santa Rita, each have market shares of about 30 percent. Large wine firms also have dominant positions in other New World countries, where Distell (South Africa), Peñaflor (Argentina), Treasury Wine Estates (Australia), and Gallo (U.S.) have domestic market shares of between 18 and 34 percent.

Organizational Structure of Wine Firms

Like those in the United States, foreign wine firms are legal entities that organize and coordinate the production and sale of wine to consumers. The dominant form of business organization in the U.S. wine industry is the corporation, which accounts for more than 75 percent of wine sales. The relatively few public corporations are owned by a large number of shareholders; the more prevalent private corporations are often family-controlled firms. The rest of the nation's wine is produced by a large number of proprietorships, partnerships, and limited liability companies with one or relatively few owners. An important type of wine-firm organization in European countries, but nonexistent in the United States, is the cooperative.[22] Estimates suggest that cooperatives produce about 35 percent of the volume of wine in Germany, 50 percent in France and Italy, and 70 percent in Spain.[23] Cooperatives also account for a significant fraction of wine output in Argentina and South Africa. In Argentina, the cooperative FeCoVitA is the second-largest wine producer by volume, with a market share of 14 percent, and the sixteenth-largest wine firm in the world.[24] In South Africa, wine cooperatives were instrumental in the development of the wine industry during the 1900s, but today play a somewhat smaller role. The wine economist Mike Veseth estimates that European wine cooperatives produce as much as 25 percent of the world's wine.[25]

Like any wine firm, a typical cooperative organizes and coordinates grape growing, wine production, and wine distribution. The critical feature that makes it different from wine firms in the United States is that it is owned by a relatively large number of grape growers, called members.[26] A cooperative may have hundreds or even thousands of members. In many cooperatives, a majority of the individual growers produce a small quantity of grapes on a tiny plot of vineyard land. For example, in Germany about 58,000 grape growers are members of 214 cooperatives, of which 130 produce wine. A typical member farms less than three acres of vines, and many are part-time grape growers that produce grapes to supplement their incomes.[27] A wine cooperative produces wine made from grapes purchased from members; most are also actively involved in distributing the wine. Winery plant and equipment are financed by the equity investments of members, sometimes supplemented by government subsidies. This allows a large number of small grape growers to pool their resources to take advantage of economies of scale in wine production and marketing, and to employ the services of a professional winemaker. Each member has an equal ownership share of the cooperative, regardless of size. The members elect directors, who conduct operations or hire managers to do so. The revenue generated by the cooperative from selling wine is used to pay grower-members for the grapes they supply and cover other expenses associated with producing and distributing wine. Any revenue over and above these costs is available to reinvest in such things as new winemaking equipment, improvements in product quality, and brand development.[28] Cooperatives also have explicit or implicit contractual rules, which may affect economic incentives and behavior. For example, in a traditional cooperative, membership is open to all growers willing to accept the rules and make the required investment; however, membership may be restricted to residents of a particular geographic location. The cooperative is required to sell only the wine products of its members; it cannot buy and sell the products of other wineries. The cooperative must purchase whatever quantity and quality of grapes the member-growers choose to deliver. In some cases, growers are allowed to decide the amount of grapes they will sell to the cooperative; if they choose, they can sell grapes to private wine firms or use the grapes to make their own wine. Alternatively, growers may be required to sell all of their grapes to the cooperative.

Many observers believe that the large surplus of low-quality wine that exists in many European countries is exacerbated by the behavior of traditional cooperatives, which often have organizational and contractual incentives to maximize the quantity of wine produced at the expense of quality. For years, major European wine-producing countries have produced more wine than consumers in the domestic and foreign market desire to purchase. Estimates suggest that France, Italy, and Spain generate an excess supply of wine of about 500,000 cases each year.[29] This surplus is the result of wine consumption falling faster than production in these countries. Much of this excess is low-quality table wine produced by cooperatives, for which there is insufficient demand. To rid the market of this surplus, the European Union buys wine that cannot be sold commercially and uses the ethanol for gasoline and manufacturing; however, this contributes to the perpetuation of the surplus.

What economic incentives may induce traditional cooperatives to produce large quantities of low-quality wine for which there is inadequate demand on the commercial market? A unique economic characteristic of a cooperative is that owners of this type of wine firm, the growers, also supply the most important input used to produce the wine. The higher the price the cooperative pays the owners for the grape input, the more money they make, regardless of their investment in the wine firm. This creates an economic incentive for the member-owners to seek high grape prices from the cooperative to maximize revenue from grape growing. However, the higher the price the cooperative pays for members' grapes, the higher its cost, the lower its profit, and the less money it has to make investments necessary to improve wine quality and satisfy the shift in European consumer demand towards higher-quality wine. Several common contractual rules reinforce and compound this problem. If members are contractually obligated to sell their entire grape output to the cooperative at a fixed price, then each grower individually has an incentive to maximize the quantity of low-cost, low-quality grapes he delivers to the cooperative to maximize his income. However, when all growers collectively behave this way, this results in an excess supply of low-quality wine that commands a low price. The low wine price then leads to a low future grape price and smaller payments for growers. All growers would benefit if they decreased grape production, because the cooperative would get a higher price enabling it to make higher grape payments to members; however, individually each grower has no incentive to limit output. Moreover, if members are allowed to decide what grapes to sell to the cooperative, they have an incentive to offer their highest-quality grapes to other wine firms willing to pay higher prices, or use these grapes to make their own wine products, and deliver their low-quality grapes to the cooperative at the fixed, agreed-upon price.[30] As a result, it is not uncommon for European wine firms that are legally organized as traditional cooperatives to overproduce low-quality wine for which there is little market demand that is ultimately purchased by government for industrial use. Without government subsidies, these cooperative wine firms would not be viable.

A new generation of wine cooperatives have recognized the problems associated with the traditional cooperative model and have implemented changes in their organizational and incentive structure that have enabled them to compete successfully in both the national and global markets. These cooperatives have market-oriented professional managers who reinvest profit in long-term winery-related investments rather than maximizing grape price payments to members in the short run. A number have evolved from bulk wine producers to cooperatives that sell bottled wine under their own brand names, and have implemented programs to reduce grape yield and increase quality. The most successful cooperatives are selling a growing share of their output on foreign markets. The Italian cooperative Cavit, with 4,500 grower-members, is one of the top wine exporters to the United States. The 300-member French cooperative Cave de Tain produces premium wine products that have received high scores from wine critics, and exports wine to the United States and other foreign markets. These are only a few examples of wine cooperatives that have been able to thrive in the global wine market by producing products that consumers want and selling them at competitive prices.

Rising Concentration and Consolidation of Wine Firms

The beginning of the new millennium brought with it rising global market shares of the world's biggest wine firms. From 2003 to 2009, the thirty largest firms increased their share of volume wine sales by 5 percent; today, about one of every four bottles of wine sold in the world is a product of one of these firms. Almost half of the increased market share during this period was accounted for by three firms: Constellation, Foster's, and Pernod Ricard.[31] All are multinational firms, with wineries in more than one country. Constellation is based in the United States, Foster's in Australia, and Pernod Ricard in France. These firms have increased their global market shares through mergers and acquisitions. A similar growth strategy has been used by a number of other wine firms, resulting in increased consolidation of the global wine industry. A brief look at these large global players and their evolution will help illuminate the way in which firms are attempting to grow bigger and capture a larger share of the world wine market.

Constellation, Foster's, and Pernod Ricard are (or were) alcoholic beverage conglomerates with wine, beer, and spirits operations in multiple countries. Each is a publicly traded corporation with a large number of shareholders. They are among the top five wine producers in the world, and Pernod Ricard is the world's second-largest spirits producer. In 2008, wine sales accounted for 74 percent of Constellation's revenues, 44 percent for Foster's, and 23 percent for Pernod Ricard.[32] Each has more than 3,500 employees, more than forty wine brands, and sells its products in a large number of countries. While they possess common attributes, they have significantly different histories.

Constellation was founded in 1945 as the Canandaigua Wine Company, a family-owned wine firm that produced bulk wine in a converted sauerkraut factory in New York.[33] By the 1950s, it was selling wines under its own labels, including Richard's Wild Irish Rose. It used the profits from this popular fortified wine to acquire several wine firms on the East Coast. In 1973, it became a public corporation and embarked on a strategy of accelerated growth through acquisition of wine firms and brands. By the mid-1990s, it had become a large producer of non-premium wine products with popular brands like Almaden, Paul Masson, Inglenook, and Taylor California Cellars. During the latter part of the 1990s, Constellation transformed itself into an alcoholic beverage conglomerate by acquiring beer and spirits producers and importers. At the same time, it entered the premium segment of the wine market by acquiring well-regarded wine firms like Simi, Franciscan, Ravenswood, Blackstone, and in 2004, the iconic Robert Mondavi, along with others, including the Beam Wine Estates portfolio of wineries in 2007. After 2000, Constellation started to expand its operations in foreign countries by acquiring BRL Hardy in Australia, Vincor in Canada, Ruffino in Italy, and several wineries in New Zealand. However, the period of rapid growth did not generate the expected profit. In 2008, Constellation began to reduce its portfolio of brands and wineries selling two nonpremium brands, Almaden and Inglenook, to The Wine Group, and eight mostly premium brands to Ascentia Wine Estates.[34] In 2010, facing vigorous competition in the Australian and U.K. markets, Constellation sold all of its wineries and brands in these two countries to the Australian-based private equity firm Champ. Champ proceeded to form a new wine firm, Accolade Wines, which is now one of the ten largest wine companies in the world, with annual sales of more than 30 million cases. Even after downsizing, Constellation still has more than fifty wine brands and global sales of 62 million cases in 2011.[35]

Foster's history of producing beer in Australia dates back to 1886. Over the years, it grew through mergers and acquisitions, becoming Australia's biggest brewer. With beer consumption falling in the 1990s, Foster's entered the wine market in 1996 by purchasing the Australian wine firm Mildara Blass. In 2000, it became a multinational wine firm by acquiring the venerable U.S. wine producer Beringer Wine Estates for $1.5 billion. At the time, Beringer was one of the few public corporations in the U.S. wine industry and it owned well-known wineries like Chateau St. Jean, Meridian, and Stag's Leap.[36] Foster's continued to grow its multinational wine business by acquiring additional wine firms in Australia, the United States, Chile, Italy, and New Zealand. By 2010, its wine division had a portfolio of more than fifty brands, including Beringer, Etude, Penfolds, Rosemont, and Lindemans. However, many stock market analysts argued that Foster's multi-beverage strategy was a failure, and that the wine division had become a financial albatross preventing its stock price from rising. In 2011, Foster's implemented a demerger of its wine business and spun it off as a separate company called Treasury Wine Estates. Today, Australia-based Treasury Wine Estates is the world's largest public corporation that produces wine products only, with global wine sales of 37 million cases in 2011; U.S consumers accounted for half of these sales.[37] In 2012, SABMiller acquired Foster's beer and other businesses.

Pernod Ricard began its corporate life in 1975 as a spirits producer, resulting from a merger between two existing French spirits companies. It became an alcoholic beverage conglomerate in 1989 when it purchased the Australian wine firm Orlando Wyndham. Unlike Constellation and Foster's, its strategy has been to largely ignore its home market and establish winemaking facilities in foreign countries.[38] By 2009, after making a number of acquisitions, it was the largest wine firm in New Zealand, the second-largest in Spain, and the third-largest in Australia; however, it continues to be a minor player in France.[39] Its best-known brand is Jacob's Creek, one of the world's largest-selling wine products, produced in Australia and sold in more than sixty countries.

It is useful to make a distinction between three types of acquisitions used by wine firms to pursue a growth strategy. One option is for one wine firm to acquire another along with all of its assets, such as wine brands, wineries, vineyards, and vineyard contracts. Examples include Foster's acquisition of Beringer in 2000 and Gallo's acquisition of Louis Martini in 2002. A second possibility is for one wine firm to purchase assets such as a winery and wine brands from another. For example, in 2007 Gallo purchased the William Hill Winery, wine brand, and vineyard land from Beam Wine Estates, only one of Beam's many brands and wineries. Finally, a third alternative is for a wine firm to make a brand-only acquisition. This involves purchasing one or more brands along with the existing inventory of wine without any additional real assets such as a winery or vineyard. As an example, in 2012 Constellation purchased the Mark West wine brand and existing inventory from the Purple Wine Company for an estimated $160 million. Mark West is the top selling Pinot noir in the United States, with estimated sales of 600,000 cases in 2011.[40] This transaction did not include a winery in which to produce Mark West wine or vineyards to source grapes for its production.

What is the motivation for wine firms to grow through acquisitions? One possible reason is to reduce cost by gleaning economies of scale in production and input purchases. Through acquisitions, a wine firm can specialize production tasks such as bottling and blending in separate plants, eliminate inefficient and underutilized wineries, and utilize the most efficient wineries to produce multiple wine brands at optimal capacity. Cost reductions can also be obtained through large-volume purchases of grapes, equipment, packaging materials, and other inputs.

Another possible motive is related to the portfolio, distribution, and marketing of wine products. Acquisitions enable a firm to offer a broader array of wine brands and products. For example, largely through acquisitions, Constellation has developed a diverse portfolio of commodity, premium, and luxury wine brands and adjusts this portfolio to satisfy changing market demand. This circumvents the high cost and relatively long time required for developing new brands internally. It also allows a wine firm to offer a variety of product choices to distributors and retailers who often prefer "one-stop shopping" for all their wine product needs rather than dealing with multiple firms. An important trend occurring in the wine industry is the global consolidation of the wholesale and retail sectors. In Europe, five large supermarkets account for more than 50 percent of wine sales.[41] In the United States, the largest twenty distributors have a market share of about 75 percent, and it is not uncommon for a state to have only a handful of distributors. In this market environment, it has become increasingly difficult for small and medium-sized wine firms to sell their products through these large distributors and retailers who prefer to transact with relatively few suppliers to minimize cost. Big wine firms with large and varied portfolios of wine products and the bargaining power that comes with size are better able to market their products through wholesalers and secure increasingly scarce retail shelf space. A wine firm can also use acquisitions to build a global distribution network to increase worldwide sales. For example, when Foster's acquired Beringer, this gave Beringer access to Mildara Blass's established wine distribution infrastructure in Australia and Asia, and Mildara Blass gained access to Beringer's distribution channels in the United States. This allowed each firm to increase its sales abroad. Moreover large wine firms can realize economies of scope in distribution and marketing. For example, Constellation can use its existing large global distribution and marketing network to expand sales of the Mark West brand at minimal cost. It is becoming more common for smaller wine firms to specialize in developing wine brands, use their limited marketing resources to gain a foothold in the market, and then sell them to large wine firms that have the distribution and sales infrastructure necessary to make them high-volume national or global brands.

Acquisitions may also be motivated by a wine firm's desire to reduce risk through diversification. By making acquisitions, large wine firms have developed diversified portfolios of wine brands at different price points, which they sell in a variety of countries through their global distribution channels. They also source grapes and produce wine in a number of different locations throughout the world. This reduces the financial risk of consumers "trading up" or "trading down," and variations in wine sales across countries. In addition, the firm is better able to manage production risks associated with weather.

Growth through merger and acquisition does not guarantee that a wine firm will be successful. As a wine firm continues to grow bigger, it may eventually experience diseconomies of scale associated with the difficulties of managing a large global operation that result in inefficiencies and higher cost. This may place a limit on the efficient size of wine firms and may have been a factor contributing to Constellation's recent decision to downsize. Large conglomerates that enter the wine market often find that they do not realize the expected synergies between wine and other products that increase shareholder value. In providing the rationale for the Treasury Wine Estates demerger, Foster's concluded that wine and beer are different businesses that operate in industries with different dynamics, which could be produced and marketed more efficiently by separate firms, resulting in substantial cost savings. Modern wine history offers plenty of examples of conglomerates that have entered and exited the wine market. These include Nestlé, Coca-Cola, Pillsbury, R.J. Reynolds, John Hancock Insurance, Schlitz Brewing Company, and Newcastle Breweries, as well as others. George Taber maintains that the wine industry is "a graveyard for large corporations with little experience in wine."[42] If this is true, then domination of the global wine industry by relatively few large conglomerates like the beer and spirits industries, predicted by many, may never materialize.

Conclusion

The purpose of this book has been to explore wine in America from an economic perspective. The principal goal has been to explain the economic organization of the U.S. wine industry, and how individuals interact and behave in their role as wine producers and consumers. A set of fundamental economic concepts and principles have been used to organize the approach taken to the study of wine. This chapter highlights and summarizes insights from these guiding principles and the results of empirical studies presented in this book.

Economics recognizes that resources are scarce relative to wants and desires, and wine producers and consumers must therefore choose among alternative uses for their money, time, and other resources. Whenever a choice is made, a cost is incurred because a valued opportunity must be forgone. In the world of wine, as well as in every other dimension of life, trade-offs are inevitable. Nowhere is this more evident than in the trade-off between wine quality and cost. Increasing the yield per acre of vineyard land lowers grape cost, but there is a long-standing belief among winegrowers that it also compromises wine quality. Many winegrowers believe that grape quality is sacrificed when adopting cost-minimizing methods of vineyard technology such as mechanical harvesters and machine pruners. The cost of oak treatment can be significantly reduced by maturing wine in a stainless steel vessel with oak staves or chips, but many winemakers believe that more costly maturation in oak barrels yields a wine of higher quality. These and many other perceived trade-offs have a significant influence on grape-growing and winemaking decisions. Unfortunately, the exact nature of these trade-offs is often uncertain.

Economics assumes that given their limited resources, wine consumers and wine-firm owners act in their own self-interest and maximize the satisfaction of their wants by making rational decisions and choosing an alternative only if the benefit outweighs the opportunity cost. Empirical studies of the demand for wine verify that the law of demand applies to the purchase of wine products, and typical wine consumers therefore behaves as though rational when making wine-buying decisions. While many wine consumers appear to make irrational choices, much of this behavior can be explained as the outcome of rational decision-making based on expected benefits and costs under conditions of uncertainty and imperfect information. Obtaining information about wines requires the expenditure of time and money, and rational consumers will therefore acquire more only as long as the marginal benefit exceeds the marginal cost. What appears to be irrational wine-buying behavior is often a manifestation of "rational ignorance." As the Internet continues to lower the cost of obtaining information, less of this seemingly uneconomic behavior should be observed.

Many wine producers also appear to display uneconomic behavior. Some purposely use cluster pruning to reduce grape yield, even though the cost of doing so may well exceed the revenue gain. Others use oak-barrel maturation, but could make more money by employing alternative oak treatments. Still others choose to invest in a winery and vineyard land when they could generate more profit by purchasing grapes from a commercial vineyard and contracting with a custom-crush producer or investing their financial resources in another line of business. If the objective of the wine-firm owner is to maximize profit, these choices are indeed irrational if the incremental cost exceeds the revenue. However, there is much evidence that many proprietors are willing to trade profit for other sources of utility associated with ownership of a wine firm, such as the status, prestige, and the aesthetic value of producing a high-quality wine, or the enjoyment they get from pleasurable aspects of the wine lifestyle. Proprietors with nonprofit objectives weigh both the pecuniary and nonpecuniary benefits against the cost, and what may appear to be uneconomic behavior is therefore a rational choice. What is more, not only can these non-profit-maximizing wine firms survive in an economic environment with profit-maximizers, but there is some evidence that they are able to outcompete profit-maximizers in the sale of high-quality premium and luxury wines.

To satisfy their wants, wine producers and consumers interact in an institutional setting called the wine market and exchange wine products for money. When making market exchanges, wine firms and consumers incur transaction costs, which include the cost of acquiring information and negotiating and enforcing contracts. These transaction costs, along with production costs, product-quality considerations, and owner preferences, influence wine firms' decisions in organizing and coordinating the activities necessary to produce and sell wine. Asymmetric, imperfect information and incomplete contracts that do not specify all possible contingencies of an exchange create an economic incentive for wine firms and input suppliers to engage in opportunistic behavior. Opportunistic behavior is more likely when an exchange involves specialized assets and uncertain conditions. This increases the transaction costs of negotiating and enforcing a contract. The relative production cost of insourcing or outsourcing a task is largely determined by economies and diseconomies of scale and scope, and a wine firm's capabilities, determined by the knowledge and skills of its owner and employees and its endowment of vineyard land and winemaking capital. A wine firm's capabilities and the degree of control it has over grape growing or winemaking affect wine quality and the net benefits of insourcing or outsourcing. Higher transaction costs, lower internal production costs, and improved wine quality as a result of handling the task internally, rather than contracting with another firm to perform it, increase all wine firms' incentive to insource grape growing, wine production, or wine distribution. Non-profit-maximizing proprietors also have more incentive to insource wine-related activities that give them personal satisfaction.

In a wine-market transaction, the utility-bearing characteristics of wine products are known to producers but not to consumers until they purchase and consume them. Because of this information asymmetry, wine firms have an economic incentive to provide quality signals to consumers. Without this information, consumers may not be willing to pay a price commensurate with the higher quality of the wine products that many firms offer for sale. To signal quality, a wine firm can build a reputation based on past performance, take actions to establish a brand-name reputation, obtain high scores from wine critics, and provide quality information on a wine label, as well as other ways. Because many consumers rely on established brand names when making wine purchases, brand names are a stand-alone intangible asset with market value that wine firms buy and sell on a regular basis. The economic value of a brand name can be considerable, as evidenced by the sale of the Mark West brand name for $160 million. Wine firms may also engage in opportunistic behavior and attempt to exploit their informational advantage. This may explain why they make systematic errors when providing information about the alcohol content of wine on the label.

The buying and selling decisions of wine consumers and producers give rise to a demand for and supply of wine products. Prices emerge from the market interactions that take place in this institutional setting; these prices make the decisions of wine firms and consumers consistent so that an equilibrium obtains.

The buying decisions of consumers depend upon the price of wine, prices of goods related to wine, income, tastes and preferences, and the sensory and nonsensory qualities of wine. A typical wine consumer is willing and able to buy more at a lower price and less at a higher price. The aggregate demand for all wine products is price inelastic, and the total amount of wine purchased by consumers in the United States is therefore not very responsive to changes in the average level of wine prices. This suggests that consumers do not view beverages such as beer, spirits, and soda as close substitutes for wine. Within the class of wine products, buying decisions are more responsive to changes in red than white wine prices, and the demand for most varietal products is price-elastic, indicating that consumers perceive different types of varietals such as Cabernet Sauvignon, Merlot, and Pinot noir as reasonably good substitutes. Consumer price responsiveness is highest for the individual commodity-wine products of different wine firms because of the large number of perceived close substitutes that are available in this segment of the market. Wine-buying decisions are quite responsive to changes in income. The business cycle has a big effect on wine demand, because consumers want to buy substantially more during periods of economic expansion, when income is rising, and less when recessions occur and income falls. However, the demand for white wine is much more sensitive to cyclical ups and downs than that for red wine. Many consumers view commodity wine and "fighting varietals" as inferior goods and tend to trade down to these lower-priced products during economic downturns, when they have less money to spend on wine, and to trade up to higher-priced "normal" premium and luxury products during upturns, when they have more cash available for wine purchases. Demographic characteristics and health considerations, as well as factors related to taste and preferences, affect wine demand. Married, middle-aged, white professionals consume more wine than unmarried, non-white, nonprofessional, older and younger individuals. Some wine-market observers argue that the perception of wine as a healthy beverage is the most important determinant of the demand for wine.

Sensory and nonsensory characteristics related to wine quality also affect wine-buying decisions. Because consumers make buying decisions with imperfect information about the appearance, smell, and taste of wine, they use a variety of nonsensory characteristics as quality indicators to provide them with information about uncertain sensory characteristics. A typical American wine consumer is willing to pay a higher price for wine products that are assigned higher scores by wine critics. Exactly why this is so is unclear. Consumers making first-time buying decisions may use scores to obtain quality information consistent with their preferences, or these scores may persuade them to buy products preferred by the critics. Wine scores may reflect the quality preferences of well-informed consumers making repeat purchases. Consumers may be willing to pay higher prices for wines with higher scores, because they are perceived as more prestigious. All of these are plausible explanations. Consumers use grape location and variety as quality indicators. A typical consumer is willing to pay a higher price for red wine and wine made with grapes that come from geographic locations with a reputation for high quality and favorable climatic conditions such as Burgundy and Bordeaux, the Napa Valley, and Tuscany. Consumers are also willing to pay higher prices for products of wine firms with a reputation for high quality, possibly reflecting viticultural practices, winemaking techniques, and winemakers' skill. Finally, there is strong evidence that vintage-related weather is an important determinant of wine quality, particularly for age-worthy wines often bought and sold on the secondary auction market. Vintages with warm, dry growing seasons and wet winters tend to produce the highest-quality wine. However, consumers and investors appear largely to ignore information on weather conditions when deciding how much they are willing to pay for young age-worthy wine products on the auction market. It may take a decade or longer for auction prices to incorporate information about vintage-related weather. When age-worthy wines exceed from twenty to thirty years, their sensory qualities may begin to decline. However, wine collectors are willing to pay an increasingly higher price as they continue to age for the sake of the prestige of owning a venerable rare wine.

The selling decisions of grape growers and wine firms are influenced by their profit or nonprofit objectives, available winegrowing technology, government regulation, and the structural characteristics of the market in which they operate. The quantity of grapes that growers supply in the current year depends in large part on decisions they made in prior years. When grape prices in previous years are high, growers have an economic incentive to plant new acreage. However, these new vines do not bear fruit for at least three years. When the grapes from this new acreage are eventually offered for sale in the current year, wine firms are willing to pay low prices because of the abundant supply. When grape prices are low in prior years, growers have an economic incentive to take acreage out of production, which eventually results in a scant supply and higher prices in the current year. As a result, the supply decisions of growers result in a repeated wine-grape supply cycle of rising production, falling prices, and below normal profits, followed by declining production, rising prices, and above normal profits. Because grapes are the most important input used to produce wine, the wine-grape supply cycle can generate wine-supply cycles.

The price and quality decisions of wine firms depend largely on the market environment in which they operate. The commodity segment of the wine market approximates an oligopoly dominated by a small number of large profit-maximizing wine firms such as Gallo, The Wine Group, and Bronco Wine Company, which strategically consider how rivals will respond to their price and quality decisions. They tend to avoid aggressive price competition and are more inclined to compete by building the reputation of their existing wine brands and introducing new brands with characteristics that better satisfy consumer wants. The premium and luxury segment of the wine market, where thousands of profit-maximizing and utility-maximizing wine firms act independently in competition with one another, resembles monopolistic competition. High-end premium and luxury wine products are produced by utility-maximizing wine firms whose owners enjoy making high-quality wine and are willing to trade off profit for the opportunity to do so. Even though they tend to have higher costs and charge higher prices than profit-maximizing wine firms, their willingness to sacrifice profit for quality enables them to drive most profit-maximizers out of the luxury segment of the market. Profit-maximizing proprietors find that they can make the most money by producing lower-end premium wines. The luxury products that utility-maximizing proprietors choose to produce reflect their tastes and preferences as well as those of consumers.

The market for bulk wine is a little known but important submarket within the wine industry. Most wine firms participate in this market, at least on occasion, as buyers or sellers to eliminate a wine surplus or shortage, which inevitably occurs from time to time. Some firms specialize in producing bulk wine, while others use it as a permanent source of wine products. As a result, it allows wine firms to increase production efficiency and offer a wider variety of products to consumers. Foreign producers located in Australia, Chile, and Argentina are important suppliers of bulk wine in the United States. A number of retailers demand bulk wine for their private-label products. Private-label wine is a fast-growing segment of the wine market and an increasingly important source of business for wine firms. Private-label wine simplifies wine choices for consumers with limited information who must select a wine from the large number offered for sale on the retail market. Many consumers view the private-label brand name as a signal of consistent quality at a bargain price. The most prominent example is the Charles Shaw wine sold by Trader Joe's supermarket, which has won a number of medals at wine competitions and can be purchased for as little as $1.99 per bottle in California.

Middlemen and information specialists such as brokers, distributors, retailers, fulfillment agents, and wine experts perform valuable economic functions by organizing the wine market, reducing transaction costs, and creating information to facilitate exchanges between producers and consumers. The information specialist that has received the most attention is the wine critic. The role of this expert is to perform a sensory evaluation of wine products to determine their quality. Information on quality is then provided to consumers in the form of a description of a wine's sensory characteristics and a quality score. However, the value of this information to consumers is unclear. Studies suggest that the preferences and quality ratings of consumers are often significantly different from those of experts. Moreover, experts are often inconsistent in the quality scores they assign to the same wines, and different experts assign significantly different scores to identical wines. It may be that wine critics provide little useful information to consumers in choosing the wines they prefer. The biggest impact of wine critics may be to affect and shape consumers' wine preferences, and by doing so create a demand for wine products with characteristics that the critics themselves prefer.

Left to its own devices, the market for wine may fail to achieve an efficient allocation of resources. The major reason is that the benefit that accrues to individuals who transact in it may exceed the benefit to the nation as a whole because of the existence of external costs wine consumers impose on other members of society. Wine is an alcoholic beverage and heavy consumption of alcohol results in automobile accidents, violent crime, child abuse, disorderly conduct, and lost productivity. This provides an economic rationale for government regulation of the wine market. However, regulation itself can be viewed as an economic good. The regulations that are instituted are the outcome of the interaction of demand by special-interest groups and supply from legislators, both of whom are rational and act in their own self-interest. As a result, government regulation may enhance the welfare of particular groups at the expense of wine consumers, and possibly reduce socioeconomic welfare. While the original intent of government regulation of the wine industry following the repeal of Prohibition may have been to enhance social welfare, there is little evidence that states have been pursuing the public interest in instituting wine regulations over the past fifty years. The vast majority of these regulations appear to be designed to benefit special-interest groups like distributors, retailers, and in-state wine firms at the expense of consumers by inhibiting competition and improving the profitability of wine suppliers. It has become increasingly difficult for regulators to justify treating wine as just another alcoholic beverage like beer and spirits, because many people choose to consume wine as part of a healthy lifestyle. Moreover, there is reason to believe the external cost of wine consumption may be smaller than it is for other alcoholic beverages. A compelling argument can be made on economic grounds that the public interest would be better served by modifying or repealing many existing wine regulations, the cost of which to the nation exceeds the benefit.

Today, the U.S. wine industry is part of an integrated global wine market. Much of the world's wine is produced in one country and consumed in another. A variety of wine products, including global wine brands characterized by an international wine style, are available to consumers worldwide. A host of multinational wine firms and winemaking consultants operate in multiple countries, spreading the latest winegrowing technology. One of every three bottles of wine consumed in the United States is an imported product, and retail store shelves are filled with wine from all over the world. Not only do U.S. wine firms compete indirectly with imports, they compete directly with foreign wine firms that own wineries in the United States. Three of the eleven largest producers in the U.S. wine industry operate under foreign ownership. Wine exports account for twenty cents of every dollar of wine sales, and foreign consumers purchase about one of every seven bottles of wine produced in the United States. Wine firms in the United States own wineries in countries around the globe, and many U.S. wine-makers are also international wine consultants. From an economic per-spective, the globalization of the wine market and increased foreign competition have made U.S. wine consumers better off, because they have a wider choice of wine products of improved quality at different price points, giving them a "bigger bang for the buck."

Wine can be, and has been, studied from a number of perspectives using different approaches. These include historical, cultural, sensory, legal, political, and business orientations. This book has investigated wine in America from an economic perspective, applying concepts and principles that define the economic approach to the study of organiza-tion and behavior. It is my hope that this approach, along with the accompanying descriptive material, have contributed to the reader's knowledge and understanding of the fascinating subject of wine and the U.S. wine industry.

Notes

1. Wine industry statistics provided in the Introduction are discussed in detail in subsequent chapters and data sources are given.

2. Throughout this book, the terms *commodity, premium,* and *luxury wine* are used to distinguish between wine products of different quality sold at different price points. Commodity wine is at the bottom of the quality-price hierarchy and is typically produced in large volume. Premium wine is considered to be of higher quality and sold at a higher price point. At the top of the hierarchy is luxury wine, which commands the highest price and typically receives the highest scores from wine critics, reflecting its high perceived quality.

CHAPTER 1: THE ECONOMIC APPROACH TO THE STUDY OF WINE

1. The value of a person's time is highly subjective and differs across individuals. At best, the wage rate is an approximation of the opportunity cost of time, and it is a better measure for some individuals than for others.

2. More generally, utility can be thought of as an index of preference. To say an individual derives more utility from a bottle of Cabernet Sauvignon than a bottle of Merlot is another way of saying she prefers the Cabernet to the Merlot because the Cabernet better satisfies her wants and desires.

3. To explain and predict individual choice and behavior, it is not necessary for people to consciously weigh the benefit and cost of each alternative; all that is necessary is that they "behave as if" they use this decision-making logic. If they do, then economic theories based on the assumption of rational decision-making will be effective in explaining and predicting the behavior of an average or typical individual, not of each and every individual.

4. The law of diminishing marginal utility is often justified by satiety and hierarchy of uses arguments. For a typical KJ consumer like Jill, drinking a first bottle when she has had none during a given week is very enjoyable, but consuming say a third bottle in the same week is less pleasurable, because she has already had two. After having consumed four bottles of KJ, opening a fifth yields no extra satisfaction; it has become tiresome. However, there are a number of different ways in which a bottle of KJ can be consumed. It may accompany a meal, serve as an aperitif, given to a friend as a gift, used for cooking, etc. A consumer values all of these uses, but some are more satisfying than others.

5. If the firm is experiencing a loss, then it reduces this loss by $30,000.

6. In this example, grapes are a self-owned variable input.

7. It should be noted that higher wine consumption at higher prices and lower consumption at lower prices does not violate the law of demand; the change in income shifts the entire demand curve, causing a change in both equilibrium price and quantity.

CHAPTER 2: THE WINE PRODUCT

1. Most of the world's wine is made from grapes; however, any fruit or vegetable that contains sugar can be fermented into a wine-like beverage. The product of interest in this book is grape wine.

2. Robinson 2006, 267–68; Kramer 2003, 79–100.

3. For a discussion of the product characteristics approach to consumer and producer behavior, see Lancaster 1966 and Rosen 1974.

4. Bottled wine sold in the United States is required by law to have a label approved by the Alcohol and Tobacco Tax and Trade Bureau. The label must provide certain information, such as a brand name, wine category, and alcohol content. Most labels also provide additional information, such as vintage and grape variety. Note that two or more wine products sold by the same wine firm can have the same brand name, and the number of wine products therefore exceeds the number of wine brands.

5. Wine products may be differentiated in a number of ways. I emphasize the qualitative differences in wine products that result from perceived differences in sensory characteristics. However, consumers might also perceive the wine product of one producer to be somewhat different from those of others because of bottle and label design, brand name, and advertising. These types of characteristics not related to appearance, smell, and taste are considered later in the book.

6. The most notable exception is when consumers sample wine at a winery's tasting room before purchase.

7. For different perspectives on the notion of wine quality, see Penn 2001, MacNeil 2001, 2–8, Kramer 2003, 21–34, Charters and Pettigrew 2003, and Robinson 2006, 557–58.

8. See McCoy 2005 for an engaging account of Robert Parker's life and his influence on the wine industry.

9. See www.erobertparker.com/info/legend.asp for Parker's rating system.

CHAPTER 3: WINE SENSORY CHARACTERISTICS

1. The material in this chapter draws largely from Robinson 2000, MacNeil 2001, Casamayor 2002, Kolpan et al. 2002, Kramer 2003, Sharp 2005, Goode 2005, Ewing-Mulligan and McCarthy 2005, Robinson 2006, and Lewin 2010.

2. Goode 2005, 181–82.

3. Mega Purple is a sweet, richly colored concentrate made from a French hybrid grape called Rubired. It is widely used by winemakers to augment the color and sweetness of red wine, but is virtually unknown to wine consumers. Some consider it winemakers' "dirty little secret" and believe its use should be prohibited, because it is an artificial way to enhance color and flavor. However, it is a less costly way to enrich the color of a red wine than blending. Lewin 2010, 124–26.

4. Robinson 2000, 13–14.

5. See Kolpan et al. 2002, 97, for a picture of the wine aroma wheel.

6. Robinson 2006, 273–74.

7. Casamayor 2002, 34–36.

8. Robinson 2006, 290.

9. Ewing-Mulligan and McCarthy 2005, 10–16.

10. For a sampling of different quality standards used by different wine professionals, see Robinson 2000, 36–41, Ewing-Mulligan and McCarthy 2005, 16–23, MacNeil 2001, 2–6, Kramer 2003, 25–28.

11. Goode 2005, 31.

12. Quandt 2007.

13. Goode 2005, 174.

14. Weil 2007.

15. Goode 2005, 180–81.

16. Ramirez 2010.

CHAPTER 4: GRAPE GROWING

1. The material in this chapter about wine grapes and viticulture comes largely from Halliday and Johnson 2007, Robinson 2006, Goode 2005, Lewin 2010, Priewe 2005, MacNeil 2001, and Law 2005.

2. To illustrate differences in varietal characteristics and affinity for blending consider two popular red grapes: Cabernet Sauvignon and Pinot noir. Cabernet Sauvignon is a small, dark blue, thick-skinned grape, with large seeds, high levels of tannin, acidity, and color pigment. It has substantial flavor compounds suggestive of blackcurrant. It is a naturally vigorous, high-yielding vine that grows best in warm climates, and the grapes ripen slowly and late in the growing season, achieving relatively high sugar and alcohol levels. Because of its high tannin, acidity, and concentrated flavor compounds, it can produce wine with the ability to age for many years. Blending with other grapes, such as Merlot and Cabernet Franc, has the potential to improve its taste profile by creating a rounder mouthfeel and providing complementary flavors. In contrast, Pinot noir is a somewhat larger, violet-colored, thin-skinned grape, with smaller seeds, higher acidity, lower tannin and color pigment, and flavor compounds reminiscent of red berry and cherry fruit. It is less vigorous, with a lower grape

yield, ripens early in the growing season, and prefers a relatively cool climate. It typically lacks the ability for long aging, and does not blend well with other grapes. Consequently, a wine labeled Pinot noir typically contains 100 percent of this grape variety, whereas a wine sold in the United States labeled Cabernet Sauvignon may consist of as little as 75 percent of the Cabernet grape with the remaining 25 percent accounted for by one or more blending grapes.

3. Kramer 2004, 61–62.

4. Clonal selection can have a significant effect on the taste profile of certain grapes, such as Pinot noir and Syrah. Depending on the clone selected, Pinot noir can have dark fruit and cola flavors in addition to the more characteristic red cherry and berry flavors. Syrah can exhibit a range of tastes from blackberry to blueberry to coffee to leather. Kramer 2004, 70.

5. Kolpin et al. 2002, 143.

6. MacNeil 2001, 25.

7. See Gale 2011 for a detailed historical account of phylloxera.

8. The precise meaning of *terroir* and its effect on wine quality are widely debated. For good discussions of the notion of terroir, see Goode 2005, 25–34, Halliday and Johnson 2007, 19–26, and Lewin 2010, 41–67.

9. Kramer 2003, 9–10.

10. Teague 2011 estimates that the Paul Hobbs winery recently paid $25,000 for a ton of Cabernet Sauvignon grapes from the To Kalon vineyard in Napa Valley, owned by the independent grape grower Andy Beckstoffer. The average price of a ton of Napa Valley Cabernet Sauvignon grapes is about $4,000. Teague also reports that Beckstoffer Vineyards recently paid $3.9 million for the thirteen-acre Hayne Vineyard in the Napa Valley.

11. Ashenfelter 2010. Studies that analyze the relationship between vintage-related weather and wine quality and price are discussed in detail in chapter 12.

12. Old World Countries are those with a long history and tradition of producing wine, including France, Germany, Italy, and Spain. New World Countries have a much shorter wine production history and include the United States, Australia, Chile, Argentina, New Zealand, and South Africa.

13. Halliday and Johnson 2007, 20. Halliday and Johnson also suggest that vineyard owners in France have an economic incentive to promote the idea that the mineral content of the soil is the most important determinant of grape and wine quality, because this results in a greater demand for mineral-rich vineyard land in France, which leads to higher land prices. Taber 2011, 14, argues that wine firms often promote the uniqueness of their vineyard soil as a marketing gimmick so that they can charge a higher price for their wine.

14. U.S. Department of Commerce 2011; Motto Kryla & Fisher and Wine Institute 2007.

15. An alternative measure of yield used in many European countries is the amount of wine that can be produced per acre of vineyard land. This productivity measure depends not only on tons of grapes per acre but also on assumptions about several wine-production-related variables. Under a reasonable set of assumptions, one ton of grapes can produce about 750 standard bottles (750 ml, or 25.4 oz, per bottle) or 62.5 twelve-bottle cases.

16. This estimate is based on data from Kramer 2004, 79.

17. Halliday and Johnson 2007, 51–53.

18. According to Alston et al. 2011b, year 2008 Cabernet Sauvignon average yield per acre for selected California North Coast, Central Coast, and Central Valley growing regions was: Napa County 2.4 tons; Sonoma County 2.8 tons; Monterey and San Benito County 4.4 tons; southern San Joaquin Valley 15.1 tons.

19. Priewe 2005, 36.

20. Robinson 2006, 134–35.

21. Kramer 2004, 78.

22. Kramer 2004, 60–61.

23. Anecdotal evidence suggests that many growers of high-quality grapes use this practice. As an example, Hudson Vineyards, a 180-acre commercial vineyard in the Carneros region of California, regularly employs cluster thinning for Syrah grapes, and in a typical year, half of the grapes are thinned and allowed to rot on the ground. Harris 2010.

24. Robinson 2006, 211.

25. See Goode 2005, 68–77, for an interesting and informative discussion of biodynamic grape growing.

26. Penn 2010.

27. Consumers may perceive that it is difficult to make a good sulfite-free organic wine. The wine literature tends to support the view that making a good wine without adding sulfites is very challenging (which is why almost all winemakers do add sulfites). Even if it can be done, to prevent the wine from deteriorating, it must be transported and stored in a temperature-controlled environment, which is difficult given the current wine distribution system.

28. A grower may consider a red grape to be mature if it looks somewhat dehydrated, stains the fingers, and easily detaches from the stem. The seeds are brown, hard, and crunchy, rather than green and soft, and the berry smells and tastes fruity, not herbaceous.

29. Goode 2005, 109.

30. Stevenson 2005b, 250.

31. Robinson 2006, 432–33.

32. Halliday and Johnson 2007, 68.

33. Goode 2005, 35–39.

34. Greenspan 2009 reports a survey of 350 vineyards—50 percent of them in California and less than 3 percent in Canada—that provides estimates of the adoption of capital-intensive methods of production and usage of advanced technology by grape growers. Twenty-three percent of growers use mechanical harvesting, 10 percent mechanical leaf removers, and only 6 percent machine pruners. Relatively few growers use machines for cluster thinning. Capital-intensive methods of production are used most by vineyards that are 200 acres or bigger and least by small vineyards that farm 25 acres or less. Eighty percent of large vineyards machine-harvest grapes, and 20 percent use mechanical pruning. Only 6 percent of small vineyards harvest by machine, and less than 5 percent use mechanized pruning. About 40 percent of vineyards use some type of weather-collection technology, while only 15 percent employ geographical information systems to construct maps of soil and landscape variation within

the vineyard. Once again, larger vineyards are much more likely to make use of more advanced vineyard technologies than smaller vineyards.

CHAPTER 5: GRAPE MARKETS AND SUPPLY CYCLES

1. This section draws heavily from Heien 2006.

2. In this chapter, the word *winery* is used to designate a wine firm.

3. Goodhue et al. 2002.

4. For example, the 180-acre Hudson Vineyards in the Napa Valley sells grapes to thirty-four different wine firms grown on fifty-four different vineyard blocks. Harris 2010.

5. Goodhue et al. 2002.

6. Lukacs 2005, 36.

7. Penn 2002.

8. These data on grape output are from the Wine Institute, www.wineinstitute .org.

9. See www.turrentinebrokerage.com/wine-business-wheel.

10. The classic paper on the cobweb theory is Ezekiel 1938. For applications of the theory to hogs and lemons respectively, see Harlow 1960 and French and Bressler 1962.

11. If the demand curve is steeper than the supply curve, then periods of overproduction and underproduction become successively larger over time and the market will move away from equilibrium point e. In this case, grape production and prices would fluctuate wildly over time. This type of unstable equilibrium seems to be inconsistent with the actual behavior of the grape market in the United States.

12. The bulk wine market is described in detail in chapter 7.

CHAPTER 6: WINE PRODUCTION

1. A production function is often expressed in general functional form as $Q = f(I_1, I_2, \ldots, I_n)$, where Q is maximum output produced and $I_1, I_2, \ldots, I_n$ are the quantities of n inputs used. For a wine firm, Q is maximum wine output, I_1 may be grapes, I_2 the services of cellar workers, etc. The functional form f represents the current state of wine-production technology. Different functional forms describe different technologies. For example, many economists believe that the multiplicative functional form $Q = \beta_0 I_1^{\beta_1} I_2^{\beta_2} I_3^{\beta_3} \cdots$, called a Cobb-Douglas production function, is a reasonable approximation of technology for some firms and industries. An empirical study of a production function would gather data on output and inputs for firms in an industry, estimate the parameters of the production function $\beta_0, \beta_1, \beta_2, \ldots$, and use these estimates to obtain various measures such as input productivity and returns to scale. From a theoretical perspective, the neoclassical theory of the firm views the firm as a "profit-maximizing, production function."

2. For detailed discussion and categorization of the variety of wine styles, see Ewing-Mulligan and McCarthy 2005.

3. McCoy 2005, 265–67.

4. The discussion of the stages of the wine-production process that follows draws largely from Bird 2005, Goode 2005, Halliday and Johnson 2007, Kolpan et al. 2002, Lewin 2010, MacNeil 2001, Priewe 2005, Robinson 2006, Stevenson 2005a, and Thach and Matz 2004.

5. Lewin 2010, 92.

6. Some very small specialty producers in the United States still crush grapes with their feet.

7. Producers have a range of mechanical presses from which to choose, among them the old-fashioned basket press, horizontal screw press, continuous screw press, pneumatic press, and tank press. They vary widely in price from the relatively inexpensive basket press to the very expensive tank press. Different presses can produce juices of different quality. The tank press is believed to produce the highest-quality juice. Many large volume producers prefer the continuous screw press, because it is the most efficient way to press large amounts of grapes, but it is generally believed to produce low-quality juice. Bird 2005, 45–53.

8. Sulfur dioxide can also enhance the extraction of aroma and pigment compounds from red grape skins during cold maceration.

9. Bird 2005, 57–58.

10. Use of reverse-osmosis filtering machines to concentrate must has become a common practice in Bordeaux, France, where many top châteaux have invested in their own equipment. Goode 2005, 113–14.

11. Stevenson 2005, 26.

12. Bird 2005, 81–88.

13. MacNeil 2001, 40.

14. Lewin 2010, 132; Robinson 2006, 491.

15. Micro-oxygenation also improves red wine by eliminating vegetal flavors, and all the large wineries in the Central Valley and as many as 33 percent of North Coast wineries in California are believed to use it, as are 66 percent of Chilean wineries and 5 percent of wineries in Australia and France. Goode 2005, 98.

16. Fining is also used by some winemakers to reduce the amount of tannin in some red wine to give it a softer mouthfeel and making it more appealing to consume at an early age.

17. Bird 2005, 132–34.

18. Lewin 2010, 104.

19. If a wine is labeled as a blend of different grape varieties, the order in which the grapes are listed typically indicates their relative proportions from largest to smallest. For example, a wine labeled Grenache Syrah Mourvedre contains more Grenache than Syrah, and more Syrah than Mourvedre.

20. Lukacs 2000, 197–99.

21. White wines are typically bottled in spring and red wines in summer.

22. Lavin 2008.

23. Pregler 2005.

24. Lewin 2010, 218.

25. Goode 2005, 148.

26. Aeppel 2010.

27. Fish 2010.
28. Pregler 2006.
29. Federal regulations require only a 75 percent grape content for a non-AVA geographic location specified on the label (e.g., Napa County).
30. For a non-AVA wine, the requirement is only 85 percent.
31. Gaiter and Brecher 2007.

CHAPTER 7: BULK WINE, PRIVATE-LABEL WINE, AND WINE ALCOHOL

1. Estimates suggest that a standard cargo ship container holds about 13,000 bottles of wine, while a bulk container of the same size holds the equivalent of 32,000 bottles. This reduces transportation cost by as much as 40 percent.
2. Pinney 2005, 88–94.
3. Ibid.,130–38.
4. Cline 2007.
5. A number of smaller specialized brokers also operate in California and other regional markets in the United States.
6. The Bronco Wine Company owns more than 30,000 acres of vineyard land and has the capacity to store more than 100 million gallons of wine. "Review of the Industry: The WBM 30—Profiles," *Wine Business Monthly,* February 2011.
7. Ibid.
8. Anderson and Nelgen 2011, tables 41, 43, 46.
9. Quackenbush 2010.
10. " News: U.S. Bulk Wine Imports Tripling as Global Producers Seek Low Cost Supplies," *Wine Business Monthly,* October 2009.
11. *Négociant* is French for *merchant.* The wine firm that sells bulk wine to a negociant may also bottle it. Negociants may also purchase shiners and resell them under their own brand names.
12. "Review of the Industry: The WBM 30—Profiles," *Wine Business Monthly,* February 2012.
13. See *www.steveheimoff.com/?s=cameron+hughes.*
14. See http://nomadeditions.com
15. Robinson 2006, 115–16.
16. Brostrom and Brostrom 2009, 159–60.
17. Tinney 2006.
18. Ibid.
19. "Interview with Doug Bell, global wine buyer for Whole Foods." http://www.rjswineblog.com/2009_09_01_archive.html.
20. Taber 2011, 116.
21. Tinney 2006.
22. Veseth 2011, 61.
23. Ibid., 60–64.
24. For discussion of these technologies, see Goode 2005, 109–14.
25. Goode 2005, 112; Alston et al. 2011b, n. 9.
26. The researchers obtained the data from the Liquor Control Board of Ontario, Canada. It measures the actual alcohol content of each wine sold in

Ontario. Recall that the actual alcohol content can differ from the content indicated on the wine label.

27. New World countries are Argentina, Australia, Canada, Chile, New Zealand, South Africa, and the United States. Old World countries are France, Italy, Spain, and Portugal.

28. From a study reported by Beekman Wines & Liquors of Glen Rock, New Jersey; see www.beekmanwine.com/prevtopbh.htm.

29. Consumers perhaps derive utility from the perceived positive health effects of consuming wine in moderation, judged, say, to be two glasses of wine containing 14 percent or less alcohol per day with dinner. Wine with a higher alcohol content is viewed as higher than moderate consumption. Recall that under federal wine-label regulations, 14 percent alcohol is the line of demarcation between a table wine and a high-alcohol dessert wine. An increasing number of sommeliers and wine merchants are refusing to purchase wine products with an alcohol content that exceeds 14 percent for a different reason: they believe these wines are not food-friendly. Teague 2010a.

30. Recall that a rational individual will acquire additional information as long as the marginal benefit exceeds the marginal cost.

CHAPTER 8: WINE DISTRIBUTION AND GOVERNMENT REGULATION

1. Cholette 2007.

2. Thach and Matz 2004, 105–6.

3. Fisher 2009.

4. Hilton 2008.

5. For an excellent discussion of alcoholic beverage and wine regulations and laws from a historical perspective, see Mendelson 2009.

6. Beliveau and Rouse 2010.

7. Riekhof and Sykuta 2005.

8. Information on state shipping laws is provided by the Wine Institute, www.wineinstitute.org, and eCompli Beverage Compliance Online, www.compli-beverage.com.

9. Mendelson 2009, 97.

10. Perdue 1999, 80.

11. A report by the Specialty Wine Retailers Association states there may be as few as 200 wine distributors in the United States; the two largest distributors in Texas account for 95 percent of the wine market. Specialty Wine Retailers Association 2008.

12. Evidence from a large body of studies suggests that one daily alcoholic beverage for women and two for men reduces the risk of heart disease, ischemic stroke, and possibly diabetes by increasing good cholesterol, stabilizing blood sugar, thinning blood, and acting as an anti-inflammatory. Some studies suggest that moderate consumption of red wine may have additional benefits such as reducing the risk of cataracts, ulcers, dental cavities, and some pulmonary conditions; see Baxter, 2009. Simon 2002, 207, provides estimates suggesting that total abstinence from alcohol consumption would reduce annual deaths from alcohol-related diseases by 100,000, but increase deaths from heart disease by 80,000.

13. As of December 2011, New York, Connecticut, Tennessee, Mississippi, Kentucky, and Wyoming allowed grocery stores to sell beer but not wine. Rickard et al. 2011.

14. In 1996, the Supreme Court struck down a Rhode Island law prohibiting advertising of alcoholic beverages. The state argued that this law increased social welfare by increasing alcohol prices and reducing excessive drinking. The Supreme Court suggested that raising alcohol taxes might be a more effective way to increase prices and decrease overconsumption. Mendelson 2009, 180.

15. Beliveau and Rouse 2010.

16. Mendelson 200, 183.

17. Perdue 1999, 77.

18. Beliveau and Rouse 2010.

19. Riekhof and Sykuta 2005.

20. Mendelson 2009, 184.

21. Wine Institute, www.wineinstitute.org.

22. Mendelson 2009, 189.

23. The principles of the economic theory of regulation were first propounded by Stigler 1971. Stigler's ideas were then formalized by Peltzman 1976 and extended by Becker 1983.

24. The per member net benefit for an interest group is the difference between the benefit per member from a regulation and the cost per member of acquiring information about the regulation and organizing the interest group to deliver political support.

25. Riekhof and Sykuta 2005.

26. Specialty Wine Retailers Association 2008.

27. Braun 2009.

CHAPTER 9: THE WINE FIRM

1. For different views of the firm, see Coase 1937, Alchian and Demsetz 1972, and Tirole 1989, chap. 1.

2. See www.ttb.gov.

3. If a firm contracts with a custom-crush producer for wine bottled under its own brand name, the label will indicate that the wine was "Produced and bottled by" the custom-crush winery, not the firm that sells the wine brand. If the firm contracts with the custom producer for bulk wine, and blends or bottles the wine in its own facility, the label will state "Cellared by" the firm selling the wine brand, not the custom producer.

4. When a wine firm registers as a legal entity, it must choose a name (e.g., XYZ Wine Company). However, it is allowed to list one or more other names as trade names and can conduct business under any of these trade names (e.g., XYZ Winery, ABC Vineyards, and LMN Vintner). When a wine firm obtains a basic alcohol permit from the TTB, it must provide a unique "operating trade name (e.g., XYZ Winery). It must also add to the permit any "bottling trade name" that it puts on a wine label (e.g., ABC Vineyards). The TTB requires that a bottling trade name appear on the label after the words "bottled by." If a brand name does not appear on the label, the bottling trade name is considered

to be the brand name. In this example, XYZ Wine Company has a basic alcohol permit under the operating trade name XYZ Winery, and sells a wine whose label states "bottled by ABC Vineyards." ABC Vineyards is the brand name if no other brand name is printed on the bottle. For a more detailed discussion, see Schorske and Heckathorn 2004.

5. Information on the wine firms discussed in this section comes from a variety of sources, including Stockton 2010, Lindblom 2010, Quackenbush 2009, Laube 2009, Heron 2010, Lewin 2010, wine firms' websites, Hoover's company profiles available on the Internet, and *Wine Business Monthly*, February 2010, February 2011, February 2012.

6. See "Interview with Doug Bell, global wine buyer for Whole Foods." http://www.rjswineblog.com/2009_09_01_archive.html.

7. This estimate is from the Wine Institute, www.wineinstitute.org.

8. *Wine Business Monthly* does not use the term *organization* in its definition; however, the notion of an organization is implied. For a verbatim definition of bonded and virtual wineries, see *Wine Business Monthly*, February 2012.

9. Ibid.

10. Anderson and Nelgen 2011, table 33.

11. *Wine Business Monthly*, February 2012.

12. Pregler 2010.

13. An alternative type of partnership that is more involved and requires formal documentation is a limited partnership. This arrangement has at least one general and one limited partner, but can have more than one of each. Limited partners differ from general partners in that they have limited liability, so that their personal assets are not at risk, and they do not participate in the management of the firm.

14. A distinction is made between a public and private corporation. A public corporation has a large number of owners and its stock is traded widely on a national exchange or over-the-counter market. A private corporation has a relatively small number of owners, typically twenty-five or fewer, and is not traded on a national market. The owners of a private corporation can be a single individual, family, group of investors, or another private or public corporation.

15. The profit of a proprietorship and partnership is taxed once as ordinary income of the proprietor or partners. The profit of a corporation is taxed twice: once as corporate profits and then a second time as the owner's dividend income.

16. This estimate is the result of an extensive search of information available about wine firms on the Internet.

17. The list of the thirty largest domestic wine companies in the United States is taken from *Wine Business Monthly*, February 2012.

18. Lewin 2010, 229.

19. Large U.S. wine firms have a number of brands and wineries. For example, Constellation sells more than seventy wine brands and owns nineteen wineries in the United States, as well as wineries in Canada and New Zealand. Its portfolio includes such well-known wineries as Robert Mondavi, Franciscan,

Simi, Clos du Bois, and Hogue. Treasury Wine Estates' portfolio includes Beringer, Stag's Leap, Chateau St. Jean, Etude, Penfolds, and Lindemans.

20. Goodhue et al. 2002.

21. For a contract to be legally enforceable it must satisfy the criterion of consideration. Consideration means that there is evidence that the wine firm and the other party have considered the terms of the transaction agreement and accepted them. A legal contract does not exist if either the wine firm or the other party does not understand or agree to the terms of the exchange, or the terms are unduly vague, in which case the courts have no basis for enforcing the agreement. A court may have to decide whether a legal contract exists, and, if so, what its specific terms are. See Posner 1977, chapter 4.

22. Ibid.

23. Milgrom and Roberts 1992, 127–40.

24. Williamson 1985, 47.

25. Stevenson 2006, 250.

26. In general, a moral hazard exists when a decision maker does not bear the full cost of his actions, and therefore makes choices that increase his own welfare but reduce the welfare of others in society. In this example, the grower does not bear the full cost of his decision to shirk, which reduces the welfare of the wine firm.

27. Price and viticultural provisions may also be included in a grape contract for reasons unrelated to information asymmetry such as risk sharing. For instance, if a wine firm is risk averse, it may want to tie the price of grapes to the price of wine to share the risk of uncertain wine market conditions with the grower. A wine firm that can observe quality and grower effort may desire to include provisions for viticultural practices to obtain greater consistency from one year to the next.

28. Billikopf and Norton 1992. A wine firm also has an informational disadvantage when it contracts with a distributor to transport, store, and sell wine to retailers. The wine firm wants the distributor to ensure wine quality, put forth maximum effort to sell the wine, determine the best price, and provide information on which wine products are selling and where. However, the wine firm cannot perfectly observe the transportation, storage, and sales effort of the distributor. This lack of information creates a moral hazard, and the distributor may therefore attempt to benefit at the expense of the wine firm by skimping on the services agreed to in the contract and pricing the wine to its own advantage.

29. This line of reasoning implies that the primary objective of a large public corporation should be to make as much money as it can for the owners. However managers, like consumers, seek to maximize utility. What if managers derive utility from some aspect of running the firm, such as the prestige of controlling a gigantic but inefficient firm, or perquisites like posh offices, private planes, and inflated salaries? What is to prevent managers from making decisions that trade profits for these sources of personal utility? Incentives exist for managers of public corporations that may be sufficient to induce them to make maximizing profit their top priority and minimize the extent to which they pursue nonprofit objectives. First, many public corporations tie managers' salaries to the firm's profits. Second, if managers don't make profit-maximizing decisions, the board of directors, acting

on behalf of the stockholders, may replace them. Finally, if managers fail to make profit-maximizing decisions and the board of directors fails to take action, the firm may be acquired by another firm that sees an opportunity to make money by replacing both the existing management and the board of directors with new decision makers who pursue maximum profit.

30. See, e.g., Conaway 2003.

31. Scott Morton and Podolny 2002.

32. For example, suppose the proprietor of a wine firm owns a vineyard and uses his own time to manage the firm. Assume he could rent the land for $20,000 per year and work as a winemaker for another winery at an annual salary of $80,000. His normal profit is $100,000 per year; this is the amount of money he could make if he used his land and time resources in their next best area of employment. If his accounting profit for the year is $125,000, he has an economic profit of $25,000, and he is earning $25,000 more than he could by using his land and time in their best alternative lines of employment. If his accounting profit for the year is $75,000, his economic profit is negative $25,000, and he could make $25,000 more by devoting his resources to their next best uses. Finally, if his accounting profit is $100,000, he earns zero economic profit. In this case, he makes the same amount of money using his resources in the wine firm or in their next best areas of employment.

33. A method of production is a particular combination of labor services, capital equipment, and other inputs that can be used to produce a specific amount of output of a good such as grapes and wine, or a service such as transportation and storage.

34. Anderson and Nelgen 2011, table 43.

35. Folwell et al. 2001. These authors' estimates are in 1998 dollars. I have adjusted them for inflation and report year 2010 dollar estimates. Folwell et al. assume that the wine firm produces premium table wine without a vineyard operation. The investment for a winery that produces a commodity wine may be somewhat smaller.

36. Gallo, The Wine Group, and Trinchero Family Estates also produce and sell spirits. I do not include these as conglomerates, since a relatively small proportion of their revenues come from these non-wine products.

37. Brown-Foreman was the tenth-largest wine firm in the United States in 2009, with annual sales of 4.5 million cases. In 2011, it sold all but one of its wine brands, including Fetzer Vineyards, to the Chilean wine firm Concha y Toro. At present, Brown-Foreman sells only one still wine brand, Sonoma-Cutrer.

CHAPTER 10: WINE-FIRM BEHAVIOR

1. The discussion of wine-firm behavior in this chapter includes concepts from neoclassical economics, transaction-cost economics, and firm-capabilities theories.

2. Akerlof 1970.

3. Arnold 2007.

4. McCoy 2005, 225–27.

5. See "Constellation Simply Naked Wine Brand Off to Fast Start, Selling 180,000 Cases in First Half Year," *Shanken News Daily,* April 30, 2012; and see also ibid., April 5 2012, "Constellation Sales Slip in Fiscal Year, Raft of New Products Coming." www.shankennewsdaily.com.

6. Williamson 1979, 1985.

7. Goodhue et al. 2004.

8. See https://wikis.nyu.edu/xdesign/mediawiki/index.php/Wine_Bottle.

9. Folwell et al. 2001. A premium wine is defined as wine sold at no less than $6.70 per 750 ml bottle (in 2010 dollars). The authors assume that the winery produces four or more different varietal wines. The average cost per case is for a "mixed case." Estimates are for five wineries of different sizes, with annual case production of 2,000, 5,000, 10,000, 50,000, and 500,000 respectively. Because average cost declined over the entire range of the study output, minimum efficient scale was not determined.

10. Ibid. The authors' estimates are in 1998 dollars. I have adjusted these estimates for inflation and report them in 2010 dollars.

11. Intardonato 2010.

12. Thach and Matz 2004, 42–44; Penn 2002.

13. Cook 2007.

14. For discussion of firm-capabilities theory applied to the sourcing decision, see Parmigiani 2007.

15. An often used example of tacit knowledge is riding a bicycle.

16. The estimates used for this example are taken from Folwell et al. 2001, rounded off, adjusted for inflation, and given in 2010 dollars. The variable cost of producing wine is inflated for Firm B to reflect its lower productivity in producing wine.

17. The information for this story is from http://teatown.com.

18. The information for this story is from Teague 2010b and the Cameron Hughes Wine website, www.chwine.com.

19. The information for this story is from Conaway 2003, 85, and Robert Parker's website, www.erobertparker.com.

20. Claburn 2004.

21. Brostrom and Brostrom 2009, 100.

CHAPTER 11: THE WINE CONSUMER AND DEMAND

1. The data for the number of wine drinkers and total wine consumption come from www.winemarketcouncil.com/?page_id=35 and are for 2012. The estimate of the number of bottles consumed per year and the number of glasses consumed per week were calculated using this data.

2. The information and data sources for this section come from the Wine Market Council, www.winemarket council.com, and wine market council data reported in Nichols 2011; Gallup and Stonebridge Research data reported in Insel 2009; and Constellation Brands' Project Genome data reported in Tinney 2008a.

3. Wine Institute, www.wineinstitute.org.

4. These market shares are calculated using Nielson Company data reported in *Wine Business Monthly,* May 2012.

5. For a formal analysis of consumer snob behavior and conspicuous consumption, see Leibenstein 1950.

6. See Fogarty 2008 for a summary of the price-elasticity estimates.

7. If demand is unit-elastic, the dollar value of wine sales remains the same regardless of whether price rises or falls.

8. For linear and most types of nonlinear demand curves, elasticity varies over different price ranges. Specifically, as price rises, elasticity increases in magnitude.

9. Income elasticity of demand is defined as the ratio of the percentage change in the quantity of wine demanded to the percentage change in income. Demand for wine is income-elastic (inelastic) and consumers' buying decisions are relatively responsive (unresponsive) to a change in income if the absolute value of this elasticity measure is greater (less) than one. A positive algebraic sign indicates that wine is a normal good; a negative sign informs us that wine is an inferior product.

10. See Fogarty 2008 for a summary of the income-elasticity estimates.

11. They report a negative income-elasticity estimate for Merlot, but the p-value indicates a high probability that this is the result of chance.

12. Perdue 1999, 25.

13. Cross-price elasticity is defined as the ratio of the percentage change in the quantity demanded of a good to the percentage change in the price of a related good. If the algebraic sign of cross-price elasticity is positive, then the good is a substitute; a negative algebraic sign indicates that the good is a complement. If cross-price elasticity is zero, then the good is unrelated in consumption. The larger the magnitude of cross-price elasticity, the more closely the good is related.

14. The California wine groups also included wines produced in the state of Washington.

15. Perdue 1999, 21–23.

16. Cuellar et al. 2009.

17. Perdue 1999, 17.

18. Studies include Heien and Pompelli 1989, Gao et al. 1995, Nayga 1996, Blaylock and Blisard 1993, and Hussain et al. 2006.

CHAPTER 12: THE WINE CONSUMER, QUALITY, AND PRICE

1. This is consistent with the version of hedonic price theory developed by Rosen 1974 and Nerlove 1995.

2. An implicit price is also called a hedonic price.

3. Tinney 2008a.

4. Soklin and Bruce 2008, 23.

5. For a good description of the wine auction market, see Soklin and Bruce 2008.

6. See, e.g., Prial 2000.

7. Weil 2001.

8. Thach 2008.

9. See chapter 11 for an explanation of p-value.

10. This equation is linear in parameters, and therefore allows for a variety of functional forms such as linear in variables, log-linear, and quadratic forms. An intercept term is often included in the equation.

11. Lattey et al. 2007.

12. Rosen 1974.

13. Combris et al. 1997, Combris et al. 2000, Cardebat and Figuet 2004, and Lecocq and Visser 2006.

14. Kramer 2003, 108.

15. Reuter 2009.

16. All but one of these studies assume no interaction effects between wine score and wine type; that is, the effect of a one-point increase in score on price does not depend upon grape variety or blend. For example, a one-point increase in score for a Cabernet Sauvignon will have the same effect on price as a one-point increase in Merlot or Chardonnay.

17. This is the average elasticity estimate for three separate periods reported by Schamel.

18. For more detailed descriptions of the Bordeaux futures market, see Soklin and Bruce 2008, and McCoy 2005.

19. Schamel 2009.

20. Bombrun and Sumner 2003.

21. Schamel 2009.

22. Landon and Smith 1998.

23. Davis and Ahmadi-Esfahani 2006.

24. San Martin et al. 2008.

25. Lewin 2010, 73.

26. Ayres 2007, 1–6.

27. Zraly 2008, 297.

CHAPTER 13: THE GLOBALIZATION OF WINE

1. Anderson and Nelgen 2011.

2. Lewin 2010, 201.

3. Drinks International 2011.

4. Bostrom and Bostrom 2009, 273.

5. Veseth 2011, 139.

6. Taber 2011, 138; Veseth 2011, 140.

7. Anderson and Nelgen 2011, table 55.

8. For an interesting discussion of the impact of government policy on wine globalization, see Veseth 2011, chapter 4.

9. Anderson and Nelgen 2011, table 16.

10. Ibid., table 41.

11. The data for this estimate were obtained from the Wine Institute, www .wineinstitute.org, and it includes territories such as the Virgin Islands.

12. For a good discussion of the development of the Chinese wine industry, see Taber 2011, chapter 9.

13. Anderson and Nelgen 2011, table 151.

14. Veseth 2011, chapter 5.

15. Taber 2011, 145.

16. Anderson and Nelgen 2011, tables 118 and 121.

17. Lukacs 2000, chapter 9, provides an interesting historical account of foreign investment in the U.S. wine industry.

18. Coleman 2008, 107.

19. Anderson and Nelgen 2011, table 120.

20. Export data for 2011 were obtained from the Wine Institute, www .wineinstitute.org.

21. Esterl 2012; Anderson and Nelgen 2011.

22. Wine cooperatives existed in the United States until 2002. Between 1934 and 1975, forty-four cooperatives were created; in the 1940s, those located in California produced one-third of the state's wine. By 1980, only eight cooperatives remained, and the last one exited the wine industry in 2002. Pinney 2005, 394n68.

23. The estimate for Germany is from Hanf and Schweickert 2007; for France, Saïsset et al. 2011; for Italy, Malorgio et al. 2008; and for Spain, Martínez-Carrión and Medina-Albaladejo 2010.

24. Anderson and Nelgen 2011, tables 34 and 35.

25. See www.wineeconomist.com/2011/08/02/invisible-wineries-europes-controversial-cooperatives.

26. Most wine cooperatives were created by small grape growers whose objective was to get a higher price for their grapes by collectively processing them into wine themselves rather than selling them to wineries or merchants.

27. Hanf and Schweickert 2007.

28. Couderc and Marchini 2011.

29. Lewin 2010, 221.

30. Veseth 2011, 173–74.

31. Anderson and Nelgen 2011, table 35.

32. Lewin 2010, 229.

33. The Canandaigua Wine Company changed its name to Constellation Brands in 2000.

34. A group of wine industry veterans established Ascentia by borrowing more than $200 million to purchase the portfolio of eight brands and wineries from Constellation, which included Geyser Peak, Atlas Peak, XYZ Zin, Gary Farrell, Buena Vista, Columbia Winery, Covey Run, and Ste. Chapelle. In 2008, Ascentia was the thirteenth-largest wine firm in the United States with annual sales of 2 million cases. However, it had difficulty paying its debt and proceeded to sell off its brands to Gallo, Accolade, and several other wine firms. It eventually went out of business in 2012. Accolade's purchase of Geyser Peak in 2012 allowed it to expand its operations to the United States.

35. *Wine Business Monthly,* February 2012.

36. Foster's acquisition of Beringer was a mutually agreeable merger between two publicly traded corporations, not a hostile takeover. Beringer was merged with Mildara Blass to create Beringer-Blass Wine Estates, a subsidiary of Foster's. Gilinsky et al. 2004.

37. *Wine Business Monthly,* February 2012.

38. In 2009, Constellation was the third-largest wine firm in the United States, and Fosters was the second-largest in Australia. Anderson and Nelgen 2011, table 34.

39. Ibid.

40. Bussewitz 2012.

41. Lewin 2010, 226.

42. Taber 2011, 25.

References

Aeppel, Timothy. 2010. "Show Stopper: How Plastic Popped the Cork Monopoly." *Wall Street Journal,* May 1.

Akerlof, George A. 1970. "The Market for Lemons: Qualitative Uncertainty and the Market Mechanism." *Quarterly Journal of Economics* 84: 488–500.

Alchian, Armen A., and Harold Demsetz. 1972. "Production, Information Costs, and Economic Organization." *American Economic Review* 62: 777–95.

Alston, Julian M., Kate B. Fuller, James T. Lapsley, George Soleas, and Kabir P. Tumber. 2011a. *Splendide Mendax: False Label Claims about High and Rising Alcohol Content of Wine.* American Association of Wine Economists Working Paper No. 82.

———. 2011b. "Too Much of a Good Thing? Causes and Consequences of Increases in Sugar Content of California Wine Grapes." *Journal of Wine Economics* 6, 2: 135–59.

Anderson, Kym, and Signe Nelgen. 2011. *Global Wine Markets, 1961 to 2009: A Statistical Compendium.* Adelaide: University of Adelaide Press.

Arnold, Eric. 2007. "Rodney Strong Vineyards Buys Davis Bynum Wine Brand." *Wine Spectator,* August 16. www.winespectator.com/webfeature /show/id/Rodney-Strong-Vineyards-Buys-Davis-Bynum-Wine-Brand_3706.

Ashenfelter, Orley. 2010. "Predicting Quality and Prices of Bordeaux Wine." *Journal of Wine Economics* 5, 1: 40–52.

Ashenfelter, Orley, David Ashmore, and Robert LaLonde. 1995. "Bordeaux Wine Vintage Quality and the Weather." *Chance* 8, 4: 7–14.

Ayres, Ian. 2007. *Super Crunchers: Why Thinking-by-Numbers Is the New Way to Be Smart.* New York: Bantam Books.

Baxter, Richard A. 2009. *Age Gets Better with Wine.* South San Francisco: Wine Appreciation Guild.

Becker, Gary S. 1983. "A Theory of Competition among Pressure Groups for Political Influence." *Quarterly Journal of Economics* 93: 371–400.

Beliveau, Barbara C., and M. Rouse. 2010. "Prohibition and Repeal: A Short History of the Wine Industry's Regulation in the United States." *Journal of Wine Economics* 5, 1: 53–68.

Billikopf, Gregory E., and Maxwell V. Norton. 1992. "Pay Method Affects Vineyard Pruner Performance." *California Agriculture* 46, 5: 12–13.

Bird, David. 2005. *Understanding Wine Technology*. Newark, Notts, UK: DBQA Publishing.

Blaylock J.R., and W.N. Blisard. 1993. "Wine Consumption by US Men." *Applied Economics* 24: 645–51.

Bombrun, Helene, and Daniel A. Sumner. 2003. *What Determines the Price of Wine? The Value of Grape Characteristics and Wine Quality Assessments*. University of California Agricultural Issues Center, AIC Issues Brief No. 18 (January).

Braun, Ken. 2009. "Grapes of Wrath (Short Version)." Mackinac Center for Public Policy.www.mackinac.org/10264.

Brostrom, Geralyn G., and Jack Brostrom. 2009. *The Business of Wine: An Encyclopedia*. Westport, CT: Greenwood Press.

Buccola, Steven T., and Loren VanderZanden. 1997. "Wine Demand, Price Strategy, and Tax Policy." *Review of Agricultural Economics* 19, 2: 428–40.

Bussewitz, Cathy. 2012. "Mark West Wine Brand Sold for $160 Million." *Press Democrat*, June 30. www.pressdemocrat.com/article/20120629 /business/12062946I/1339/business?Title = Mark-West-wine-brand-sold-for-160-million.

Byron, R.P., and Orley Ashenfelter. 1995. "Predicting the Quality of an Unborn Grange." *Economic Record* 71, 212: 40–53.

Cardebat, Jean-Marie, and Jean-Marc Figuet. 2004. "What Explains Bordeaux Wine Prices?" *Applied Economics Letters* 11: 293–96.

Casamayor, Pierre. 2002. *How to Taste Wine*. London: Octopus Publishing.

Charters, Stephen, and Simone Pettigrew. 2003. "I Like It, but How Do I Know if It's Any Good? Quality and Preference in Wine Consumption." *Journal of Research for Consumers*, no. 5.

Cholette, Susan. 2007. "A Novel Problem for a Vintage Technique: Using Mixed-Integer Programming to Match Wineries and Distributors." *Interfaces* 37, 3: 231–39.

Cholette, Susan, and Kumar Venkat. 2009. "The Energy and Carbon Intensity of Wine Distribution: A Study of Logistical Options for Delivering Wine." *Journal of Cleaner Production*, June: 1–13.

Claburn, Thomas. 2004. "Top of the List: Recipe for a Better Winery." *InformationWeek*, September 20. www.informationweek.com/top-of-the-list-recipe-for-a-better-wine/47900073.

Cline, Harry. 2007. "California Wine Grapes Sold for Bulk Market before Bottled or Bagged." *Western Farm Press*, March 15.

Coase, Ronald. 1937. "The Nature of the Firm." *Economica*, n.s., 4, 16: 386–405.

Colman, Tyler. 2008. *Wine Politics: How Governments, Environmentalists, Mobsters, and Critics Influence the Wine We Drink.* Berkeley: University of California Press.

Combris, Pierre, Sebastien Lecocq, and Michael Visser. 1997. "Estimation of a Hedonic Price Equation for Bordeaux Wine: Does Quality Matter." *Economic Journal* 107, 441: 390–402.

Combris, Pierre, Sébastien Lecocq, and Michael Visser. 2000. "Estimation of a Hedonic Price Equation for Bordeaux Wine." *Applied Economics,* 32: 961–67.

Conaway, James. 2002. *The Far Side of Eden: New Money, Old Land, and the Battle for Napa Valley.* Boston: Houghton Mifflin.

Cook, Doug. 2007. "Review of the Industry: Consolidation of the Industry." *Wine Business Monthly,* February.

Couderc, Jean-Pierre, and Andrea Marchini. 2011. "Governance, Commercial Strategies and Performances of Wine Cooperatives." *International Journal of Wine Business Research* 23, 3: 235–57.

Cuellar, Stephen S., and Ryan Huffman. 2008. "Estimating the Demand for Wine Using Instrumental Variable Techniques." *Journal of Wine Economics* 3, 2: 172–84.

Cuellar, Stephen S., Dan Karnowsky, and Frederick Acosta. 2009. "The *Sideways* Effect: A Test for Changes in the Demand for Merlot and Pinot Noir Wines." *Journal of Wine Economics* 4, 2: 219–32.

Cuellar, Stephen S., and Aaron Lucey. 2005. "Forecasting California Wine Grape Supply Cycles." *Wine Business Monthly,* December.

Cuellar, Stephen S., Aaron Lucey, and Mike Ammen 2006. "Understanding the Law of Demand." *Wine Business Monthly,* March.

Davis, Tim, and Fredoun Ahmadi-Esfahani. 2006. "Hedonic Modeling for Australian Wine." Paper presented at the Forty-Ninth Annual Conference of the Australian Agricultural and Resource Economics Society.

Drinks International. 2011. "Most Admired Wine Brands." www.drinksint.com/news/categoryfront.php/id/193/World_s_Most_Admired_Wine_Brands.html.

Dubois, Pierre, and Céline Nauges. 2007. *Identifying the Effect of Unobserved Quality and Experts' Reviews in the Pricing of Experience Goods: Empirical Application on Bordeaux Wine.* American Association of Wine Economists Working Paper No. 10.

Ellig, Jerry, and Allan E. Wiseman. 2007. "The Economics of Direct Wine Shipping." *Journal of Law, Economics, and Policy* 3, 2.

———. 2011. *Competitive Exclusion with Heterogeneous Sellers: The Case of State Wine Shipping Laws.* American Association of Wine Economists Working Paper No. 90.Esterl, Mike. 2012. "Stars Align for Constellation in Deal." *Wall Street Journal,* July 2.

Ezekiel, Mordecai. 1938. "The Cobweb Theorem." *Quarterly Journal of Economics* 52, 2: 255–80.

Ewing-Mulligan, Mary, and Ed McCarthy. 2005. *Wine Style: Using Your Senses to Explore and Enjoy Wine.* Hoboken, NJ: Wiley.

Fish, Tim. 2010. "Cork Screwed: Screw Caps Ace Test." *Wine Spectator,* May 31.

Fisher, Cathy. 2009. "Direct to Consumer: 2009 Tasting Room Report." *Wine Business Monthly,* May.

Folwell, R. J., T. A. Bales, and C. G. Edwards. 2001. "Cost Economies and Economic Impacts of Pricing and Product Mix Decisions in Premium Table Wine Wineries." *Journal of Wine Research* 12, 2: 111–24.

Fogarty, James. 2008. *The Demand for Beer, Wine, and Spirits: Insights from a Meta Analysis Approach.* American Association of Wine Economists Working Paper No. 31.

French, Ben C., and Raymond G. Bressler. 1962. "The Lemon Cycle." *Journal of Farm Economics,* 444: 1021–36.

Gale, George. 2011. *Dying on the Vine: How Phylloxera Transformed Wine.* Berkeley: University of California Press.

Gaiter, Dorothy, and John Brecher. 2007. "Boxed Wines Face the Six-Week Challenge." *Wall Street Journal,* June 15.

Gao, X. M., Eric J. Wailes, and Gail L. Cramer. 1995. "A Microeconometric Model Analysis of US Consumer Demand for Alcoholic Beverages." *Applied Economics* 27: 59–69.

Gergaud, Olivier, and Victor A. Ginsburgh. 2010. "Natural Endowments, Production Technologies, and the Quality of Wines in Bordeaux: Does Terroir Matter?" *Journal of Wine Economics* 5, 1: 3–21.

Gilinsky, Armand, Raymond H. Lopez, and Richard Castaldi. 2004. *The Globalization of Beringer Blass Wine Estates.* Lubin Business School Case Studies Paper No. 5.http://digitalcommons.pace.edu/business_cases/5.

Goldstein, Robin, Johan Almenberg, Anna Dreber, John W. Emerson, Alexis Herschkowitsch, and Jacob Katz. 2008. "Do More Expensive Wines Taste Better? Evidence from a Large Sample of Blind Tastings." *Journal of Wine Economics* 3, 1: 1–9.

Goode, Jamie. 2005. *The Science of Wine: From Vine to Glass.* Berkeley: University of California Press.

Goodhue, Rachael E., Dale M. Heien, Hyunok Lee, and Daniel A. Sumner. 2002. "Contract Use Widespread in Wine Grape Industry." *California Agriculture,* May–June: 97–102.

Greenspan, Mark. 2009. "Vineyard Survey Report: Mechanization and Technology." *Wine Business Monthly,* November.

Haeger, John W., and Karl Storchmann. 2006. "Prices of American Pinot Noir Wines: Climate, Craftsmanship, Critics." *Agricultural Economics* 35: 67–78.

Halliday, James, and Hugh Johnson. 2007. *The Art and Science of Wine.* Buffalo, NY: Firefly Books.

Hanf, Jon H., and Eric Schweickert. 2007. *Changes in the Wine Chain—Managerial Challenges and Threats for German Wine Co-ops.* American Association of Wine Economists Working Paper No. 7.

Harlow, Arthur A. 1960. "The Hog Cycle and the Cobweb Theorem." *Journal of Farm Economics* 42, 4: 842–53.

Harris, Jessamyn. 2010. "Lee Hudson: A Highly Regarded Grower Makes the Case for Carneros as a Site for Syrah." *Wine Spectator,* March 31.

Heien, Dale. 2006. "Price Formation in the California Winegrape Economy." *Journal of Wine Economics* 1, 2: 162–72.

Heien, Dale, and Greg Pompelli. 1989. "The Demand for Alcoholic Beverages: Economic and Demographic Effects." *Southern Economic Journal* 55: 759–68.

Heron, Katrina. 2010. "Try the Red: Napa Learns How to Sell." *New York Times,* February 17.

Hilton, M. L. 2008. "Case Study: Winery's DTC Overtakes Wholesale Division." *Wine Business Monthly,* December.

Hodgson, Robert T. 2008. "An Examination of Judge Reliability at a Major Wine Competition." *Journal of Wine Economics* 3, 2:105– 13.

———. 2009. "An Analysis of the Concordance Among 13 U.S. Wine Competitions." *Journal of Wine Economics* 4, 1: 1–9.

Hussain, Mahmood, Richard Castaldi, and Susan Cholette. 2006. "Determinants of Wine Consumption of U.S. Consumers: An Econometric Analysis." Paper presented at the Third International Wine Business & Marketing Conference, Montpellier, France, July 6–8.

Insel, Barbara. 2009. "Understanding Wine Demographics in a Down Market." *Wine Business Monthly,* February.

Intardonato, John. 2010. "How the WBM 30 Make Wine: Closer to the Source." *Wine Business Monthly,* October.

Jenster, Per V., David E. Smith, Darryl J. Mitry, and Lars V. Jenster. 2008. *The Business of Wine: A Global Perspective.* Copenhagen: Copenhagen Business School Press.

Jones, Gregory V., and Karl Storchmann. 2001. "Wine Market Prices and Investment under Uncertainty: An Econometric Model for Bordeaux Crus Classes." *Agricultural Economics* 26, 2: 115–33.

Kolpan, Steven, Brian H. Smith, and Michael A. Weiss. 2002. *Exploring Wine: The Culinary Institute of America's Complete Guide to Wines of the World.* New York: Wiley.

Kramer, Matt. 2003. *Making Sense of Wine.* Rev. ed. Philadelphia: Running Press.

———. 2004. *California Wine : Making Sense of Napa Valley, Sonoma, Central Coast, and Beyond.* Philadelphia: Running Press.

Lancaster, Kelvin J. 1966. "A New Approach to Consumer Theory." *Journal of Political Economy* 74, 2: 312–56.

Landon, Stuart, and Constance E. Smith. 1998. "Quality Expectations, Reputation, and Price." *Southern Economic Journal* 64, 3: 628–47.

Lattey, Kate A., Belinda R. Bramley, I. Leigh Francis, Markus J. Herderich, and Sakkie Pretorius. 2007. "Wine Quality and Consumer Preferences: Understanding Consumer Needs." *Australian & New Zealand Wine Industry Journal* 22, 1: 31–39.

Laube, James. 2009. "From Tips to Riches." *Wine Spectator,* November 30.

Lavin, Kate. 2008. "Going Mobile, Wineries Outsource Bottling to Save Space and Capital." *Wines and Vines,* December.

Law, Jim. 2005. *The Backyard Vintner. The Wine Lover's Guide to Growing Grapes and Making Wine at Home.* Gloucester, MA: Quarry Books.

Lecocq, Sebastien, and Michael Visser. 2006. "What Determines Wine Prices: Objective vs. Sensory Characteristics." *Journal of Wine Economics* 1, 1: 42–56.

Leibenstein, Harvey. 1950. "Bandwagon, Snob, and Veblen Effects in the Theory of Consumers' Demand." *Quarterly Journal of Economics,* May: 183–207.

Lewin, Benjamin. 2010. *Wine Myths and Reality.* Dover, UK: Vendange Press.

Lindblom, John. 2010. "A Passion for Making Wine." *Napa Valley Register,* September 30.

Lukacs, Paul. 2005. *American Vintage: The Rise of American Wine.* New York: Norton.

———. 2005. *The Great Wines of America.* New York: Norton.

MacNeil, Karen. 2001. *The Wine Bible.* New York: Workman.

Malorgio, Giulio, Anna Hertzberg, and Cristina Grazia. 2008. "Italian Wine Consumer Behavior and Wineries Responsive Capacity." Paper presented at the Twelfth International Congress of the European Association of Agricultural Economists, Gent, Belgium, August 26–29.

Manning, Willard G., Emmett B. Keeler, Joseph P. Newhouse, Elizabeth M. Sloss, and Jeffrey Wasserman. 1989. "The Taxes of Sin: Do Smokers and Drinkers Pay Their Way?" *Journal of the American Medical Association,* March 17: 1604–9.

Martínez-Carrión, J.M., and F.J. Medina-Albaladejo. 2010. "Evolution and Recent Developments of Spanish Wine Sector, 1950–2008." Paper presented at the Thirty-Fifth Annual Economic and Business Historical Society Conference, Braga, Portugal, May 27–29.

McCoy, Elin. 2005. *The Emperor of Wine: The Rise of Robert M. Parker, Jr. and the Reign of American Taste.* New York: Harper Collins.

Mendelson, Richard. 2009. *From Darling to Demon: A Legal History of Wine in America.* Berkeley: University of California Press.

Milgrom, Paul, and John Roberts. 1992. *Economics, Organization, and Management.* Englewood Cliffs, NJ: Prentice-Hall.

Motto Kryla & Fisher [firm] and Wine Institute. 2007. *The Impact of Wine, Grapes, and Grape Products on the American Economy 2007: Family Businesses Building Value.* St. Helena, CA: MKF Research LLC.

Nayga, Rodolfo M. 1996. "Sample Selectivity Models for Away from Home Expenditures on Wine and Beer." *Applied Economics* 28: 1421–25.

Nerlove, Marc. 1995. "Hedonic Price Functions and the Measurement of Preferences: The Case of Swedish Wine Consumers." *European Economic Review* 39: 1697–1716.

Nichols, Rachel. 2011. "U.S. Wine Consumer Trends: Boomers' Tastes Evolve, Millennials Continue to Drive Market Growth." *Wine Business Monthly,* January.

Parmigiani, Anne. 2007. "Why Do Firms Both Make and Buy? An Investigation of Concurrent Sourcing." *Strategic Management Journal* 28: 285–311.

Peltzman, Sam. 1976. "Toward a More General Theory of Regulation." *Journal of Law and Economics* 19: 211–40.

Penn, Cyril. 2001. "What Is Quality?" *Wine Business Monthly,* May.

———. 2002. "Andy Beckstoffer." *Wine Business Monthly,* May.

———. 2010. "Research Shows Organic Practices Raise Wine Scores and Prices (if the Wineries Don't Talk about Them)." *Wine Business Monthly,* October.

Perdue, Lewis. 1999. *The Wrath of Grapes: The Coming Wine Industry Shakeout and How to Take Advantage of It.* New York: Avon Books.

Pinney, Thomas. 2005. *A History of Wine in America,* vol. 2: *From Prohibition to the Present.* Berkeley: University of California Press.

Posner, Richard A. 1977. *Economic Analysis of Law.* Boston: Little, Brown.

Pregler, Bill. 2005. "Buying Your First Bottling Line." *Wine Business Monthly,* November.

———. 2006. "Product Review: Mobile Bottling Services." *Wine Business Monthly,* April.

———. 2010. "Survey Report: 2010 Winery Equipment." *Wine Business Monthly,* March 15.

Prial, Frank. 2000. "Wine Talk: So Who Needs Vintage Charts." *New York Times,* February 9.

Priewe, Jens. 2005. *Wine: From Grape to Glass.* 3rd rev. ed. New York: Abbeville Press.

Quackenbush, Jeff. 2009. "Kosta Browne First, but Not Last." *North Bay Business Journal,* September 21.

———. 2010. "Two Winemakers from M. Draxton to Market Bulk Wine." *North Bay Business Journal,* August 9.

Quandt, Richard E. 2007. "On Wine Bullshit: Some New Software?" *Journal of Wine Economics* 2, 2: 129–35.

Ramirez, Carlos D. 2008. "Wine Quality, Wine Prices, and the Weather: Is Napa Different?" *Journal of Wine Economics* 3, 2: 114–31.

———. 2010. "Do Tasting Notes Add Value? Evidence from Napa Wines." *Journal of Wine Economics* 5, 1: 143–63.

Reuter, Jonathan. 2009. "Does Advertising Bias Product Reviews? An Analysis of Wine Ratings." *Journal of Wine Economics* 4, 2: 125–51.

Rickard, Bradley J., Marco Costanigro, and Teevrat Garg. 2011. *Regulating the Availability of Beer, Wine, and Spirits in Grocery Stores: Beverage-Specific Effects on Prices, Consumption, and Traffic Fatalities.* American Association of Wine Economists Working Paper No. 95.

Riekhof, Gina M., and Michael E. Sykuta. 2005. "Politics, Economics, and the Regulation of Direct Interstate Shipping in the Wine Industry." *American Journal of Agricultural Economics* 87, 5: 439–52.

Robinson, Jancis. 2000. *How to Taste: A Guide to Enjoying Wine.* New York: Simon & Schuster.

———, ed. 2006. *The Oxford Companion to Wine.* 3rd ed. New York: Oxford University Press.

Rosen, Sherwin. 1974. "Hedonic Prices and Implicit Markets: Product Differentiation in Pure Competition." *Journal of Political Economy* 82, 1: 34–55.

Saïsset, Louis-Antoine, Jean-Pierre Couderc, and Mario Saba Bou. 2011. "Cooperative Performance Measurement Proposal." Paper presented at the Sixth Academy of Wine Business Research International Conference, Bordeaux, France, June 9–10.

San Martin, Guillermo S., Bernhard Brummer, and Javier L. Troncoso. 2008. "Determinants of Argentinean Wine Prices in the U.S. Market" *Journal of Wine Economics* 3, 1: 72–84.

Schamel, Günter. 2000. *Individual and Collective Reputation Indicators of Wine Quality.* University of Adelaide Centre for International Economic Studies Policy Discussion Paper No. 0009.

———. 2009. "Dynamic Analysis of Brand and Regional Reputation: The Case of Wine." *Journal of Wine Economics* 4, 1: 62–80.

Schorske, S., and A. Heckathorn. 2004. "The Rules of the Winery Name Game." *Vineyard and Winery Management,* September–October.

Scott Morton, Fiona M., and Joel M. Podolny. 2002. "Love or Money? The Effects of Owner Motivation in the California Wine Industry." *Journal of Industrial Economics* 50, 4: 431–56.

Sharp, Andrew. 2005. *Winetaster's Secrets: A Step-by-Step Guide to the Joy of Winetasting.* Toronto: Warwick Publishing.

Simon, Harvey B. 2002. *The Harvard Medical School Guide to Men's Health.* New York: Free Press.

Sinton, Peter. 2001. "Growing Grapes for Other Companies Products: GSV Supplies Most Top Vintners." *San Francisco Chronicle,* July 31.

Sokolin David, and Alexandra Bruce. 2008. *Investing in Liquid Assets: Uncorking Profits in Today's Global Wine Market.* New York: Simon & Schuster.

Specialty Wine Retailers Association. 2008. "Wholesale Protection: Alcohol Wholesalers Control and Weakening of the American Wine Market through $50,000 in Campaign Contributions." www.specialtywineretailers.org.

Stevenson, Tom. 2005a. *The Sotheby's Wine Encyclopedia.* 4th ed.. New York: Penguin Group.

———. 2005b. *Wine Report 2006.* London: Dorling Kindersley.

———. 2006. *Wine Report 2007.* London: Dorling Kindersley.

Stigler, George J. 1971. "The Theory of Economic Regulation." *Bell Journal of Economics and Management Science* 2: 137–46.

Stockton, Diana. 2010. "Ric Forman." *Napa Valley Library Report,* Summer.

Taber, George M. 2011. *A Toast to Bargain Wines: How Innovators, Iconoclasts, and Winemaking Revolutionaries Are Changing the Way the World Drinks.* New York: Scribner.

Teague, Lettie. 2010a. "Wines That Pack a Little Extra Kick." *Wall Street Journal,* April 17–18.

———. 2010b. "Taking Advantage of the Wine Glut." *Wall Street Journal,* May 1.

———. 2011. "The Most Powerful Grower in Napa." *Wall Street Journal,* March 19.

Thach, Liz. 2008. "How American Consumers Select Wine." *Wine Business Monthly,* June.

Thach, Liz, and Tim Matz, eds. 2004. *Wine: A Global Business.* New York: Miranda Press.

Thrane, Christer. 2004. "In Defense of the Price Hedonic Model in Wine Research." *Journal of Wine Research* 15, 2: 123–34.

Tinney, Mary-Colleen. 2006. "The Impact of Private Label Brand Growth." *Wine Business Monthly,* December.

———. 2007. "Retail Sales: Highest Price Segments Show Strongest Growth." *Wine Business Monthly,* February.

———. 2008a. "Addressing the Consumer's Desire." *Wine Business Monthly,* November.

———. 2008b. "Retail Sales Report: Highest Price Points Growing Despite Economic Concerns, Shifting Buying Habits." *Wine Business Monthly,* November.

Tirole, Jean. 1988. *The Theory of Industrial Organization.* Cambridge, MA: MIT Press.

Tsolakis, D., Paul C. Riethmuller, and Geof Watts. 1983. "The Demand for Wine and Beer." *Review of Marketing and Agricultural Economics* 51, 2: 131–35.

United States. Department of Commerce. 2011. *U.S. Wine Industry – 2011.* Prepared by Donald A. Hodgen. http://ita.doc.gov/td/ocg/wine2011.pdf.

Veseth, Mike. 2011. *Wine Wars: The Curse of the Blue Nun, the Miracle of Two Buck Chuck, and the Revenge of the Terroirists.* Lanham, MD: Rowman & Littlefield.

Weil, Roman. 2001. "Parker vs. Prial: The Death of the Vintage Chart." *Chance* 14, 4: 27–31.

———. 2007. "Debunking Critics Wine Words: Can Amateurs Distinguish the Smell of Asphalt from the Taste of Cherries?" *Journal of Wine Economics* 2, 2: 136–44.

Williamson, Oliver E. 1979. "Transaction-Cost Economics: The Governance of Contractual Relations." *Journal of Law and Economics* 22: 233–61.

———. 1985. *The Economic Institutions of Capitalism: Firms, Markets, Relational Contracting.* New York: Free Press.

Wood, Danielle, and Kym Anderson. 2006. "What Determines the Future Value of an Icon Wine? New Evidence from Australia." *Journal of Wine Economics* 1, 2: 141–61.

Yang, Nan, Jill J. McCluskey, and Carolyn Ross. 2009. "Willingness to Pay for Sensory Properties in Washington State Red Wines." *Journal of Wine Economics* 4, 1: 81–93.

Zraly, Kevin. 2008. *Windows on the World Complete Wine Course.* New York: Sterling.

Index

Italicized page numbers indicate tables or figures.